# FREEDOM
# DEMOCRACY AND
# ECONOMIC
# WELFARE

# FREEDOM DEMOCRACY AND ECONOMIC WELFARE

LORD BAUER
RAMON DIAZ
MILTON FRIEDMAN
RAYMOND D. GASTIL
TIBOR R. MACHAN
DOUGLASS NORTH
SVETOZAR PEJOVICH
ALVIN RABUSHKA
INGEMAR STAHL
LINDSAY M. WRIGHT

EDITED BY
MICHAEL A. WALKER

PROCEEDINGS OF
AN INTERNATIONAL
SYMPOSIUM

THE FRASER
INSTITUTE

Proceedings of an International Symposium on Economic, Political and Civil Freedom, held October 5-8, 1986 in Napa Valley, California. This event is part of the programme of Liberty Fund Inc., under the direction of its President, Dr. W.W. Hill. This Symposium was managed by The Fraser Institute and organized by its Director, Dr. Michael A. Walker.

Canadian Cataloguing in Publication Data

Main entry under title:
Freedom, democracy and economic welfare

    Symposium held Oct. 5-8, 1986 in Napa Valley, Calif.
    Includes bibliographical references.
ISBN 0-88975-116-1
    1. Capitalism - Congresses. 2. Liberty - Congresses. 3. Economics - Political aspects - Congresses. 4. Economics - Philosophy - Congresses. I. Walker, Michael, 1945- II. Fraser Institute (Vancouver, B.C.)

HB501.F74 1988   330.12'2   C88-091102-6

Printed in Canada.

# CONTENTS

# PARTICIPANTS

**Lord Bauer**

Professor Emeritus of Economics, London School of Economics and Political Science and a Fellow of the British Academy. Lord Bauer has written six books including *Equality, the Third World and Economic Delusion* (1981) and *Reality and Rhetoric: Studies in the Economics of Development* (1984).

**Ramon P. Diaz**

Editor, *Busqueda*, and Lecturer on Political Economics at the University of the Republic, Montevideo, Uruguay. Ramon Diaz has a Doctorate in Law and Social Sciences and has written many articles which have appeared in U.S., U.K., and Latin American publications as well as two books, *The Long-Run Terms of Trade of Primary-Producing Countries* (1973) and *Enfoque de la Balanza de Pagos en la Economía Uruguaya* (1981).

**Milton Friedman**

Senior Research Fellow, The Hoover Institution, Stanford University; Professor of Economics Emeritus, University of Chicago; 1976 Nobel Laureate in Economic Sciences. Author of numerous books including *A Theory on the Consumption Function* (1957); *Capitalism and Freedom* (1962); *The Optimum Quantity of Money (1969); Free to Choose* (1980); and *Tyranny of the Status Quo* (1984).

**Raymond D. Gastil**

Director of the Comparative Survey of Freedom which has been published annually (since 1972) by Freedom House and is entitled *Freedom in the World: Political Rights and Civil Liberties.* He is the author of *Cultural Regions of the United States* (1976), *Social Humanities: Toward an Integrated Discipline of Science and Values* (1977) and numerous scholarly articles.

**Tibor R. Machan**

Professor of Philosophy at Auburn University in Alabama. He has published in numerous scholarly journals, magazines and newspapers including the *Review of Metaphysics, Theory and Decision, Southern Economic Journal* and *Economic Affairs.* Machan wrote, among other things, *Human Rights and Human Liberties* (1975) and edited, again among other works, *The Main Debate: Communism vs. Capitalism* (1987).

## Douglass C. North

Luce Professor of Law and Liberty in the Department of Economics at Washington University, St. Louis and Director of the Center for Political Economy. He edited the *Journal of Economic History* for five years and is the author of over fifty articles and seven books including *The Rise of the Western World: A New Economic History* with R.P. Thomas (1973) and *Structure and Change in Economic History* (1981).

## Svetozar Pejovich

Professor of Economics and Director, Center for Education and Research in Free Enterprise, Texas A & M University. Among his many publications, Dr. Pejovich has written *Co-Determining Movement in the West* (1978), *Fundamentals of Economics: A Property Rights Approach* (1979) and *The Economic, Philosophical and Economic Foundations of Capitalism* (1982). More recently he has edited *Socialism: Institutional, Philosophical and Economic Issues* (1987).

## Alvin Rabushka

Dr. Rabushka is Senior Fellow of The Hoover Institution at Stanford University and specializes in domestic policy research. He is author or co-author of fourteen books ranging from race and ethnic politics to aging and housing policy, state, local and federal taxation, the political economy of Hong Kong's free market and politics in plural societies.

## Ingemar Stahl

Department of Economics, Lund University, Sweden. He is a member of the Nobel Prize Committee in economic science and has contributed to an earlier book published by The Fraser Institute entitled *Unemployment Insurance: Global Evidence of Its Effects on Unemployment* (1978).

## Lindsay M. Wright

Lindsay M. Wright is a Ph.D. candidate in political science at the University of Pennsylvania where she is completing her dissertation on gender and political power. She is a former research assistant with the Freedom House Comparative Survey of Freedom and has authored essays on economic freedom, corporatism and pluralism in Western Europe which have been published in *Freedom in the World: Political Rights and Civil Liberties*.

# PREFACE

## I. ORIGINS

This book had its origins in a discussion paper which I was asked to write for the 1984 meetings of the Mont Pèlerin Society in Cambridge, England. The paper upon which I was asked to comment, "1984—A False Alarm?," by journalist and historian Paul Johnson, presented the view that George Orwell's predictions about the demise of democracy had proven to be too pessimistic. In commenting on Johnson's paper, I raised a number of points which I thought demonstrated the accuracy of Orwell's analysis even if he had been wrong in the extent to which totalitarian forces would exert themselves by 1984.

For example, the increase in the aggregate tax rate borne by the citizens in the Western democracies has gone hand in hand with the decline in their ability to individually control their economic destinies. The use of social insurance numbers to trace every financial transaction in which individuals engage has increasingly exposed private affairs to the potential scrutiny of the State. The fact that one of the economic transactions that is subject to scrutiny is contributions to political parties led me at the time to note that this intrusiveness of the State might eventually challenge the political freedom which in Western democracies we take for granted. Ultimately it is the wide dispersal and availability of financial resources which enables citizens to challenge the political power of governments. In other words, I opined, there is a connection between the extent of economic freedom and the dispersal of economic purchasing power and the extent of political freedom enjoyed by people.

In support of my comment, I referred to a passage in the ground-breaking book *Capitalism and Freedom* by Milton Friedman with the assistance of Rose Friedman, in which the authors note "historical evidence speaks with a single voice on the relation between political freedom and a free market. I know of no example in time or place of a society that has been marked by a large measure of political freedom, and that has not also used something comparable to a free market to organize the bulk of economic activity."

At the meeting in Cambridge, there then ensued a discussion about the relationship between economic and political freedom. It became clear during the course of this discussion that while Milton and Rose Friedman's comment had been extant for more than several decades, there had been no serious attempt to explore the relationship between economic and political freedoms in a scholarly way. I decided at that time that such an investigation should be undertaken and was able to convince Rose and Milton Friedman to co-host a symposium to investigate these relationships. In discussion, it soon became clear that the focus of the symposium should be somewhat broader than economic and political freedoms. As Milton Friedman noted at the time, in some important cases it is civil freedoms and not political freedoms which are of most significant interest and concern. Hong Kong, which has a trivial amount of political freedom, but enjoys civil and economic freedoms, is a case in point.

We were extremely fortunate to attract to the symposium some of the finest minds in the world, representing a broad cross-section of disciplines, including history, philosophy, political science, economics and the law. The papers which were presented and the very rich discussion and debate which ensued provide a fascinating exploration of this important topic.

## II. A CONCEPTUAL, HISTORICAL AND STATISTICAL OVERVIEW

Part One of the book provides a conceptual, historical and statistical overview of the relationship between political, economic and civil freedoms.

The historical paper by Douglass North provides fascinating insights about the role which institutional developments and cultural heritage play in the evolution of democratic process. By comparing and contrasting the evolution of Britain and Spain, North casts into sharper relief the factors that have been important in the evolution of economic growth in the Western world. This paper is followed by excerpts from the book by Milton Friedman, with Rose Friedman, *Capitalism and Freedom* which as I have noted above were in some sense the instigation for the symposium. The conceptual exploration of the relationship between economic and political freedom contained in the excerpts provides a timeless exploration of the subject and this is evident from the discussion led off by Professor Gordon Tullock. There is also a considerable range of opinion about the issues, and certainly no consensus. There was, however, considerable progress made in isolating the issues which have to be considered in forming a judgement on the importance of economic and civil freedoms.

For example, it was noted that economic and civil freedoms have in common the fact that they are freedom from coercion by others, whereas political freedom, at least according to some of the discussants, was a process whereby people relinquish their rights in a collective majoritarian decision-making process. According to some participants, if civil and economic freedoms are guaranteed then participation in the political process is almost irrelevant in this sense.

While the direction of causality was not established, evidence introduced in the course of the conversation led to the definite impression that there is a correlation between the level of affluence and the likelihood that a nation will be politically tolerant and be respectful of democratic institutions. Professor Alvin Rabushka, referring to earlier work, noted that he had correlated the level of incomes with the political freedom indices produced by Raymond Gastil in his paper in Part One. The unmistakable conclusion from Rabushka's work is that countries which have a high rate of growth and a high level of income are also likely to have political and civil freedoms.

An examination of the global record seems to strongly suggest that the existence of political freedom is not a prerequisite to the existence of civil and economic freedoms. Singled out for particular consideration by the participants was the fact that most people tend to associate political freedom with the existence of some sort of majority rule. That is to say that legislation is determined by a simple majority of the populace and that all have the opportunity to participate in the electoral process. It was determined by the consideration of a number of examples that majority rule of itself has no particular virtues, especially if the majority decides to abuse the rights of minorities.

## III.  CASE STUDIES

### Hong Kong and Singapore

Part Two of the book consists of a collection of case studies in which countries from different parts of the world and existing in different cultural and environmental contexts are analyzed to discern how economic, political and civil freedoms coexist in those environments. The first paper in Part Two, by Alvin Rabushka, deals with the two city states of Hong Kong and Singapore. The paper, and the subsequent discussion, confirms the impression that both these countries have done remarkably well in protecting economic and civil freedoms without access to political freedoms in the ordinary sense. In the case of Singapore, a one-party government has denied the citizens effective political choice whereas in Hong Kong the colonial status has meant that people have not engaged in internal political activities of any significant nature.

Not only is the conclusion that countries have been able to prosper in spite of having no political institutions, the judgement is that they have prospered because there have been no political institutions. Much of the discussion centres on the unfortunate proclivity of the political system to be used for what Gordon Tullock described and Anne Kruger has dubbed "rent-seeking behaviour." This involves the use of regulations and legislation to benefit one group of citizens at the expense of another.

While enjoying substantial amounts of economic freedom, neither Hong Kong nor Singapore are completely free of government interventions, particularly Singapore which has had a long tradition of governmental activism with regard to such institutions as the Central Provident Fund and other social engineering types of policies. On the other hand, it was also noted that while Hong Kong is subject to economic regulation, by comparison with any other developing country, it is undoubtedly the most economically free country in the world.

While the lack of political institutions has been an important ingredient in Hong Kong's past economic success, as the end of colonial status approaches and the beginning of the People's Republic of China hegemony becomes important after 1997, the conclusion is that political institutions may be the only thing that can act as a buffer between the PRC and Hong Kong's economic and civil freedoms.

## Africa

The second paper in Part Two by Lord Peter Bauer examines the interaction of economic growth, political sovereignty and freedom in black Africa. Bower notes that the colonial managers of black African states left an administrative residue which has subsequently become the "ready-made framework of economic totalitarianism." Also according to Lord Bauer the subsequent behaviour of Western politicians, civil servants, academics and people in the media, have tended to reinforce totalitarian economic attitudes and encourage despotism and lawlessness in black Africa. Economic aid has largely underwritten unsuccessful and intrusive economic policies which in the absence of aid would have led to economic collapse and the necessity to face the consequences of those policies. But aid has also shored up totalitarian political behaviours of the region as time and again Western countries have provided military, financial and moral support for leaders engaged in the systematic elimination of economic, political and civil freedoms.

Ironically, according to Bauer, it was the economic apparatus of marketing boards and import controls erected by colonial managers which have been the principal instrument of economic destruction in these countries. The fact that the same basic policy apparatus could under colonial administration lead to relative prosperity and in the context of political and tribal rivalry lead to economic demise is a telling commentary on the relationship between political and economic freedom. But, as Bauer notes, an even more poignant comment on the consequences of providing African states with their sovereignty is the large numbers of blacks from all over Africa who travel long distances to attempt to get into South Africa where black peoples are said to be enslaved by the current system.

As Sir Isaiah Berlin noted in 1958, the notion of liberty is a concept of such porosity that there is practically no interpretation that it is capable of resisting. The confused identification of the sovereignty of African governments with the freedom of Africans is an example.

During the course of discussion, while there were no firm conclusions, there was a kind of consensus that Africa does provide a large number of examples of the misuse of political power by incumbent governments and the crucial role which protection of civil rights and economic rights has for economic development and political stability. The resounding message from Africa is that those who are seriously interested in the freedoms enjoyed by people must not be misled to believe that political freedom, in the sense of freedom to cast votes in an election can in any sense guarantee freedom that is meaningful for citizenry, and in particular, civil rights and freedom from capricious violence administered by the state. The economic success stories of Africa occur in those jurisdictions where civil rights are preserved and where a measure of economic freedom has been ensured.

## South America

The paper by Ramon Diaz dealing with the puzzle of economic, political and civil freedoms in South America is in some ways a melting pot for many of the concepts and notions which emerged in previous discussions and in previous papers. It reflects the insights about institutional and cultural attitudes contained in the first paper by Douglass North. Diaz sets for himself the task of explaining why an area with such economic promise as South America could have lapsed into the economic and political difficulties which are endemic to the region.

Diaz hypothesizes and the subsequent discussion confirms that, in part, the difference between South America and North America is that South America was inspired by a Rousseaunian concept of the appropriate role of government whereas in North America the Lockean notion of limited government was much more prevalent. Cultural differences have also apparently proved important, particularly the pervasive impact of mythological thought and romanticism in Latin society.

## Sweden

The paper by Ingemar Stahl notes that many of the discussions about the relationship between rights and freedoms is often marred by a lack of precision in the terminology used. Stahl proposes an approach to the discussion about freedoms and civil rights which relates these to contractual relationships between individuals and between individuals and the State. Freedoms in this sense are bundles of rights which will be more or less extensive in different states depending on the regime pursued.

This was found to be quite a useful classification system and it sharpened somewhat the nature of the discussion. The discussion itself focused more on the extent to which the relations between the State and the individual really are voluntary in the modern welfare state and, in particular, focused on the issue of Sweden's economic performance in the light of the fact that it is a highly redistributive state.

In discussion it emerged that the Swedish case is not, in many respects, what it appears because much of the economic success in Sweden occurs within the export sector which is very lightly regulated. This is one of the reasons why the Swedish economy has performed so well notwithstanding a significant welfare state apparatus. Another point which arose from the discussion was the very important question of the extent to which the modern welfare state apparatus really is coercive. If citizens believe that other citizens are bearing the cost of the programmes which they themselves particularly subscribe to then they are, in effect, voluntarily concurring with arrangements which, while not in their interest, seem to be in their interest because of a lack of transparency of the costs and benefits associated with their actions. Discussion of the Swedish case, in particular, revealed that there are many lapses and many imperfections in the conceptual framework which economists and political scientists bring to the analysis of the relationship between economic, political and civil freedoms.

## Yugoslavia

The final paper in the volume by Svetozar Pejovich deals with innovation in economic systems and while at first blush seems to be unconnected with the rest of the papers in the volume, in fact initiated a discussion which neatly enveloped much of the discussion which had proceeded. Innovation—the introduction of something new—occurs in economic, political and scientific as well as other aspects of human existence. The amount of innovation, in its broad sense, that can occur in a society depends to a considerable degree on the relationships between individuals and on the relationship between the individual and the State.

As emerged in the conversation, as long as people are free to make contracts with each other about how they will treat each other and even if those contracts involve restrictions they nevertheless enhance the amount of freedom in the sense of the amount of choice that people have. It was noted, for example, that contracts between inventors and those given the rights to use their inventions, while often quite demanding contracts, in effect are intended to provide the user with sufficient latitude to use the innovation in a creative and potentially novel way. The only way the inventor will be inclined to encourage this to happen is if there is some equitable sharing, from the inventor's point of view, of the fruits of that arrangement.

One of the kinds of innovation that can occur in a society where people are free to contract and recontract and make choices is new institutions. Elections are a process whereby people change governments and the freedom to do that is the freedom to innovate in the political area. Freedom of speech is the freedom to bring new ideas or new perspectives on old ideas to a society, while the range of civil rights which are often the concern of civil libertarians and libertarians are the rights to be innovative in personal behaviours as long as those behaviours don't impose costs on others. From the point of view of society's economic growth and development, the most unimportant right is the right to innovate, to bring new products, new methods of production and new pricing information to individual interactions.

The papers and discussions contained in this volume are by no means presented as a final or definitive word on the relationship between economic, political and civil freedoms. The ideas recorded here are both novel and hackneyed in the sense that the themes are some of the oldest which have occupied thinking people for the course of human history. They are novel in the sense that little attention is paid to them by formal economists, by political scientists, or by others into whose realm of analysis the issues do not quite squarely fall.

For those who have an interest in pursuing the issues discussed in this volume, I am pleased to say that the symposium on which this book is based is the beginning of a process which will continue for many years. Thanks to the agreement of the Liberty Fund, Inc. to provide funding, a series of discussions about economic freedom will be conducted at The Fraser Institute during 1988 and 1989. For that reason, this book has been entitled Volume 1 and subsequent excursions in the series will be published in subsequent years.

The papers and the opinions expressed in this volume have been independently arrived at by the authors and as a consequence may not reflect the views of the members, the trustees or others who financially support The Fraser Institute. Nevertheless, the Institute is especially pleased to have the opportunity to present the views of these learned scholars in the hope that it will stimulate further discussion and research by others.

Michael A. Walker
Director
The Fraser Institute

# PART ONE

## POLITICAL, ECONOMIC AND CIVIL FREEDOMS: AN HISTORICAL, CONCEPTUAL AND STATISTICAL OVERVIEW

# Chapter 1

# Institutions, Economic Growth and Freedom: An Historical Introduction

## Douglass C. North

This essay* uses an exploratory analytical framework to examine the origins of modern economic growth in the Western world. This growth was inextricably involved with the emergence not only of secure property rights but of political, religious, and "civil" freedoms. Because the Western world evolved in two widely divergent directions, I wish to explore both the "successful" story of Britain (and the Netherlands) and the unsuccessful story of Spain (and Portugal). My objective is not simply to demonstrate that the freedoms were mutually reinforcing aspects of the pattern of successful countries; but, more important, to explore the dynamics of long-run societal change in terms of the evolution of contrasting institutional environments. One story takes us to British North America, the thirteen colonies, independence, and the growth of the United States; the other, to Spanish imperial policy in the Indies, Latin American colonial development, independence, and the subsequent relative failure of Latin American countries.

In the sections that follow, I explore the issues that are involved in the history (I); the nature of institutions (II); the sources of institutional change (III); the initial historical conditions in England and Spain (IV); English development (V); Spanish development (VI). In the final section, I briefly examine the consequences in the New World. Of necessity, the historical sections are little more than outlines, illustrating the framework developed in Sections II and III.

---

* I wish to thank Elizabeth Case for improving this essay.

## I.  HISTORY

I shall not tarry long over the definition of freedom. While a lengthy analysis should go into the complexities of this issue, here I simply assert that the freedoms I am concerned with are uniformly applied rules with respect to the security of persons and property over a range of civil, political, religious, and economic activities. They include freedom of religious and political expression; protection against arbitrary imprisonment; the right to bailment; protection against impairment of the right to use, derive income from, or alienate property. None of these freedoms is absolute; nor are they ever perfectly enforced. At the margin they can lead to anarchy, or tyranny, or a reduction in the choices of others. Hence, they are always relative to their consequences upon others.

Their connection to economic growth is straightforward. The more secure are these freedoms, the lower the costs of transacting; and declining transaction costs are (given relatively non-controversial behavioural assumptions) a critical historical source of economic growth. The implications of this assertion are that one can understand neither the nature of freedom nor economic growth in a traditional neo-classical framework, since this framework is devoid of institutions; and that institutions are at the heart of a meaningful understanding of freedom and determine transaction costs in a society.[1]

## II.  THE NATURE OF INSTITUTIONS

Institutions are rules, enforcement characteristics of rules, and norms of behaviour that structure repeated human interaction. Hence, they limit and define the choice set of neo-classical theory. We are interested not in the institutions per se, but in their consequences for the choices individuals actually make.

Constitutions, statute and common laws, contracts specify in formal terms the rules of the game, from the most general constitutional cones to specific terms of exchange. Rules (and their enforcement) are constrained by the costliness of measuring the characteristics or attributes of what constitutes rule-compliance or violation. Hence, the technology of measurement of all the dimensions (sight, sound, taste, etc.) of the human senses has played a critical role in our ability to define property rights and other types of rules. Moreover, since we receive utility from the various attributes of goods and services rather than from the entities themselves, it is the costliness of measuring the separable dimensions that is critical in this study.[2] The relationship between the benefits derived from rule-specification and the costs of measurement not only has been critical in the history of property rights (common property vs. private property) but is at the heart of many of the issues related to the structure and effectiveness of enforcement.

If it were costless to measure the performance of agents or the attributes of goods and services as well as the terms of exchange, then enforcement would not be a problem. We would be back in the neo-classical world of the instantaneous exchange of a unidimensional good or service. But because measurement is costly and the parties to exchange stand to gain by receiving the benefits without incurring all of the costs of exchange, not only is enforcement typically imperfect, but the structure of the enforcement process will affect outcomes and hence choices. Let me elaborate both points.

Enforcement is typically imperfect for two reasons: 1) measurement is costly; and 2) the interests of principals and agents are not identical. The costliness of measurement implies that at the margin the benefits from additional monitoring or policing will be balanced against the incremental costs. Moreover, as I shall discuss below, the marginal benefits and costs of policing will be weighed against those of investing at the margin in ideological persuasion. Rules are enforced by agents (police, foremen, judges, juries, etc.), and therefore the standard problems of agency theory obtain. It is important to stress here that both the structure of the enforcement mechanism and the degree of imperfection of enforcement are important in the choices that are made.[3]

Rules and their (imperfect) enforcement are not the complete story. If they were, the modeling of institutions and hence the costs of transacting could be made, at this stage of our knowledge, much more precise. But norms of behaviour also matter; and we know very little about them.

As a first approximation, norms are informal constraints on behaviour that are in part derivative from formal rules; that is they are extensions of such rules and apply to specific issues. These informal procedures, deriving as they do from formal organizational structures and agendas, are important but still relatively easy to analyze.[4] Much more important, norms are codes of conduct, taboos, standards of behaviour, that are in part derived from perceptions that all individuals form both to explain and to evaluate the world around them. Some of these perceptions are shaped and molded by organized ideologies (religions, social and political values, etc.). Others are honed by experience, which leads to the re-affirmation or rejection of earlier norms.

However they are formed, and however they evolve, norms play a critical role in constraining the choice set at a moment of time and in the evolution of institutions through time. They are important at a moment of time precisely because of the costliness of measurement and the imperfect enforcement of rules. To the degree that individuals believe in the rules, contracts, property rights, etc., of a society, they will be willing to forego opportunities to cheat, steal or engage in opportunistic behaviour. In short, they live up to the terms of contracts. Conversely, to the degree that individuals do not believe in the rules, regard them as unjust, or simply live up to the standard wealth maximizing behavioural assumption we typically employ in neo-classical economics, the costs of contracting, that is transactions costs, will also increase. Empirical evidence suggests the price we are willing to pay for our convictions is a negatively sloped function, so that ideological attitudes are less important as the price increases; but both the slope of the function and shifts in the functions are subjects about which we know very little.[5]

The foregoing paragraphs suggest that ideas and value matter at a moment of time. They do so because of "slack in the system," "agency costs," "consumption on the job," etc., all of which result from the costliness of measurement and enforcement. But how do they change through time? Certainly fundamental changes in relative prices lead not only to rule (and enforcement) changes; but to changes in ideas and values, and the rate of these two kinds of change may be markedly different. This subject will be explored below, but first let me raise some specific issues about institutions, transaction costs, and the consequent choices of the "players" which bear on the subject of this essay.

Let me start with a quotation from Bill Riker.

> ...Every time I convince myself that I have found an instance in which constitutional forms do make a difference for liberty, my discovery comes apart in my hands...Professor Ostrom believes that at least part of the reason we believe we are a free people is that we have certain constitutional forms, but it may just as easily be the case that the reason we have these constitutional forms is that we are a free people.[6]

Now let me quote Bill Riker again, a decade later.

> The Constitution was in a formal sense a necessary condition for the achievement, that is had the Articles [of Confederation] survived, the nation would not have flourished. To see this, note the Constitution was, in a formal sense, necessary for political unity and the consequent political dominance of the United States, first in America and its expansion westward, then in the western hemisphere by restraining European empirical expansion and finally in the world, helping to destroy in two world wars Western European monarchies and empires and later in countering the Soviet empire. All this depended on political unity. Yet without the

Constitution, North America might very well have been as Balkanized as South America.[7]

Rules themselves are not a sufficient condition for determining outcomes even though they are, on occasion, critical. Indeed, the second quotation is from an extraordinarily insightful analysis of the formation of the Constitution, in which Riker makes the convincing case that its creation results from a rather unique concatenation of events that, as the quote implies, changed the destiny of the thirteen confederated states. But it is important to remember that a number of Latin American countries patterned their constitutions after that of the United States with radically different results.

It may be a slight exaggeration to assert that enforcement is always imperfect, but this statement focuses our attention on a critical and neglected aspect of economic history: the essential role of third party enforcement of contracts for human economic progress. There is a large literature in the new industrial organization on self-enforcing contracts, etc.; but as with so much of modern economics, it misses the larger issues involved in exchange in a specialized world. Personal exchange solves the problems of contract fulfillment by repeat dealings and a dense network of social interaction. But the key to the high-income societies of the western world is still the one that Adam Smith propounded more than two hundred years ago. And increasing specialization and division of labour necessitates the development of institutional structures that permit individuals to take actions involving complex relationships with other individuals far removed from personal knowledge and extending over long periods of time.

The essential institutional reliability means that we have confidence in outcomes increasingly remote from our personal knowledge. As the network of interdependence widens, the institutional requirements necessary to realizing the productivity gains arising from specialization are efficient factor and product markets and a medium of exchange with reliable features. The establishment and enforcement of property rights conducive to the creation of such markets would then allow individuals in highly complex, interdependent situations to have confidence in their dealings with individuals with whom they have no reciprocal and ongoing exchange relationships. This is only possibly as a result of a third party to exchange, government, which specifies property rights and enforces contracts.

Let me emphasize that while third party enforcement is far from perfect, there are vast differences in the relative certainty and effectiveness of contract enforcement, temporally over the past five centuries in the Western world, and more currently between modern Western and third world countries. The evolution of government from its medieval mafia-like character to that embodying modern legal institutions and instruments is a major part of the history of freedom. It is a part that tends to be obscured or ignored because of the myopic vision of many economists, who persist in modeling government as nothing more than a gigantic form of theft and income redistribution.

In a recent paper, Robert Axelrod tells the story of Alexander Hamilton writing, on the last night of his life, all of the reasons why he should not engage in a duel with Aaron Burr.[8] They were rational and overwhelmingly convincing reasons but in the end not sufficient to overcome the dishonour that he perceived would result from a code of conduct that required such a solution of disputes amongst gentlemen. Axelrod's purpose in telling this story was to illustrate that norms of behaviour, which are not legal rules, are enforced by the attitudes and behaviour of others in the society.

But this is surely only part of that complex of ideas, customs, dogmas, values, ethical standards, etc., which make up our understanding of the world around us, establish our normative standards, and help define the choices we make. While some norms are externally enforced, others are internally enforced codes of conduct, like honesty, integrity, etc. It would be an immense contribution to have a testable general theory of the sociology of knowledge and therefore an understanding of the way overall ideologies emerge and evolve.[9] In the absence of such a theory, we can still derive an important and potentially testable implication about norms at a more specific micro-level of analysis, which is derived from an understanding of institutions. Specifically, the structure of rules and their enforcement help define the costs we bear for ideologically determined choices; the lower the costs, the more will ideas and ideologies matter. Let me provide three illustrations.

A basic paradox of public choice is that individual votes don't matter, but lots of people still vote. Brennan and Buchanan point out this dilemma in a recent paper but do not satisfactorily resolve it.[10] Surely one of the things voters are doing is expressing strongly held convictions at low cost to themselves. Moreover, in the aggregate votes do of course matter. The expression "putting your money where your mouth is" characterizes neither voters nor for that matter academics. Both can afford to be in the literal sense, "irresponsible."

Recently a large volume of literature has grown up around agency theory applied to legislators, with the voter as principal and the legislator as agent. Empirical work suggests that legislators frequently vote their own conviction rather than principals' interests.[11] Other empirical work suggests that the institutional structure of Congress permits legislators to engage in strategic voting behaviour that effectively conceals their true objectives.[12]

Finally, judges with lifetime tenure can and do vote their own convictions, as even the most casual study of courts in general and the Supreme Court in particular testifies. Moreover, this is not an accident. The constitutional provisions, as interpreted by the Marshall Court (1801-1835), were deliberately designed to remove judges from interest group pressures.[13]

It is one thing to be able to show that ideas matter; but as noted above, it is much more difficult to trace the way they have evolved. For example, the demise of slavery, one of the landmarks in the history of freedom, is simply not explicable in an interest group model. Surely the micro argument described above is important to understanding its end. That is, most of those who voted for its elimination, either directly or indirectly, paid little or no costs; they could simply express their abhorrence of one human being owning another. There was no institutional way for the slave owner to buy off the voters. On the other hand, the *way* in which the anti-slavery movement grew (and frequently was used by interest groups) so that it could lead to these votes is a much more complex story.

It's time we took stock. The neo-classical model describes the output of an economy as a function of the quantity and costs of a set of inputs of land, labour, capital, and entrepreneurship, given some production function derived from the state of technological knowledge. But this formulation is, if not incorrect, largely misleading, since if that were all there were to the output of societies, they would all be rich (given again some rather non-controversial behavioural assumptions). If we make the story more complex by introducing transportation costs as an obstacle to realizing the gains from trade, then we should observe with the decline in those transportation costs, which has been going on for several thousand years, a corresponding growth in wealth and income. As a matter of fact, at the time of the Roman Empire in the first two centuries A.D., there was a Mediterranean-wide market, which disappeared with the empire's demise after the Fifth Century A.D. Here, transportation costs had not risen; rather, the costs of transacting had risen with the disappearance of a unified political system of rules and laws (at least partially) enforced over the Mediterranean world. Restated more usefully, the costs of production are a function of the costs of the traditional inputs listed above and the costs of transacting.

It is important to stress that economic growth can and has occurred as a consequence of increasing productivity associated with either decline in production costs or decline in transaction costs. But while falling production costs are a result of technological change or economies of scale, reduced transaction costs are a consequence of the development of more efficient institutions;[14] and since political institutions are the source of the specification and enforcement of property rights, our examination must encompass both political and economic institutions.

The measurement of transaction costs is beset with all of the problems of measurement in traditional national income accounting. To the extent that transactions occur in the market economy, they can be measured.[15] However, costs of transacting arising from queuing, waiting, rationing, bribery, etc., which are substantial in all economies but particularly in Third World and socialistic economies, are unmeasured.

In considering historical measurement we must remember that the costs of transacting have frequently been so high that no production or exchange occurred. The lack of institutions and instruments to facilitate production and exchange in factor and product markets (as well as the existence of institutions designed to raise the costs of transacting) resulted in predominantly personalized (and localized) production and trade. The development of institutions to facilitate transacting is marked not only by expansion of production and exchange in particular factor markets, but by a subsequent decline in transaction costs as the institutions develop. The dramatic decline in real interest rates in 17th Century Netherlands and early 18th Century Britain followed the development of capital market institutions; it is probably the best quantitative measure (and the most critical indicator) of improving productivity in the transactions sector.

The foregoing discussion profiles transactions costs in a growing economy. The emergence of political institutions that specify "efficient" property rights and provide increasingly effective enforcement should show up in terms of the development of economic institutions to facilitate market exchanges. As a result, costs per transaction will be falling; but the size of the transaction sector in the aggregate will be a growing proportion of GNP, as increasing specialization and division of labour multiplies the aggregate volume of exchanges. This is precisely the pattern for the United States, where the measured size of the transaction sector in 1870 is about one-quarter of GNP and in 1970 is almost one-half.

## III.  THE SOURCES OF INSTITUTIONAL CHANGE

There are two issues I wish to address on institutional change: 1) What causes the change; and 2) what determines its path. In neither case have I a completely satisfactory answer.

Before we turn to these two issues, we must examine the role institutions play in reducing uncertainty in human interaction, since it is this stabilizing role of institutions which separates clearly the framework of analysis being developed here from the traditional neo-classical approach. We can most readily understand the difference if we have ever visited a foreign country and attempted to "do business" with them. We will find that of necessity we must learn their "way of doing things." The structural forms of human interaction that characterize societies are a combination of rules, enforcement features, and norms of behaviour. Until we learn what these are, the costs of transacting are high. Once we understand them, we can effectively communicate and engage in varieties of social, political, and economic exchange. The function of institutions is to provide certainty in human interaction, and this is accomplished by the inherent features of rules and norms. Rules are typically nested in a hierarchical structure, each more costly to change. But even in the absence of the hierarchical institutional structure, the status quo typically has an advantage over changes in a variety of political structures, as a consequence of agenda control and committee structure.

However, it is norms of behaviour that probably provide the most important sources of stability in human interaction. They are extensions, elaborations, and qualifications of rules that have tenacious survival ability, because they become an integral part of habitual behaviour. The reduction of uncertainty, in consequence, makes possible regular human interaction; but it in no way implies that the institutions are efficient, only that they dampen the consequences of relative price changes.

But institutions do change, and fundamental changes in relative prices do lead to institutional change. Historically population change has been the single most important source of relative price changes, though technological change (including and importantly, changes in military technology) and changes in the costs of information have also been major sources. Moreover, as briefly noted in the previous section, changes in norms of behaviour, while certainly influenced by relative price changes, are also influenced by the evolution of ideas and ideologies.

A stylized characterization of the process of institutional change could proceed as follows: As a result of a relative price change, one or both parties to an exchange (political or economic) perceives that he (they) could do better with an altered agreement (contract). Depending on his relative (and presumably changed) bargaining power, he will, as a consequence of the changed prices, re-negotiate the contract. However, contracts are nested in a hierarchy of rules. If the re-negotiation involves alteration of a more fundamental rule, he (or they) may find it worthwhile to devote resources to changing it; or gradually, over time, the rule or custom may simply become ignored and/or unenforced. Agenda power, free-rider problems, and norms of behaviour will add meat (and lots of complications) to this skeletal outline.

An important distinction in this argument is made between absolute bargaining power and changes at the margin. To illustrate this distinction, I turn to the medieval world. The "agreement" between lord and serf on the medieval manor reflected the overwhelming power of the lord vis-a-vis the serf. But changes at the margin, as a consequence of 14th Century population decline, altered the opportunity costs, increased the relative bargaining power of serfs, and led to the gradual evolution of copyhold.[16]

While institutional evolution may proceed in the above manner, without explicit intent or design, dramatic changes in the rules (or their enforcement) occur as well. The gathering in Philadelphia in 1787 is a clear example. Riker, in the essay referred to above, makes clear that the instigators of the convention were Federalists and that their opposition both misunderstood and misjudged their ability to write and ratify a new constitution. Indeed, it was the promised addition of the Bill of Rights as the first order of business under the new constitution that made ratification possible (Riker, forthcoming). Perhaps it is worth noting that the writers were "gentlemen" and that their promise was both believed and carried out.

A special note should be made of the role of military technology in institutional change. Not only have changes in military technology resulted in different, efficient (survival) sizes of political units, but, as in the story that follows, they have consequently induced fundamental changes in other institutions, so that fiscal revenues essential to survival could be realized.

The second issue of institutional change is what determines the direction of change. From what must have been quite common origins several million years ago or even as recently as the hunting and gathering societies that predate the "agricultural revolution" in the 8th millennium B.C., we have evolved in radically different directions (and at radically different rates). How have we evolved such divergent patterns of social, political, and economic organization? To consider a specific example, as I will do in the subsequent sections of this paper, how do we explain the divergent paths of British and Spanish development, both at home and in the contrasting histories of North and South America?

I believe the answer lies in the way that institutional structures evolve. The closest (although by no means perfect) analogy is the way we perceive that the common law evolved. It is precedent-based law: Past decisions become embedded in the structure of rules, which marginally change as cases arise involving some new or, at least in the terms of past cases, unforeseen issue, which when decided becomes, in turn, a part of the legal framework. However, I don't intend to imply by this analogy that the result is "efficient." In fact, as we shall see, Spanish institutional evolution moved in the direction of stagnation.

Let me illustrate institutional evolution by reference to a specific act, which was almost as important as the Constitution in United States history. This was the Northwest Ordinance, passed by the Congress (when it was under the Articles of Confederation) in 1787, at the very time that the Constitutional Convention was meeting in Philadelphia. It was the third act dealing with the issues that arose with respect to the settlement, governance, and integration of the vast lands to the west in the new nation. Where did the rules incorporated in these acts come from and how were they arrived at?

The Ordinance is quite simple and brief. It provided for rules of inheritance and fee-simple ownership of land; it set up the basic structure of the territorial governments and provided for the mechanisms by which territories gradually became self-governing. Additionally, it made provisions for when a territory could be admitted as a state. Then there were a series of Articles of Compact, in effect a bill of rights for the territories (i.e., provisions for religious freedom, the writ of habeas corpus, trial by jury, bailment, enforcement of contract and compensation for property). There were additional provisions about good faith to the Indians, free navigation on the Mississippi and the St. Lawrence, public debt, land disposal, the number of states that could be divided up within the Northwest Territory, and finally a provision prohibiting slavery (though the return of run-away slaves was provided for) in the territories.

It is easy to trace most of the provisions. They had evolved and become a part of the rules of political units of the colonies during the previous 150 years (described in more detail below). These included inheritance laws, fee simple ownership of land, and many of the provisions of the Bill of Rights. Some, however, were precedent-based but had become controversial because of new issues. This was particularly true of the size and the conditions for admittance of new states. The precedence base derived from the original provisions of charters and the Articles of Confederation. Controversies arose from the implications of changing political power with the new government. One of the rules, the prohibition of slavery, appears to have been the result of vote-trading between the authors of the Northwest Ordinance and the writers of the Constitution; slavery was prohibited in the former bill in return for counting slaves as 3/5 of a person in the Constitution, which increased the representation of Southern slave states in Congress (a major issue of the period).[17]

The Northwest Ordinance provided the basic framework dictating the pattern of expansion of the American nation over the next century. While its provisions were at times modified by new issues and controversies, it provided a clear, "path-dependent" pattern of institutional evolution. It is only understandable in terms of precedent, new issues, and the bargaining strength of the parties. It is essential to note that precedent not only defined and determined many of the provisions but also dictated the existing agenda, decision rules, and method of resolution. the larger point of this illustration is that we can only understand historical change by modeling the way institutions evolved through time. That brings us to the following brief outline of English and Spanish institutional change, from the 1500s to the 19th Century in North America and Latin America.

## IV. THE INITIAL HISTORICAL CONDITIONS IN ENGLAND AND SPAIN

Despite the similarities between England and Spain (discussed below) at the beginning of the Sixteenth century, the two countries had evolved very differently. Spain had just emerged from seven centuries of Moorish domination of the peninsula. It was not really a unified country. Although the marriage of Ferdinand and Isabella brought Castile and Aragon together, they continued to maintain separate rules, Cortes, and policies. England, in contrast, had developed a relatively centralized feudalism, as a result of the Norman conquest, and had recently established the Tudors with the Battle of Bosworth (1485).

Yet, in common with the rest of the emerging european nation states, they each faced a problem with far-reaching consequences. That is, that a ruler required additional revenue to survive. The tradition was that a king was supposed to live on his own, which meant that the income from his estates, together with the traditional feudal dues, were his total revenue. The changes in military technology associated with the effective use of the cross-bow, long-bow, pike, and gun powder enormously increased the cost of warfare and led to a fiscal crisis first described by Joseph Schumpter (1919). In order to get more revenue, the king had somehow to make a bargain with constituents. In both countries this initially led to the development of some form of representation on the part of the constituents in return for revenue. In both countries, the wool trade became a major source of crown revenue; but thereafter their stories diverge. We can better appreciate these divergent stories in the framework of a very simple model of the state, consistent with the framework developed int he previous sections of this essay.[18]

The king acts like a discriminating monopolist, offering to different groups of constituents "protection and justice," or at least the reduction of internal disorder and the protection of property rights, in return for tax revenue. Since different constituent groups have different opportunity costs and bargaining power with the ruler, there result different bargains. But there are also economies of scale in the provision of these (semi) public goods of law and enforcement. Hence, total revenue is increased, but the division of the incremental gains between ruler and constituents depends on their relative bargaining power; changes at the margin in either the "violence" potential of the ruler or the opportunity costs of the constituents will result in re-divisions of the incremental revenues. Moreover, the rulers' gross and net revenues differ significantly as a result of the necessity of developing agents (a bureaucracy) to monitor, meter, and collect the revenue; and all the inherent consequences of agency theory obtain here. The initial institutional structure that emerged in order to solve the fiscal crisis therefore looked similar in all the emerging nation states of Europe. A representative body (or bodies) or constituents, designed to facilitate exchanges between the two parties, was created. To the ruler it meant the development of a hierarchical structure of agents, which was a major transformation from the simple (if extensive) management of the king's household and estates to a bureaucracy monitoring the wealth and/or income of the king's constituents. Let us see how this initial institutional framework evolved in the two cases.

## V.  ENGLISH DEVELOPMENT

The tension between rulers and constituents (although that would hardly describe the situation at Runnymede in 1215) surfaces with the Magna Carta; but the fiscal crises come to a head with Edward I and Edward III during the Hundred Years War. Stubbs in his *The Constitutional History of England* summarizes the consequences.

> The admission of the right of parliament to legislate, to inquire into abuses, and to share in the guidance of national policy, was practically purchased by the monies granted to Edward I and Edward III.

A logical consequence was that in the 16th Century under the Tudors the structure of Tudor government was revolutionized, as Geoffrey Elton has described in *The Tudor Revolution in Government*. This revolution transformed the government from an elaborate household structure to a bureaucracy increasingly concerned with overseeing and regulating the economy. It had early on been the wool trade which had served as the basis for a good deal of tax revenue; and, as told by Eileen Powers (1941), the wool trade involved a three-way relationship between the exporters, the wool growers as represented in Parliament, and the Crown. In this agreement, the Merchants of the Staple achieved a monopoly of the export trade and a depot in Calais. Parliament received the right to set the tax and the

Crown obtained the revenue. In England the combined mix of the growth of the wool trade, the development of fee-simple ownership in land, and the development of arable lands and new crops imported from the Dutch all contributed to an expansion of agriculture. At the same time, in the non-agricultural sector the economy became increasingly diversified. Although the Tudors continued to attempt to control the economy and to freeze the structure of economic activity into guilds and monopolistic activities, their efforts were relatively ineffective. They were ineffective because 1) the statutes only covered existing industries, so that new industries escaped rule; 2) despite opposition by town guilds, industries moved to the countryside and effectively escaped guild control; 3) the control of wages and labourers in the Statute of Artificers of 1563 was only partially and sporadically enforced; 4) enforcement in the countryside was typically in the hands of unpaid justices of the peace who had little incentive to enforce the law.

The cloth trade therefore grew in the countryside. The interplay between the expansion of diverse economic activities escaping from guild restrictions and the pressures for the development of parliamentary control over the sovereign came to a head with the Stuarts, with the fumbling efforts of James I, the continuing fiscal crises that occurred under Charles I, and the articulate opposition of Coke and others. It was Coke who insisted that the common law was the supreme law of the land, and who repeatedly incurred the anger of James I. It was Coke who led the parliamentary opposition in the 1620s, which established common law control over commercial law. By the end of Elizabeth's reign a changing benefit cost pattern of economic activity was emerging with the widening of domestic and foreign markets; the result was the expansion of voluntary organizations in the form of joint stock companies, and growing resentment against the crown sponsored monopolies which excluded private companies from many of these growing markets. *Darcy vs. Allein* was only the most celebrated case reflecting this ongoing struggle to create a set of rights that would be outside the control of the monarchy. Passing the Statute of Monopolies was just another step in the ongoing process.

Yet the issue of the supremacy of Parliament hung in the balance for much of the 17th Century; and as the struggle continued, Parliament not only attempted to wrest from the King's control the granting of monopolies (as in the Statute of Monopolies), but also to protect itself from the King's wrath by establishing religious, civil, and political freedoms as well (such as the Petition of Right in 1629). It distorts the story, however, to think of it as a clear-cut struggle between an absolutist "oriented" king and a unified Parliament concerned with economic, civil, and political liberties.[19] As the Civil War attests, a complex of religious, economic, and political interests coalesced into armed caps. Moreover, the winning coalition one day could be in the minority the next day. Hence, there was persistent interest and concern with broadly based and impersonally guarded rights.

Sixteen eighty-nine produced the final triumph of Parliament, and in rapid consequence came a set of economic institutions reflecting the relatively increasing security of property rights. The creation of the Bank of England (1694) and the development of new financial instruments led to a dramatic decline in the cost of transacting and has been described as the English financial revolution. Both institutions and consequent falling transaction costs reflect increased security of the time dimension of property rights, a dimension critical to both the long-term capital market and to economic growth itself.

In terms of the very simple political model outlined in Section II, the original trade of certain rights to Parliament in return for revenues was a product of the fiscal crises of the One Hundred Years War. In the 17th Century the Tudors' tripartite arrangement between the Crown, Parliament, and merchants granted further rights to Parliament in return for tax revenues (and still further rights were granted to the Commons by Henry VIII for support in his controversial seizure of church properties). In consequence, the Tudors required an organized bureaucracy to oversee tax collection and to regulate other parts of the economy. The triumph of Parliament in 1689 simply shifted the locus of decision-making to Parliament, which raises the issue of why Parliament would not then proceed to act just like the King. Tollison and Ekelund argue:

> Higher costs due to uncertainty and growing private returns reduced industry demands for regulation and control in England. All this strengthened the emergent Constitutional democracy, which created conditions making rent-seeking activity on the art of both monarch and merchant more costly. When the locus of power to rent-seeking shifted from the monarch to Parliament...the costs of supply and regulation through legislative enactment rose, for reasons suggested by the theory of public choice.[20]

The framework of institutional evolution I have described suggests a somewhat more complicated story than Ekelund and Tollison provide. They assert, "While it is flattering to think that intellectuals affect public policy—surely they do to some extent—it seems completely out of character for economists to think that intellectual arguments could affect real magnitudes so strongly."[21] But the embedding of economic and political freedoms in the law, the interests of principals (merchants, etc.) in greater degrees of freedom, and the ideological considerations that swept England in the 17th Century combined to play a role in institutional change.

## VI.  SPANISH DEVELOPMENT

While the major steps in Spanish institutional evolution are not in question, nor is the final result, I do not believe that the specific steps along the way have been as clearly delineated as in the English story. [It should be emphasized that I am not nearly as familiar with the Spanish literature as with the English; but it is my impression that an explicit analysis of the evolution of property rights and their political origins has not been a focus of Spanish economic history.] However, some sketch is possible.

Prior to the union of Ferdinand and Isabella the kingdom of Aragon (comprising approximately Valencia, Aragon, and Catalonia) had a very different character than Castile. Aragon had been reconquered from the Arabs in the last half of the 13th Century nd had become a major commercial empire extending into Sardinia, Sicily, and part of Greece. The Cortes, reflecting the interests of merchants, "had already secured the power to legislate and even to limit the king's power to issue legislation under certain conditions" (Veliz, 1980, p. 34). In contrast Castile was continually engaged in warfare, either against the Moors or in internal strife. While the Cortes existed, it was seldom summoned,

> and as nobility and clergy were exempt from financial exactions that could conceivably join them with representatives of the town in resisting additional levies by the Crown, they did not pose (that is the towns did not pose) a credible challenge...(Veliz, 1980, p. 35).

In the fifteen years after their union, Isabella succeeded in gaining control not only over the unruly war-like barons but over church policy in Castile as well. The result was a centralized monarchy in Castile; and it was Castile that defined the institutional evolution of both Spain and Latin America.

A major source of fiscal revenues was the Mesta (the sheepherders guild), which in return for the right to migrate with their sheep across Castile provided the Crown with a secure source of revenue, but also with consequences adverse to the development of arable agriculture and the security of property rights, as well as with soil erosion.[22]

Within Castile the other chief source of revenue was the alcaba, a sales tax. But as the Spanish empire grew to become the greatest empire since Roman times, its major sources of revenue were increasingly external, derived from Sicily, Naples, the low countries, and the New World. Control internally over the economy and externally over the far-flung empire entailed a large and elaborate hierarchy of bureaucrats armed with an immense out-pouring of royal edicts. [Over 400,000 decrees had been issued concerning the governance and economy of the Indies by 1635, an average of 2,500 a year since Columbus sailed first to the Indies (Veliz, 1980, p. 43)]. Designed to provide minute regulation of the economy, guilds also provided a vehicle for internal economic regulation. Price ceilings were imposed on grain and state-owned trading companies, and monopolistic grants provided control of external trade.

As the military costs of controlling the empire outstripped revenues (which declined with the revolt of the Netherlands and the gradual decrease in receipts of treasure), the Crown raised the internal tax (alcaba) from 1.2 percent to 10 percent and repeatedly went into bankruptcy, which it resolved through the seizure of properties and financial assets. The consequence was the decline of the Spanish economy and economic stagnation.[23]

In terms of the foregoing model of the polity, the bargaining position of the Crown, vis-a-vis the Cortes, shifted in favour of the Crown and consequently resulted in the decline of the Cortes. The governance structure then became a large and elaborate bureaucracy and there were endless efforts by the Crown to control its far-flung agents. Indeed, the history of the control of the Indies is an elaborate story in agency theory, beginning as early as Isabella's recision of Columbus' policies towards the Indians in 1502. Distance magnified the immense problem of monitoring agents in the New World; but despite the dissipation of rent at every level of the hierarchical structure, the Crown maintained effective control over the polity and over the economy of the New World.[24]

## VII. CONSEQUENCES IN THE NEW WORLD

It is likewise much easier to trace the institutional evolution of the English North American colonies than their Latin American counterpart. The initial conditions are in striking contrast. English America was formed in the very century when the struggle between Parliament and the Crown was coming to a head. Religious diversity, as well as political diversity in the mother country, was paralleled in the colonies. In the Spanish Indies, conquest came at the precise time that the influence of the Castilian Cortes was declining. The conquerors imposed a uniform religion and a uniform bureaucratic administration on an already existing agricultural society.[25]

In the English colonies there was substantial diversity in the political structure of crown proprietary and charter colonies. But the general development in the direction of local political control and the growth of assemblies was clear and unambiguous. Similarly, the Navigation Acts placed the colonies within the framework of overall British imperial policy, and within that broad framework the colonists were free to develop the economy. Indeed, the colonists themselves frequently imposed more restrictions on property rights than did the mother country. (The exception was the effort of proprietors to obtain quit-rents from settlers in proprietary colonies, such as that of Lord Penn. The problem of enforcement and collection in the context of the availability of land resulted in very indifferent success.)

In the Spanish Indies, a bureaucracy detailed political and economic policy.

> ...the 'residencia' was the principal means employed by the king to keep viceroys and other functionaries under control. On the expiration of their term of office, all officials had to undergo the official investigation of their conduct. The fear of the residencia was frequently an incentive to serve the monarch well; it also limited any autonomous inclination of ambitious civil servants in the periphery of the empire. [Veliz (1980), p. 73.]

As for the economy, the Marquis of Pombal, who was the Secretary of State for Foreign Affairs and War and "ruled like a virtual dictator" Portugal and its empire from 1755-1777, is said to have stated:

> I find it absolutely necessary to bring all the commerce of this kingdom and its colonies into companies, then all merchants will be obliged to enter them, or else desist from trading, for they certainly may be assured that I know their interests better than they do themselves and the interest of the whole kingdom. [Veliz (1980), pp. 108-109.]

Some merchants and the Lisbon Chamber of Commerce protested.

> Pombal properly dissolved the chamber and had several of its leading members imprisoned; the rest were regrouped under direct government supervision into a 'Juntado Commercio' that dutifully approved all the minister's decisions. [Veliz (1980), p. 109.]

The French and Indian War (1755-63) is the familiar breaking point in American history. British efforts to impose (very modest) taxes on colonial subjects, as well as to curb westward migration, produced a violent reaction that led through a sequence of steps to the Revolution, the Declaration of Independence, the Articles of Confederation, the Northwest Ordinance, and the Constitution: a sequence of institutional expressions that formed a consistent evolutionary institutional pattern, despite the precariousness of the process.

In the Spanish Indies the recurrent crises were over the efficiency and control of the bureaucratic machinery. The decline under the Hapsburgs and the revival efforts under the Bourbons led to restructuring of the bureaucracy and even some liberalization of trade (under the Bourbons) within the empire. But the control of agents was a persistent problem, compounded by efforts of the Creoles to take over the bureaucracy in order to pursue their own interests. To whatever degree the wars of independence in Latin America were a struggle between colonial control (of the bureaucracy and consequent polity and economy) and imperial control, the struggle was imbued with the ideological overtones that stemmed from the American and French revolutions. Independence brought United States inspired constitutions, but with radically different consequences. In contrast to the United States, in Latin America, "The imaginative federal schemes and courageous attempts at decentralization had one thing in common after the first few years of republican independence: they were all tried but none worked. Some were disastrous; none survived."[26]

The contrasting histories of North and South America is perhaps the best comparative case that we have of the consequences of divergent institutional paths for political and economic performance. We are only just beginning to extend economic and political theory to the study of institutions.[27] I hope this "Historical Introduction" gives some indication of the promise of this approach for the study of economic growth and the history of freedom.

# NOTES

1. In a neo-classical world, economic growth is a function of the growth of the capital stock, broadly conceived to include not only physical and human capital, but the stock of resources, technology, and pure knowledge. Moreover, in this frictionless world one would equalize the rate of return at the margin by investing in whatever part of the capital stock yielded the highest return. Hence, there is not a fixed factor and diminishing returns as in the classical economic result. In this world the rate of growth is a function of the savings rate and the rate of growth per capita is a function of that rate over the rate of growth of population. In this neo-classical world growth is not a very interesting problem, and the distance between that formulation and the economic history of the world is vast and is determined by the cost of transacting.

2. See Lancaster (1966) and Becker (1965) for the origination of this consumer theory argument. It has been extended into the transaction cost framework by Cheung (1074), North (1981) and Barzel (1982).

3. Oliver Williamson's approach is basically deficient for several reasons, but principally because he takes imperfect enforcement as a given (otherwise opportunism would never pay) rather than recognize that both the characteristics of the enforcement process and the degree of imperfection are essential in modeling institutions and to the costs of transacting.

4. See for example Kenneth Shepsle and Barry Weingast, "The Institutional Foundations of Committee Power," 1986.

5. See Kalt and Zupan (1984) for discussion of these issues.

6. *Public Choice*, 1976.

7. "The Lessons of 1787," *Public Choice*, forthcoming.

8. Robert Axelrod (1985).

9. The immense literature on the subject from Marx and Mannheim to Merton is not very convincing, although Robert Herton's chapters written in 1949 are still a good summary of the state of the art.

10. Brennan and Buchanan (1983).

11. Kalt and Zuppan (1984).

12. Denzau, Riker and Shepsle (1985).

13. Landes and Posner (1975) provide an interest group model of the Supreme Court, but the evidence simply does not support such an argument. See Buchanan (1975) and North (1978).

14. For an analysis of the contribution of falling transactions costs on productivity growth in ocean transportation between 1600 and 1850, see North (1968).

15. See North and Wallis (1987) for a lengthy discussion of the issues and measurement of the transaction sector in the American economy between 1870 and 1970.

16. See North and Thomas (1973) for a description of this process.

16. For an elaboration of these issues, see "The Northwest Ordinance in Historical Perspective," North (forthcoming).

17. This simple "neo-classical theory of the state" is elaborated in North (1981), Chapter 3.

18. Moreover it should be noted that the rights that Parliament had in mind were those of the nobility and the gentry.

19. Ekelund and Tollison (1981), page 149.

20. Ekelund and Tollison (1981), page 151.

21. The history of the Mesta (Klein, 1920) is an exception to my assertion that the history of Spanish property rights has not been told. For a summary of the effects of the Mesta on the development of property rights in Spain, see North and Thomas (1973), Chapter 10.

22. For a more detailed account and sources, see North and Thomas (1973), Chapter 10.

23. For a more detailed account, see Veliz (1980), Chapter Three, "The Regalist Indies."

24. "The Indian population was subdued and subordinated by the new ruling class of Encomenderos. But the Encomendero class itself was the target of a royal program that reduced its political significance by installing a class of state office holders" (Lang, 1975, p. 220).

25. Veliz (1980), p. 151. Veliz provides a country-by-country summary account of the decline of democratic government and the revival of the "centralist" bureaucratic structure and tradition in Latin America (Chapter 7).

26. See North (1986) for an analysis of the "New Institutional Economics."

24

## BIBLIOGRAPHY

Axelrod, Robert (1985) "Modeling the Evolution of Norms," Working Paper.

Barzel, Yoram (1982) "Measurement and the Organization of Markets," *Journal of Law and Economics.*

Becker, Gary (1965) "A Theory of the Allocation of Time," *Economic Journal.*

Brennan, Geoffrey and James Buchanan (1982) "Voter Choice and the Evolution of Political Alternatives: A Critique of Public Choice," Center for the Study of Public Choice: mimeo.

Buchanan, James (1975) "Comment on the Independent Judiciary in an Interest group Perspective," *The Journal of Law and Economics.*

Cheung, Stephen (1974) "A Theory of Price Control," *Journal of Law and Economics.*

Denzau, Art, William Riker, and Kenneth Shepsle (1985) "Farquharson and Fenno: Sophisticated Voting and Homestyle," *American Political Science Review.*

Ekelund, Robert and Robert Tollison (1981) *Mercantilism as a Rent Seeking Society*, College Station: Texas A & M Press.

Elton, Geoffrey (1953) *The Tudor Revolution in Government*, Cambridge: The University Press.

Kalt, Joseph and Mark Zuppan (1984) "Capture and Ideology in the Economic Theory of Politics," *American Economic Review.*

Klein, Julius (1920) *The mesta*, Cambridge: Harvard University Press.

Lancaster, Kelvin (1966) "A New Approach to Consumer Theory," *Journal of Political Economy.*

Landes, William and Richard Posner (1975) "The Independent Judiciary in an Interest Group Perspective," *The Journal of Law and Economics.*

Lang, James (1975) *Conquest and Commerce: Spain and England in America*, New York: Academic Press.

North, Douglass (1968) "Sources of Productivity Change in Ocean Shipping, 1600-1850," *Journal of Political Economy.*

North, Douglass and Robert Thomas (1973) *The Rise of the Western World*, Cambridge: The University Press.

North, Douglass (1978) "Structure and Performance: The Task of Economic History," *Journal of Economic Literature.*

North, Douglass (1981) *Structure and Change in Economic History*, New York: W.W. Norton.

North, Douglass (1986) "The New Institutional Economics," *Journal of Institutional and Theoretical Economics* (March).

North, Douglass and John Wallis (1987) "Measuring the Transaction Sector in the American Economy, 1870-1970," in *Long-Term Factors in American Economic Growth*, Volume 51 of the Income and Wealth Series, Stanley L. Engerman and Robert E. Gallman, eds., University of Chicago Press.

Powers, Eileen (1941) *The Wood Trade in English Medieval History*, London: The Clarendon Press.

Riker, William (1976) "Comment on Vincent Ostrom," *Public Choice*.

Riker, William (1986) "1787 and Beyond," *Public Choice*.

Shepsle, Kenneth and Barry Weingast (1986) "The Institutional foundations of Committee Power," Washington University: Political Economy Working Paper #105.

Stubbs, William (1896) *The Constitutional History of England*, London: The Clarendon Press.

Veliz, Claudio (1980) *The Centralist Tradition of Latin America*, Princeton University Press.

# Discussion

## Edited by Michael A. Walker

**Herbert Grubel** I accept without quarrel as valid North's proposition that economic growth is encouraged by a legal environment that assures present and future property rights and keeps the costs of transactions and contracts low. I am also sympathetic to North's more general point that governments have important roles to play in modern industrial societies and that these functions may well be among the most important.

However, in the few minutes available to me here I want to raise some questions about the validity of his assertion on page nine: "This (the creation of an environment for dealing in confidence) is only possible as a result of a third party to exchange, government, which specifies property rights and enforces contracts."

Put starkly, my argument is that in some circumstances government is not needed to establish property rights and that in other circumstances government is detrimental to the maintenance of assured property rights. It all depends and, as we might expect, the optimal role of government in this enterprise is one of costs and benefits, which are determined by a wide range of factors.

As Anderson and Hill (Anderson, T. and P.J. Hill, "An American Experiment in Anarcho-Capitalism," *The Journal of Libertarian Studies,* III, 1, 1979) have shown, in the Wild West of the United States in the 19th century, private arrangements very effectively took the place of government in creating an institutional framework for the maintenance of property rights and the enforcement of contracts. When wagon trains to the West entered territory that had no effective government, they typically adopted a constitution and sets of laws that guided their relationships. Settlers in these areas similarly adopted systems for the settlement of land-claims and other disputes that resembled closely those which governments would have introduced. However, it is interesting to note that the decentralized private process permitted variations in legal structures and was able to accommodate ranges of settlers' preferences impossible under centralized government programmes.

On the other hand, it is not clear to me that the many laws passed by modern industrial societies in recent decades have been conducive to the assured maintenance of property rights and low transactions costs. Progressive income taxation, capital gains taxes and the wide range of regulation symbolized by rent-controls are equivalent to forced expropriation of property. Moreover, their adoption has created uncertainty about future laws that may be as important as the direct consequences of the expropriation.

The many laws in all countries that govern financial markets have vastly increased the cost of establishing a global capital market which has been made possible by the development of modern electronic technology. One could blame this problem on the absence of a world government and the global provision of laws and regulations that lower the cost of contracts. But in the light of the Law of the Sea and its effect on the cost of deep-sea mining I am not optimistic about the ability of a global government to generate an efficient legal environment.

These considerations lead me to the conclusion that the issue of when and where the government is an optimal supplier of property rights systems depends on the costs and benefits of the specific conditions. In the wild West the U.S. government simply did not have the technical and financial means to do so. At the same time, the common cultural and religious backgrounds of the settlers made it relatively easy to reach agreement on the preferred laws and enforcement institutions. In the literature on libertarian anarchism, this commonality is known as the Schelling point, after the analysis in Schelling (Schelling, T.C., *The Strategy of Conflict,* Harvard University Press, Cambridge, 1960).

It is very likely that after substantial population and economic growth, efficiency in the definition and administration of property rights was increased by the substitution of government for private institutions in the wild West of the United States. On the other hand, I interpret the current trend towards deregulation in so many industries as the outcome of mainly technical developments which have caused the government to be less efficient than the private determination of property rights. Comparative advantage appears to have moved back to the private provision of rules, regulations and the assurance of property rights.

The perspectives I just presented are of some relevance to North's interpretation of the causes of different development patterns in North and South America. In the absence of reliable knowledge on this matter let me postulate as a hypothesis that throughout the process of settlement of these regions, private institutions for the establishment and preservation of property rights preceded governments and that these governments more or less just accepted the private institutions, much like they have done in the U.S. West.

Under these conditions we should look to the different Schelling points of the settlers in the two continents for the causes of the different evolutionary patterns. I need not repeat here North's analysis of the differences in the strength of democratic rights enjoyed in the countries from which the settlers came predominantly. I would only add that perhaps the organized religions of the two regions reinforced the differences in the traditions of the secular governments. Settlers of South America who came mainly from Spain and Portugal probably were accustomed to the hierarchical and authoritarian organization of the Catholic church and therefore were more tolerant of centralized institutions and arbitrariness in property rights than were the North American settlers who were accustomed to the more decentralized and democratic protestant religions.

I think that it is obvious from my remarks that I find North's paper stimulating and dealing with important issues which deserve much greater attention than economists have given them in the past. We should be grateful to him for this stimulation and a penetrating analysis of the issues he raised.

**Raymond Gastil** It's a very small point, but it seems to me that what your example of the West illustrates is that if there isn't a government, you have to create a government. In other words, it is just a semantic issue to call this "private" arrangements as opposed to "governmental" arrangements. If they got beyond U.S. jurisdiction, they essentially created a new jurisdiction which then handled their problems for them. So it seems to me it reinforces the point of the paper rather than detracts from it.

**Gordon Tullock** Actually, in a way I was going to say the same thing. But I have something else. As it happens in the West, the American government was far, far more important. If it had not been for the U.S. Army, the Mexicans and the Indians would have wiped all of these things out. Their property depended entirely on the battles of Buena Vista and things of that sort and the continuing existence of this military force. Now Heaven knows it wasn't as efficient as one might like, particularly in dealing with the Indians, but it was a necessary condition for the existence of that property. Remember the Mexican War? How did they keep the Mexican Army out?

**Herbert Grubel** I accept your point, but it seems to me that you are talking about external defence. The issue is clearly whether certain types of government functions are carried out more efficiently and with the loss of less freedom at different levels of organization. The examples from Anderson and Hill that I have given are very persuasive to me. The optimum level of government for wagon trains travelling through a wilderness without effective government is the assembly of members of the train, not some far-away government. This is not inconsistent with your view that once the wilderness was encroached upon by the representatives of an organized state like Mexico, there was a need for a higher level of government to assert its rights there. It did so by sending troops and, I would surmise, using them as agents for later claims and the establishment of a formal government.

**Voice** I'd bet you would regard the two honourable East India companies as private enterprises.

**Voice** Dirty question!

**Ingemar Stahl** When I read this interesting paper I found the Latin American and U.S.A. case very convincing. But if we looked at a larger universe of observation, taking all the colonial powers and all the colonial areas, what would happen? If you have a regression function, including the West Indies, Indonesia and Netherlands, Belgian Congo and Belgium, will your conclusion still be true, that the British property rights system and the British institution transferred to North America was better than taking the Spanish and the Portuguese traditions to Latin America? If you include Netherlands, which was a very democratic country, and look at Indonesia, what would then happen? Or is the determining factor also the share of population that came from the original structure, and the number that were not wiped out in the colonial countries?

**Douglass North** I was originally going to respond on this point. There is a big literature on all kinds of contracting that can be done without third party enforcement; we all are familiar with this literature. But none of it, it seems to me, really survives when you have very complex economic systems that we think of as associated with high income countries. I know of no high income country that has managed to do without government once it gets into that complexity. It is very easy to think of ways of enforcing property rights by hostages or ways of having repeat dealings and so on in small settings; it is very hard to think of ways to do this when you have the complex world we are talking about.

Ingemar's point is a very good one. In fact, Gordon and I talked about this last December, and I have not confronted the issues of complexities that might arise when I start to look at a lot of places in the world where you had settlement—in this case the Dutch, which is a very good case of other societies. Part of it—and I think Gordon and I have talked about this—rests with the kind of indigenous populations you have and the kind of society that is already in existence. That makes the American case unique, and you can compare the North American case with those parts of Latin America which had sparse populations like Argentina and so on. There, it seems to me, there is some similarity; you are imposing a set of rules with settlers coming in. Where you have large indigenous populations, I think the problems are most complex and are ones I really haven't dealt with very satisfactorily in this paper.

**Walter Block** With regard to the settling of the West, certainly there was a cavalry, but I think it was a question, in many cases, of too little and too late. There was a vast area, there were very few cavalrymen. I think an awful lot of the supposed government function, namely defence, was provided not by the cavalry—although some was—but by the people themselves. In this regard I am especially out of sympathy with Raymond Gastil's point, namely that these settlers, when they engaged in self-defence and property rights definitions, were just another government. This would seem to eliminate libertarian anarchism, not through any flaws in it but merely by definition. I think this is a mistake, since government should be defined as a monopoly of coercion. These settlers were not engaged in a monopoly and were not engaged in coercion, but rather just in self-defence.

Now with regard to the point of a complex world requiring government, this seems to me to be the argument that is used by many of our friends on the left who are always saying, well, for simple problems we don't need much government planning or central control, but in the modern world there is much complexity, so we need lots of government. Then they go on to justify rent control, minimum wage or whatever on that basis. If we have such a complex world where we need government, why not world government? But we don't have world government; we now have anarchy between nations. I think the anarchy between nations is a very good thing, because a world government would certainly interfere with economic growth. So I don't see these attacks on the libertarian version of anarchism as overwhelmingly convincing.

**Alan Walters** The striking thing in Latin America over the last 30 years is the difference between the Portuguese and Spanish colonies. The Portuguese performed much better than the Spanish colonies. The reasons for this are unclear to me, but one surely is the absence, in the Portuguese colonies, of the sort of concessionaire system which dominated the Spanish colonies. I would like to see a sort of comparative history since the Portuguese and Spanish are similar in their nature, similar in family structure, similar in mores and so on. But the critical ingredient is the absence of the concessionaire system, which is ubiquitous in the rest of Latin America but not in the Portuguese colonies.

**Assar Lindbeck** The topic is so broad it lends itself to rather speculative comments. Herbert Grubel said that one point against North's exposition would be that many governments are destroying property rights, as a matter of fact. I don't think that is really hitting North very much. Douglass is saying that governments are a necessary condition for stable property rights in a complex society. But it is not a sufficient condition and, of course, governments can destroy property rights as well as establish them. So I don't think that hits him. But I think a distinction between necessary and sufficient conditions here might be in place.

You hear that the British culture was good for the colonies, and that Latin America was a failure by contrast to the U.S. But how would you explain that British culture didn't work very well in Britain? Britain started her downfall at the turn of the century or even earlier and has gone down, relatively speaking, all the time.

**Douglass North** Very briefly, Britain does experience a very high rate of growth. We think of it as the Industrial Revolution that followed on the period that I am talking about, in the late 18th and through the 19th century. You don't predict any society is going to keep growing forever. In fact, one of the things we know very little about is that all of them at some point begin to stagnate and certainly that happened to Britain. But it is long after the period where I am looking at the set of property rights and rules evolving that produced *high* rates of growth in Britain and in its colonies.

**Tibor Machan** I would like to make the point, somewhat against Walter Block in defence of Raymond Gastil, that it is not the size of the enforcement of rules that determines whether something is a government or not, it is certain structural features. Libertarian anarchists rule out of court John Locke's concept of government by consent of the governed. If that concept is to stay intact and be intelligible, then it should be possible to have a government which is entirely consensual, something the libertarian anarchist refuses to acknowledge. He defines government as inherently coercive and this is not in the tradition of liberalism that we are familiar with.

**Raymond Gastil** That is pretty much what I was going to say. Essentially, the point being made about government in the West was a point that certainly has some validity in the sense that small, decentralized governmental units may have more flexibility or be better adjusting to situations than large governments at a distance. But that is rather different from bringing up an argument about libertarian anarchism, which I imagine would have to be based on something other than simply small, decentralized government units, which it seems to me we are talking about in this case.

If I could make another remark in regard to the paper that we are discussing, I found that the argument was convincing enough except that I wasn't sure that it showed exactly what was related to what. There was, of course, a British tradition and a Spanish tradition, with many different features. The result was, in its particular application to North America, that we had a more developing, rapidly growing society, and in Latin America you had lots of problems, both economic and political. But what precisely was in that heritage? I think that maybe some more amorphous and harder to find things in that heritage played a large part, rather than what was mentioned here. Look, for example, at the Portuguese heritage. Certainly, in Africa it hasn't had the effect it had in Brazil. So I find the whole discussion a little hard to pin down.

**Armen Alchian** I want to call attention to a paper by Ronald Batchelder who was at Texas A & M and is now at Pepperdine. I don't recall details precisely enough to state his position correctly, but he did look at the Spanish method of governing their areas in the Americas, where I believe he was emphasizing there they had a system which induced exploitative immediate expropriation of wealth. I think he said the Portuguese—and here I may be doing him a disservice or putting words in his mouth— enabled people there to acquire the land and to hold it in their own name, and had incentive to invest in it. I don't know where it appeared, but I thought it was quite a good paper, and I just wanted to call it to your attention.

**Arnold Harberger** Latin America seems to be destined to come up a number of times in this meeting. A couple of points. First of all on what Alan was saying, the actual story, to me, is that Brazil is a late bloomer in Latin America and it was developmentally, far behind Argentina, Uruguay and Chile by the 1930s. The estimates that I have seen on per capita incomes around the world place Argentina, Sweden, Canada and Australia pretty much in one package, well ahead of many of the countries of Europe.

Uruguay, as Ramon Diaz has emphasized in another paper, in its early growth was doing beautifully in a very free, open market setting. It is hard to lay the responsibility for what has subsequently happened to them on the Spanish heritage. The Spanish heritage was there before.

**Ingemar Stahl** As far as I can understand, when the United States was founded it was a rather large free trade area for that time. In Latin America, was there anything similar to a customs union or free trade area, or was the interstate trade in Latin America insignificant, and were there obstacles for that type of trade? It could be a kind of supplementary explanation if you have one area that was a free trade area and one that was not.

**Douglass North** The Latin Americans can probably answer the Latin America one better than I can. Certainly, the U.S. was always a free trade area. Actually, there were some barriers between colonies before they became independent; after independence there was a free trade area. In Latin America, it is my impression that there was some trade between areas, but I don't think there was a great deal of trade. But I am not sure about that.

**Ramon Diaz** I think that in the origins of Latin America as a set of independent countries, with tariffs impeding trade between them, that was not a very important development. I think more important was the failure of the greater part of Latin America to have stable government and predictable policies.

**Svetozar Pejovich** I don't have comments, but I have two questions for Doug. What do you mean when you say "freedom"? That's one question. And the second is, you use the terms "economic growth" and "economic performance." Do you really mean the same thing, or do you distinguish? The reason I am asking is because I know of some high growth states, like Russia during the Stalin years, that have not performed that well.

**Douglass North** Let's take "freedom" first. Milton Friedman intimidated me on freedom, and so I wrote just one page on it to cover myself. I have nothing more at this point to say except that one page—particularly as I look at Milton across the way. But I thought that was satisfactory. I don't think there is any short way to define it. I was at a conference about what we meant by freedom, for four days last year, and I listened to Rousseauians and libertarians and all kinds of other philosophers and the only conclusion we could come to was that freedom isn't easy to define. So I tried to define it very briefly and therefore somewhat arbitrarily.

On "economic performance" I am really using just some standard measures of what we consider growth—growth in output, real per capita income, real output, stability of output, things like that. There is nothing elegant about it.

**Brian Kantor** The point about Argentina did occur to me as well. Argentina was really one of the great success stories until about 1930, I think. At the start of the Second War the Argentineans were still, perhaps, among the first five groups of people in terms of per capita incomes. Argentina developed her resources with the aid of lots of British capital, and British capital was certainly very much attracted to Argentina. But what is also true of Argentina, as I think is true of the U.S., is that the indigenous population certainly weren't important; they had been wiped out. The plains were empty.

This is not true, of course, of other areas which were nominally conquered. In fact they weren't fully conquered ever. If you think of India, the British ruled India indirectly, as they ruled much of Africa. This is a point I am going to make again when I discuss Peter Bauer's paper. When you rule *indirectly* you leave many of the institutions in place, and those indigenous institutional arrangements are often inimical to economic development.

**Milton Friedman** Well, Alan and Brian have more or less taken the words out of my mouth, because I was going to refer back to the case of Argentina, particularly in relation to Australia. One of the fascinating things to me has always been that Argentina and Australia were so largely parallel in so many respects. Neither one of them had a large indigenous population; both of them were largely settled by Europeans. In both cases, you had very rapid growth in the late 1930s as you were speaking of. Maybe Argentina would have been a little ahead of Australia, but I am not sure—Al could tell us better about that—but they would have been pretty close don't you think?

**Arnold Harberger** They were very close as of 1929.

**Milton Friedman** They both were countries which had large grazing areas, very similar in their characteristics. It seems to me it is very hard to argue that what happened after Peron came in derives from the Spanish institutions, while what happened in Australia derived from the British institutions. The question arises of trying to interpret why Argentina went one way—and Argentina isn't the only one—and Australia went the other.

It looks as if what happened each time is that when you get a man on horseback you have one problem, and when you don't have a man on horseback you have another problem.

**Ramon Diaz** On the subject that Milton has just raised, I think that the Spanish heritage may have been instrumental in Peron's success and therefore may, by the back door, have been important at a deep ideological or philosophical level. What we find is a great success story in Argentina, to some extent also in Uruguay. But they were both very vulnerable at a conceptual level. There had been no great national debates about these issues, and there was no intellectual heritage. When Peron came with his new outlook, there was no defence. The country very easily followed this brash populist leader who then led it to destruction.

I think, therefore, that we can say that the destruction of Argentina was in the broadest sense due to a lack of education. It also had to do with institutions that were not solid enough. In that sense I think, not in any more direct a manner, the different cultural background was probably quite material.

**Assar Lindbeck** Is it really the institutional framework inherent in a country that is important? Isn't it rather a kind of immature political culture in Latin American countries that has been important? Maybe the British brought some maturity of political culture to North America and to Australia rather than the institutional frameworks, if you don't include political culture in the institution, so to speak.

I also have a comment for Walter Block. He said that governments are not necessary conditions for stable rules and property rights in a complex society because we have international property rights without international government. That is not a very strong argument, because what do we mean by "international property rights"? When private agents operate in many countries, they are protected mainly by the national legal system in each country where they operate. Every country has a legal system, and to the extent that you have international rules that regulate interactions between countries in terms of trade, for instance, you have agreements between governments like IMF or the GATT agreements or bilateral agreements. So that is government again. You have not really given an argument on why governments would not be needed here, because it is governments and agreements between governments that guarantee the system.

**Tibor Machan** Quickly, on freedom. In the paper the term is defined in terms of protection of security. I think that is a little bit more than what it should be. Security might be threatened by earthquakes or a lot of sources other than human beings. We don't want to give government the right to intervene just because it says, "we are protecting freedom by protecting people against hardship or earthquakes or disease." That is just a minor point, but worth making.

**Lindsay Wright** I just wanted to register a strong disagreement with Walter that we do not have anarchy between world governments. We actually have a very well organized world order that functions to uphold and maintain and preserve consensus about a world capitalist market. I think that the lack of formal institutions does not mean that a consensus on the rules or procedures that govern those procedures does not exist. We need to beware of purely legalistic interpretations of what government entails.

**Gordon Tullock** I want to go back to Argentina and Uruguay. In the first place, Argentina has an immense Italian population, not Spanish. I think that is true of Uruguay, but my only evidence of that is the fact that Garibaldi fought much more in Uruguay than he did in Italy. Chile and Colombia also had large North European immigration. Another point worth noting is that Southern America was very, very heavily dependent on England for a long time. They used to refer to Argentina as the "sixth dominion." I don't know any positive evidence about it at all, but I suspect that if Argentine governments through most of this time had decided to, let's say, confiscate the railroad, they would have found the British Navy in their ports the following day. It was the weakening, I think, of England after World War II that permitted a reaction back.

**Douglass North** Well, my point is new, but it turns out that it is going to touch on some of the things that have been said around the table. What I was trying to do in this paper, and in this bigger book that I am trying to write is to really answer two questions that bother me about institutional change, and have bothered me ever since I became concerned about it. One is why there are such divergent patterns of evolution of societies through time, and under what conditions do they converge again? That is, there is a radical change in relative prices or something which causes divergence in institutional development and sometimes we observe some convergence, and sometimes we observe them diverging through time persistently. That is a puzzle that economic historians ought to solve.

The second question is one, of course, that came out of Armen's article of 1950 and that is, if we think of institutions as existing in a world in which there is competition and scarcity, why don't inefficient ones fail? And why do societies appear to be persistently not doing well over long periods of time?—however defined in terms of Steve's concerns.

It is those two questions that are bothering me right now, that I am trying to at least get an initial handle on. It seems to me that some of you have taken me way beyond the scope of the paper. The paper only went up to the beginning of the 19th century; it did not go up to 1900 and what Assar was talking about, or to the present time. It just says, how did we get such very different beginnings in North America and Latin America, and can we say something intelligible about those origins. Can we develop a framework that is going to say something intelligible about those things in terms of looking at the incremental changes, and it is mostly incremental.

One of the things that I am doing now on another paper on the Northwest Ordinance is looking in great detail at the small changes that existed in most specific kinds of property rights and legislation as it evolved in colonial and newly independent North America over the late 18th and early 19th centuries. They *are* small changes, and I want to know where they came from, how they came about, how they link up and what kinds of bargaining strengths produced divergences.

Brian, I think, made the point that is most bothering me now. That is, invading powers come into a society where there is a large indigenous population with existing institutions, as in Peru and other places in Latin America. Then, no matter how hard you try to impose some sort of institutions on them, they are going to get intermingled with the existing ones. You are going to produce some very divergent results, and that is something I am just starting to work on.

**Walter Block**  I wanted to make a point on Doug's paper with regard to economic growth. I accept with alacrity his rejection of the neoclassical view which speaks in terms of capital stock and take-off periods and all sorts of things that really have little to do with economic growth. One of the forerunners of this type of analysis is certainly Peter Bauer, who has directed our attention on institutions and incentives and culture and matters of that sort. I also think that Doug's directing our attention to transactions costs is very helpful, but I don't think transactions costs tell the whole story. It is conceivable to imagine cases where transactions costs were reduced but still there was not a great amount of growth because of the culture. Peter Bauer talks about India, where they have a culture which is against wealth; it is hard to see how reducing transactions costs would help in such a society. Also we can conceive of a situation where transactions costs were reduced and yet we had marginal tax rates of 99 percent or something like that, which would certainly reduce incentives.

**Michael Parkin** I would like to come back to Doug's main point, though I'm finding it difficult to keep track of what the main point is and what the sideline points are. I want to go back to the notion that the goal of this research is to try to explain why we see the patterns of divergence and convergence in institutional forms and why we see what Doug called inefficient institutions.

My first thought is that this is such an ambitious undertaking that I would like Doug to give us some clue as to why he thinks that it is an achievable programme of research. It seems to me that we are tackling questions that are, in the nature of things, too big to be successfully pursued with our current technology and ways of thinking about things. I hope I am wrong about that, but if I am I would like some guidance on why this might be a hopeful line of inquiry.

Two things make me worry about this particular attempt, particularly in the context of the late 19th century. What I think we need to do, if we are going to look at the sorts of questions that are being addressed here, is to try to find reasonably isolated environments in which we can observe what happens in these environments. By the late 19th century the world was already a pretty open society with a lot of interaction between the various groups. Gordon's point about the British Navy not being too far away from Argentina underlines the point. I would worry whether you have the sort of independent, isolated data bases that you require.

Second—and this is related but a slightly different point—I worry when people talk about inefficiencies surviving. It seems to me much more fruitful to talk about trying to find explanations for why bad situations are persistent equilibria. Unemployment is a bad situation, but it is something that can persist. Political institutions that are very corrupt and that impose heavy costs on the people are a bad situation, but frequently persist. I would like to see a refocusing of the question. Not why does inefficiency persist, but what is it that makes the apparently inefficient, in fact, the best of a bunch of bad outcomes. In this respect, I suppose that one has to start to look at the sorts of things that the new micro-economists are looking at when trying to explain peculiar situations—things like informational asymmetries and costs of doing business with each other—that are hidden, in some sense. If we could put our fingers on them, we would stand a chance of making some sense of this big class of phenomena. So, I am really appealing for a more micro, nitty-gritty, get down to some of the tighter issues, rather than this broad-brush approach. But I hope that I am wrong. I hope the broad-brush look at a huge and ambitious period of history will work, and I wonder if you have any words of hope and encouragement.

**Douglass North** Transactions costs are not institutions, the way I look at it. Transactions costs are a consequence of institutions, and I want to make that clear. It is a misunderstanding of what I conceive transactions costs to be to think of them as institutions. Transactions costs arise as a consequence of the kinds of institutions and market structures and so on that you have. But I want to spend however much time you will give me on Michael's point, because this is what I spend my life on.

What I have been doing, Michael, over the last 15 or 20 years is working backwards towards this set of issues. I started out as a straight neoclassical type of economist applying it to economic history and asking what I could learn. From that, and with inspiration from people like Armen, I moved into thinking that property rights gave me a clue as to how to get behind prices and things to get an idea as to the relative incentive structures in societies. From looking at property rights I moved behind to enforcement of property rights, because it turns out that that in turn can make a big difference in how property rights work. And I keep going backwards.

It seems to me that is the way to go. It is an infinite regress, I am sure, and you never arrive at some point when the Holy Grail is sitting there and you grab it. But I do think you get more understanding of the way in which societies evolve if you move in this direction, and that is what I am trying to do—not, perhaps, altogether successfully, but I don't know any other way to go.

We ought to be modelling and trying to theorize about the things that economists typically hold constant in their models, and that is demographic change, institutional change, technological change. This is where I am going, only I concentrate on institutional change and other people concentrate on demographic change. Whether it is possible to really say something more significant is up to all of you. I think I am getting somewhere, but that is something I will leave to other people to decide finally.

**Raymond Gastil** I would like to go back to the cultural issue which has been brought up. This paper basically addresses the effects of some cultural differences in regard to institutions that were imposed. The point has been made, of course, that in many of the colonies in Latin America there was a mixture between what was brought in by the Spanish and what was there before, so one should look at the pure examples. But what strikes me more strongly is that in different periods people of different backgrounds seem to have shown the greatest economic performance. At one time it was the people of British tradition, and wherever you looked around the world, the purer the British impact, the better the performance.

Right now it seems to be the Chinese societies—Japan, South Korea, Taiwan, Singapore, Hong Kong—that are showing the best kind of performance. Sometimes you can point to certain groups of people, even within *other* cultures, who have had outstanding performance at certain times—Parses in India, for example. So it seems to me that it may be that we have a real problem in deciding whether it is particular institutional patterns, definable in the way this paper does it, or something else which is involved in the culture of a people that is really determining the outcome.

I would suggest what one might try to do in this situation is concentrate on examples where you can keep the general culture constant and vary the institutions that are tried in different places at that same time, and then compare that with situations where you can keep the institutions constant and vary the cultures that are operating those institutions.

**Alvin Rabushka** Just to embellish that, Tom Sowell has written two books on that subject. One looks at a dozen ethnic groups in the United States, a common institutional, legal, political system, and he finds their economic performance varies largely as a result of different backgrounds and up-bringings and attitudes and mores. The other is a book in which he shows that the Chinese do brilliantly everywhere, the Japanese do well everywhere, and certain ethnic groups do awful everywhere.

It may just be that an institutional framework is the necessary but not sufficient condition, subcultural norms are necessary but not sufficient, and the two together give you a better overall handle on this.

I agree with what Doug said in response to Michael. I think his approach wouldn't get you anywhere either, worrying about technology and regression leaves out things that can't be modelled in modern economic technology. And I think one has to get at some of these things because they are important.

**Milton Friedman** I wanted to raise three very broad comments which are peripheral to much of what has been going on. The first of them is the fact that chance—pure chance—plays an enormous role. It wasn't necessary that Peron come on the scene in the Argentinean case. It would be very hard to argue that his arrival was anything more than chance.

The case that has always impressed me the most is the one of the United States at the time of the Revolution. In his biography of George Washington, James Flexner makes the point that the United States was on the verge of establishing a military dictatorship, and it was prevented from doing so only by George Washington's personal characteristics.

There was a military junta of the revolutionary officers, including Alexander Hamilton, incidentally, who were trying to persuade Washington to assume headship of the junta so that they could get their salaries paid and be compensated. They had a fallback candidate whom they were prepared to go to if Washington didn't agree. But not only didn't Washington agree, he was effective enough in his personal intervention with the officer corps to put an end to it. Now, after all, you can't say that that was because of a British influence of democracy when Britain at the time was ruled by George III. Where do you get democracy out of that? So, I think we have to put enormous emphasis on chance at certain crucial points.

That leads to my second point, which has come up in an indirect way several times here. That is, the way to look at things in these respects is that there are often situations in which there are multiple stable equilibria with great difficulty in getting from one to the other. A valley with a hill and a valley. One may be a better one than the other, but you can't easily get to it. Very obvious examples: metric system versus English weights and measures; the Chinese calligraphy, an ideographic versus a phonetic script. Now the phonetic script is, from one point of view, far more efficient, certainly for science, mathematics and so on. Yet, once you have established an ideographic script as in China, it is hell and all to go from one to the other.

In the same way, once Peron emerged in Argentina, once he established that pattern, it was extremely hard to go from there to something else. So that you do have stable equilibria, it seems to me, which may be perfectly consistent with the same cultural background, the same institutions, same reactions.

And the third point is the one that was just raised here about how you shift from one area to another. Social and economic arrangements, political arrangements, have a life history. Alfred Marshall, always used to talk about the "life history of enterprises," of birth, growth, fall—the same as human life. The same thing is true of institutions. You have the theory, indeed, of Mancur Olson which attempts to explain the world in exactly this fashion.

We talk about the Dutch having been leaders at one point, the Portuguese at another point, the English at another point. In each case the process is a kind of a life history in which these develop.

When we talk about necessary and sufficient conditions—obviously we are always much better at necessary conditions than we are at sufficient conditions—they are not conditions which are without a time dimension relative to some kind of an origin. Often that origin was a major chance event that started them off in one direction rather than the other, whether the chance event is finding gold in California or the emergence of a particular person like Peron, who was able to take over, or the emergence of a particular person like George Washington, who was able to prevent something.

**Gordon Tullock**  This is very brief. I don't think you can use Olson any more for this. I would say the statistical studies, of which I get tons because of my particular journal, have killed him. Weede, the German scholar, is still trying to argue that Olson's theory is correct, but I think the evidence is overwhelming. This I regard as very unfortunate, because I like his theory. But I think you have to say that as of now it is demonstrated not to be true.

**Herbert Grubel**  Do you have any ideas on what causes these life cycles? Is this an inevitable form.

**Milton Friedman**  I don't know. I only say that the fact that you have the leadership shift from one area to another, one group to another, suggests that there must be something.

This is a different issue, but I have always been interested in the "golden ages" of history, and all golden ages have limited lives, whether it is 5th century B.C. Greece, or whether it is the early stage of Rome, whether it is the first Elizabethan era—they all last about 75 to 100 or 150 years.

**Peter Bauer**  The life cycles of societies and institutions are both significant and paradoxical. They are paradoxical because you would expect that successful societies and institutions would have cumulative advantages over their neighbours in know-how and capital. These life cycles therefore raise some far-reaching questions and problems. They refute much of modern development economics, including Gunar Myrdal's notion of circular cumulative causation.

Steve introduced the problem of measuring economic growth. There are very real problems here which should not be pushed aside. Since World War II, the U.N. statistics on the East European countries have registered impressive rates of growth. At the same time, many people in the West received begging letters from these countries asking for the simplest consumer goods such as razor blades, sewing cotton and the like. Alan Walters has some very informative stories about that.

Next, a few remarks on world government and property rights. In the contemporary political climate, a world government with world sovereignty is likely to be utterly destructive of property rights because such a government would try to standardize conditions world-wide. That would involve massive redistributive taxation and confiscation of property.

On Michael Parkin's point, I think there is much to be said for studying the nitty-gritty of processes and also phenomena on a small scale. Francis Bacon said that it "cometh often to pass that mean and small things discover great better than great can discover small." I might also quote a beautiful phrase by Sir Lewis Namier: "In a drop of dew can be seen the colours of the sun." Again, major cultural matters affecting economic performance, such as refusal to take sentient animal life, widespread in South Asia, are matters which one can observe, on which one can reflect, and about which one can draw inferences, but which are hard to discuss sensibly in macro terms or by means of regression analysis.

**Milton Friedman** On world government, I just want to tell a story of Bertrand de Juvenelle. Bertrand de Juvenelle, 30 years ago, said he had always been an ardent advocate of world government until the day he crossed the border into Switzerland ahead of the pursuing Nazis.

**Assar Lindbeck** I too think the life cycle aspect of countries and civilizations is crucial, even if you cannot explain it and even if Mancur Olson might not have an explanation. It is what I call Budenbrook's model. The first generation of a family creates wealth with very hard work and with strong purpose connected with it; the second administrates it; and the third takes it as manna from heaven and consumes and destroys it. There is a possibility that after a while a rich society may take as exogenously given sources of wealth that can be consumed, and you get a different attitude. I think most countries seem to believe it.

Let me just make a very casual observation myself that might be wrong. I came to the U.S. for the first time in 1957 as a student. What impressed me in the U.S. at that time was the hard work in the service sector. I had never before seen people working that hard in shops and stores. I said to myself, this is so different from Sweden. But now, it is just the opposite—such sloppiness! I go into a drug store and ask, "do you have commodity X?" and always get the same answer, "I don't know." Over the last 30 years, I have seen a marked difference in discipline in the stores and in the work ethic in general in the U.S. So I think you are perhaps in the third generation in Budenbrook's model.

**Brian Kantor**  My point is related. Clearly, the life cycle must have something to do with institutions that initially tolerate accumulation˙ and differences in wealth, because everybody doesn't accumulate at the same rate. Some must be allowed to accumulate much faster and, at a later stage the wealth is attacked through processes of redistribution, which spread it around and take away the incentives to accumulate. Therefore growth slows down. I think one sees that pattern.

When societies get rich enough, they certainly become vulnerable to the politics of redistribution. They don't *get* rich unless accumulation is acceptable, at least over some stages of their development. So, I think one needs a theory of redistribution that will explain why people vote for redistributive policies. That is what we need.

**Walter Block**  I wanted to offer an aphorism for what Assar said. The expression is "from shirtsleeves to shirtsleeves in three generations."

Also, on the matter of political life cycles, John Glubb Pasha has written a book where he discusses the rise and fall of about 25 different civilizations. He mentioned that typically each polity lasts about 200 years. This is an analogue to what Assar was saying, only for nations instead of people. According to Glubb: conquer them, but they are strengthened by this experience. The first settlers in the land meet harsh conditions and this resolve and strong character carries over until the third or the fourth generation. But eventually later generations get weaker. They become involved in pornography and rights for homosexuals and things like that. They lose their fervour for nation-building and even to defend themselves.

**Douglass North**  All kinds of things have occurred to me. I want to enter a few caveats, however, to some of the things I have heard around the table, particularly lately. I think you should be cautious about this sort of cycle pattern. Rome really persisted for a thousand years, and it was certainly a very corrupt society for at least four or five hundred of those years. That we do see the rise and fall of nations is correct, but the idea that there is some neat pattern to it I don't think is true—even though I can find some that fit that sort of pattern. We just don't know a lot about this set of issues.

The other thing is, surely we want to draw lessons from history, but to think that the world we are evolving in now is in every sense like the ones in the past is very misleading to say the least. We are a very different world than any we have experienced before. That's frustrating, particularly for an economic historian—although it's easier to "predict" the past than to worry about what is going to happen next. Easy analogues with the past can be very facile, but I think they are terribly dangerous.

# Chapter 2

# Capitalism and Freedom*

# Milton Friedman

## Introduction

In a much quoted passage in his inaugural address, President Kennedy said, "Ask not what your country can do for you—ask what you can do for your country." It is a striking sign of the temper of our times that the controversy about this passage centered on its origin and not on its content. Neither half of the statement expresses a relation between the citizen and his government that is worthy of the ideals of free men in a free society. The paternalistic "what your country can do for you" implies that government is the patron, the citizen the ward, a view that is at odds with the free man's belief in his own responsibility for his own destiny. The organismic "what you can do for your country" implies that government is the master or the deity, the citizen, the servant or the votary. To the free man, the country is the collection of individuals who compose it, not something over and above them. He is proud of a common heritage and loyal to common traditions. But he regards government as a means, an instrumentality, neither a grantor of favors and gifts, not a master nor god to be blindly worshipped and served. He recognizes no national goal except as it is the consensus of the goals that the citizens severally serve. He recognizes no national purpose except as it is the consensus of the purposes for which the citizens severally strive.

---

*Excerpts from *Capitalism and Freedom* by Milton Friedman, with Rose D. Friedman, University of Chicago Press, Chicago, 1962.

The free man will ask neither what his country can do for him nor what he can do for his country. He will ask rather "What can I and my compatriots do through government" to help us discharge our individual responsibilities, to achieve our several goals and purposes, and above all, to protect our freedom? And he will accompany this question with another: How can we keep the government we create from becoming a Frankenstein that will destroy the very freedom we establish it to protect? Freedom is a rare and delicate plant. Our minds tell us, and history confirms, that the great threat to freedom is the concentration of power. Government is necessary to preserve our freedom, it is an instrument through which we can exercise our freedom; yet by concentrating power in political hands, it is also a threat to freedom. Even though the men who wield this power initially be of good will and even though they be not corrupted by the power they exercise, the power will both attract and form men of a different stamp.

How can we benefit from the promise of government while avoiding the threat to freedom? Two broad principles embodied in our Constitution give an answer that has preserved our freedom so far, though they have been violated repeatedly in practice while proclaimed as precept.

First, the scope of government must be limited. Its major function must be to protect our freedom both from the enemies outside our gates and from our fellow-citizens: to preserve law and order, to enforce private contracts, to foster competitive markets. Beyond this major function, government may enable us at times to accomplish jointly what we would find it more difficult or expensive to accomplish severally. However, any such use of government is fraught with danger. We should not and cannot avoid using government in this way. But there should be a clear and large balance of advantages before we do. By relying primarily on voluntary co-operation and private enterprise, in both economic and other activities, we can ensure that the private sector is a check on the powers of the governmental sector and an effective protection of freedom of speech, of religion, and of thought.

The second broad principle is that government power must be dispersed. If government is to exercise power, better in the county than in the state, better in the state than in Washington. If I do not like what my local community does, be it in sewage disposal, or zoning, or schools, I can move to another local community, and though few may take this step, the mere possibility acts as a check. If I do not like what Washington imposes, I have few alternatives in this world of jealous nations.

The very difficulty of avoiding the enactments of the federal government is of course the great attraction of centralization to many of its proponents. It will enable them more effectively, they believe, to legislate programs that—as they see it—are in the interest of the public, whether it be the transfer of income from the rich to the poor or from private to governmental purposes. They are in a sense right. But this coin has two sides. The power to do good is also the power to do harm; those who control the power today may not tomorrow; and, more important, what one man regards as good, another may regard as harm. The great tragedy of the drive to centralization, as of the drive to extend the scope of government in general, is that it is mostly led by men of good will who will be the first to rue its consequences.

The preservation of freedom is the protective reason for limiting and decentralizing governmental power. But there is also a constructive reason. The great advances of civilization, whether in architecture or painting, in science or literature, in industry or agriculture, have never come from centralized government. Columbus did not set out to seek a new route to China in response to a majority directive of a parliament, though he was partly financed by an absolute monarch. Newton and Leibnitz; Einstein and Bohr; Shakespeare, Milton, and Pasternak; Whitney, McCormick, Edison, and Ford; Jane Addams, Florence Nightingale, and Albert Schweitzer; no one of these opened new frontiers in human knowledge and understanding, in literature, in technical possibilities, or in the relief of human misery in response to governmental directives. Their achievements were the product of individual genius, of strongly held minority views, of a social climate permitting variety and diversity.

Government can never duplicate the variety and diversity of individual action. At any moment in time, by imposing uniform standards in housing, or nutrition, or clothing, government could undoubtedly improve the level of living of many individuals; by imposing uniform standards in schooling, road construction, or sanitation, central government could undoubtedly improve the level of performance in many local areas and perhaps even on the average of all communities. But in the process, government would replace progress by stagnation, it would substitute uniform mediocrity for the variety essential for that experimentation which can bring tomorrow's laggards above today's mean.

This book discusses some of these great issues. Its major theme is the role of competitive capitalism—the organization of the bulk of economic activity through private enterprise operating in a free market—as a system of economic freedom and a necessary condition for political freedom. Its minor theme is the role that government should play in a society dedicated to freedom and relying primarily on the market to organize economic activity.

The first two chapters deal with these issues on an abstract level, in terms of principles rather than concrete application. The later chapters apply these principles to a variety of particular problems.

An abstract statement can conceivably be complete and exhaustive, though this ideal is certainly far from realized in the two chapters that follow. The application of the principles cannot even conceivably be exhaustive. Each day brings new problems and new circumstances. That is why the role of the state can never be spelled out once and for all in terms of specific functions. It is also why we need from time to time to re-examine the bearing of what we hope are unchanged principles on the problems of the day. A by-product is inevitably a retesting of the principles and a sharpening of our understanding of them.

It is extremely convenient to have a label for the political and economic viewpoint elaborated in this book. The rightful and proper label is liberalism. Unfortunately, "As a supreme, if unintended compliment, the enemies of the system of private enterprise have thought it wise to appropriate its label,"[1] so that liberalism has, in the United States, come to have a very different meaning than it did in the nineteenth century or does today over much of the continent of Europe.

As it developed in the late eighteenth and early nineteenth centuries, the intellectual movement that went under the name of liberalism emphasized freedom as the ultimate goal and the individual as the ultimate entity in the society. It supported laissez faire at home as a means of reducing the role of the state in economic affairs and thereby enlarged the role of the individual; it supported free trade abroad as a means of linking the nations of the world together peacefully and democratically. In political matters, it supported the development of representative government and of parliamentary institutions, reduction in the arbitrary power of the state, and protection of the civil freedoms of individuals.

Beginning in the late nineteenth century, and especially after 1930 in the United States, the term liberalism came to be associated with a very different emphasis, particularly in economic policy. It came to be associated with a readiness to rely primarily on the state rather than on private voluntary arrangements to achieve objectives regarded as desirable. The catchwords became welfare and equality rather than freedom. The nineteenth-century liberal regarded an extension of freedom as the most effective way to promote welfare and equality; the twentieth-century liberal regards welfare and equality as either prerequisites of or alternatives to freedom. In the name of welfare and equality, the twentieth-century liberal has come to favour a revival of the very policies of state intervention and paternalism against which classical liberalism fought. In the very act of turning the clock back to seventeenth-century mercantilism, he is fond of castigating true liberals as reactionary!

The change in the meaning attached to the term liberalism is more striking in economic matters than in political. The twentieth-century liberal, like the nineteenth-century liberal, favors parliamentary institutions, representative government, civil rights, and so on. Yet even in political matters, there is a notable difference. Jealous of liberty, and hence fearful of centralized power, whether in governmental or private hands, the nineteenth-century liberal favored political decentralization. Committed to action and confident of the beneficence of power so long as it is in the hands of a government ostensibly controlled by the electorate, the twentieth-century liberal favors centralized government. He will resolve any doubt about where power should be located in favor of the state instead of the city, of the federal government instead of the state, and of a world organization instead of a national government.

Because of the corruption of the term liberalism, the views that formerly went under that name are now often labeled conservatism. But this is not a satisfactory alternative. The nineteenth-century liberal was a radical, both in the etymological sense of going to the root of the matter, and in the political sense of favoring major changes in social institutions. So too must be his modern heir. We do not wish to conserve the state interventions that have interfered so greatly with our freedom, though, of course, we do wish to conserve those that have promoted it. Moreover, in practice, the term conservatism has come to cover so wide a range of views, and views so incompatible with one another, that we shall no doubt see the growth of hyphenated designations, such as libertarian-conservative and aristocratic-conservative.

Partly because of my reluctance to surrender the term to proponents of measures that would destroy liberty, partly because I cannot find a better alternative, I shall resolve these difficulties by using the word liberalism in its original sense—as the doctrines pertaining to a free man.

### The Relation Between Economic Freedom and Political Freedom

It is widely believed that politics and economics are separate and largely unconnected; that individual freedom is a political problem and material welfare an economic problem; and that any kind of political arrangements can be combined with any kind of economic arrangements. The chief contemporary manifestation of this idea is the advocacy of "democratic socialism" by many who condemn out of hand the restrictions on individual freedom imposed by "totalitarian socialism" in Russia, and who are persuaded that it is possible for a country to adopt the essential features of Russian economic arrangements and yet to ensure individual freedom through political arrangements. The thesis of this chapter is that such a view is a delusion, that there is an intimate connection between economics and politics, that only certain combinations of political and economic arrangements are possible, and that in particular, a society which is socialist cannot also be democratic, in the sense of guaranteeing individual freedom.

Economic arrangements play a dual role in the promotion of a free society. On the one hand, freedom in economic arrangements is itself a component of freedom broadly understood, so economic freedom is an end in itself. In the second place, economic freedom is also an indispensable means toward the achievement of political freedom.

The first of these roles of economic freedom needs special emphasis because intellectuals in particular have a strong bias against regarding this aspect of freedom as important. They tend to express contempt for what they regard as material aspects of life, and to regard their own pursuit of allegedly higher values as on a different plane of significance and as deserving of special attention. For most citizens of the country, however, if not for the intellectual, the direct importance of economic freedom is at least comparable in significance to the indirect importance of economic freedom as a means to political freedom.

The citizen of Great Britain, who after World War II was not permitted to spend his vacation in the United States because of exchange control, was being deprived of an essential freedom no less than the citizen of the United States, who was denied the opportunity to spend his vacation in Russia because of his political views. The one was ostensibly an economic limitation on freedom and the other a political limitation, yet there is no essential difference between the two.

The citizen of the United States who is compelled by law to devote something like 10 per cent of his income to the purchase of a particular kind of retirement contract, administered by the government, is being deprived of a corresponding part of his personal freedom. How strongly this deprivation may be felt and its closeness to the deprivation of religious freedom, which all would regard as "civil" or "political" rather than "economic," were dramatized by an episode involving a group of farmers of the Amish sect. On rounds of principle, this group regarded compulsory federal old age programs as an infringement of their personal individual freedom and refused to pay taxes or accept benefits. As a result, some of their livestock were sold by auction in order to satisfy claims for social security levies. True, the number of citizens who regard compulsory old age insurance as a deprivation of freedom may be few, but the believer in freedom has never counted noses.

A citizen in the United States who under the laws of various states is not free to follow the occupation of his own choosing unless he can get a license for it, is likewise being deprived of an essential part of his freedom. So is the man who would like to exchange some of his goods with, say, a Swiss for a watch but is prevented from doing so by a quota. So also is the Californian who was thrown into jail for selling Alka Seltzer at a price below that set by the manufacturer under so-called "fair trade" laws. So also is the farmer who cannot grow the amount of wheat he wants. And so on. Clearly, economic freedom, in and of itself, is an extremely important part of total freedom.

Viewed as a means to the end of political freedom, economic arrangements are important because of their effect on the concentration or dispersion of power. The kind of economic organization that provides economic freedom directly, namely, competitive capitalism, also promotes political freedom because it separates economic power from political power and in this way enables the one to offset the other.

Historical evidence speaks with a single voice on the relation between political freedom and a free market. I know of no example in time or place of a society that has been marked by a large measure of political freedom, and that has not also used something comparable to a free market to organize the bulk of economic activity.

Because we live in a largely free society, we tend to forget how limited is the span of time and the part of the globe for which there has ever been anything like political freedom: the typical state of mankind is tyranny, servitude, and misery. The nineteenth century and early twentieth century in the Western world stand out as striking exceptions to the general trend of historical development. Political freedom in this instance clearly came along with the free market and the development of capitalist institutions. So also did political freedom in the golden age of Greece and in the early days of the Roman era.

History suggests only that capitalism is a necessary condition for political freedom. Clearly it is not a sufficient condition. Fascist Italy and Fascist Spain, Germany at various times in the last seventy years, Japan before World Wars I and II, czarist Russia in the decades before World War I— are all societies that cannot conceivably be described as politically free. Yet, in each, private enterprise was the dominant form of economic organization. It is therefore clearly possible to have economic arrangements that are fundamentally capitalist and political arrangements that are not free.

Even in those societies, the citizenry had a good deal more freedom than citizens of a modern totalitarian state like Russia or Nazi Germany, in which economic totalitarianism is combined with political totalitarianism. Even in Russia under the Tzars, it was possible for some citizens, under some circumstances, to change their jobs without getting permission from political authority because capitalism and the existence of private property provided some check to the centralized power of the state.

The relation between political and economic freedom is complex and by no means unilateral. In the early nineteenth century, Bentham and the Philosophical Radicals were inclined to regard political freedom as a means to economic freedom. They believed that the masses were being hampered by the restrictions that were being imposed upon them, and that if political reform gave the bulk of the people the vote, they would do what was good for them, which was to vote for laissez faire. In retrospect, one cannot say that they were wrong. There was a large measure of political reform that was accompanied by economic reform in the direction of a great deal of laissez faire. An enormous increase in the well-being of the masses followed this change in economic arrangements.

The triumph of Benthamite liberalism in nineteenth-century England was followed by a reaction toward increasing intervention by government in economic affairs. This tendency to collectivism was greatly accelerated, both in England and elsewhere, by the two World Wars. Welfare rather than freedom became the dominant note in democratic countries. Recognizing the implicit threat to individualism, the intellectual descendants of the Philosophical Radicals—Dicey, Mises, Hayek, and Simons, to mention only a few—feared that a continued movement toward centralized control of economic activity would prove *The Road to Serfdom*, as Hayek entitled his penetrating analysis of the process. Their emphasis was on economic freedom as a means toward political freedom.

Events since the end of World War II display still a different relation between economic and political freedom. Collectivist economic planning has indeed interfered with individual freedom. At least in some countries, however, the result has not been the suppression of freedom, but the reversal of economic policy. England again provides the most striking example. The turning point was perhaps the "control of engagements" order which, despite great misgivings, the Labour party found it necessary to impose in order to carry out its economic policy. Fully enforced and carried through, the law would have involved centralized allocation of individuals to occupations. This conflicted so sharply with personal liberty that it was enforced in a negligible number of cases, and then repealed after the law had been in effect for only a short period. Its repeal ushered in a decided shift in economic policy, marked by reduced reliance on centralized "plans" and "programs," by the dismantling of many controls, and by increased emphasis on the private market. A similar shift in policy occurred in most other democratic countries.

The proximate explanation of these shifts in policy is the limited success of central planning or its outright failure to achieve stated objectives. However, this failure is itself to be attributed, at least in some measure, to the political implications of central planning and to an unwillingness to follow out its logic when doing so requires trampling rough-shod on treasured private rights. It may well be that the shift is only a temporary interruption in the collectivist trend of this century. Even so, it illustrates the close relation between political freedom and economic arrangements.

Historical evidence by itself can never be convincing. Perhaps it was sheer coincidence that the expansion of freedom occurred at the same time as the development of capitalist and market institutions. Why should there be a connection? What are the logical links between economic and political freedom? In discussing these questions we shall consider first the market as a direct component of freedom, and then the indirect relation between market arrangements and political freedom. A by-product will be an outline of the ideal economic arrangements for a free society.

As liberals, we take freedom of the individual, or perhaps the family, as our ultimate goal in judging social arrangements. Freedom as a value in this sense has to do with the interrelations among people; it has no meaning whatsoever to a Robinson Crusoe on an isolated island (without his Man Friday). Robinson Crusoe on his island is subject to "constraint," he has limited "power," and he has only a limited number of alternatives, but there is no problem of freedom in the sense that is relevant to our discussion. Similarly, in a society freedom has nothing to say about what an individual does with his freedom; it is not an all-embracing ethic. Indeed, a major aim of the liberal is to leave the ethical problem for the individual to wrestle with. The "really" important ethical problems are those that face an individual in a free society—what he should do with his freedom. There are thus two sets of values that a liberal will emphasize—the values that are relevant to relations among people, which is the context in which he assigns first priority to freedom; and the values that are relevant to the individual in the exercise of his freedom, which is the realm of individual ethics and philosophy.

The liberal conceives of men as imperfect beings. He regards the problem of social organization to be as much a negative problem of preventing "bad" people from doing harm as of enabling "good" people to do good; and, of course, "bad" and "good" people may be the same people, depending on who is judging them...

The existence of a free market does not of course eliminate the need for government. On the contrary, government is essential both as a forum for determining the "rules of the game" and as an umpire to interpret and enforce the rules decided on. What the market does is to reduce greatly the range of issues that must be decided through political means, and thereby to minimize the extent to which government need participate directly in the game. The characteristic feature of action through political channels is that it tends to require or enforce substantial conformity. The great advantage of the market, on the other hand, is that it permits wide diversity. It is, in political terms, a system of proportional representation. Each man can vote, as it were, for the colour of tie he wants and get it; he does not have to see what colour the majority wants and then, if he is in the minority, submit.

It is this feature of the market that we refer to when we say that the market provides economic freedom. But this characteristic also has implications that go far beyond the narrowly economic. Political freedom means the absence of coercion of a man by his fellow men. The fundamental threat to freedom is power to coerce, be it in the hands of a monarch, a dictator, an oligarchy, or a momentary majority. The preservation of freedom requires the elimination of such concentration of power to the fullest possible extent and the dispersal and distribution of whatever power cannot be eliminated—a system of checks and balances. By removing the organization of economic activity from the control of political authority, the market eliminates this source of coercive power. It enables economic strength to be a check to political power rather than a reinforcement.

Economic power can be widely dispersed. There is no law of conservation which forces the growth of new centers of economic strength to be at the expense of existing centers. Political power, on the other hand, is more difficult to decentralize. There can be numerous small independent governments. But it is far more difficult to maintain numerous equipotent small centers of political power in a single large government than it is to have numerous centers of economic strength in a single large economy. There can be many millionaires in one large economy. But can there be more than one really outstanding leader, one person on whom the energies and enthusiasms of his countrymen are centered? If the central government gains power, it is likely to be at the expense of local governments. There seems to be something like a fixed total of political power to be distributed. Consequently, if economic power is joined to political power, concentration seems almost inevitable. On the other hand, if economic power is kept in separate hands from political power, it can serve as a check and a counter to political power.

**NOTE**

1. Joseph Schumpeter, *History of Economic Analysis* (New York: Oxford University Press, 1954) p. 394.

# Discussion

## Edited by Michael A. Walker

**Milton Friedman** I am going to make a couple of comments. In reading all of these papers, including our own, we have been impressed with the problems that arise out of confusing ends and means. This is a symposium on three things: economic, political and civil freedoms. Each of those in turn can be viewed either as ends or means. But if you look at them first as ends, they are by no means exclusive, they by no means cover the major ends that have moved people or societies. You would have to include in any such list, today at least, and earlier, egalitarianism or equality, which many people would regard as an ultimate end, with economic, political or civil freedom as means toward that end. You can look at the question of nationalism. Certainly nationalistic sentiment has served a more important role in moving peoples and producing major changes and conflicts than has the search for economic, political or civil freedom! And prosperity or economic growth can be viewed something as an end in itself rather than as a means.

But I was going to limit my comments to the three we have chosen for topics for this session. And for us, each of these separately can be an end or a means, and I thought the papers illustrated that divergence quite well. For Rose and me, civil freedom is the end—a single end—and economic or political freedom are means toward that end. Our position is fundamentally that of the Declaration of Independence: that we hold these truths to be self-evident; that all men are created equal; that they are endowed by their Creator with certain unalienable rights; that among these are life, liberty and the pursuit of happiness (which of course should have been property, as it was in the original source); that to secure these rights governments are instituted among men.

Well and good, but if governments are instituted among men to secure *these* rights, then political freedom or political arrangements can't be an ultimate end; they are a means. Economic arrangements are more complicated, because economic freedom is part and parcel of civil freedom, as we have argued and everybody would agree. But in addition to that, economic arrangements are a means toward the end of civil freedom. They are a means towards the end not only of economic freedom but of all other freedoms. From that point of view, we regard emphasis on market arrangements not as an end in itself but as a means toward a much greater end.

On the other hand, to Gastil and Wright, as I interpret their paper, *political* freedom is the essential component, and they regard civil freedom and economic freedom as means toward political freedom. For example, the freedom to speak is not an ultimate right at all; it is simply a necessary condition for achieving representation in political government, as I interpret their argument. In the same way, in their argument, economic freedom is not part of an ultimate end, it is purely a means. I think these two approaches lead to very different kinds of conclusions and very different ways of analysing the material.

If we take the third, economic freedom, to many people that seems to be an ultimate end in itself. You want growth or prosperity, you want to have a great, wealthy country, or for that matter, prosperous people. Many of the people who live in the United States who are called conservatives belong in this category. They are strong believers in free markets and what is called capitalism, while not being concerned at all with maintaining a large number of other freedoms, particularly civil freedoms, or, for that matter, political freedoms. That draws a sharp line in which Gastil and Wright and we agree—that the issue is not capitalism, whatever that may mean, versus socialism.

Capitalism isn't a guarantee of human freedom. It is only competitive capitalism that serves fundamentally as a means toward human freedom or civil freedom, which we regard as the ultimate objective. That is why in our book, *Capitalism and Freedom*, we almost never refer to capitalism alone—we refer to "competitive capitalism" in order to make the distinction. But again, the Gastil and Wright point of view is very different. From their point of view, the only role of capitalism is as a means to permit sufficient decentralization of power in order to be able to have a political structure under which the leadership can change from time to time.

I am not going to come out anywhere. We were reminded, when we came to this point of thinking about what we would say, about that famous story about the high official who had a speech written for him. He read page after page, and he said, "Now the solution to all these problems is..." and the next page said, "Now you're on your own!" (Laughter)

So now *you* are on *your* own.

**Gordon Tullock** I want to make two supplementary comments. The first is that that Declaration of Independence, which you read, was written by a man who was a very large-scale slave holder, and a large number of the people who signed it—and perhaps a majority, I don't know—were also large-scale slave holders.

I had the good fortune to attend the Volker Fund Conference at Wabash College where Milton Friedman first presented the lectures which became *Capitalism and Freedom.* I can assure him that these lectures had a major impact on my thought. This impact was reinforced when I later read the book. The book, of course, was a major extension of the lectures, but so close in style and reasoning that I am unable to remember now what it was that I heard and what I only read. Nevertheless, as discussant, it is my duty to criticize.

Fortunately, as the Friedmans will no doubt be happy to hear, my criticisms are the same as for *The Road to Serfdom,* another book which had a major intellectual impact on me. The authors of both of these books, I now think, had cloudy crystal balls. The basic problem with *The Road to Serfdom* was that it offered predictions which turned out to be false. The steady advance of government in places such as Sweden has not led to any loss of non-economic freedoms. This is particularly impressive because I doubt that any government before 1917 had obtained control of anything even close to the 65 percent of GNP now flowing through the Swedish government. I know many Swedes (and also Norse, Danes, Dutch and English) who are very upset with the sacrifice of control over so much of their earnings, but none who regard themselves as unfree in any other sense.

But let me digress to another point. The Friedmans say, "the great advances of civilization, whether architecture or painting, in science or literature, in industry or agriculture, have never come from centralized government." No one who has ever passed through the Gate of Heavenly Peace will deny that centralized despotism can produce brilliant architecture. There is, of course, the collection of churches in Byzantium, of Mosques in Isfahan and the great hypostyle hall at Karnak as further evidence. Indeed, if you are, as I am, an inveterate tourist, in Europe you will frequently find yourself in architectural gems that were put up by despotic governments.

It isn't only architecture. El Greco lived in the Toledo of the high Inquisition. The French regard the period of Louis XIV as in many ways the high point of their culture. Chinese painting and poetry flourished over 2000 years of centralized despotism. With respect to agriculture, the development of large centralized systems of irrigation supported most of the human race (Europeans were a small minority until recently). These systems either were developed by the government or their masters became the government.

As far as science is concerned, we believe that it began in Babylonia under the control of rather centralized despotic governments, but the early history is still rather poor. The flourishing of Greek science is of course well known. The later period of Greek science in which it was controlled by the despotic and centralized Ptolemid state was far from contemptible. Euclid, after all, wrote in Alexandria.

The revival of science after the Middle Ages occurred in Western Europe and originally in rather despotic states, although the trailing off of feudalism meant that they weren't centralized. Galileo did a good deal of his work in Medici Florence, and indeed, the first scientific academy was founded there. Further, with time, France and Spain became highly centralized. It would be extremely difficult to argue that science progressed more rapidly in the rather decentralized environment of England than in the highly centralized French monarchy. Lavosier, to name but one example, was a subject of Louis XVI who was executed by the Republic.

In general, in the 19th century most of Europe developed fairly strong democratic trends, although not necessarily decentralization, and this was a great scientific period in Europe. The regression to despotic governments in the 20th century, however, did not necessarily change that. Mussolini's Italy retained its high scientific traditions, particularly in physics. Even in Hitler's Germany, the two-thirds of the scientific community who stayed (the ones who were permitted to stay) continued to do distinguished and important work.

I suspect that both Friedman and Hayek have been very much affected by the Communist and Nazi dictatorships. It should be kept in mind, however, that these are extremely bizarre and unusual forms of government. Most of the human race has lived under what can only be described as mild autocracies. (I have just finished a book on autocracies, so I feel authoritative on this subject.[1]) These autocracies were far, far from mild with respect to those people who chose to take an active role in politics. For the average citizen, however, the government was neither very oppressive nor very beneficial.

Indeed, the economic policy followed by most of these despots doesn't differ too much from what has been followed by most historic democracies. Athens and Rome, after all, had price control over basic necessities. Indeed, the bread of Rome was largely provided directly by the Roman state. Anyone living today realizes that democracies muddle around a good deal in their economies, just like despots.

Most despots have, to repeat, not done a great deal in their economy, not because they have any theoretical objections to it, but because they are busy with other things, such as their harem. I recently acquired a book[2] which is a translation of a general guide for local officials under the old Chinese Empire. The official slogan of the Chinese Empire from the time of Mencious was: "The government should own all important industries and carefully control the rest." No doubt the author of this book believed in that slogan, but as a matter of fact, in this very thick book he devotes almost no attention to economic control. The only conspicuous example of intervention in the economy was his decision that the wine shops located directly across from the entrance of his Yamen were overcharging their customers. He imposed price control on them.

Mainly, however, he was occupied in holding court, collecting taxes, and performing the many other duties of governing about 100,000 people. Once again, despots, like democracies, when they do engage in government intervention in the economy, tend to be responding to rent-seeking activities of well-organized political groups rather than carrying out anything we would refer to as planning. As far as I know, none of the early despotisms engaged in anywhere near as much detailed economic intervention into their economics as is normal in present day democracies.

As I remarked, the type of dictatorship we tend to think of as totalitarian—Stalin, Hitler, Mao Tse Tung, et cetera—is a very unusual phenomenon historically. So is democracy. It is not surprising then that there are no coincidences. I should say, however, that I doubt that this kind of government could operate with a true democracy, not because it would necessarily be able to strangle the democracy but because the voters would surely throw the rascals out.

Having said that I disagree with *this* aspect of what we may call the Hayek-Friedman argument, there is another sense in which there is no doubt that capitalism and freedom are closely connected. This is a sense which the Friedmans emphasize much more than Hayek. My freedom to spend my income as I wish is surely of great importance to me. It is equally surely a freedom, although many people on the left would deny that. Further, my freedom to move from one government system to another without too much inconvenience is another freedom, and it puts governments into competition with each other.

With respect to the last, I should say that it does not really require democracy. I have recently seen an investigation of the situation in Germany before the unification of that state, and discovered the individual princes, counts, et cetera behaved very much as businessmen do today. They realized they had no monopolistic power because the peasant could move down the road a few miles, and they attempted to maximize profits on their "enterprise" using low production costs and a high level of service in order to attract customers.

One of the arguments for a free economy is false. It doesn't follow that the free economy is not important or that it does not lead to individual freedom. The freedom that it gives, however, is economic freedom. There is no reason why we should be ashamed of that, or regard that as in any sense a criticism of the system. Arguments for political freedom are strong, as are the arguments for economic freedom. We needn't make one set of arguments depend on the other.

But the principal problem I wish to talk about is not about economic but political freedom. At the time I read Hayek's book and heard Friedman's lecture, it seemed to me very reasonable that a government which completely dominated the economic system would suppress political freedom. Alas, for those of us who follow another aspect of Friedman's work and believe in empirical testing, in present-day Sweden the government takes control of 63 percent of the GNP. Most of the other North European countries have somewhat similar shares. It is hard to argue that there is any lack of political freedom in any of these countries, nor does there seem to be any evidence that political freedom is declining. This should not be taken as praise of these governments; indeed I think they are very objectionable. But the apparent logical connection between government control of a large part of the economy and the loss of political freedom is only apparent.

**Milton Friedman** I only want to point out one thing, and that is one of the major reasons why this conference was called and took the approach it did was precisely because of the kind of empirical evidence you end up with— which leads us to the conclusion that our initial belief, that these went together as closely as they did, was wrong. I would cite as my main example Hong Kong rather than Sweden, in the sense that there is almost no doubt that if you had political freedom in Hong Kong you would have much less economic and civil freedom than you do as a result of an authoritarian government.

**Raymond Gastil** The biggest difference between our approach and Milton's has to do with the difference between emphasis on the individual and emphasis on the group. I will turn to that more in the discussion of our own paper later on.

Specifically, in regard to Milton's discussion today, the first point to be made is that it is quite possible that none of these three should be regarded as the end—neither economic, political nor civil freedoms or rights. I would think the end lies outside those three. I am not going to define what it is, but there are a lot of words around like joy and love and human betterment with which one can go in various directions. But the fact that I do a survey of political and civil rights doesn't mean I think those are ends.

The second point is that I think one should distinguish between absolutes and ends. One could say, for example, that freedom of speech is an absolute. But I don't think freedom of speech should be regarded as an end.

The third point is that it is true that as far as the Survey is concerned, we talk about those civil rights that are supportive of political rights. So, we emphasize one group of civil rights or civil liberties and de-emphasize other kinds of civil liberties because they don't really contribute as directly to the legitimacy of political rights. That doesn't mean we regard them as less important. It just means that for the purpose of the Survey that is what we do, because that seems to make a neat package which goes together nicely. But the other civil liberties might, in fact, be just as important in the general scheme of things.

**Assar Lindbeck** I would like to follow up on a very strong statement made by Gordon Tullock: "There is an intimate connection between economics and politics, in that only certain combinations of political and economic arrangements are possible, and that, in particular, a society which is socialist cannot also be democratic in the sense of guaranteeing individual freedom." I don't see any reasons why that should be true, either from an a priori point of view or from empirical experience. I have no difficulty imagining a society where the means of production are owned by the government but you still have elections every year, where state-owned newspapers publish articles on people from different parties, et cetera, provided there were pluralistic political structures in the country from the very beginning. I agree that there may be a low probability of a pluralistic political culture under those circumstances, but I really see no impossibility.

Sweden was mentioned as an example where 65 percent of the GNP goes through the government budget, half with transfer payments and the other half in public spending on goods and services, and we are going to discuss that another day. Austria is another example where some 40 percent of the manufacturing sector is owned by the public sector. I could imagine that even if 95 percent or one hundred percent were owned by government, you could still have civil liberties, elections and freedom of speech.

A crucial point is control over or the ownership of mass media and newspapers. It is very tempting for a ruling party to control mass media, as it tried to do with television in France, for instance. If the government owns all mass media, then civil liberties and freedom of speech might go down considerably. But if you make an exception and let private individuals, organizations and political parties own mass media, I think you could very well have a democratic society.

**Voice**  Where would they get their paper from?

**Assar Lindbeck**  That is an open question. I agree with you that there are larger risks for authoritarian regimes if government owns the mass media. But I don't see it as logically impossible. That's my only point.

What I see as threatened by government ownership is, first of all, pluralism. You could have freedom of speech, but a pluralistic political culture might be difficult because people would be afraid to use freedom of speech if there were only one career in society, that is, through the government. You could have non-pluralistic democracies with elections every four years and freedom of speech, but they would not be very vital political cultures. Mexico might be such an example, where everybody has to make a career through the same political party. If one party completely dominates, political democracy might not be very vital, but I think it could still exist.

In my opinion, where a very big government really intrudes on individual freedom—that is really what Gordon Tullock said—is through its impact on disposable income. If you pay tax at 90 percent of your income, you cannot influence your own economic situation by your own effort. Or, if government rations goods and services, you don't have much freedom of choice. If there are government monopolies, you cannot choose different types of services; you have to rely on government services. So it is really pluralism and freedom of choice rather than civil liberties that are threatened.

**Tibor Machan**  One of the points raised by Milton Friedman and Raymond Gastil has to do with ends versus means. I think only individual persons can have ends. They may get together with others in their pursuit of ends. But individuals have ends, and thus social and political institutions are means for individuals to pursue certain ends of theirs.

The other thing upon which I want to comment is whether a society that has socialist or statist laws must thwart freedom in all areas. Let me take the analogy of a zoo. There are zoos with very small cages where the animals can't do anything, and there are zoos like the San Diego Wild Animal Park which is practically not a zoo. Nevertheless there are certain limits; both are zoos.

In Hungary, for example, there is officially a Soviet-style socialism, but most bureaucrats don't bother to implement it. So people go to Hungary and come away and say, "See, the thawing of socialism." It has nothing to do with the thawing of socialism; there is practically no socialism going on in many parts of Hungary. I don't think that the fact they give lip service to socialist ideology should be taken seriously in our discussion of the practical effects of political and economic institutions.

**Walter Block** I would like to approach the original Friedman thesis from a different perspective, although I think Tibor's points are very well taken. I would like to attempt to make a serious bifurcation between economic and civil freedom on the one hand and political freedom on the other hand. I claim that the former two are legitimate forms of freedom but that the latter is not. I would go so far as to say that political freedom is an oxymoron or a contradiction in terms.

By freedom, what I mean is the absence of initiatory coercion, or that there is no violation of personal legitimate property rights. Now, economic freedom under this rubric is easy to understand; it defends the right to trade or to engage in any consensual activity of an economic sort. Civil freedom would mandate that there be no laws against pornography, prostitution, drugs, religion, free speech, et cetera.

But political freedom is very different. Economic and civil freedom are just capitalist acts or non-capitalist acts between consenting adults. Now, if politics is, as I contend, just a futures market in stolen goods, then political freedom is only a right to get in on this ganglike behaviour. If we do not have it, all we are kept away from is the right to control other people's lives—and that, improperly. If there are no elections, and we have no government, or we have a benevolent government that doesn't violate economic or civil freedoms, then we are free.

On the other hand, we can have all the political freedom we want, and if the majority votes for rent control, as it does in the People's Republic of Santa Monica or New York City, then we have "political freedom," which is a misnomer. What we have really is a warlike activity where people gang up on other people and determine what they can or cannot do with their own property. This is not political freedom; this is just licence. This is allowing people to control other people unjustly. Economic and civil freedom are legitimate freedoms, political freedom is not.

**Ingemar Stahl** If I remember my history, most of the constitutions and political systems we call democratic were instituted to control a despot or a king with a very limited size of the public sector. We are now using exactly the same system to run economies where 65 percent of the economy is channelled through the public sector. So, of course, it would be remarkable if political freedom in the sense of controlling a despot would apply to the situation of controlling 65 percent of GNP.

While Tullock made a plug for public choice, I want to make a plug for Wicksell. This is the 90-year anniversary of the publishing of his text wherein he proposed the unanimity rule as the basic rule for government. We must remember that political freedom in everyday talk, even including the Friedmans' paper, is a kind of acceptance of a democratic system where the majority rules. But I think we could sharpen the conditions and say that we should also include protection of minorities, for example, by qualified majorities, or that there should be some restrictions on the competence of government. It is a little bit dangerous here—and I will take that up later when we come to the Gastil/Wright paper—to put an equals sign between democratic institutions where the majority rules and political freedom.

I think we should be more interested, as economists, in looking at the u-nanimity principle as the basic principle of democracy, which can then be compromised by accepting a qualified majority or certain restrictions on all government behaviour. Majority rule has created 40 percent ownership of industry in Austria. Majority rule has created 65 percent channelled through the public sector and most of the services and transfers in Sweden. There is a lot of coercion included in the majority rule concept, even though we find it somewhat difficult to accept the strong statement of the point in the form that Walter Block, for example, is inclined to make it. If we say lack of coercion is the most basic political freedom, we are back to having to advance the unanimity principle.

**Milton Friedman** I just wanted to clarify that in *Capitalism and Freedom* we explicitly take the position you just took. We take the position that the only real principle is unanimity. The majority rule is an expedient, and various forms of qualified majorities are various forms of expedients. So there is absolutely no difference between your view and the one we expressed in *Capitalism and Freedom*.

**Peter Bauer** Autocracy is compatible limited government. I should like to refer to two sayings, one from the 18th century, the other contemporary. Dr. Johnson said, in the 18th century, "Public affairs vex no man." He meant two things by that. First, that when people complain about the government they more often than not project their own private unhappiness in various ways. But it was also an apt comment in the middle of the 18th century, because government was so limited in its impact on people that this statement had much greater validity then than now. Second, it used to be said before the war in British Malaya that the Chinese there did not mind who owned the cow as long as they could milk it.

This last statement reflects the familiar misconception, namely that wealth is extracted not created. The Chinese on Malaya had created their wealth; they didn't take it from the Malays. But the saying also embodies the important truth, namely that when a country is relatively lightly governed, people are not so desperately anxious who has the government. The Chinese in today's Malaysia would not say that they did not mind who had the government. We should remember this vital distinction between elected government or non-elected government on the one hand and limited and unlimited government on the other.

Second, I think Gordon reminded us of a very important consideration which we are apt to overlook, namely that much of the world's greatest art was created in autocracies of various kinds.

There is an asymmetry between the size of the public sector and government control of the economy. A large public sector implies government control over much of the economy. But the converse doesn't apply. Even if public spending is small, the government can still control the economy closely by licensing, ethnic quotas, price and wage regulation and the like.

The last point is the question of how fundamental is freedom of speech or freedom of expression of ideas. Academics habitually insist on the freedom of ideas and their expression. Simultaneously they often insist on the need for government control of the production and distribution of other goods and services. Some years ago Coase published a very informative article on this dichotomy titled "The Market for Goods and the Market for Ideas."

**Brian Kantor** I wouldn't want to abandon the links between economic and political freedoms. I come from a country where democracy, that is, political freedoms, are greatly feared because of the economic outcomes that are expected from it. In other words, the popular government is feared because of the great power that government would have and exercise. There is thus a violent competition to control economic outcomes through government. Clearly, unless you can get people to agree to limit those powers, you won't get democracy, political freedoms or civil freedoms either. So, I think the links are extremely important, although some of the evidence, as Gordon has pointed out, seems rather unclear.

I suggest trying to save the hypothesis that there are these links between economic and political freedom by looking at the realities again, and governments may be very important in that their share of the economy may be very large, especially if the amount of transfer payments they indulge in are included. Yet, despite this, the economic outcomes may not be terribly much affected by it. For example, you may have a very high level of taxation, but when you look at the benefits of government expenditure, how are they distributed? Aren't the people who proportionately pay much of the taxation, in fact, actually getting a lot of the benefits? We know that educational expenditure goes largely to the middle class. So, the reality is rather different than what it may appear as. That is, even though governments are big, maybe they don't affect the economic outcomes very much, especially when people are free to move their capital and are free to migrate.

**Douglass North** I guess I am going to be supporting Gordon a lot. This goes against my grain, but, truth will out.

I do think there is confusion, as I hear it around the table, about really what you mean by institutions and freedoms or the outcome of institutions, which is part of what we are talking about. It seems to me what we are always interested in is not the institutions *per se*; we are interested in the outcomes. That is, we are interested in the set of choices that follow from this. One of the things that I have been at pains over the years in learning about institutions is that it isn't just rules, it isn't just enforcement characteristics, it is also this illusive thing that I call "norms of behaviour."

Restraints on behaviour by individuals in society really exist, and they exist above and beyond rules and enforcement characteristics. We don't know a lot about them, but they make a lot of difference in the outcomes we get. That means that the same rules imposed on different societies produce very different results. What would be a rule that would deny freedoms in one society wouldn't be exercised in that way at all in another society.

I remember, Alan, when we had that conference on immigration that you gave a paper at, and I commented on. A critical question at this conference was this bill that was before Congress which was going to have everybody having an identification card, and it was immediately raised, and properly so, that this sounded like the Soviet Union. In fact, what you would be having was people being done the same way. But it is not clear that in the United States it would produce that result at all, or that in a lot of other countries it would produce that result. You cannot make simple, facile statements in which you shift and talk about the consequences of a rule in one place and another place without thinking about the fact that they are also constrained both by enforcement characteristics and the norms of behaviour in different societies.

**Raymond Gastil** The discussion has gone in many different directions since I originally raised my hand, but let me make a few points on what has been going on. The first point is that very clear majorities can be very coercive, and what they do may ruin society. For example, one man one vote could ruin South Africa, no doubt about it. Nevertheless, in most situations there is very little alternative, (1), to having governments and, (2), if you accept certain principles about equality, to having majority rule, in spite of some of the results that may accrue from that.

It seems to me that majority government, as oppressive, coercive, and so on as it may be and in spite of all the theory that one might have that unanimity or something else is a possibility or would be nicer, is really for most situations the only available solution to the problem of power. From that perspective, I find the remarks by Walter, for example, reminiscent more than anything of listening to Marx speak about the terrible things that were going on in the world. It is utopianism to say that something that has never been anywhere on any scale—and probably because of the nature of people will *not* be anywhere on any scale—is the way in which we should organize our relationships.

The second point is just a thought in regard to Tibor's point that only individuals really have ends. That may be true in some philosophical sense, nevertheless, in a practical sense, if we think about the fact that we as Americans are very interested in the survival of certain values over the future centuries that stretch out in front of us, it isn't as appropriate to think of those in terms of our individual wants and desires as to think of those in terms of group wants and desires. I don't think it is we as separate individuals that are really interested in that long-range future, but we as members of a collectivity.

The point that I was really going to talk about when I raised my hand was Assar's point having to do with the media. Let me just point to National Public Radio in the United States, which is the closest thing to a government-owned and controlled media we have in this country, and yet is the most consistently critical of the United States government.

**Voice** Republican government!

**Ramon Diaz** Assar Lindbeck said that he didn't find it difficult to think of a regime where all property was social and yet political and civil liberties remained. I think that is perfectly right, as a logical point of view. If we think of society as made up of so many chessmen, we can arrange them in a logical way in that sense. But I doubt that this is a very relevant statement.

Actually, what we are talking about here has to do with the rule of law and with competitive capitalism, and this is a very unique circumstance. As the Friedmans say in their paper, the typical state of mankind is tyranny, servitude and misery. We are in a very, very special circumstance. I think it is inconceivable that we could have come to this special and privileged historical circumstance if the society had been made up of civil servants. Civil servants will *not* produce a society that upholds freedom. We have a character in this great play that is enacted in Western society, and this hero of our play is a property owner. Therefore, I think that we have to focus on the very special characteristics that have prevailed in the West which have produced a particular individual who thinks of himself as a separate private individual with property rights and not as an employee of the government.

**Michael Parkin** I would like to go back to the sentence that begins the thesis of this chapter and which several people have picked up on. It seems to me that if we think about what is being said there in just a slightly different way from the precise words that are used, we see that the statement really has a lot of strength. Milton and Rose distinguish between socialism and capitalism, but they always—or almost always (as Milton has said)—qualify the word "capitalism" with the word "competitive." It seems to me to be useful to think about a two-fold classification—competitive and non-competitive arrangements; and capitalistic and socialistic arrangements—and then ask ourselves, which is the key dimension?

We know that scarcity means that every situation has to be fundamentally competitive, but using the word in the more limited sense, to talk about how we explicitly organize our social institutions, I wonder whether it is the competitive rather than the socialist/capitalist dimension that makes the difference? Think about competitive as being a situation in which there is freedom of entry and exit. That is what makes competition different from other arrangements. There might be only one (producer, government or whatever), but the fact that that one got there through a process that could have resulted in any one, or more than one, being there, doing whatever it is, makes the situation different from a situation in which there is one and only one there because others are excluded by explicit rules and procedures.

If we think of things in this way, I think we see that Assar is wrong in the inferences he draws from Sweden. Sweden is an example of *competitive* socialism. It is competitive in the sense that it competes on the world market to sell its output. We wouldn't want to say that IBM is in some sense a socialist country, but Sweden is a big organization, a big corporation, like IBM, that produces goods and services by means that do not use the market very extensively, internally, but that sell the output competitively on the world market.

I don't know the fraction of Swedish GNP that is traded internationally, but it must be pretty high. That puts a discipline on the Swedish economy that would not be there if this were a closed economic system.

Secondly, a feature of the freedom of entry and exit view was touched on by Brian Kantor, that is, individuals who don't want to put up with the arrangements that are in place in Sweden are, in fact, pretty reasonably free to take their human and physical capital and locate it somewhere else. That also makes it a competitive environment in the same sense as before.

I will summarize very quickly just by saying that if we think about the words "competitive" and "noncompetitive" as being more important for this particular point than the words "socialist" and "capitalist," we make more sense of the original thesis and it emerges as a much more powerful thesis.

**Svetozar Pejovich** I have three points. The absence of private ownership is what I understand to be socialism. In that sense, Sweden is not a socialist state and, in that sense, Hungary is. If I have a car that belongs to the state, I cannot sell it. And for that reason there is no market for capital goods.

On the second point, I want to ask Mr. Friedman. What I observe is that people trade freedom for other things, like security, marriage, the priesthood, and if this is so, then there must be diminishing marginal returns to the freedom that people enjoy. If so, then a perfectly free society will be an inefficient society. To me, what is important seems to be the ease of exit, the cost of exit.

**Assar Lindbeck** I think we all agree that there are very important links between political and economic systems. We are trying to discover the character of those links. What I tried to say is that those links are much more complex than earlier thought by Hayek and the Friedmans in their expositions. Moreover, they are not deterministic, but they are highly probabilistic. I think Milton should include chance and risk in these considerations as well.

There is not a monotonic relation between the size of the public sector and individual freedom. If you go to a society where public ownership is 10 percent and increase it to 40, 50, 60 or 70 percent, you could not predict what would happen to civil liberties in that society. If public spending increased to 65 percent of GNP in Sweden, I couldn't say that there are fewer civil liberties now than when the sector was 20 percent or in countries where it is presently 20 percent.

As the size of the public sector grows, freedom of choice—the possibility for an individual to change his own life situation by his own effort—decreases. But I think that is very different from civil liberties. By civil liberties I mean that you have elections, you have freedom of speech, you have a competitive political system—you can feel free to criticize the government as much as you like. That is different from the fact that it is difficult to change your own disposable income by your own effort. I am not saying that the latter is less important, only that it is different. We should make distinctions between those different aspects of freedom—freedom of choice versus civil liberties.

Lastly, in Sweden there is no big risk in criticizing the government, with some exceptions. Research institutes, for instance, that live on government funds, might think for awhile before they criticize government. There could be some limitations there. What is more important is that people hesitate much more to criticize labour unions, because labour unions can influence the career of a person in the sense of affecting promotions. Labour unions do not have a truly competitive political system for choosing their leaders. You can get a new government after two or three years, but it is very difficult to get a new political party to rule the labour union. That is ruled by the same group of people decade after decade. So there is a private organization besides the state which I think is much more detrimental to freedom of speech in my country than is the government because of the lack of a competitive political system between the unions.

Finally, it is very misleading to call Sweden a socialist state. I think 7 percent of manufacturing is owned by the government—less than in practically any country in the world. It is a transfer state rather than a socialist state.

**Gordon Tullock**    I think we have three different things: economic freedom, which is the right to work, et cetera; civil freedom or personal freedom, which is a large collection of things which, really on traditional grounds we think are important, like the right to speak, and so forth; and then finally there is the use of the voting system in some variant. I spend most of my time trying to think of ways to make it work better, so I say "some variant." I agree with Block, that the use of freedom for the third kind of freedoms is a somewhat odd use of language. It doesn't follow from that that I don't think it is important. I do think it is important, but I don't think, strictly speaking, that freedom is the correct term to use with it.

If you go back to the 19th century you will find the opposite of what I am calling here the Friedman/Hayek position. You find people saying that if you want a free economy you have to have democracy. This point of view vanished in the 1920s and '30s for rather obvious reasons. There has been an effort to simply reverse it. I don't see any strong reasoning for doing so. In fact, in the 19th century I think it was essentially an accidental coincidence that economic freedom and democracy coexisted. I also think it is essentially an accidental coincidence now.

We can be in favour of all of these freedoms without feeling that we have to allege that they come out of each other. Some of the personal freedoms come out of the use of some kind of voting system, because you can't do it unless you have freedom of speech and things like that. That is part of the voting system. But other than that, they seem to be three different things—all of which are desirable—and I don't see any strong reason for arguing that they are correlated.

**Alan Walters** I think the sort of distinction which Milton makes in his book somewhere between totalitarianism and despotism is a very important one. Hong Kong is ruled by a despot, by the governor, but it is completely opposite to a totalitarian society. I think that distinction tends to be lost sometimes.

I would like to go back and support a point that Gordon made in a positive sense, and that is, it isn't just that great art comes from these despots. It is also true that those despots, to a very large extent, had competitive art systems supplying them.

The second point I think is very important too. For all of their many successes, America and Britain in their capitalist heydays have been pretty much an artistic desert. It is tragic and it is something we cannot easily explain. There is no good art, no good music produced during these long periods.

**Raymond Gastil** I made most of my points before, but let me just add that there is a great difference between different contexts as to what are the important and significant issues of freedom. As you move from capitalist to socialist, from government control to private control and so forth, you have different problems arising. One thing that we have not spent enough time on is that if you don't have government controls that limit freedom, you very often find that the controls come from other sources. They might come from unions, from religion, or from business.

**Walter Block** Gordon agrees with me that we should put economic and civil liberties on the one side and political freedom on the other, and even that political freedom is sort of a misnomer. But he insists that it is important, nonetheless. I would urge that it is not quite so important. Certainly the Hong Kong example of the despotism not ruining economic liberty is one example. Another example would be British colonial rule over Africa and India, which was despotic in many ways but which was very beneficial in terms of economics.

Second, I don't regard unions as private enterprises. I regard them as bits of government or "overmighty subjects," as Peter has called them. I regard them as bands of criminals who compete with the government gangs. Somehow they have wrested some legitimacy and some ability to initiate coercion from the government. But, just like government, they do provide some legitimate services. So they are neither fish nor fowl. But to call them private institutions is a misnomer.

Third, about Sweden being like IBM. I am very reluctant to accept this analogy. I see a vast difference between a voluntary organization such as IBM, which receives its capital from the voluntary choices of investors, and Sweden, which obtains its revenue from the involuntary taxation system.

My last point is with regard to utopians. I accept happily the notion that I am a utopian, if, by utopian you mean all that is good and pure! And I do mean it just that way, at least in one sense: a utopian is someone who does not care much whether something is or is not politically feasible. A utopian says what is right and what is not right is much more important than what is politically feasible. Certainly, a free enterprise system now is not really politically feasible, but I think that is really unimportant. My concerns are for what is right and just and not for what is likely to occur in the next couple of years.

**Milton Friedman** There are so many things here I don't know quite what to react to. But I want to start by making a few comments in connection with Assar Lindbeck's various comments.

I believe that Assar neglected to read the whole of the sentence which he criticized, because it says, "A society which is socialist cannot also be democratic, *in the sense* of guaranteeing individual freedom" (italics added). And the next sentence goes on, "Economic arrangements play a dual role...On the one hand, freedom in economic arrangements is itself a component of freedom broadly understood." So when Assar says that socialism is not compatible with freedom of choice, he is agreeing with us that it is not possible to have a democratic socialism which guarantees individual freedom. Because in our view economic choice is an extremely important component of economic freedom, and not simply a means toward another end.

I agree thoroughly with Ingemar that government spending as a fraction of income is an imperfect measure of the role of government and is not necessarily closely related to most of the other things that we talk about. But government influence, in the sense of controlling the activities of individuals, including redistribution of income, does severely interfere with freedom of individuals as such. Therefore, I am not going to retreat from believing that that sentence is basically a correct sentence.

I also will agree with him, and with Michael, that what is really relevant is pluralism and competitiveness, and that is why in an earlier page on this little document we got out we said that "The second broad principle is that government power must be dispersed...If I do not like what my local community does...I can move to another local community." I have no doubt that a world of small, dispersed governments—even if governments in that case owned all the means of production—could be, in principle, competitive as among the different governments and could, in principle, produce exactly the same results as what we call a free enterprise, private enterprise, situation.

With respect to Raymond's various comments, I want to separate myself completely from the notion of group values. Again, if I may just go back to show that I am not making this up anew. If we say, *he*—and by that I mean a liberal in my sense of the term liberal—"recognizes no national goal except as it is the consensus of the goals that the citizens severally serve." I believe there *are* such things, very important things, as consensus about values, agreement about values, but I think the notion of group values is a dangerous notion that inevitably leads to an organismic concept of society and in a direction I don't think Raymond would want to go.

As to some of the other comments, I will make one more comment only. I have no doubt that the best of all forms of government is benevolent dictatorship. I am not going to quarrel with that at all, and we have had some examples in history of good, benevolent dictatorships, as in Hong Kong, in Singapore with Lee Kuan Yew—he's been a benevolent dictator. The problem with benevolent dictators is that they don't stay benevolent, which goes to Herbert's point of what is the time period. They don't stay benevolent, and they tend to be replaced by people who aren't so benevolent, and the benevolent people tend to get corrupted as well.

On to Gordon's point about the notions contained in Hayek's *Road to Serfdom* and our *Capitalism and Freedom*. The key feature of Hayek's *Road to Serfdom*, as I see it, is the chapter which says the worst rise to the top. In that respect I believe that he has been completely right. I don't believe you can say he has been wrong. He was wrong in predicting that the increase in the size of government measured by government spending would lead to dictatorship and totalitarianism, but what happened in the course of the next 20 years is that the character of government expenditures and control changed. It started out in the direction of nationalization and then it changed into redistribution. And there is no doubt that—and this is a point Assar has been making—the effect on the tendency toward dictatorship is quite different as between these two modes of government expenditure.

**Douglass North**  I want to pick up on Milton's point about competitiveness. Actually, it relates to something Michael said earlier. It seems to me that what is crucial about competitiveness is two aspects of it that make institutions have greater viability. One is that competition maximizes the chance to make mistakes and, therefore, perhaps the chance of finding successful ways to do things. Since we don't know which ways work, we want to maximize those opportunities. Certainly, the kind of institutions that do that are very crucial.

Secondly, competitiveness eliminates the losers, and that is equally important. If you let the losers continue and persist in the society, then you build into it structural weaknesses. I have a term that is not original, "adaptive efficiency," which is very different I think from allocative efficiency as we use it in economics. But it is related to institutions that do maximize both the choice set that is available to people and the competitiveness, so that you wipe out losing sets of institutions.

The Northwest Ordinance, which I talk about in my paper, is a marvellous illustration of it. It provided for some very simple things like fee simple ownership of land, easy transferability of title, inheritance laws that were clear and simple. The result was that while downstream in U.S. history we made terrible ways of distributing land, it didn't make much difference because with these institutions in place we could transfer land, as we did, to more efficient uses and ones that solved our problems better. So the competitiveness is something that has a precise meaning in the way I want to think about it that relates to your point and to Milton's.

**Arnold Harberger**  As I have been listening through the discussion this morning and also from the very beginning, looking at the title of the conference, I felt that this was a topic that could easily fall prey to semantics and definitions, to creating categories and arguing between them. Now, there is nothing wrong with all of that, but I think we should recognize, for the efficiency of *our* discussion, that it is a trap that we could easily fall into.

I would like to try to help the discussion get a bit more concrete by speaking a little from my own experience. I float around in Latin America a lot, and I also try to study economic growth around the world a fair amount. There is a question that really gets me sometimes, especially in ideological discussions in Latin America. They keep pounding me. They say, in effect, that the kind of economics I am selling is okay, but it is only dictatorial, autocratic governments that can really do it.

It has been bothersome to me to have to agree with this view to some extent. The problem is that we all like all the freedoms. If we only liked one, it would be easy. I look at the actual historical record of Hong Kong, Singapore, Korea, Indonesia, Taiwan, Spain in the latter decade of Franco, Portugal, Brazil, in each case, its economic miracle took place under an autocratic government. Chile has had two spates (of which it is currently in one) where it has outperformed its neighbours, largely as a consequence of this type of policy. While not many seem to be aware of the fact, Guatemala and Nicaragua, starting around 1950, had very good growth under autocratic government. The reality is that these governments have had better than average economic performance under that kind of rule.

My first response is, we are economists, we know that other freedoms are a part of our value system; we have to be willing to pay a price. And that is really where I sit when I have to. But at the same time I wonder what is the secret there? Why are these essentially autocratic regimes seemingly more successful than other regimes?

First of all, let me note that most of these autocracies seem to turn into technocracies. They tend to acquire a higher proportion of technocrats, and this transition seems in some way to be important for the growth process. The reason appears to be that the technocracy in turn imposes a discipline and self-restraint on government. It keeps government small when a lot of populist and other pressures are trying to make it bigger. Autocratic government seems to be able to impose self-restraint and to avoid doing a lot of things that it would be pressured to do in a more open political system. Moreover, and perhaps more importantly, autocratic governments often bring discipline, restraint and predictability to the economic scene, which before had been chaotic. It is this transition that is the common thread in these various success stories.

But, I can also think of three cases of democratic governments which have been successful in the growth encouraging game—Switzerland, Japan, and Panama. Switzerland is an old democracy but very self-restrictive by the nature of its constitution; nothing can happen in Switzerland, hardly. Japan in the modern world is a democracy, but they have a lot of built-in self-restraint by their culture. Panama had built-in restraint by having the dollar as a circulating medium and having a prohibition against having a central bank. But during the 1960s, when it led the Western Hemisphere in the rate of growth, it didn't have the tendency to populism that later infected and ultimately overwhelmed it in the late 1970s and early 1980s.

So, here are three cases where democracy has worked to produce high rates of growth, in all of which the elements of discipline and restraint, and in a certain sense predictability, have been present.

**Raymond Gastil** I think insofar as that is true, I would have some questions about the democracies in each case, and particularly in the case of Panama. But perhaps we don't wish to get into that at the moment.

**Alvin Rabushka** First of all, I don't have a dictionary with me, but I think the word "despotic" conveys some norms and modes of behaviour. Hong Kong is *not* despotic; please stop calling it despotic. Call it regulated, call it night watchman, call it authoritarian, call it unrepresentative, call it administrative no-party state, but stop calling it despotic.

The second thing is precisely the point that Arnold was making—this notion about semantics and language and what these words mean. Words have meanings, and we have to talk about them in some way or we can't talk about the subject. I think we all have a sense about what civil liberties are, and I'd buy the Freedom House list intact. I think we have some pretty good senses of what economic freedoms are, and in my own paper I basically enumerate the Friedman bill of rights and add three or four more, which I think he might be willing to buy as well. So I think we can get around that.

Now we get to the political problem, and Block is right. But I think we can amend that a little bit. The way I would like to talk about it is to talk about political freedoms having imbedded within them, shall we say, some kind of constitutional, written or unwritten custom limitations on the abilities of those majorities to take away the rights of individuals and minorities. If we can do something like that, I think we would get a better handle on what we mean by political freedom that won't bother us all that much.

But the last point is this whole question of running around the world looking at other countries, and Latin America is one of the few places I haven't gone to look at. One thing I did do at a prior Liberty Fund Symposium and in some other papers was take a hundred countries in the developing world in the post-war period and then take the Freedom House data and look at their scores on civil liberties and look at their scores on political rights, and I discovered the following.

First of all, civil liberties and political freedoms come out reasonably similar when you simply do a cross classification against some economic factors (I will tell you what those are in a minute), which means there is a very high internal overlap between the presence of political rights and civil liberties as measured in the Freedom House scores. And that is very encouraging. It means that if you are going to have political rights, you can have civil liberties, and vice versa. You don't have to choose one over the other. So you don't have to worry about the majorities tyrannizing civil liberties out of existence.

Now, in terms of what these economic variables were, I used two: one was per capita income, and the other was rates of growth over the last 20 years, that is, per capita rates of growth in income. The results come out reasonably the same; that is, countries that have had very high rates of economic growth for 20 years now have a reasonably high per capita income. Countries that have had very low growth rates don't. The results came out reasonably similar, and they are as follows.

Where there is zero or low growth—I mean negative growth up to 1 or 2 percent—and per capita incomes are $400 and under, there are almost no civil liberties and political rights. In countries that have high rates of economic growth and per capita incomes over a thousand, or seven hundred and up, there is a fifty-fifty mix, between countries that have high civil liberties and not and countries that have high political rights and not. So stagnation and poverty are just iron-clad guarantees of not having any freedoms. Prosperity gives you some chance of getting some of the liberties.

In this context, I think what Arnold has described as a cross-sectional phenomenon also is exhibited longitudinally. What is clearly happening in Taiwan and in Korea—for that matter, mainland China and some other places—is there is a gradual emerging of civil liberties and political rights that didn't exist in the first instance. So affluence is a kind of nice breeding ground in many of these countries for a much looser society, a much less restricted, a much less controlled society. On the basis of the evidence, I am willing to go on the line and simply say that if one can impose the kinds of growth-oriented policies that work, one will get—down the road a generation later, in those places where it has had a chance to work—probably many more rights and freedoms than there were in the beginning or than there are in other countries which are similar except for the growth experience.

**Gordon Tullock**  I would deduce from these numbers that you have given that a country that has a per capita income of about $150 a year could never have freedom. I am, of course, referring to the United States in 1776. But going on from that, actually what I wanted to talk about is that we observe that a dictatorship sometimes is successful economically and democracy sometimes is successful economically. As a result of the fact that a lot of democracies in the great 19th century were leading countries, both in economy and politics, a lot of them are still pretty wealthy. I am sure that is the reason the United States is still pretty wealthy. Although we had the advantage that the 19th century, in our case, lasted right through to the 1930s. So we left the 19th century somewhat later than anyone else.

There is another possible explanatory variable, an unpopular one. Again, this is found in pre-World War II or even pre-World War I literature. The anthropologists divide the European culture up into three main groups, by language, actually: Slavic, Latin and Teutonic. There is an overwhelming correlation between being members of that Teutonic group and being both prosperous and democratic, and also, I should say, being protestant. It may be that we are simply talking about a characteristic of one particular subculture within the European collection. I sincerely hope not.

## NOTES

1. *Autocracy*, Kluner, Hingham, Mass. 1987.

2. *A Complete Book Concerning Happiness and Benevolence*. Huang Liu-Hung. Translated and edited by Djang Chu. University of Arizona Press, Tucson, 1984.

# Chapter 3

## The State of the World
## Political and Economic Freedom

## Raymond D. Gastil and Lindsay M. Wright

The Comparative Survey of Freedom may contribute to this seminar in two respects. First, it has provided a running account of the status of the traditional, liberal democratic, political and civil freedoms in the world. Second, it has attempted on several occasions to address the problem of the relationship of these freedoms to economic freedoms. This paper considers both of these efforts by presenting an overview of the present status of political democracy in the world and a discussion of how *in these terms* we have come to consider the relationship of economic systems or of government controls to freedom.

### The Status of Freedom in the Comparative Survey

Freedom, like democracy, is a term with many meanings. Its meanings cover a variety of philosophical and social issues, many of which would carry us far beyond the discussion of political and economic systems. Unfortunately, linguistic usage is such that the meanings of "freedom" infect one another, so that a "free society" may be taken to be a society with no rules at all, or a free man may be taken to be an individual with no obligations to society, or other individuals. Yet freedom, when addressed in a narrow political sense, is the basic value, goal, and, to a remarkable degree, attainment of successful democratic regimes.

The Comparative Survey was begun in the early 1970s as an attempt to give a more standardized and relativized picture of the situation of freedom to the world.[1] Experience suggested that the world media and, therefore, informed opinion often misevaluated the level of freedom in countries with which Westerners had become particularly involved. In many countries oppressions were condemned as more severe than they were in comparative terms. On the other hand, the achievements of the post-war period in expanding freedom were often overlooked. Many small countries had quietly achieved and enjoyed democracy with relatively little media attention. The purpose of the Comparative Survey is to give a general picture of the state of political and civil freedoms in the world. By taking a consistent approach to the definition of freedom, distinctions and issues that are often overlooked are brought out. In particular, its comparative approach brings to the reader's attention the fact that the most publicized denials of political and civil liberties are seldom in the most oppressive states. These states, such as Albania and North Korea, simply do not allow relevant information to reach the world media. There may or may not be hundreds of thousands in jail for their beliefs in North Korea; few care because no one knows.

## The Categories of the Survey

The two dimensions of the Survey—political rights and civil liberties—are combined summarily for each country as its "status of freedom." Political rights are rights to participate meaningfully in the political process. In a democracy this means the right of all adults to vote and compete for public office, and for elected representatives to have a decisive vote on public policies. Civil liberties are rights to free expression, to organize or demonstrate, as well as rights to a degree of autonomy such as is provided by freedom of religion, education, travel, and other personal rights. The Status of Freedom is used to differentiate those countries that are grouped toward the top, middle, or bottom of the political rights and civil liberties scales.

The Comparative Survey of Freedom is built around the construction of a table rating each country on seven-point scales for political and civil freedoms (see Appendix One). It then provides an overall judgement of each as "free," "partly free," or "not free." In each scale, a rating of (1) is freest and (7) least free. Instead of using absolute standards, standards are comparative. The goal is to have ratings such that, for example, most observers would be likely to judge states rated (1) as freer than those rated (2). No state, of course, is absolutely free or unfree, but the degree of freedom does make a great deal of difference to the quality of life.

In political rights, states rated (1) have a fully competitive electoral process, and those elected clearly rule. Most West European democracies belong here. Relatively free states may receive a (2) because, although the electoral process works and the elected rule, there are factors that cause us to lower our rating of the effective equality of the process. These factors may include extreme economic inequality, illiteracy, or intimidating violence. They also include the weakening of effective competition that is implied by the absence of periodic shifts in rule from one group or party to another.

Below this level, political ratings of (3) through (5) represent successively less effective implementation of democratic processes. Mexico, for example, has periodic elections and limited opposition, but for many years its governments have been selected outside the public view by the leaders of factions within the one dominant Mexican party. Governments of states rated (5) sometimes have no effective voting processes at all, but strive for consensus among a variety of groups in society in a way weakly analogous to those of the democracies. States at (6) do not allow competitive electoral processes that would give the people a chance to voice their desire for a new ruling party or for a change in policy. The rulers of states at this level assume that one person or a small group has the right to decide what is best for the nation, and that no one should be allowed to challenge the right. Such rulers do respond, however, to popular desire in some areas, or respect (and therefore are constrained by) belief systems (for example, Islam) that are the property of the society as a whole. At (7) the political despots at the top appear by their actions to feel little constraint from either public opinion or popular tradition.

Turning to the scale for civil liberties, in countries rated (1) publications are not closed because of the expression of rational political opinion, especially when the intent of the expression is to affect the legitimate political process. No major media are simply conduits for government propaganda. The courts protect the individual; persons are not imprisoned for their opinions; private rights and desires in education, occupation, religion, and residence are generally respected; and law-abiding persons do not fear for their lives because of their rational political activities. States at this level include most traditional democracies. There are, of course, flaws in the liberties of all of these states, and these flaws are significant when measured against the standards these states set themselves.

Movement down from (2) to (7) represents a steady loss of civil freedoms. Compared to (1), the police and courts of states at (2) have more authoritarian traditions. In some cases they may simply have a less institutionalized or secure set of liberties, such as in Portugal or Greece. Those rated (3) or below may have political prisoners and generally varying forms of censorship. Too often their security services practise torture. States rated (6) almost always have political prisoners; usually the legitimate media are completely under government supervision; there is no right of assembly; and, often, travel, residence, and occupation are narrowly restricted. However, at (6) there still may be relative freedom in private conversation, especially in the home; illegal demonstrations do take place; and underground literature is published. At (7) there is pervading fear, little independent expression takes place even in private, almost no public expressions of opposition emerge in the police-state environment, and imprisonment or execution is often swift and sure.

The generalized checklist for the comparative Survey is presented in Appendix 4. Although there is not room to consider the checklist in full, it might be useful to look at some of the considerations involved in just the first two items.

Political systems exhibit a variety of degrees to which they offer voters a chance to participate meaningfully. At the antidemocratic extreme are those systems with no formal opportunities, such as inherited monarchies or purely appointive communist systems. Little different in practice are those societies that hold elections for the legislature or president, but give the voter no alternative other than affirmation. In such elections there is neither a choice nor the possibility—in practice and sometimes even in theory—of rejecting the single candidate that the government proposes for chief executive or representative. In elections at this level the candidate is usually chosen by a secretive process involving only the top elite. More democratic are those systems, such as Zambia's, that allow the voter no choice, but do suggest that it is possible to reject a suggested candidate. In this case the results may show ten or twenty percent of the voters actually voting against a suggested executive, or even on occasion (rarely) rejecting an individual legislative candidate on a single list. In some societies there is a relatively more open party process for selecting candidates. However the list of preselected candidates is prepared; there is seldom any provision for serious campaigning against the single list.

The political system is more democratic if multiple candidates are offered for most positions, even when all candidates are government or party selected. Popular voting for alternatives may exist only at the party level—which in some countries is a large proportion of the population—or the choice may be at the general election. Rarely do such systems extend voter options to include choice of the chief authority in the state. Usually that position, like the domination by a single party, is not open to question. But many legislators, even members of the cabinet, may be rejected by the voters in such a system. Campaigning occurs at this level of democracy, but the campaigning is restricted to questions of personality, honesty, or ability; for example, in Tanzania campaigning may not involved questions of policy.

A further increment of democratic validity is effected if choice is possible among government-approved rather than government-selected candidates. In this case the government's objective is to keep the most undesirable elements (from its viewpoint) out of the election. With government-selected candidates there is reliance on party faithfuls, but self-selection allows persons of local reputation to achieve office. More generally, controlled electoral systems may allow open, self-selection of candidates for some local elections, but not for elections on the national scale. It is also possible for a system, such as that of Iran, to allow an open choice of candidates in elections, but to draw narrow ideological limits around what is an acceptable candidacy.

Beyond this, there is the world of free elections as we know them, in which candidates are both selected by parties and self-selected. It could be argued that parliamentary systems such as are common outside of the United States reduce local choice by imposing party choices on voters. However, independents can and do win in most systems, and new parties, such as the "Greens" in West Germany and elsewhere, test the extent to which the party system in particular countries is responsive to the desires of citizens.

The checklist for civil liberties is longer and more diffuse than that for political rights. While many civil liberties are considered in judging the atmosphere of a country, primary attention is given to those liberties that are most directly related to the expression of political rights, with less attention being given to those liberties that are likely to primarily affect individuals in their private capacity.

Again, let us just take the first item in this category, the question of the freedom of the communications media. We want to know whether the press and broadcasting facilities of the country are independent of government control, and serve the range of opinion that is present in the country. Clearly, if a population does not receive information about alternatives to present leaders and policies, then its ability to use any political process is impaired. In most traditional democracies there is no longer any question of freedom of the press: no longer are people imprisoned for expressing their rational views on any matter—although secrecy and libel laws do have a slight effect in some countries. As one moves from this open situation, from ratings of (1) to ratings of (7), a steady decline in freedom to publish is noticed: the tendency increases for people to be punished for criticizing the government, or papers to be closed, or censorship to be imposed, or for the newspapers and journals to be directly owned and supervised by the government.

The methods used by governments to control the print media are highly varied. While pre-publication censorship is often what Westerners think of because of their wartime experience, direct government ownership and control of the media and post-publication censorship through warnings, confiscations, or suspensions are more common. Government licensing of publications and journalists and controls over the distribution of newsprint are other common means of keeping control over what is printed. Even in countries with some considerable degree of democracy, such as Malaysia, press controls of these sorts may be quite extensive, often based on an ostensible legal requirement for "responsible journalism." Control of the press may be further extended by requiring papers to use a government news agency as their source of information, and by restricting the flow of foreign publications.[2]

Broadcasting—radio or television—is much more frequently owned by the government than the print media, and such ownership may or may not be reflected in government control over what is communicated. It is possible, as in the British case, for a government-owned broadcasting corporation to be so effectively protected from government control that its programs demonstrate genuine impartiality. However, in many well-known democracies, such as France or Greece, changes in the political composition of government affects the nature of what is broadcast to the advantage of incumbents. (Very recently France has been developing private alternatives.) The government-owned broadcasting services of India make little effort to go beyond presenting the views of their government.

In most countries misuse of the news media to serve government interests is even more flagrant. At this level, we need to distinguish between those societies that require their media, particularly their broadcasting services, to avoid criticism of the political system or its leaders, and those that use them to "mobilize" their peoples in direct support for government policies. In the first case the societies allow or expect their media, particularly their broadcasting services, to present a more or less favourable picture; in the second, the media are used to motivate their peoples to actively support government policies and to condemn or destroy those who oppose the governing system. In the first, the government's control is largely passive; in the second it is directly determinative of content.[3]

The comparison of active and passive control by government brings us to the most difficult issue in the question of media freedom—self-censorship. It is fairly easy to know if a government censors or suspends publications for content, or punishes journalists and reporters by discharge, imprisonment, or worse; judging the day-to-day influence of subtle pressures on the papers or broadcasting services of a country is much more difficult. Perhaps the most prevalent form of government control of the communications media is achieved through patterns of mutual assistance of government and media that ensure that, at worst, reports are presented in a bland, non-controversial manner—the practice until this last year, at least, of the largest newspapers in Pakistan and the Philippines.

Some critics believe that most communications media in the West, and especially in the United States, practise this kind of censorship, either because of government support, or because this is in the interest of the private owners of the media. In the United States, for example, it is noteworthy that National Public Radio, financed largely by the state, is generally much more critical of the government in its commentaries than are the commercial services. The critics would explain this difference by the greater ability of commercial stations to "police" their broadcasts and broadcasters. The primary explanation, however, lies in the gap between the subculture of broadcasters and audience for public radio and the subculture of broadcasters and especially audience for commercial stations.[4]

After countries are rated on seven-point scales for levels of political rights and civil liberties, these ratings are summarized in terms of overall assessments as free, partly free, and not free. This categorization is interpreted to mean that the list of operating democracies in the world is made up of those countries given the summary status of "free." In these terms about 36 percent of the people of the world, in 56 countries, live in democracies, 23 percent live in part-democracies, and 40 percent of the world's population live in 55 countries without democracy. The more important ratings are the basic ones for political rights and civil liberties. The Status of Freedom is such a generalized measure that it necessarily groups countries together that are actually quite far apart in their democratic practices—such as Hungary or South Africa at the lower edge of partly free, and Malaysia or Mexico at the upper edge.

## The Record of Gains and Losses: 1973-1985

Since the Survey began, the world has experienced a number of gains and losses of freedom, either immediate or prospective. Most generally there has been an advance of Soviet communism in Southeast Asia after the fall of South Vietnam, and at least its partial institutionalization in South Yemen, Ethiopia, and the former Portuguese colonies of Africa. In the Americas there has arisen an imminent danger of the spread of communism to Nicaragua and an erstwhile danger in Grenada. Perhaps equally significant has been the amelioration of communism in many areas. While mainland China is still a repressive society, it has increased freedom through the support of private initiative, through more open discussion in some areas, and through the sending of thousands of students overseas. While Poland suggests the immediate limits of change, nearly every country in Eastern Europe is freer today than it was at the beginning of the 1970s. Unfortunately, the same cannot be said of the Soviet Union.

In Western Europe gains for democracy in Spain, Portugal, and Greece were critical to its continued advancement everywhere. After a setback in Chile, gains have been achieved in many parts of Latin America. Argentina, Bolivia, Brazil, Dominican Republic, Ecuador, Honduras, Peru, and Uruguay re-established democratic institutions. Several countries that the Survey listed as "free" at the beginning are now more authentically free. Colombia is an example. African democracy has not fared well during these years. In many areas there has been a noticeable decline, especially in countries such as Ghana, Nigeria, Burkina Faso (Upper Volta), and Kenya in which great hopes were placed in the 1970s. In sub-Saharan Africa only Senegal seems to have made progress. Recently we have seen a modest resurgence of free institutions in the Middle East, but the destruction of Lebanese democracy will be hard to make up. Further to the east there has been remarkably little advance. The people of Sri Lanka have lost freedoms; those of Thailand and Nepal have made some hopeful progress. Maintaining Indian democracy has been a remarkable achievement.

During this period many new small states successfully achieved independence as democracies—in the South Pacific from Papua New Guinea to the east, and among the islands of the Caribbean.

In 1985-86 the stabilization of freedom continued in a number of new or emerging democracies. Against considerable odds the Brazilians, Argentineans, Bolivians, Uruguayans, Peruvians, and Ecuadorans have overcome, at least temporarily, the serious problems that beset them both politically and economically. A major reason for their success was the mutual support that each of these adjacent societies was able to give its neighbours. In maintaining their freedoms these states implicitly put additional pressure on Chile and Paraguay, the states in their midst that continue to have oppressive systems.

The record in Central America was more mixed than it was last year. Significant advances continued in El Salvador and Guatemala. In the latter, the degree of success that progress toward more freedom and a rule of law appears to be making is as surprising as President Duarte's victory over the right in El Salvador may have been reassuring. Elsewhere, the democratic institutions and elections in Honduras were once again attended by the uncertainty of constitutional and factional confusion, while rights went down in Nicaragua and Panama. In many of these states a key issue remains the degree to which men under arms are able to remain the arbiter of politics— whether the arms be in the hands of leftists or those who vow their hatred of the left.

In Asia, Pakistan and Bangladesh made hesitant moves toward more democratic and open systems, although there was still a long way to go. Thailand's increasing ability to surmount overt military interventions suggests a further institutionalization of democracy. Further east the development of an East and Southeast Asian model of modern, noncommunist autocracy was shaken by the ability of the Korean people to demonstrate a growing commitment to democracy, in spite of the controls that are exerted over the expression of their political and civil freedoms. A similar fighting spirit was demonstrated throughout Philippine society in the struggle to restore the openness that once characterized its political system. The people of one province in Malaysia were able to vote in a regional government uncontrolled by that country's ruling front. They appeared willing to withstand pressure from a central government intent on preserving its monopoly of power.

We must not forget that in spite of certain positive trends, most of the world continues to live in non-democracies, or what at best might be called semi-democracies. Where armed force determines the outcome, as in so much of Africa or the Middle East today, there is still little room for democratic forms. As more and more people come to realize, however, that they need not live under repression, maintaining repressive systems in many countries appears to require ever more violence.

**Political and Economic Freedom**

Our approach to the relationship of political and economic freedom has been to first establish the nature of political freedom or democracy, and then place economic choice within this framework.

For the present discussion a pertinent way to conceptualize democracy is to begin with the theoretical approach developed by Alfred Kuhn in *The Logic of Social Systems.*[5] Organizations, for Kuhn, are means by which individuals can more effectively achieve their individual objectives. From this theoretical viewpoint, "democracy" is the name for a particular way to organize a political system. Any organization—government, corporate, or private—can be seen as consisting of Sponsors, Staff, and Recipients. The sponsors are the ones that bring the organization into being, and maintain or institutionalize it. In simple organizations and primitive communities, everyone is a sponsor. Larger organizations hire a staff that carries out the work for the sponsors. For such organizations, the recipients are the clients or customers the organization sells to, or "acts upon," whether for good or ill. In a private corporation, it is fairly easy to see that the sponsors are the stockholders, the staff the employees, and the recipients the customers who both receive the corporation's service or product and pay for it. In a consumers co-operative, on the other hand, the usual recipients of the product—goods or services—hire a staff to provide it. The customers of a consumers co-operative are both the sponsors and the recipients. Achieving this identity—and the reduced costs that go with it—is the reason for forming consumers co-operatives.

In these terms Alfred Kuhn helps us understand the concept of democracy by contrasting government as a co-operative organization with government as a profit-making organization. In the co-operative (or democratic) organization all citizens are both sponsors and recipients of the actions of government staff. They pay the costs and receive the benefits of the organization. Since the staff works for the sponsors, attempts of the staff to coerce sponsor decisions or defy sponsor control will ultimately result in staff dismissal. Sponsor members—that is, the public—pursue their personal interests in the state organization through political organizations, elections, pressure groups, educational campaigns, and other means.

Political rights may be defined as the freedom of citizens to fully exercise their sponsor function—that is, their oversight function in regard to government. Civil liberties consist of limitations on the power of staff to interfere with sponsors either in their sponsor or recipient roles. For some contexts we may say that political rights define input; civil liberties control output.

In contrast to government as a co-operative organization or democracy, Kuhn describes some governments as profit-making organizations. In this model, the sponsors of the system are a small minority of the public, but the whole public is the recipient of the output of the system. Through both positive and negative inducements, the sponsors try to get as much out of the system as they can. Here the staff works for the non-majority sponsors. All governments use force to ensure the continuity of the state organization, but the profit-making government also uses force to keep particular leaders in power. In this model political rights are essentially nonexistent for the majority which by definition does not control the sponsoring group, while civil liberties are granted only to the extent that they do not interfere with sponsor objectives.

Kuhn applies the profit-making model to both exploitative dictatorships or oligarchies, such as that in Haiti, and the ideological dictatorships of communist or one-party socialist states. In either case society is dominated by a small group with special interests that can be fulfilled only through non-majority rule over the population. The most important benefits for the sponsors in the ideological state are achieved through forcing the population to build the society the sponsors desire. Of course, exploitative and ideological profit-making systems become indistinguishable to the extent that ideological leaders shift from pursuing their ideals to manipulating the system for selfish personal objectives.

Both co-operative and profit-making models are pure forms; systems that actually exist in the world will lie in between. But these models help to make clear the essential distinction between democracy and its alternatives, a distinction too often obscured by the rhetoric of the spokesmen and apologists for nondemocratic systems. Kuhn's contrast is instructive in that it casts doubt on the assumption that the values of Western democracy are similar to those of capitalistic organization while the values of communism or one-party socialism are similar to those of co-operative institutions. If we look at the relationships involved instead of the rhetoric, we discover that the values of liberal democracy are most congruent with those of co-operatives. Communitarian values are democratic values.

One advantage of approaches such as Kuhn's is that they assume no more than that individuals will pursue their own interests, whether as leaders or followers. Kuhn assumes that leaders must be institutionally forced by threats of dismissal to consistently respond to the interests of the people they govern. Otherwise, they will soon respond primarily to their own interests. This has been a basic assumption of most social thinkers from Madison to Marx. If we define interests in the broadest sense, elected representatives will generally reflect popular interests more surely than any elite or vanguard. That voters will pursue their interests through the electoral processes of democracy, and that political parties will respond by trying to match these interests with programs has been shown by both theoretical and empirical evidence. There is a crushing burden of proof on those who assert that a small vanguard party will rule indefinitely in the interests of the majority that it excludes from rule.

The objective of Kuhn's description of democracy is primarily scientific, to describe the relation of democracy to other forms of organization. However, from a humanistic point of view, of natural law or natural right, democracy also seems to be an intuitively required form for state organization. The reason is that states have a fundamentally different relationship to people than other organizations. Most organizations can be freely joined or abandoned. We can choose to relate to them as sponsors, recipients, staff, or not at all. For most people state organizations are not avoidable. We are born to the state we live in. This would seem to give us a prima facie right to be a sponsor of that state—as is assumed by many contract theorists, including most recently John Rawls.[6]

Only democracies provide institutionalized means for all adults to be the sponsors as well as the recipients of the state organization. As our model suggests, democracies provide these means in two ways. First, they provide political rights. Political rights define the relation of the sponsors—the people—to the staff or administration. In a democracy every person has a right to periodically vote for candidates representing different policy positions, and, in some cases, to vote directly on policy issues. In addition, everyone has a right to become a candidate, and thus to serve as staff—as a legislator or administrator—of the organization of which he is a recipient. Democracies provide those elected with the primary power to direct the political system.

Secondly, democracies provide civil liberties that define the relation of the staff or administration to the recipients, the people. Civil liberties are necessary if a society is to develop and propagate new ideas. Civil liberties include freedom of the press, freedom of organization, and freedom of demonstration. Democracies guarantee a neutral judicial system that mediates between the attempt of the government's staff to enforce the law and the rights of citizens to challenge the staff's interpretation of the law. Political rights without such civil liberties would have little meaning; new ideas would be stifled before larger audiences could accept or reject them, and potential leaders with new values and interests would have no way to influence the policies of the system through challenging and even defeating incumbents.

Democracy in the co-operative organization is based on the theory of political equality, and assumes a continuing struggle to equalize the influence of each person in the determination of public policy. It does not mean that all people are equal in ability or worth, but that all people have certain fundamental rights that no one has a right to deny. It does not mean that all people have or should have equal incomes or benefits from society, but that all people have a right to help establish the political rules determining how economic or other benefits shall be attained or divided.

A democracy need be neither liberal nor conservative; it will be as liberal or conservative as its sponsors. All minorities have a right to be heard and to press for their own interests, but the majority has the right to determine the public way of life for any society; only the majority has the right to forbid obscenity on television or billboards on highways. The majority may decree land reform or do away with welfare benefits. The makeup of majorities varies from subject to subject, but at any one time and on a particular issue the majority acts as the temporary sponsor of the society for the people as a whole. But, as long as a society is democratic, it cannot forbid rational discussion or political organization in favour of any alternative for the future regulation of the society.

Democracy is social, but it is also private and individual. To preserve the generation of alternatives for discussion, and thereby the meaning of this right, all democracies must grant an arena of privacy to its individuals in which they may live as they feel best. Only such privacy allows the autonomy necessary for creativity, and thus guarantees functioning political rights for all.

Democracy is neither capitalist nor socialist. Liberal democracy is not libertarian democracy, nor is it necessarily liberal in the nineteenth century European sense of "liberal economics." The struggle between democracy and totalitarianism is not the struggle between capitalism and communism, although many people of both right and left would have us think so. This misunderstanding results in part from the materialist tendency of many of those on both ends of the ideological spectrum. They see "things" determining "ideas" rather than the other way around. In this view material changes must produce changes in society and ultimately in the ideas that guide it. Marxists argue that capitalist society in which ownership is often very unequal inevitably produces a tyrannical concentration of power in the hands of the few, while socialism that grants ownership to society as a whole inevitably produces an egalitarian distribution of power—and thereby a more "democratic" society. Capitalists, on the other hand, argue that historically political democracy and capitalism developed together because only capitalism supports a pluralistic distribution of power. The dynamism of capitalism is said to continually break down the concentrations of power that are unavoidable in noncapitalist states. Socialism, then, inevitably tends to concentrate power in the hands of the few.

There is some truth in both positions, but enough falsehood to cast doubt on the assumption of any necessary relationship. Unless a society has functioning, self-corrective political mechanisms, those who attain power and authority will tend toward increasing concentration and monopolization regardless of the official theory. Even in communist China, a relatively egalitarian communist state, Party leaders ride in shuttered limousines to special stores and suburban elegance in walled compounds.[7] "Public ownership" is no more than a slogan to such leaders. Similarly, many capitalist leaders will gladly use government to suppress labour leaders, force out smaller businesses, or suppress critical news media—unless there are countervailing forces capable of exposing and eliminating the worst of these abuses.

To illustrate the point, we might distinguish between two sorts of capitalism and two sorts of socialism, with the differences within each category of economic system due to the presence or absence of adequate political mechanisms to defend or create democracy.

Capitalist-democratic states, such as those of Europe and North America, and including a range of states from Japan to Barbados, have functioning democratic systems, with a free press, competitive parties, and effective means for exposing abuses. We also find capitalist-autocratic states, such as Singapore, Haiti, Chile, or South Africa where political freedoms are quite limited or absent. Political control remains concentrated in these states by denying large sections of the population a political voice, by banning opposition parties, forcing the media into silence, or the general brutalization or even execution of those who oppose the system.

Similarly, socialist-democratic societies, such as those in Scandinavia, manage to preserve a wide variety of opposing and countervailing organized groups. Regardless of socialization, by and large they remain effective, functioning democracies. The socialist-autocratic systems of communist and socialist one-party states, such as the Soviet Union or Algeria, are associated with the denial of democratic rights. But an examination of the evidence does not suggest that the one produced the other inexorably. Rather, the political and economic systems of such states appear to have been "exported" and accepted together as a Marxist-Leninist package. The role of the Soviet Communist Party in the export of socialist ideas has probably had more to do with the antidemocratic nature of its offspring than with the nature of the economic system that was espoused.

Finding inevitable linkages between economic and political systems is also rendered implausible by the mixed nature of all economic systems in the real world. The "capitalists" of the world are frequently characterized by narrow anti-market allegiances between small ruling cliques and closely related economic or military elites (and often their foreign friends). Perhaps the outstanding recent example was President Somoza of Nicaragua who controlled government, army, and large sections of the economy directly, although ostensibly his was a "capitalist" state. More general is the tendency of the governments of many "capitalist" countries to amass government holdings in transportation, communications, agriculture, and even industrial production. The state plays a decisive role in the so-called capitalist economies of Japan, Singapore, Taiwan, South Korea, and the Philippines, as well as such capitalist states as France or Italy. This is less true of the United States, but the major role of the U.S. government in economic development since the inception of the Republic is too often ignored.

A democratic economy is simply one that the people as sponsors develop, promote, or shape through their political institutions. All other things being equal, the free society will wish to allow individuals or groups the largest scope for developing their particular economic interests. However, everything else is not equal. Eventually the voters may find unlimited industrial pollution, or life-threatening differences in health care un-acceptable. If so, within broad limits it will have a democratic respon-sibility and capability to exert control.

Theoretically, then, a majority might have the right to decide on any policy or any degree of government control that it wished. In fact all democracies emerged from traditional societies that understood certain rights to be the natural property of all citizens and so insulated from majority rule. For example, the assumption in our tradition that everyone has a right to a fair trial limits absolute parliamentary or plebiscitary sovereignty.

A modern democracy accepts limits to majority rule by accepting the principle that every individual has a right to a private realm distinct from the public realm and, thus, outside the purview of government. This right to privacy has a considerably history and stems in part from our Judeo-Chris-tian tradition, although discussions by Alan Westin, Charles Fried, and others suggest that the status of privacy in formal law is surprisingly weak and insecure.[8] Everyday and judicial references to "private matters" attest to the general acceptance in our culture that there is a basic right to privacy comparable to the public right to political equality. It can also be argued that democracy as defined here requires privacy. In a totally public society those with minority views would be so quickly identified and at least subtly punished that they would find it extremely difficult to develop their minority political positions into majority positions.

In considering the boundaries of a right to privacy we must begin again with the rights of the majority. The majority has the decisive role in defin-ing the nature of social life: defense, transportation, education, sanitation and the allocation of property are among the areas in which it achieves this definition. As long as the majority's decisions do not unduly restrict the possibility of new majorities to progressively change the definition, there is no basis to deny its right to legislate in these areas. Similarly, there is a plausible case for the majority intervening in other more subtle aspects of public life. If the majority cannot control the nature of the public places in which its members live, then its will is being thwarted quite undemocrati-cally by minorities. For example, if on one's way to work each morning, one had to witness overt sadomasochism among consenting adults, and it was not possible for the majority to use the law to control this environment, one would justifiably think that his rights as a member of the majority were unduly restrained. A minority would be making a basic decision about the quality of public life for the majority.

It should be noted that in outlining the majority's rights we have not said anything about what the majority should do, about the areas in which it should legislate. There are good reasons for accepting extremely restrictive views of government, based on arguments such as those of Nozick.[9] There are also good reasons for a society to take on special responsibilities such as those toward the underprivileged and the environment. Advocates on both sides of this argument need to be more modest, to realize that their arguments are not concerned with the (natural) rights of individuals in communities to particular privileges or services, but with whether it would be morally or practically desirable for majorities to decide to allocate public attention or money to specified persons or causes. The proliferation of claims to rights (of children, refugees, disabled, poor, aged, animals, trees, religious sects, and property, for example) threatens to bring the concept of rights into disrepute in the political community. When too many claims on society are labeled rights, all rights become open to question, including those to the free discussion of such claims. When special interests are labeled "rights" their effective denial by the majority—and many such rights will be ignored or slighted in all societies—will add unnecessarily to the disaffection of those who identify with special interests.

### The Comparison of Political-Economic Systems

Against this background the Comparative Survey has made two approaches to the question of the relationship of political democracy to economic freedom. The first has been to develop a rather simple-minded classification that will allow for the cross tabulation of political and economic systems. The second has been a more courageous attempt to understand what might be meant from the Survey's perspective by the term "economic freedom."

Economic freedom is on one level hardly separable from political freedom. It is useful in this regard to note that "socialism" in the informed discussion of the last generation has two quite different faces. On the one hand, socialism is a doctrine suggesting that all property should be held in common, or that the community is the custodian of all property, or perhaps only productive property. Its implicit assumption is that all differences in economic level, and particularly in the availability of services such as education or health, are unjust or, at the least, must be carefully justified by exception. This is an attitude or faith that sets implicit goals toward which the political community can move. Socialism in Western Europe, for example, in a country such as Sweden, has been introduced progressively through the political system by legislating ever higher taxes and ever-expanding government services.

"Socialism," or more commonly "socialist," is used in the international community today to also refer primarily to those countries that have adopted a "Marxist-Leninist" political system. This system is based on the premise that for the transformation to a more just society a single dominant political party is required to lead that society toward fundamental change. Thus, "socialist" in this sense means the one-party state with a well-organized and disciplined vanguard party—in practice a party dominated from the top down by a small ideological elite. While socialist in the first sense may or may not mean direct government ownership of the means of production, in the second political sense it means that the government dominates and determines all aspects of life from the top down. Although concerned with the economy, this form of socialism is also concerned with security, religion, and family life. Its goal is the making of a "new man." This political socialism is what dominated Nazi Germany as well as what determines the nature of the Soviet Union.

With this in mind, the Survey of Freedom has published for many years a Table of Political-Economic Systems (Appendix 2), in which "socialist" is used as a label along both the political and economic dimensions. Admittedly, states labeled "socialist" politically tend to be socialist economically, but the most obvious result is that no country with a socialist or communist political system could rank very high on political freedom. On the other hand, a number of states with a considerable degree of socialism economically stood at the top of the ratings for political and civil freedoms. From this standpoint it is the way in which the decisions about the economy are arrived at that determines the presence or absence of freedom.

The Survey has noted the correlation of capitalism and political freedom. On first appraisal, it would appear that some degree of capitalism is a necessary but not sufficient condition for democracy. There are no states that have adopted a thoroughgoing economic socialism that are free, and there are many states that are largely capitalist that are free. However, there are capitalist states that are distinctly unfree. Unhappy lands such as Haiti or Malawi have little freedom, although they are certainly capitalist. Many states of the Middle East, regardless of the labels they place on themselves, are capitalist or capitalist-statist. Saudi Arabia is an example. Yet, they are not free politically or civilly. South Africa is a capitalist bastion, but there are severe problems for freedom there, as in Taiwan, South Korea, and Indonesia.

We should not expect capitalism and freedom to automatically determine one another. Capitalism is a way of organizing economic production, while political liberties are a way of expressing the dominance of people over the state. Political freedom means that the dominance of the people over the state should be primary. This dominance implies, in turn, that the economic regulations the state enjoins shall be determined by popular government.

Economic organization has always been regulated by the political system. The tax farms of the ancients, the feudal estates of the Middle Ages, the guilds, the unions, and the corporations have all operated under political supervision. In democracies economics is placed under the control of majorities. Government intervention under majority rule has been characteristic rather than exceptional in modern democracies, just as it was characteristic before their emergence. Economically, socialism and communism can be thought of as systems that transfer property from private holders of capital or property not directly in use by its owners, to workers, peasants, or the state itself. A democracy could in theory establish such a system without changing its nature.

For example, on May 30, 1984, the Supreme Court decided in favour of the right of the State of Hawaii to force the division of the great estates of the islands. In its opinion the Court saw the purpose of the Hawaiian Land Reform Act as "[reducing] the perceived social and economic evils of a land oligopoly." The Court added: "On this basis we have no trouble concluding that the Hawaii Act is constitutional. The People of Hawaii have attempted, much as the settlers of the original Thirteen Colonies did, to reduce the perceived social and economic evils of land oligopoly traceable to their monarchs. The oligopoly has, according to the Hawaii legislature, created artificial deterrents to the normal functioning of the state's residential land market and forced thousands of individual homeowners to lease, rather than buy, the land underneath their homes. Regulating oligopoly and the evils associated with it is a classic exercise of the state's police powers."[10]

### The Search for Economic Freedom

The foregoing discussion suggests that the dependent relationship should really be between political democracy and economic freedom. The result of exploring this relationship was the development of a measure of economic freedom that included separate measures for freedom to have property, freedom of association, freedom of movement, and freedom of information.[11] Initially economic freedom was then judged on the basis of ratings from high to low on these characteristics. (This work is summarized in Appendix 3 as the Table for Economic Freedom.)

It is useful to briefly describe what might be included under each heading. A country received a high rating for freedom of property if taxes were not confiscatory, or if there was not undue concentration of ownership of either land or industrial property. Acceptable levels of taxation or concentration depends, in part, on the type of economy and level of development. On freedom of property, Spain and Australia score well, Brazil and Sri Lanka toward the middle, communist countries toward the bottom. Not all limitations on property were due to government actions. In countries such as Bangladesh or Guatemala there have been private attempts to restrict freedom and unfairly confiscate land. Thus, while government interference with land rights generally diminishes economic freedoms, often the preservation of a legal structure against private greed, or reform of the property structure may serve to increase freedom of property for most people.

Freedom of association is measured in terms of the evident ability of workers, owners, professionals, and other groups to form organizations to pursue common interests, whether these be in the form of co-operatives, business firms, labour unions, professional organizations, consumers groups, or many other economically relevant organizations. In most of the world, even the "free world" of propagandists, restrictions on union and business organization are significant, for their independent development poses a threat to local power structures. For example, the unions of Singapore have their leaders appointed by the government. Business is slightly freer, but in some areas of business, particularly newspapers, it is the Singapore government that decides on the number of companies and their composition.

Freedom of movement and information are basic civil rights that have a special meaning in the economic arena. If individuals are not free to change employment, or to seek work elsewhere, even in other countries, then they are much easier to repress or exploit. If one is unable to learn about conditions elsewhere in the country or world, or unable to know what the government is doing and contemplating, or unable to learn what others think and plan, then it will be very difficult for the individual or his group to gain control over their economic lives. Control over movement and information particularly characterizes communist states.[12] These controls are not necessary for economic socialism, but they are necessary if one small elite is to effectively shape a society.

Few readers should be surprised to learn that the Survey has found a good correlation between economic freedom, understood in this sense, and political and civil freedom. While a country such as Sweden might not score "high" on freedom of property, the high regard of freedom of association, information, and movement in that country raises its overall freedom to a high rating. The correlation of economic freedom with political freedom is particularly high when we bring into consideration a supporting category of the "legitimacy" of the economic system. For an economic system to be legitimate the people must have continual opportunities to discuss it, learn about it, and vote on it through the election of representatives or more direct means. This will occur only in a system that is free politically.

Still, a contradiction in this analysis needs to be resolved. On the one hand, we are considering economic freedom to be analyzable in terms of a series of economic ratings such as that for freedom of property, while on the other hand we are considering economic freedom to be determinable from the extent to which the majority in a democracy decides on the rules that produce the economic ratings. If, then, a society were to vote in a free and well-debated election or referendum for the confiscation of all productive property, and there were no courts to reverse such a vote, would this represent a diminution of economic freedom? Would such a society be less free economically than one that had a Supreme Court, for example, that ruled such confiscation was illegal and unenforceable?

As phrased, there is no way to decide whether an economic system freely decided on by a majority can be called an unfree economy because of its denial of separate economic freedoms through massive taxation or the confiscation of other property. But if we divide the question we may come to a more satisfactory conclusion. To do this we need to think of rights as individual and collective, and to imagine that societies must maintain two sets of rights—two sets of books, if you will—without searching for a full resolution in favour of either. For an economy to be individualistically free the individuals must be allowed opportunities to control, for example, a fair degree of property, as well as the results of their labours. They must have not unreasonable restrictions placed on their movement or search for useful information.

When we use "collective" rights it is important to note that we refer to the rights of the majority in a free political system to determine the nature of any public system, including the economic. We are not using "collective" in the vague Marxist sense of a group desire or right that may be defined outside the political process by reference to general principles. "Individualistic" refers to the "natural rights" that individuals may feel they have, or be taught they have, or have enshrined in particular laws, such as our Constitution and Bill of Rights, that make them, as minorities, able to curb the expression of unlimited majoritarian rights. Individualistic here does not mean "more selfish" or more limited in ethical content. Indeed, what the individual wishes to protect against the group may be more in the group's interest than what the group wants. This would certainly be the position of the conservative economist when he argues against the advocates of interventionist government.

Many would argue that economic freedoms, such as the right to property, to organize workers, or to freely make bargains for labour or products are basic rights equivalent to those to privacy and freedom of expression. However, the argument seems to be much the same as that against unduly restricting the rights of majorities to enforce regulations and laws that determine the quality of public life. It is our position here that while accepting individualistic economic rights might be good for the economy and would be desirable in many societies, as basic rights, individual economic rights should be very narrowly defined. Such a definition will not be attempted here.

Collectively, then, there is a scale for economic freedoms that is determined primarily by the extent to which the nature of the economic system has been legitimized by free democratic institutions. Individualistically, however, there is a scale for economic freedoms that is determined by the extent to which certain economic natural rights—which will be defined differently by different commentators—are protected from political attack. For private property the difference between the two scales could be considerable, but for many economic rights, such as association, information, or movement, the ratings will be very similar. Freedom must be individual and collective, economic and political, if it is to be effective.

## Conclusion

These considerations suggest that the struggle of systems in the world, between the free and the unfree, is not between capitalism and communism. The struggle is between those free systems that let peoples decide on the degree and quality of public and private, group or individual, ownership, and those that by fiat demand the particular economic system or mix of systems that a small leadership clique prefers. Chile and China, Vietnam and Mauritania are all tyrannies from this perspective, regardless of the labels they may place on their economic arrangements.

To see the ideological struggle as one between communism and capitalism is to play by communist rules. Economic equality is identified with communism according to these rules and equality is always attractive. Unfortunately, this is a game that Western businessmen too often support, for they unwittingly carry their slogans from internal political disputes over regulations and taxes into the international arena. It is past time we consistently defined the struggle as one between political freedom and tyranny. This is a game we can win, for political equality, too, is always attractive.

The general picture that political and civil freedoms and economic freedoms go together in the world leads many to believe the United States should be primarily interested in supporting pluralistic, open, capitalistic economies in the Third World, for these are, after all, the ones that hold values closest to our own, and the ones most likely to support rapid economic development and the achievement of freedom in all senses.

However, the record suggests that there are many Third World countries that are able to imitate the methods of capitalism and the forms of democracy, but are unable to move toward effective political or civil freedoms. Indonesia and Saudi Arabia are examples. The tendency of business, labour, military, and political leaders to club together into a small, graft-ridden ruling clique is likely to hold back both political and economic development in the long run. The denials of rights today are the denials of rights tomorrow, and not the preparation of the ground for their development. Unfortunately, in many cases the willingness of Western representatives, whether of government or business, to find dealing with the small, stable, entrenched elites of such societies reassuring and profitable reinforces their longevity and makes further advancement difficult without painful explosions. When the comfortable relation of Americans and the Shah's court blew apart, everyone was hurt, including the Iranians. An economy without freedom of association—there were practically no free unions—without freedom of information, and without political freedoms failed through lack of organized feedback to respond to changing trends. Many Americans had been deluded into thinking of Iran as a country with economic freedoms, just as others had come to see Somoza's Nicaragua as a capitalist bastion.

Today another group of authoritarians has taken over Nicaragua, this time in the name of socialism. But just as capitalist competition did not thrive under Somoza, equitable socialist distribution has quickly failed under the Sandinistas. The specially privileged elite has rapidly been corrupted by its assumption of both military and economic power, and its unwillingness to accept or allow popular feedback.[13]

It is very difficult to have great concentrations of political power for many years without this power being transformed into economic power, and when the two are closely intertwined, all freedoms suffer. It is hard for American businessmen to deal effectively with countries with such power concentrations without themselves adding to the concentration, and thus implicating themselves and our country in a political-economic tyranny foreign to our traditions and foreign to the desires of the businessmen themselves.[14] Unfortunately, this tends to occur as easily in China and Angola as in South Africa and Chile.

## Appendix 1

### Independent Nations: Comparative Measures of Freedom

|  | Political Rights[1] | Civil Liberties[1] | Status of Freedom[2] | Inf.Mort./ GNP/Cap.[3] |
|---|---|---|---|---|
| Afghanistan | 7 | 7 | NF | 205/170 |
| Albania | 7 | 7 | NF | 47/840 |
| Algeria | 6 | 6 | F | 118/2100 |
| Angola | 7 | 7 | NF | 154/800 |
| Antigua & Barbuda | 2 | 3 | F | 11/1443 |
| Argentina | 2 | 2 | F | 45/2600 |
| Australia | 1 | 1 | F | 11/12200 |
| Austria | 1 | 1 | F | 14/10300 |
| | | | | |
| Bahamas | 2 | 2 | F | 32/3600 |
| Bahrain | 5 | 5 | PF | 53/7500 |
| Bangladesh | 5 + | 5 | PF | 136/150 |
| Barbados | 1 | 2 | F | 25/3500 |
| Belgium | 1 | 2 | F | 11/12000 |
| Belize | 1 + | 1 | F | 34/1100 |
| Benin | 7 | 7 | NF | 154/300 |
| Bhutan | 5 | 5 | PF | 150/80 |
| Bolivia | 2 | 3 | F | 131/600 |
| Botswana | 2 | 3 | F | 83/900 |
| Brazil | 3 | 2 + | F + | 77/2200 |
| Brunei | 6 | 5 + | PF + | 20/11900 |
| Bulgaria | 7 | 7 | NF | 20/4200 |
| Burkina Faso[5] | 7 | 6 - | NF | 211/250 |
| Burma | 7 | 7 | NF | 101/200 |
| Burundi | 7 | 6 | NF | 122/250 |
| | | | | |
| Cambodia[4] | 7 | 7 | NF | 212/100 |
| Cameroon | 6 | 7 | NF | 109/800 |
| Canada | 1 | 1 | F | 11/11200 |
| Cape Verde Islands | 6 | 7 | NF | 82/300 |
| Central African Rep. | 7 | 6 | NF | 149/300 |
| Chad | 7 | 7 | NF | 149/100 |
| Chile | 6 | 5 | PF | 38/2600 |
| China (Mainland) | 6 | 6 | NF | 45/300 |
| China (Tiawan) | 5 | 5 | PF | 24/2500 |
| Colombia | 2 | 3 | F | 56/1300 |
| Comoros | 6 · - | 6 · - | NF · - | 93/300 |

| | | | |
|---|---|---|---|
| Congo | 7 | 6 | NF | 129/1100 |
| Costa Rica | 1 | 1 | F | 24/1500 |
| Cuba | 6 | 6 | NF | 19/700 |
| Cyprus (G) | 1 | 2 | F | 18/3800 |
| Cyprus (T) | 3 + | 3 | PF | NA |
| Czechoslovakia | 7 | 6 | NF | 17/5800 |
| | | | | |
| Denmark | 1 | 1 | F | 9/12800 |
| Djibouti | 6 · | 6 | NF · | 63/480 |
| Dominica | 2 | 2 | F | 20/750 |
| Dominican Republic | 1 | 3 | F | 68/1300 |
| | | | | |
| Equador | 2 | 3 - | F | 82/1200 |
| Egypt | 4 | 4 | PF | 103/650 |
| El Salvador | 2 + | 4 + | PF | 53/650 |
| Equatorial Guinea | 7 | 7 · | NF | 143/200 |
| Ethiopia | 7 | 7 | NF | 147/150 |
| | | | | |
| Fiji | 2 | 2 | F | 37/1900 |
| Finland | 2 | 2 | F | 8/10400 |
| France | 1 | 2 | F | 10/12100 |
| | | | | |
| Gabon | 6 | 6 | NF | 117/3900 |
| Gambia | 3 | 4 | PF | 198/350 |
| Germany (E) | 7 | 6 | NF | 12/7200 |
| Germany (W) | 1 | 2 | F | 13/13500 |
| Ghana | 7 | 6 | NF | 103/400 |
| Greece | 2 - | 2 | F | 19/4500 |
| Grenada | 2 + | 3 | F + | 15/900 |
| Guatemala | 4 + | 4 + | PF | 70/1200 |
| Guinea | 7 | 5 | NF | 165/300 |
| Guinea-Bissau | 6 | 6 | NF | 149/200 |
| Guyana | 5 | 5 | PF | 44/700 |
| | | | | |
| Haiti | 7 | 6 | NF | 115/300 |
| Honduras | 2 | 3 | F | 88/600 |
| Hungary | 5 + | 5 | PF | 23/4200 |
| Iceland | 1 | 1 | F | 8/12600 |
| India | 2 | 3 | F | 123/250 |
| Indonesia | 5 | 6 | PF | 93/500 |
| Iran | 5 | 6 | PF | 108/1900 |
| Iraq | 7 | 7 | NF | 78/3000 |

| | | | | |
|---|---|---|---|---|
| Ireland | 1 | 1 | F | 12/5400 |
| Isreal | 2 | 2 | F | 14/5500 |
| Italy | 1 | 1 | F | 14/6800 |
| Ivory Coast | 6 | 5 | PF | 127/1200 |
| | | | | |
| Jamaica | 2 | 3 | F | 16/1200 |
| Japan | 1 | 1 | F | 7/10300 |
| Jordan | 5 | 5 | PF | 69/1600 |
| | | | | |
| Kenya | 6 | 5 | PF | 87/400 |
| Kiribati | 1 | 2 | F | 42/440 |
| Korea (N) | 7 | 7 | NF | 34/1100 |
| Korea (S) | 4 + | 5 | PF | 34/1700 |
| Kuwait | 4 | 4 | PF | 39/26000 |
| | | | | |
| Laos | 7 | 7 | NF | 129/100 |
| Lebanon | 5 | 4 | PF | 41/1900 |
| Lesotho | 5 | 5 | PF | 115/500 |
| Liberia | 5 + | 5 | PF | 154/500 |
| Libya | 6 | 6 | NF | 100/8600 |
| Luxembourg | 1 | 1 | F | 12/14000 |
| | | | | |
| Madagascar | 5 | 6 | PF | 71/350 |
| Malawi | 6 | 7 | NF | 172/200 |
| Malaysia | 3 | 5 | PF | 31/1800 |
| Maldives | 5 | 5 | PF | 120/400 |
| Mali | 7 | 6 | NF | 154/200 |
| Malta | 2 | 4 | PF | 16/4000 |
| Mauritania | 7 | 6 | NF | 143/500 |
| Mauritius | 2 | 2 | F | 33/1300 |
| Mexico | 4 - | 4 | PF | 56/2300 |
| Mongolia | 7 | 7 | NF | 55/800 |
| Morocco | 4 | 5 | PF | 107/900 |
| Mozambique | 6 | 7 | NF | 115/250 |
| | | | | |
| Nauru | 2 | 2 | F | 31/21000 |
| Nepal | 3 | 4 | PF | 150/150 |
| Netherlands | 1 | 1 | F | 9/11100 |
| New Zealand | 1 | 1 | F | 13/7600 |
| Nicaragua | 5 | 5 | PF | 90/900 |
| Niger | 7 | 6 | NF | 146/350 |
| Nigeria | 7 | 5 | NF | 135/900 |

| | | | | |
|---|---|---|---|---|
| Norway | 1 | 1 | F | 9/13800 |
| Oman | 6 | 6 | NF | 128/5900 |
| Pakistan | 4 + | 5 | PF + | 126/350 |
| Panama | 6 - | 3 | PF | 34/1900 |
| Papua New Guinea | 2 | 2 | F | 104/800 |
| Paraguay | 5 | 5 | PF | 47/1600 |
| Peru | 2 | 3 | F | 88/1100 |
| Philippines | 4 | 3 + | PF | 55/800 |
| Poland | 6 | 5 | PF | 21/3900 |
| Portugal | 1 | 2 | F | 26/2500 |
| Qatar | 5 | 5 | PF | 53/28000 |
| Romania | 7 | 7 | NF | 32/2500 |
| Rwanda | 6 | 6 | NF | 107/250 |
| St. Kitts-Nevis | 1 | 1 | F | 43/1000 |
| St. Lucia | 1 | 2 | F | 33/850 |
| St. Vincent | 2 | 2 | F | 38/500 |
| Sao Tome & Principe | 7 | 7 | NF | 50/400 |
| Saudi Arabia | 6 | 7 | NF | 114/12700 |
| Senegal | 3 | 4 | PF | 147/500 |
| Seychelles | 6 | 6 | NF | 27/1800 |
| Sierra Leone | 5 - | 5 | PF | 208/400 |
| Singapore | 4 | 5 | PF | 12/5200 |
| Solomons | 2 | 3 | F | 78/600 |
| Somolia | 7 | 7 | NF | 147/300 |
| South Africa | 5 | 6 | PF | 96/2300 |
| Spain | 1 | 2 | F | 11/5800 |
| Sri Lanka | 3 | 4 | PF | 37/300 |
| Sudan | 6 | 6 | NF | 124/400 |
| Suriname | 6 + | 6 | NF | 36/3000 |
| Swaziland | 5 | 6 | PF | 135/850 |
| Sweden | 1 | 1 | F | 7/14500 |
| Switzerland | 1 | 1 | F | 9/17200 |
| Syria | 6 | 7 | NF | 62/1600 |
| Tanzania | 6 | 6 | NF | 103/300 |
| Thailand | 3 | 4 | PF | 55/800 |
| Togo | 6 | 6 | NF | 109/400 |

| | | | |
|---|---|---|---|
| Tonga | 5 | 3 | PF | 21/500 |
| Transkei | 5 | 6 | PF | NA |
| Trinidad & Tobago | 1 | 2 | F | 26/5300 |
| Tunisia | 5 | 5 | PF | 100/1400 |
| Turkey | 3 | 5 | PF | 123/1500 |
| Tuvalu | 1 | 2 | F | 42/680 |
| | | | | |
| Uganda | 5 - | 4 + | PF | 97/350 |
| USSR | 7 | 7 | NF | 36/4600 |
| United Arab Emirates | 5 | 5 | PF | 53/26000 |
| United Kingdom | 1 | 1 | F | 12/9000 |
| United States | 1 | 1 | F | 12/12500 |
| Uruguay | 2 + | 2 + | F + | 37/2800 |
| | | | | |
| Vanuatu | 2 | 4 | PF | 97/585 |
| Venezuela | 1 | 2 | F | 42/4200 |
| Vietnam | 7 | 7 · | NF | 100/200 |
| | | | | |
| Western Samoa | 4 | 3 | PF | 40/850 |
| | | | | |
| Yemen (N) | 5 | 5 | PF | 162/450 |
| Yemen (S) | 6 | 7 | NF | 146/500 |
| Yugoslavia | 6 | 5 | PF | 33/2800 |
| | | | | |
| Zaire | 7 · | 7 | NF | 112/200 |
| Zambia | 5 | 5 | PF | 106/600 |
| Zimbabwe | 4 | 6 - | PF | 74/800 |

## NOTES

1. The scales use the numbers 1-7, with 1 comparatively offering the highest level of political or civil rights and 7 the lowest. A plus or minus following a rating indicates an improvement or decline since the last yearbook. A rating marked with a raised period ( · ) has been reevaluated by the author in this time; there may have been little change in the country.

2. F designates "free," PF "partly free," and NF "not free."

3. Data for infant mortality per 1000 live births and GNP per capita from J.P. Lewis and V. Kallab (eds.) *U.S. Foreign Policy and the Third World: Agenda 1983* (New York: Praeger, 1983), supplemented by the *Encyclopedia Britannica: 1985 Book of the the Year*.

4. Also known as Kampuchea.

5. Formerly Upper Volta.

# Appendix 2

| POLITICAL SYSTEM: | Multiparty | | | Dominant-Party |
|---|---|---|---|---|
| | centralized | | decentralized | |
| **ECONOMIC SYSTEM:** | | | | |
| **Capitalist** **inclusive** | Antigua & Bar. F<br>Bahamas F<br>Barbados F<br>Belize F<br>Colombia[4] F<br>Costa Rica F<br>Cyprus (G) F<br>Cyprus (T) PF<br>Dominica F<br>Dom. Rep.[4] F<br>El Salvador[1/3] PF | Iceland F<br>Ireland F<br>Japan F<br>Korea (S)[1] P<br>Luxembourg F<br>Mauritius F<br>New Zealand[3] F<br>St.Kitts-Nevis F<br>St.Lucia[3] F<br>St. Vincent[3] F<br>Spain F | Australia F<br>Belgium F<br>Canada F<br>Germany(W)[3] F<br>Lebanon PF<br>Switzerland F<br>United States F | Malaysia PF |
| **non-inclusive** | Ecuador F<br>Fiji[4] F<br>Gambia[4] PF<br>Guatemala[1] PF<br>Honduras[1/4] F | Thailand[1] PF | Botswana F<br>Papua New Guinea F<br>Solomons[2] F | Haiti NF<br>Lesotho PF<br>Liberia[1] PF<br>Transkei PF |
| **Capitalist-Statist** **inclusive** | Argentina F<br>Grenada F<br>Italy F<br>Jamaica[3] F<br>South Africa PF | Sri Lanka PF<br>Turkey[1/4] PF<br>Venezuela F<br>Panama[1] PF | Brazil[3/4] F<br>Trinidad & Tobago F | China(Taiwan) PF<br>Mexico PF |
| **non-inclusive** | Bolivia F<br>Morocco[3] PF<br>Pakistan[1/2] PF<br>Peru[4] F<br>Uganda[1/3] PF | | India F<br>Vanuatu PF | Indonesia[1/4] PF<br>Iran[2/4] PF<br>Paraguay[1/3/4] PF<br>Philippines PF |
| **Mixed Capitalist** **inclusive** | Austria F<br>Denmark F<br>Finland F<br>France F<br>Greece F<br>Israel F<br>Malta PF | Netherlands F<br>Norway F<br>Portugal F<br>Sweden F<br>U.K.[3] F<br>Uruguay F | | Egypt[3/4] PF<br>Nicaragua PF<br>Senegal[3/4] PF<br>Singapore PF<br>Tunisia[4] PF<br>Zimbabwe[5] PF |
| **Mixed Socialist** **inclusive** | | | | Guyana PF<br>Syria[1/4] NF |
| **non-inclusive** | | | | Madagascar[1/2] PF |
| **Socialist** **inclusive** | | | | |

Notes to the Table

**non-inclusive**

1. Under heavy military influence or domination. (All countries in the Nonparty Military column are military dominated.)
2. Party relationships anomalous.
3. Close decision along capitalist-to-socialist continuum.
4. Close decision on inclusive/noninclusive dimension.
5. Noninclusive.

Source: *Freedom in the World: Political Rights and Civil Liberties, 1985-1986,* Freedom House, Inc., New York, N.Y., 1986.

# Political-Economic Systems

| One-Party | | Non-Party | | |
|---|---|---|---|---|
| socialist | communist | nationalist | military | nonmilitary |
| | | Djibouti NF | Chile[3] PF<br>Suriname NF | Jordan[2/3/4] PF<br>Western<br>  Samoa[2/4] PF |
| Sierra<br>  Leone[1] PF | | Cameroon[3] NF<br>Comoros NF<br>Gabon NF<br>Ivory Coast[4] PF<br>Kenya PF<br>Malawi NF | Chad NF<br>Niger NF<br>Yemen (N) PF | Bhutan[3] PF<br>Maldives PF<br>Nepal[3] PF<br>Swaziland PF<br>Tonga PF<br>Tuvalu F |
| | | | Ghana NF<br>Nigeria[3/4] NF | Bahrain PF<br>Brunei PF<br>Kuwait PF<br>Nauru F<br>Qatar PF<br>Saudi Arabia NF<br>Un. Arab Emirs PF |
| | | Zaire[1] NF | Bangladesh PF<br>Central Afr.<br>  Republic[3] NF<br>Eq. Guinea[3] NF<br>Mauritania NF | Kiribati F<br>Oman NF |
| Burundi[1/5] NF | | | | |
| Libya[1/2/3] NF<br>Seychelles[3] NF | China (M)[3] NF<br>Poland[1] PF<br>Yugoslavia[3] PF | | | |
| Burma[1] NF<br>Cape V[3/4] NF<br>Congo[1/3] NF<br>Guinea NF<br>Somalia[1/3] NF<br>Zambia[3] PF | | Mali[1] NF<br>Rwanda[1/3] NF<br>Sudan[1] NF<br>Togo[1] NF | Burkina Faso NF | |
| Algeria[1] NF<br>Sao Tome &<br>  Prin.[3/4] NF | Albania NF<br>Bulgaria NF<br>Cuba NF<br>Czecho-<br>  slovakia NF<br>Germany(E) NF | Hungary[3] PF<br>Korea (N) NF<br>Mongolia NF<br>Romania NF<br>USSR NF<br>Vietnam NF | | |
| Angola NF<br>Benin[1/3] NF<br>Guinea-<br>  Bissau[1/3] NF<br>Iraq[1/3/4] NF<br>Mozambique NF<br>Tanzania NF<br>Yemen (S) NF | Afghanistan NF<br>Cambodia NF<br>Ethiopia[1] NF<br>Laos NF | | | |

114

# Appendix 3

| ECONOMIC FREEDOM: | High | | Medium-High | Medium |
|---|---|---|---|---|
| **ECONOMIC SYSTEM:** **Capitalist** **inclusive** | Antigua & Barbuda F<br>Australia F<br>Bahamas F<br>Barbados F<br>Belgium F<br>Belize F<br>Canada F<br>Costa Rica F<br>Cyprus(G) F<br>Dominica F<br>Germany(W) F<br>Iceland F | Ireland F<br>Japan F<br>Luxembourg F<br>Mauritius F<br>New Zealand F<br>St. Kitts & Nevis F<br>St. Lucia F<br>St. Vincent F<br>Spain F<br>Switzerland F<br>United States F | Cyprus(T) PF<br>Djibouti NF<br>Dominican Republic F<br>Lebanon PF<br>Western Samoa PF | Chile PF<br>Colombia F<br>El Salvador PF<br>Jordan NF<br>Korea(S) PF<br>Malaysia PF |
| **non-inclusive** | Fiji F<br>Papua New Guinea F<br>Solomon Islands F | | Botswana F<br>Ecuador F<br>Gambia PF<br>Honduras PF<br>Kenya PF<br>Thailand PF<br>Tuvalu F | Bhutan PF<br>Cameroon NF<br>Gabon NF<br>Haiti NF<br>Ivory Coast PF<br>Lesotho PF<br>Liberia PF<br>Maldives PF |
| **Capitalist-Statist** **inclusive** | Greece F<br>Italy F<br>Nauru F<br>Trin. & Tob. F<br>Venezuela F | | France F<br>Jamaica F<br>Kuwait PF<br>Malta PF<br>Panama PF<br>Sri Lanka PF | Argentina PF<br>Bahrain PF<br>Brazil PF<br>China(T) PF<br>Ghana NF |
| **non-inclusive** | Kiribati F | | Bolivia F<br>Morocco PF<br>Nigeria F<br>Peru F<br>Vanuatu PF | Bangladesh PF<br>Cen. Afr. Rep. NF<br>India F |
| **Mixed Capitalist** **inclusive** | Austria F<br>Denmark F<br>Finland F<br>Netherlands F | Norway F<br>Sweden F<br>United Kingdom F | Israel F<br>Portugal F<br>Senegal PF | Nicaragua PF<br>Singapore PF<br>Tunisia PF |
| **non-inclusive** | | | | Egypt PF |
| **Mixed Socialist** **inclusive** | | | | Grenada NF<br>Yugoslavia PF |
| **non-inclusive** | | | | Cape Verde Islands NF<br>Madagascar PF<br>Rwanda NF |
| **Socialist** **inclusive** | | | | |
| **non-inclusive** | | | | Guinea-Bissau NF |

Source: *Freedom in the World: Political Rights and Civil Liberties, 1983-1984,* Freedom House, Inc., New York, N.Y., 1984.

# Economic Freedom

| Medium(cont.) | Low-Medium | Low |
|---|---|---|
| | Suriname NF | |
| Nepal PF<br>Niger NF<br>Sierra<br>  Leone PF<br>Swaziland PF<br>Tonga PF<br>Transkei PF<br>Yemen(N) NF | Chad NF<br>Comoros PF<br>Guatemala NF<br>Malawi NF | |
| Mexico PF<br>Qatar PF<br>Turkey PF<br>Saudi Arabia NF<br>U. Arab Ems. PF | South Africa PF | |
| Indonesia PF<br>Oman NF<br>Philippines PF<br>Zimbabwe PF | Equatorial<br>  Guinea NF  Pakistan NF<br>Iran NF  Paraguay PF<br>Mauritania NF  Uganda PF<br>  Zaire NF | |
| | Uruguay PF | |
| | Burundi NF | |
| | Guyana PF  Seychelles NF<br>Libya NF  Syria NF<br>Poland PF | |
| Sudan PF<br>Upper Volta PF<br>Zambia PF | Burma NF  Togo NF<br>Congo NF<br>Mali NF<br>Somalia NF | |
| | Algeria NF<br>Hungary NF<br>Sao Tome &<br>  Principe NF | Albania NF Korea(N) NF<br>Bulgaria NF Mongolia NF<br>China(M) NF Romania NF<br>Cuba NF USSR NF<br>Czecho-  Vietnam NF<br>  slovakia NF<br>Germany(E) NF |
| | Benin NF Tanzania NF<br>Guinea NF<br>Iraq NF<br>Mozambique NF | Afghanistan NF Laos NF<br>Angola NF Yemen(S) NF<br>Cambodia NF<br>Ethiopia NF |

## Appendix 4

## Checklist for Freedom Ratings

### Political Rights

1. Chief authority recently elected by a meaningful process
2. Legislature recently elected by a meaningful process

   Alternatives for 1 and 2:
   a. no choice and possibility of rejection
   b. no choice but some possibility of rejection
   c. choice possible only among government or single-party selected candidates
   d. choice possible only among government-approved candidates
   e. relatively open choices possible only in local elections
   f. open choice possible within a restricted range
   g. relatively open choices possible in all elections

3. Fair election laws, campaigning opportunity, polling and tabulation
4. Fair reflection of voter preference in distribution of power
      --parliament, for example, has effective power
5. Multiple political parties
      --only dominant party allowed effective opportunity
      --open to rise and fall of competing parties
6. Recent shifts in power through elections
7. Significant opposition vote
8. Free of military control
9. Free of foreign control
10. Major group or groups denied reasonable self-determination
11. Decentralized political power

--including: groups or factions other than the national government having legal regional or local power

12. Informal consensus; de facto opposition power

## Civil Liberties

13. Media/literature free of political censorship

    a. press independent of government

    b. broadcasting independent of government

14. Open public discussion

15. Freedom of assembly and demonstration

16. Freedom of political or quasi-political organization

17. Nondiscriminatory rule of law in politically relevant cases

    a. independent judiciary

    b. security forces respect individuals

18. Free from unjustified political terror or imprisonment

    a. free from imprisonment or exile for reasons of conscience

    b. free from torture

    c. free from terror by groups not opposed to the system

    d. free from government-organized terror

19. Free trade unions, peasant organizations or equivalents

20. Free businesses or cooperatives

21. Free professional or other private organizations

22. Free religious institutions

23. Personal social rights: including those to property, internal and external travel, choice of residence, marriage and family

24. Socioeconomic rights: including freedom from dependency on landlords, bosses, union leaders, or bureaucrats

25. Freedom from gross socioeconomic inequality

26. Freedom from gross government indifference or corruption

NOTES

1. First published in the Freedom House publication *Freedom at Issue* in its January 1973 edition, the Survey has appeared annually. Since 1978 it has also appeared in a yearbook. The latest in this series is Raymond D. Gastil, *Freedom in the World: Political Rights and Civil Liberties 1985-86* (Westport: Greenwood Press, 1986). Most of the following discussion is adapted from the yearbooks.

2. For example, *Keesing's Contemporary Archives*, 1984, pp. 32782-85; *Far Eastern Economic Review*, September 20, 1984, pages 40ff, as well as Leonard Sussman, "No Detente in International Communications," in *Freedom in the World: 1985-86*, pp. 89-128.

3. William Rugh, *Arab Press: News Media and Political Process in the Arab World* (Syracuse: Syracuse University Press, 1979).

4. For an attempt to suggest the relatively greater importance of subcultural as opposed to class or other interests in determining the opinions of people in our own society, see Raymond D. Gastil, "'Selling Out' and the Sociology of Knowledge," *Policy Sciences*, 1971, 2, pp. 271-77.

5. Alfred Kuhn, *The Logic of Social Systems* (San Francisco: Jossey-Bass, 1975), 330-61.

6. John Rawls, *A Theory of Justice* (Cambridge, Massachusetts: Belnap Press, 1971).

7. See Butterfield, *China, Alive in the Bitter Sea* (New York: New York Times Books, 1982).

8. Alan Westin, *Privacy and Freedom* (New York: Atheneum, 1967); Charles Fried, "Privacy," *Yale Law Review*, 77, 1968, 475-493.

9. Robert Nozick, *Anarchy, State, and Utopia* (New York: Basic Books, 1974).

10. Quoted from Robert C. Kiste, "Hawaii land: A revolution ahead?," *Pacific Islands Monthly*, August 1984, pages 29-30.

11. This discussion is based on Wright, "A Comparative Survey of Economic Freedoms," in *Freedom in the World, 1982*, pages 51-90. It was summarized and the table (Appendix 3) added in the 1983-84 edition.

12. The detailed rules for the censors as to what information to control in Poland, a relatively free communist state, were detailed in "Polish

Censors Secret Restrictions Revealed," *Freedom at Issue*, March-April 1978, pages 7ff. The government was extremely sensitive to anything published on what we would call consumer issues, such as the expected prices of food or accusations of pollution dangers.

13. Robert S. Leiken, "Nicaragua's Untold Stories," *The New Republic*, October 10, 1984, pages 16-23.

14. Compare, Grace Goodell, "Conservative Principles and Multinational Companies in Economic Development," in the *Heritage Lectures*, No. 25, The Heritage Foundation, 1983.

# A Statistical Note on the
# Gastil-Wright Survey of Freedom

## Milton Friedman

In their recent Survey of Freedom, Raymond Gastil and Lindsay Wright assign to 167 countries a ranking ranging from 1 to 7 in respect of their so-called "political rights" and "civil liberties," with 1 denoting the highest degree of attainment of each and 7 the lowest. In addition, for 165 of the 167 countries they provide quantitative estimates of infant mortality and gross national product per capita. They point out the generally significant relation between the qualitative characteristics of the countries and the quantitative characteristics but make no attempt at a detailed statistical analysis. In particular, since the rankings for political rights and civil liberties are highly correlated with one another, they eschew any effort to isolate their separate influence on the quantitative measures. The purpose of this note is to present some statistical calculations bearing on that issue.

In addition to the categories Gastil and Wright consider, one other variable is relevant to such an analysis, namely, whether the country in question is one of those that has recently benefited from the effects of OPEC on the price of oil. For example, Qatar, with a GNP per capita of $28,000 has the highest GNP per capita of any of the 165 countries, and Kuwait and the United Arab Emirates are close behind with a recorded figure of $26,000. Clearly, these have very little if any relation to either political rights or civil liberties.

The standard statistical technique of sorting out the separate influences of correlated variables is multiple regression. Accordingly, I calculated two multiple regressions, one for infant mortality and one for GNP per capita, using three independent variables, the rankings for political rights and civil liberties, and a dummy variable assigned the value of 1 for the 14 countries I identified as oil countries, and 0 for all other countries. As dependent variables, I used the logarithms of reported infant mortality and GNP per capita in order to avoid what statisticians call heteroscedasticity, or the wider absolute variability of the observations for high absolute levels than for low ones. One correction that I did not make, but that in principle would be desirable, would be to weight the observations in accordance with the likely accuracy of reported infant mortality and GNP per capita. Population might well serve as a proxy for the likely degree of accuracy, but I had no such figures readily available and was unwilling to devote the effort required to collect them. In any event, it is my considered opinion that the results would not be materially affected by introducing such a weighting scheme.

With these preliminaries out of the way, the computed equations are as follows:

$$\text{LogIM} = \underset{(20.0)}{2.6250} - \underset{(0.6)}{0.0380\text{PR}} + \underset{(4.5)}{0.3417\text{CL}} - \underset{(0.2)}{0.0335\text{PC}},$$
$$R^2 = .42 \quad \text{S.E.E.} = .706,$$

$$\text{LogGNP} = \underset{(44.6)}{8.7761} + \underset{(0.8)}{0.0839\text{PR}} - \underset{(4.3)}{0.4913\text{CL}} + \underset{(6.9)}{2.0790\text{PC}},$$
$$R^2 = .432 \quad \text{S.E.E.} = 1.060,$$

where IM stands for infant mortality, GNP for GNP per capita, PR for ranking by political rights, CL for ranking by civil liberties, PC for the dummy variable for whether or not an oil country, $R^2$ for the square of the multiple correlation coefficient corrected for degrees of freedom, S.E.E. for the standard error of estimate, and the numbers in parentheses below the coefficients are the absolute t-values.[1]

In interpreting the results, recall that 1 represents the highest degree of achievement for political rights or civil liberties, so that a positive coefficient means that a deterioration in rights or liberties is associated with a rise in infant mortality or GNP per capita, and conversely for a negative coefficient.

I find the results fascinating. When civil liberties are held constant, political rights show no statistically significant association at all with either infant mortality or GNP per capita. On the other hand, when political rights are held constant, there is a highly significant association between civil liberties and both infant mortality and GNP per capita: the greater the liberties, the lower the infant mortality and the higher the GNP per capita. Understandably, being or not being an oil country has no determinable effect on infant mortality but clearly does on level of GNP per capita.

Because the dependent variables are (natural) logarithms, the coefficients of the variables can be interpreted as comparable to percentages. Thus each one unit improvement in the ranking by civil liberties implies a 34 percent change in infant mortality and a 49 percent change in GNP per capita—down for infant mortality and up for GNP for an improvement in ranking, and conversely for a deterioration in ranking. These are clearly major changes.[2]

To avoid misunderstanding, I hasten to repeat the cliche that correlation is not proof of causation. The regression result is consistent with high income leading to a wider range of civil rights and to a lower level of infant mortality or with the kind of institutions that favour civil rights leading to high income and low infant mortality or high GNP per capita. They do establish the proposition that civil liberties, as defined in the Survey of Freedom, are a more significant variable in understanding the other phenomena than political rights, whether because of differences in the accuracy of the rankings or for other reasons.

I hasten to emphasize that my intention is not to denigrate the importance of political rights as an essential component of what I regard as a "good society." On the contrary, I strongly believe they are an essential component. But on this evidence, they cannot be regarded as an effective means to other objectives. However, my purpose is statistical, not ethical.

For the benefit of those who are distrustful of multiple correlation, I append a table for a cross-classification of the non-oil countries by the two rankings giving the number of observations and the average infant mortality and GNP per capita. These are the simple arithmetic averages, not the geometric averages that would be the counterpart of my use of logarithms in the multiple correlation. A detailed examination of these two-way tables yields results that are fully consistent with the results of the multiple correlations, and, incidentally, show how misleading the marginal distributions by themselves can be.

## Survey of Freedom:
## Cross-classification by Political Rights and Civil Liberties
## Number, Average Infant Mortality and
## Average GNP per Capita Non-oil Countries

| Political Rights | Civil Liberties | | | | | | | Total |
|---|---|---|---|---|---|---|---|---|
| | 1 | 2 | 3 | 4 | 5 | 6 | 7 | |
| *Number of Countries* | | | | | | | | |
| 1 | 20 | 10 | 1 | 0 | 0 | 0 | 0 | 31 |
| 2 | 0 | 12 | 11 | 3 | 0 | 0 | 0 | 26 |
| 3 | 0 | 1 | 0 | 5 | 2 | 0 | 0 | 8 |
| 4 | 0 | 0 | 2 | 2 | 4 | 1 | 0 | 9 |
| 5 | 0 | 0 | 1 | 2 | 15 | 3 | 0 | 21 |
| 6 | 0 | 0 | 1 | 0 | 5 | 12 | 6 | 24 |
| 7 | 0 | 0 | 0 | 0 | 2 | 11 | 19 | 32 |
| Total | 20 | 23 | 16 | 12 | 28 | 27 | 25 | 151 |
| *Average Infant Mortality* | | | | | | | | |
| 1 | 14 | 25 | 68 | | | | | 19 |
| 2 | | 35 | 70 | 55 | | | | 52 |
| 3 | | 77 | | 117 | 77 | | | 102 |
| 4 | | | 48 | 87 | 70 | 74 | | 69 |
| 5 | | | 21 | 69 | 103 | 101 | | 96 |
| 6 | | | 34 | | 61 | 83 | 114 | 84 |
| 7 | | | | | 150 | 118 | 107 | 113 |
| Total | 14 | 32 | 62 | 89 | 92 | 99 | 109 | 73 |
| *Average GNP per Capita* | | | | | | | | |
| 1 | 9845 | 4847 | 1300 | | | | | 7957 |
| 2 | | | 918 | 1745 | | | | 2730 |
| 3 | | | | 420 | 1650 | | | 950 |
| 4 | | | 825 | 925 | 2038 | 800 | | 1383 |
| 5 | | | 500 | 1125 | 1065 | 1167 | | 1059 |
| 6 | | | 1900 | | 2180 | 1003 | 608 | 1187 |
| 7 | | | | | 600 | 1514 | 908 | 1097 |
| Total | 9845 | 4623 | 965 | 953 | 1412 | 1221 | 836 | 2805 |

## NOTES

1. Incidentally, I computed the same equations excluding the oil countries and the oil dummy. The results were essentially identical.
2. In terms of conventional percentages the percentage change is different for a rise and a fall—e.g., 29 percent for a decline in infant mortality as the result of 1 unit improvement in the ranking, 40 percent for a rise in infant mortality as a result of a 1 unit deterioration. The numbers derived from the logarithms are the geometric mean of these two ways of describing the percentage change.

# Discussion

## Edited by Michael A. Walker

**Lindsay Wright** I would like to start my remarks by addressing two myths about the Survey. First, the numbers are not meant to be used for mathematical computations, even though Milton has so kindly given us a regression analysis. If people want to use the data in this way, we like to encourage them to do so with care. They are based on subjective assessments—certainly of what we believe are fundamental rights—but they are our, and mainly Ray's, analyses of how the countries fit into the categories that he has developed. Second, the Survey is based on trends, not on singular events, so that something that may occur late in the year is not necessarily given any more emphasis—unless it signifies an important trend or a change in patterns in political and civil freedoms.

I would like to clear up one misunderstanding about the Economic Systems Table where we make cross tabulations between political-economic systems and economic systems, and economic freedom. The economic systems, grouped on a capitalist to socialist dimension, were developed prior to my analysis of economic freedoms, so economic systems are defined in the traditional sense of private ownership versus public ownership of property, and not on degree of economic freedom.

I would like to make a couple of comments on economic freedoms. With reference to Assar's earlier comments about the logic of democracy existing with socialism, the distinction that we make is really between ownership and control of property. One of the four freedoms that I use to develop an overall status of economic freedom for a particular country is the freedom to *control* property, as distinct from the freedom to *own* property.

You may also have seen an inherent contradiction in our examination of economic freedoms. On the one hand we have defined individual economic freedoms—specifically freedom to have property, freedom of association, freedom of information, and freedom of movement—as they relate to economic matters. We have also defined economic freedom on a collective level. A country that has a democratic process that legitimates the economies that develop is also considered economically free.

**Raymond Gastil** I just want to make a few quick points, going beyond the paper, really, of what has to do with the point Rabushka makes later on in regard to Hong Kong. The Survey tries to make a re-evaluation of what is going on in the world every year. If you see a period in front of the rating, that means it has been changed from the past year without anything happening in the country, only something happening in *me*. It may be that the Hong Kong change should have had a period by it, because that is something that is going on in me, not something going on in Hong Kong.

The second point along that line is that judgements are necessarily in terms of some fairly obvious and overall categories, and they hide a lot of problems. For example, I think there may be serious problems in freedom in Japan, Sweden, Switzerland and so forth in political rights and civil liberties, but superficially there are not. Therefore, the Survey tries to stay on that plane and not go into these deep problems, because if it did, it would have to do it for 167 different countries and that would be too many deep problems to solve. So that is just a warning.

Next, we need to separate desirability of something for growth from ethical acceptability. Sometimes in the discussion those two get mixed up. People seem to think that because something is good for growth, then it should be something that is approved in terms of ethical standards of goodness. It may be that those two things are not necessarily connected.

The third point is, if political rights are to be fully developed, then the list of *human* rights should be as short as possible. I often make that point to my friends on the left, and I think I also, in regard to this group, would make it in regard to their favourite rights. Every right you add to the basic rights takes away from the ability of the population to decide things for itself through a political process. We should be very wary of doing that.

Finally—and this is a critical point that we went into in the last discussion, and we will come back to here—individual rights and collective rights must both be emphasized and must be balanced. And let me, on that point, offer a very short story. Imagine an island with ten persons on it, and these persons have all decided they want to leave the island. Some think they will build a boat and leave the island. Some think they will build an airplane and leave the island. It is generally agreed that all the surplus for the next year, until the next hurricanes come, must be spent on one or the other of these, or neither will work. Therefore they hold a vote. Six want to build boats, and four want to fly airplanes. It seems to me that four, then, are going to be oppressed, in that sense. All their surplus is going to be taken away and given to building the boat. On the other hand, there is general agreement that if that isn't done, nothing is going to be done. Now, of course, if there wasn't general agreement on that, it would be an even more difficult problem. But I suggest that political rights mean that people have an equal right to participate in those decisions in which it is necessary that a group decision rather than an individual decision be made.

**Armen Alchian**  I will make my humorous remarks first. Where are Andora, Monte Carlo and Liechtenstein in your list? I couldn't find them any place.

**Raymond Gastil**  We regard them as dependencies.

**Armen Alchian**  Well then, why do you have Bulgaria, Cuba, Romania, Czechoslovakia, and the rest of those specified as separate countries? I would put California up here, I would put Oregon up here—on the same principle as you have included Bulgaria. It is confusing. That is not a central point, but it is a little puzzling as to how you identify countries.

I would have expected all the nondiagonal cells in appendix 3 to be zero, empty. And in table 2, I would expect to find no correlation. But I lack a good theory for that. Presumably it was some theory you had in mind that induced you to make that classification. In some way you thought there was a connection between the political-economic system and what you call an economic system. I wasn't able to find that theory anywhere, and I wasn't able to come up with one myself.

Let me turn then to make a comment that I think any economist would make who read your paper, and so it won't be new to most of you, but it is the way I looked at the issue. I don't like the word "freedom" because it is so loaded with ambiguity and different meanings to different people. It is like the word "utility" in economics. So what have economists done with that ambiguity? They have made "utility" an empty term except meaning preference-ordering. What we have done is put into that preference-ordering a lot of other dimensions.

So instead of talking about freedom itself, I would rather say the following. If the society in which I am going to live has more private property rights, I prefer it. You could add to that list. But the point is that I identify attributes of the society and specify which ones the more of which you have the better I like it. When I say I like it better, I mean it has more freedom. Now, if you have some other meaning for freedom, you are welcome to it. But as it stands in our discussion, it has been empty so far and, as a consequence, you can load in anything you want.

In addition to that, I would add into it the following elements, in the sense that if it had them I would regard the society as better, and you may therefore call it freer. Are there restrictions on the governments' political violence powers? I think of government as the monopoly power over physical force, and I want it to have that force exclusively so that others don't use it. But is the government restricted in how it uses it? Will it be used to enforce private property rights? Will it be used to solve or give decisions on dispute resolutions? If so, I would prefer that. Will it be one that uses its power to engage in more wealth transfer? If it were, then I would say I don't like that, and I would put that down as lower freedom. Does it enforce economic due process more fully? If it does, then I would put a plus sign there. In other words, does it have limited powers like, maybe, government is limited under our Constitution?

To the extent that these various elements are more prevailing or stronger, I would be tempted to say that is a preferred society and, in your language, it has more freedom. If you don't like me to say it that way, then you have to tell me more precisely what you mean by freedom.

I would also ask the question in deciding whether this society is free, in the sense of preferred, as to the competitive processes which people engage in to get government power. There are a lot of competitive processes we can engage in for that power; military competition is one of them. In a way, we just fight it out until someone gets monopoly power, and he is in charge. We use that system a lot. After all, if I take over your country, that is a political competition process. There is nothing disallowed in the competitions between countries. So, if the United States were to go and take over Switzerland, okay, then we've won that competitive process. What is there bad about a military competitive process? I suspect I don't like that kind of process for acquiring the power, but it's present. And I don't know where to put that in my category of pluses and minuses. I can imagine a system in which the Republican Party hired its army and the Democratic Party hired its army, and they would engage in a battle every four years and the survivor takes over. That might be a nice system. We might all enjoy that. We could watch the fight on television.

Another system would be hereditary and marriage. We could compete in getting the right heredity, that is, compete in being the son of the king, the first son especially; or I compete in having my daughter marry your son, and have my children then become the king. Societies competed at one time for monarchial power, and it is a pretty good system I think.

So I offer you two alternatives: military, fight it out; marriage/hereditary process. Which is competitive? There is also a plutocratic voting system where only land owners get to vote, and they get as many votes as they have acres of land or as taxable land value. I would like that system. Or you have a democratic system where anybody votes, no matter who he is, as long as he or she is 21 years of age—or 18, some number—and maybe you stop voting at 65.

Now there are some different systems of competition for political power. I don't have a clear idea which of those have greater survival value in our society, let alone which ones you prefer. So I have two questions, emerging from normative and positive considerations. Which of these competitive processes for getting power as a government is more viable, has been used more, leads to the kind of economic institutions that I prefer? I don't know. Until I get some kind of theory about those, all I can do is sit here and carp at what is being said.

But you must have some theory in mind about these things. What I thought I detected—not a theory but a premise—was that democracy and majority voting was either preferred by you or you think it is the positive one with greater survival value. It is awfully difficult for me to say, on the one hand, I prefer this system, and on the other hand say it hasn't got survival value. It is always odd for one to go around saying, "Well, you ought to have this system here, but it won't last very long." That, it strikes me, is simply a bit of daydreaming.

Let me make a couple of specific, though minor, points. As to the meaning of political freedom or political liberty, I don't know whether that relates to whether you are more or less dependent upon government or whether it means you have a greater role in influencing who becomes the government. You talk about access to political power, voting and what not, but you could also have great voting power and be very dependent upon the government. I would like to get those two cleared up rather than make my own conjectures about that.

I thought I detected the idea that democracy and majority rule was appropriate. I don't know where that comes from. What I see majorities doing in Santa Monica, California, in the California Coastal Commission just persuades me that democracy is for the birds. The trouble is, I don't know what is better than that.

And one last comment. Some people want to use freedom to mean "increased range of choice." You don't increase the range of choice; you merely reallocate who gets the choices. The question is whether a dispersed system of choices is better than a highly concentrated one for society to survive. I don't know. The main point is, it is one thing to talk about our preferences; it is something else to talk about a system that is going to survive whether we like it or not.

**Ingemar Stahl** I want to continue where Armen finished. I also got the same understanding that you have very strong preferences for a majority rule system, and that's the kind of a norm you imply when you discuss the different systems of political rights. I would like to start another way by saying the basic thing would be to keep as close as possible to a kind of unanimity principle. If that cannot be done, and we have to adopt the majority rule, then we can look at the institutions which are closest to having some political rights under the majority rule system. But any system which is closer to unanimity than majority rule would be ranked above majority rule systems.

Let us see if this criterion is fulfilled when we look at your table. Look at the table for political rights for Finland. Finland is not a full-worthy member here. Finland has a second rank on political rights, which would definitely violate the principle I just recently indicated that we should be as close as possible to the unanimity rule. Finland is one of the few countries on this list that has adopted a two-thirds majority for taxes and public expenditures, and in some cases a five-sixths majority. If you have a five-sixths majority clause, you are very close to applying the Wicksellian unanimity principle. So, I can't really understand the ranking order, unless it has to do with Finland's proximity to the Soviet Union, which has nothing to do, really, with political rights.

**Tibor Machan** I am tempted to launch into this collective rights debate. I think the characterization you give to something called collective rights or collective freedom is misleading because you would then argue that a club whose members got together, typically voluntarily, and subsequently have a democratic process for deciding about the things the club will do, like the Kiwanis Club or the Rotary Club, is engaged in something called collective freedom or collective rights or possess collective rights. I think that's just a misleading way of considering collectivity in the politically significant way. Collectivity, in a politically significant way, means that from the moment you are born you are regarded as part of an organic whole. Your individuality is denied as a human being—not that you voluntarily give it up and join a club or a church or whatever else. The question is, do you then agree to the existence of such things as collective rights or collective freedoms in this organic sense or not? If not, then I don't think the subject is even worth mentioning, because so many things fall under it—corporate life, marriage—all sorts of things fall under the notion of collective rights.

Second, democracy versus liberty. Now, to make a society a preferred one or a good one on the basis of how widespread democracy is, I think leaves too many questions unanswered. Some democracies may be extremely good if the people who are participating in the democratic process are also wise. If the people are corrupt, irresponsible, stupid, et cetera, it can bring about the most horrendous society and nevertheless it will be democratic. So I don't see that there is any correlation between democracy, which is a process, and the result which may be either good or bad.

Finally, this notion about freedom. We of course know that freedom is an ambiguous term in the sense that it has at least two clear meanings in political philosophy: freedom *from* the intrusion of other people into your lives and property versus the freedom *to do* things that you might wish to do or maybe even you ought to do. In the classical liberal tradition we are talking about negative freedom. Society is free to the extent that its individual members are not intruded upon unavoidably.

If I talk to you, that's an intrusion of a sort, but it's not unavoidable because you can turn and walk away. But if I grab you by the collar and hold you down, that is an unavoidable intrusion. In the classical liberal tradition—I think the one that is interesting to Americans and westerners in general and the one about which the big debate is still going on—this negative freedom is pervasive. If you are looking at various societies you might say art is flourishing or lots of other things are flourishing, but whether freedom is flourishing in this sense is not that difficult to determine. Are individuals by law capable of exercising their will over their own actions or are others doing that for them?

**Raymond Gastil** There is a good deal of misunderstanding of some points.

First, a technical one, having to do with the Survey. The Survey is of 167 countries and another 40 or so related territories. This is based on very traditional assumptions about what are countries and what are related territories. We get into a lot of problems on that. Hong Kong is clearly a related territory, and that is just a different classification scheme. The misinterpretation comes, for example, when Tibor says there is no necessary correlation of democracy with good things. That was the point I was trying to make, so I am glad you also made it.

On the point that Armen was making about having a favourite list of things he would like to call freedom, I have a favourite list of things I would like to call freedom too. The Survey, on the other hand, isn't a list of my favourite things, or of what I think is most important. It is a list of what I felt at the time the Survey was set up were most generally considered to characterize democracies in the Western European tradition in terms of political life and civil liberties, and I tried to see how countries came closer or went further away from that definition. I didn't set out a definition of a perfect society. The point I have often made in the Survey—perhaps you missed it over the years—is that this is not a survey of goodness versus badness; these are not necessarily the best countries versus the countries that are not so good. They are, rather, countries that meet certain criteria and countries that do not meet certain criteria. So that is the basis of my discussion.

The last point has to do with majority rule. It seems to me the point there is that if you emphasize individual rights and say everybody in the world or everybody in a nation has equal individual rights, there come certain situations in which you ask how one can best express that individual right. If he can't do it as an individual and has to do it through a group, then majority rule is the best way. Now I have found, in looking at countries with consensus—consensus has been brought up here a lot—most in the world today are the self-described African "democracies." These are the countries whose leaders keep repeating, "In Africa we don't have competing parties, we have consensus. Everybody gets together and they reach a consensus." It is a dangerous doctrine. I think pushing for consensus and assuming you are going to get consensus in society is a dangerous way to proceed.

**Lindsay Wright** I would like to add a comment on democracy and political freedom. Democracy may not create a good society, as Ray said, but that is the whole point. If we believe that democracy should exist, then we should also believe that the political and economic arrangements that evolve from that democracy are wished and desired by the majority of those who make up that democracy. That is the basic principle on which we have based our survey.

**Gordon Tullock** I don't want to talk about politics but economics. It seems to me this description of societies on the basis of a one-dimensional spectrum, socialism to capitalism, which is used throughout, is simply wrong. There are many institutional structures that simply don't fit on the spectrum. Right now I don't like the descriptions for merchantilism you find in the standard text, but let's accept that meaning for merchantilism. It is a large-scale intervention into a system which is certainly not socialist, but to call it capitalist is a little odd too. Haiti, for example, was not, to my way of thinking, a capitalist system. I certainly don't think it's socialist; it is not either.

Just by accident, I am reading a book which I recommend very highly to all of you even though I am only half through—Grace Godell's *The Elementary Structures of Political Life*, which deals with Persia under the Shah. She calls it a personalistic system, which I think is a very good description. What was valuable in that system were your connections and who you knew, some of which could be inherited. Property tended to come to you or be taken away from you in terms of changes in your personal relations with other people. It's very hard to regard this as either socialist or capitalist. Certainly, at the particular time she is writing, I think it was regarded as more socialist than capitalist, but that was an accidental fact. At the time she was writing the Shah was spending immense amounts of oil money all over the place, and therefore the economy was much under government control. I just don't like this one-dimensional distinction between capitalism and socialism. What you have is socialism—which has a fairly definite meaning—and capitalism, a term which was invented by a prominent socialist. But in actual reality there are many, many other systems, and it's very difficult to do anything except to say that there are many other systems.

**Walter Block** I have a few criticisms also. It seems that this fetish for democracy, if I can call it that, doesn't allow for the understanding of the tyranny of the majority. If the majority favoured something—automatic death penalty for all redheads or something equally silly—it is still democratic. Therefore, according to this theory, it is good. It embodies or promotes political freedom, or freedom of some sort. But this is a grievous mistake as far as I can see.

I agree with the point Armen was making that this list was arbitrary. He has his arbitrary list, and I feel like Armen's arbitrary list is a lot better than the other arbitrary list.

I don't see why organized labour should be given a plus. Unions are just institutions that engage in prohibition of entry into labour markets. They are anti-free labour markets, and I'll be damned if I can see why they get a plus. And the same goes for political demonstrations, which are often organized violations of private property rights.

I particularly resent the good treatment given to my own country of Canada. Why should Canada be considered such a great, politically free nation? It has a Canadian Broadcasting Corporation, which is a state-owned TV system. It recently had a Kent Commission report, which was an attempt to interfere with the newspaper market on the grounds that private monopolies were too powerful in those markets. It consigned to jail Ernst Zundel who had the temerity to question whether six million people died in concentration camps. It penalized him, it violated his free speech rights. I don't understand this. If I want to maintain that the earth is flat, or that two plus two is five, or that there were no Nazi concentration camps, or that Stalin was a great, benevolent person, or that World War II never occurred, you would think I would have a right to do that. There are three or four places in this conference where we talk about rational views. As I see it, Zundl's views are about as rational as these. But people still have a right to spout off irrational nonsense. And if a country violated my freedom to do this, it should go at least from a one to a two.

Now, as to Armen's claim that the California Coastal Commission and this other city are violating rights. He says he doesn't like democracy at all, but he can't think of a better system. I can think of a better system. It's called free enterprise, where there is no political voting on anything. We don't vote on whether you can keep your property or not, or on whether I can take your property away. A free enterprise system is one where the government is limited just to protecting property rights and to doing very little else. And that seems to me to be a much better system than this unbridled democracy we now have.

**Milton Friedman** I have two very different comments. One has to do with individual rights versus collective rights. I think your analysis of the island is highly defective, and you did not come out with the right solution for people who believe in human freedom. The right solution is not that the majority should win, but that the ten people should unanimously agree that they will have a lottery in which there are six chances out of ten that it will come up the one way and four chances out of ten that it will come up the other way. That is a proposition on which you can get unanimous agreement.

I do not think you would get unanimous agreement among the ten people, that either the six should have their way or the four should have their way. The fallacy in your view is the notion of collectivity; or collective rights. There are no collective rights; there are only individual rights, which may or may not be shared. There are collective agreements made among individuals. One of those collective agreements is a form of government which says that in certain cases it is more important to do something whether everybody agrees with it or not, and that in those cases we will accept majority rule as an expedient. I regard it strictly as an expedient in that sense—we all do.

There is not a person here—not even Lindsay—who thinks that if 51 percent of the people vote to shoot the other 49 percent of the people that is an appropriate exercise. Don't shake your head. If you say that is not an appropriate exercise in majority rights, then you don't believe that democracy is an ultimate value. You don't believe that majority rule is an ultimate value.

**Lindsay Wright** No. Democracy *is* an ultimate value, given protection of minority rights and basic fundamental rights.

**Milton Friedman** I know. But you can't have your cake and eat it too. You can't say that majority voting is a basic right. You cannot say, as you say here, that "theoretically then a majority *might* have the right to decide on any policy or any degree of government control that it wished." Now if I take out the weasel words from that, that is a statement that majority rule is an ultimate objective. That's a proposition I object to very strenuously.

The second comment I want to make is altogether different. I have played around on my computer with some of these data, and I think the results are fascinating. These days you can make so many calculations that would have taken months before.

What I did was run a multiple regression with two dependent variables: one was a logarithm of infant mortality and the other one was a logarithm of GNP per capita, just to get rid of heteroscedasticity. And the independent variables, obviously a constant (they are written on the left): political rights, which is just their one to seven; civil liberties, which is just their one to seven; and oil countries, which is just a dummy variable, one-zero (one for oil countries and zero for others).

The fascinating thing to me is that in neither for infant mortality or for GNP per capita do political rights exhibit any correlation whatsoever. That is, neither coefficient comes close to being significant at *any* level, nor are political rights correlated with the result. I don't think that is at all surprising, because of the fact that political rights are purely a means and don't really have any ultimate objective value, while civil liberties are something else.

Civil liberties are things that people value very highly, and you can take it either way. You can say that when people have high income they can afford to provide civil liberties, so that it may be the income that is the cause of the civil liberties. Or you can take it the other way, that any environment that promotes civil liberties is likely to promote freedom of enterprise, et cetera, which is likely to promote income growth.

As you can see, on income the oil countries dummy is very important; on infant mortality it is not. I don't regard the prosperity of the oil countries as contradicting in any way the various notions we've all expressed about what's good for growth. That's an accident, an aberration. I predict that 10 or 20 years from now they will not be as prosperous. The coefficient of that dummy variable is going to decline year by year.

At any rate, it seemed to me that those results are kind of fascinating because of the fact that if you hold civil liberties constant, political liberties as defined by you two are completely unrelated to performance. Whichever way you interpret the cause and effect relationships, I think that's an interesting empirical finding.

**Assar Lindbeck** I think the most basic criticism directed against this paper is that political freedom is identified with majority rule. The case that 51 percent decide to kill the other 49 percent may be an unnecessarily strong example. Take an example that 51 percent decide that all property above the level of subsistence should be removed from 49 percent. Moreover, that those 49 percent should be exposed to 100 percent marginal tax rates so they could not change their own economic life by their own actions. They would become completely dependent on government transfer. They would have to apply to government for more resources—transfer payments or goods and services in kind. That is one society.

In another society, the 49 percent make the decisions. They decide that marginal taxes should be very low, everybody should be allowed to keep their property, and that you should have no rent controls or exchange controls that limit your possibility to travel or to choose your housing.

How would you describe those two societies in terms of individual or political freedom? If the only important thing is majority rule, you would say that the first society is the one with political rights. But, if you emphasize the protection of freedom of choice of the minority in society, you would say that the society with 49 percent making the decisions but not discriminating against the 51 percent very much is the society with much more freedom of choice for the individual and with higher political freedom. I use this example to show the real limitation of looking at majority rule as the only dimension of political freedom or political rights.

**Armen Alchian** I'm at the University of California, and I'd like to change the institutional arrangements so they'd charge high tuition. There is not a ghost of a chance in hell that that will be done. Now, my problem is, what's the point of preferring something which I know is impossible as a practical matter? That's what I'm worried about choosing among options you think have a chance of surviving and those which just have no chance at all.

**Lindsay Wright** Are you referring to democracy?

**Armen Alchian**  No, just in general. I'm not sure democracy has survival value. It may last a hundred years and then down the drain. I think it's the least surviving of all.

**Lindsay Wright**  In this discussion, we seem to be going around repeatedly on this issue of economic success as necessarily having a higher value than political freedom. My argument is that economic success or economic growth is something that a people, as members of a state, have a natural right to determine for themselves, whether they will put a high priority on that or on other things.

**Voice**  As a collective or as individuals?

**Lindsay Wright**  As both.

**Voice**  That's the dividing point.

**Lindsay Wright**  People have a right to decide these economic issues for themselves. That is why we believe political freedom is the only way that these types of choices can be made about how society is going to be structured, as it necessarily has to be since we all live in societies that we can't avoid.

**Raymond Gastil**  Let me run over some points that have come up since the last time I spoke. One was the one-dimensionality of the capitalism /socialism dimension. Again, that was an attempt to give some information to readers who think in terms of capitalism and socialism. Most of our readers do, and therefore I tried to take that simple distinction and see how it would relate to what I was doing on the Freedom Survey. I do try to differentiate different varieties, if you will, of capitalism. I distinguish "capitalist-statism," for example, which describes the Shah's system. I also distinguish the situation where a primitive culture is operating a system, and actually most of the people are not in the system from more characteristic economics—that is where the inclusive/non-inclusive distinction comes in the table, as you noticed.

The second point has to do with Milton's lottery. It seems to me that the lottery would be a wonderful way to decide. But the only way *to decide to use* the lottery is to have a majority vote.

**Milton Friedman** No. You have a unanimous vote.

**Raymond Gastil** You made the point that you wouldn't have the unanimous vote.

**Milton Friedman** No, I didn't. Not at all.

**Raymond Gastil** At any rate, my point would be that it seems to me that the only legitimate way to use a lottery to decide between the boat and the airplane would be if each person had equal weight in the decision, and that is what a majority rule allows.

The point has been made about absolute rights. In no place can we say that the majority has absolute rights; we always are thinking in terms of political rights constrained by certain basic civil liberties. Now, as I made the point, that should be a short list. It should be a definite list, and it should control, certainly, such things, through a judiciary, as 51 percent deciding to shoot 49 percent and so on. That certainly has always been our thinking.

Now survival value—that's the point I was trying to make earlier when I talked about the anarchists. It is utopianism to talk about a system for which you don't have real historical cases with a real track record. There is a track record with democracy. It is not perfect, but it is a track record. Therefore it seems to me it has survival value in the sense that it is one of the legitimate operative alternatives. It may not be the best for certain purposes, but it is there.

Finally, on these correlations, one thing I find strange about these correlations is that other statisticians who have approached the Survey have pointed out to me that political and civil liberties have a 0.9 correlation...

**Milton Friedman** That's perfectly consistent.

**Raymond Gastil** ...between the two. So they feel that they should not treat them as separate at all; it's really the same thing.

**Tibor Machan** A couple of points here. One is that I don't think you should jump to the conclusion that the debate here is a purely ideological or an axe-grinding kind of debate. We really are taking seriously your name "Freedom House" and your "partly free," "not free," "free" categorization. I think for that reason we are trying to look into what that means and whether the characterization as abiding by some sort of a democratic rule or process or majority rule is an accurate way to gauge whether a country is free. So we could all be haters of freedom and still make that very same point, namely, whether in fact it characterizes a free society that its institutions are democratically established. So it is not entirely just an axe-grinding thing.

Second, it is arguable that when consistently examined, democracy does require its own extreme limitation. If democracy means the continued participation of people in the political process, that may indeed require a considerable amount of economic freedom. Without economic freedom, the newspapers shut down, people could be pushed out and made dependent upon political rulers, and so on. So it is arguable that the implication of democracy does indeed mean that it cannot extend way beyond, say, the selection of political representatives.

Finally, you kept using the term "people's rights" to determine for themselves, or something. Suppose I use this similarly with newspapers. Suppose I say the right of newspapers to determine for themselves what they will publish—and that means that the majority of newspapers in the country determine what all the newspapers have to publish. Surely you would not regard this as an instance of the free press. You would regard it as an instance of the free press if every individual newspaper, magazine, publishing house and so on has the full liberty, not interfered with by other people, to determine what goes into print and to sell it on an open market. Similarly, if you are going to talk about freedom of the people to make choices with respect to the distribution of property, engaging in labour, and so forth, this isn't going to be met by the conditions that you seem to be specifying; namely, that they get together and collectively decide what sort of economic institutions they are going to have. That won't do, any more than getting together the newspapers and deciding what they will collectively print will constitute freedom of the press. So I think that is just a mistake.

**Walter Block** I think Tibor is making a magnificent point on that. I agree whole-heartedly with the idea of newspaper rights and individual freedom, not a majority vote. I would like to carry this yearning for egalitarianism further. We have, I would consider, a certain area where egalitarianism is legitimate; namely, everyone has an equal right not to be aggressed against. That is, it is equally wrong to murder anyone, a rich person or a poor person. Now that is an area of positive egalitarianism or proper egalitarianism. But I think we make a category mistake when we apply that willy-nilly to every other area. Why does it follow that we should have an equal right to vote in the political process? Voting in a political process is not a negative freedom, it is a positive freedom, and it is an aspect of wealth. We don't say that everyone has an equal right to vote in IBM shares; it depends upon how many IBM shares they bought. If we look upon the polity as a voluntary organization, we must recognize the legitimacy for unequal votes.

Now with regard to these ten people on the island, I don't agree that there is a unique decision and that it must be a lottery. I think a lottery is one possibility, but the overriding principle would be whatever the people voluntarily agree upon. That would be what ...

**Voice** Unanimous?

**Walter Block** Whatever they agreed to unanimously. I don't think you would say that it must be a lottery. It could be some other form of agreement.

Now, there is a statement on page 1 of the Gastil and Lindsay paper that a free society may be taken to be a society with no rules at all. I think that this is a travesty of what freedom means. A free society means that a person's property rights are respected—that's what a free society means. Not that there are *no* rules; that's just chaos.

Now, I want to take issue with Armen on the question of survivability. I don't think that survivability has any positive value in moral analysis. For example, I yearn for a society where no murder is committed, and yet this is not survivable, it is not likely, it is not politically feasible and it has never happened. The question Armen might ask in response is, why talk about it if it is not likely? I think the answer is because that sets us toward the proper goal. Whether it is survivable or not is, I think, only of secondary importance. The much more major importance is, does it uphold rights and justice?

**Michael Parkin** I would like to go back to the much belaboured topic of majority voting, and back to the island story. It seems to me that that particular example is not a very helpful one for addressing the issues. It is not helpful because the initial set up was that it was clear to all these people that they had to decide one or another of these things, and so they weren't too far away from having a unanimous position on the critical issue. Real societies that we live in and want to try to improve, typically have as their major problem not deciding how they will do something that all are agreed can only be done by collective decision but choosing which things will be on the collective list and which things will be left on the private list. It is figuring out how that allocation will be made that is the difficult choice. I am not clear how it can be done. I *am* clear that if we could do it, and if we could have the list of things that could be done collectively, we would probably be in much less disagreement about whether we used majority as a method of delivering the actual answer, because we have already settled the really big issue as to whether or not the things about which the majority were making decisions were things that we all agreed were legitimate things for the majority or some other collective device to be choosing on.

The really tough problem is how we ought to form constitutions to sort out these allocations of decision-making power. I would like to hear the philosophers and the people who think about these things much more deeply than I do talk about that approach. I don't know whether we have to leave that to Armen's armies or some other procedure, or whether there is a trick that was learned in Philadelphia in 1776 or in some other time when the Bill of Rights was drafted—some trick that will work. I am simply agnostic and have nothing to offer on that.

Just one final point that came up concerning the statistics, the data and the regressions. I think it's very interesting to note that all our fears about the weight majority voting is getting in the political rights issue is reinforced by the data, even though the two series—political and civil liberties—may have a high correlation. We can't tell that directly from the data reported here.

A secondary point, once you control for the civil liberties that we think we can make some sense of there's not much left for this other variable to do. It's not doing any work, which suggests that it is a redundant classification.

**Peter Bauer** A few remarks about the survival of societies. Hindu society has survived for centuries, even millennia, in a largely unchanged form. Most of us here would not like many of its characteristics. Yet collapse of a society may inflict so much suffering that we may wish for its survival even in the face of undesirable characteristics.

Gordon raised the question of the division of societies into capitalist and socialist categories. But many societies are largely custom-dominated. The extent and strength of customs differ and vary, but classification solely in terms of capitalist and socialist societies can be misleading. This applies in much of Asia and Africa.

Two practical questions in connection with majority rule. First, what is the unit within which you count majority? For example, is it Ireland as a whole or Northern Ireland? Second, how do you assess or compute votes?

In Britain there are single-member constituencies, a system which brings very different results from proportional representation. Thus, apart from basic philosophical issues, there are practical matters also to consider.

**Milton Friedman** I want mostly to say that the notion that because each person has equal weight implies majority rule is, I think, an utter fallacy. All that each person has equal weight implies is that nobody has a right to violate anybody else's rights. And it really implies unanimity about such questions. They may be unanimous that they are going to use majoriιy rule, but it is an utter non sequitur to convert "each person has equal weight" to "majority rule"; it doesn't follow. That leaves you absolutely in the dilemma that if 51 percent of the people vote to kill the other 49 percent, that's okay. You cannot get out of that by saying you are going to serve many gods at once. What you are trying to do is to say you are going to serve many gods at once, and it seems to me that ultimately you can only serve one god.

**Alan Walters** A lot of our discussion wavers around between basic voting rules and other very pragmatic things like the selection of variables. It seems to me it is a mistake to mix up those two. When we are talking about the ideal constitution, we generally talk about unanimity. But what happens if you don't get unanimity? You can have millions of decisions, and you would never get unanimity on any one. Therefore, unanimity cannot be the thing by which you will, in fact, decide anything.

But getting down to the pragmatic side, look at a list of variables as indicators of liberty. How many people are in jail? Those are people being deprived of freedom. You can take them as a fraction of the population over some given age. One has to count gulags as well as jails with bars. But I think that one can get pretty close to the truth on that.

And the second element that you can argue about a bit, but I would say in terms of judging what I would consider the freedom of a society, I think it relevant to know how many people die from violence, whether that violence is publicly imposed or privately imposed. It seems to me when you feel yourself at risk of violence, that is a severe infringement on freedom. We can get data on the victims of violence in a wide range of different societies. This ought to be the focus in some of these quantitative studies.

**Gordon Tullock** I want to talk about the Constitution. I should say that your lottery system has been seriously suggested. Professionally, I spend

much of my time worrying about voting methods. To confuse people completely, I will say that I myself would prefer demand revealing.

But the point that I want to make is that we do have a wide collection of ways of integrating people's preferences to get something in the way of a collective decision. Whether it's a collective preference doesn't, I think, have anything much to do with freedom. It may be the best thing that we can do. In fact, I have hopes that we can do better.

I wish you people would stop talking about majority voting because I do not regard that necessarily as the be all and end all of this thing. For one thing, to take an obvious case, the most common voting group in the United States votes by unanimity—it is a jury—and it does decide very important matters. But anyway, I don't terribly like majority rule. But there is one country in the world that has a specific provision in its constitution that says a majority vote can override anything, and which regularly and consistently enforces that position, and that country is Switzerland. Now it is very hard to argue that you are in great danger when you enter Switzerland. And speaking as somebody who has looked into these things, I myself think that widespread use of direct voting on issues, in spite of the California experience, is an improvement. It makes it very, very difficult to set up a complicated logrolling bundle if right after you get it passed your legislature there is going to be a popular referendum. Historically, pure democracies have been quite tolerant of differences of opinion and so forth. They tend to be quite inefficient because the average voter is badly informed. But they are not particularly oppressive.

But the real problem here is a deeper one and that is that we have no idea of how to design a constitution so that it is self-enforcing. If you are going to restrict the government—who is going to enforce the restrictions? Well, it always turns out, part of the government. For some obscure reason the Supreme Court is not regarded as part of the government by most people who offer that rule. What we actually have in the United States is a system under which lines of authority are extremely unclear, and there are terrific fights in Washington. Over time, it is very hard to argue that they have been, strictly speaking, enforcing the Bill of Rights. In fact, it is not even clear that the Fourteenth Amendment was ever properly ratified, let alone the more obvious difficulties.

**Raymond Gastil** There have been a lot of very strange suggestions around the table that somehow we are dealing with an abstract system of majority rule. In fact all systems of majority rule (and we are dealing with real systems) have limitations on them of all kinds. Switzerland, for example, has all kinds of limitations on majority rule. It is split up into cantons and local communities—you can't change that, you can't change the jurisdictional layout. The majority in Switzerland is more constrained that any other one country in the world. But that is true of the United States, too. Majorities are tremendously constrained by other aspects of the society.

Now when we talk about civil liberties and political rights, these two are in balance with one another and neither one, in fact, in our judgement, could really exist without the balancing mechanism of the other. I'll get back to Milton's "one god" later.

**Tibor Machan** Back to Switzerland, it is true that it is a federalist system, and as far as the majority of Swiss citizens is concerned, they are very restricted in their power. But in communes and cantons there is a great deal of majoritarianism. You can make all sorts of rules that intrude on your fellow human beings, and indeed I have argued, somewhat casually, in an article in *Reason* recently that this famous "sourness" of the Swiss has something to do with the fact that they are always afraid that their next meeting is going to result in some restriction upon them, and they are not very friendly to each other, because they are always in a state of fear. And living there for one year has in fact confirmed this view. Swiss citizens themselves complain about how they are worried about next door neighbours because of majoritarianism. But it is not the kind of majoritarianism that I think you had in mind, namely that of the whole country. There are some measures on which the federal system invokes majority rule. For example, four times they ruled against changing to Daylight Savings with the rest of Europe. After the fourth time, the government simply decided to change the time anyway! (Laughter) So they are sort of nice to them. It's like joining the United Nations. Many Swiss citizens predict that after the fourth time they reject joining the United Nations, their government will join anyway. So there is a bit of a mythology about Switzerland.

Now, I want to say something to Gordon again about constitutional restrictions. If I promise to meet you, obviously I can violate the promise, but there are certain sanctions about my violating that promise which are much stronger than if I simply say I might meet you tomorrow, but I don't show up. Well, you know, I said "might" and I was careful in my language, and so I didn't, and that was included in "might." But if I say I *will* and I don't, then I need a great deal more excuse.

Similarly, a constitution can be written with a great many restrictions which of course can be overturned, but there is a certain pain associated with overturning them, a certain kind of violating a contract almost, except of course there is not an outside enforcer. But the separation of powers, which is an interesting and ingenious mechanism for keeping the government somewhat honest within itself, is a way to keep people to those restrictions, and not just have them as a matter of periodic consensus. And I grant that you cannot guarantee that restrictions on democratic rule will be maintained, but I think to write them down and have them held up and celebrated every Fourth of July and things like that is a valuable support mechanism. To go against them then would be a major catastrophic event in that kind of political institution.

**Gordon Tullock** In the first place, I think you are wrong about the Swiss constitution. It is certainly true that if nobody bothers to force an election on such a bill, it could go through. But there is, I assure you, a specific provision in the Swiss federal constitution. In 1848 they had a revolution, the purpose of which was to impose the American constitution. And having won the revolution, they decided they would *read* the American constitution and discovered judicial review. This horrified them, so they put this specific provision in to make clear that it wouldn't happen in Switzerland. Switzerland has many fine characteristics, and this is one of the funnier stories. The other is that in the early days of the Swiss federation the secretary of the treasury used to go down every Friday and physically count the treasury.

**Ingemar Stahl** Peter's paper mentioned the concept of positive and negative rights first discussed by Berlin. I think something like that would be very good to include here. If one goes through your civil liberty rights, from a logical standpoint and even from an economic/social standpoint they are quite different. Most of these rights are what my paper calls "individual immunities." Government shall not do a lot of things toward individuals that change their position in certain ways.

Another type of rights described here are individual powers—individual liberties or privileges. An individual *may* do certain things, like start a new business or try to interfere with others through trade unions or whatever it might be.

There is a third type of right indicated by your 25th point, freedom from gross socio-economic inequality, which seems a little bit like all the service rights included in most declarations of rights. These represent a claim from individuals that government shall do different things, like providing free education or whatever it might be.

You say all these are civil rights or civil liberties, but it is obvious that they are of quite different characters. I think you could categorize them in other ways. It is very important to keep in mind that most of these rights are of the type which put restrictions on political rights, namely immunities from what government can do. If you had the unanimity rule as the basic principle, many of these civil rights would be redundant.

**Tibor Machan**  One of the things we haven't been talking about this time, and especially in the last session, is the connection that I think is held to be rather significant between what we call liberty or freedom and individual responsibility. I think it might be a nice thing to reflect on that now and then. After all, one of the interesting things about human beings is that they are deciding agents, and some connection ought to be preserved in a good society between what they think and what they will do. And to the extent that this connection is severed, I think that is a flawed society.

**Raymond Gastil**  I wanted to refer to a couple of points. Positive and negative rights, to take your point, is something we considered for a number of years. I used to always make the distinction between the civil rights of the Survey as being primarily negative, whereas many people wanted to add on certain positive rights. But I later found that it is much more difficult in the practical world to distinguish between positive and negative rights. For example, police powers, which are often necessary to enforce many civil liberties as well as to defend the civil liberties, have been thought of as both positive and negative. Voting is a positive right rather than a negative right, and so on. So I think it is more difficult than often considered to distinguish adequately between positive and negative rights.

I also wanted to go back to Milton's point about only serving one god. It seems to me that it is a mistake in philosophy or political science or whatever to assume that you can set up one principle and say everything else has to be derived from this. It seems to me that a much more realistic approach is to have a plurality of principles you see balanced against one another. I have often made the point in the Survey, as perhaps you have noticed, that without certain kinds of civil liberties, you can't really have a legitimate majority. In other words, if the majority was oppressing the minority to such an extent the minority does not feel it can express itself, develop new ideas and so forth, then very quickly the actual ability of the society to receive new ideas and decide upon the alternatives becomes destroyed by the majority's oppression. So that oppression beyond a certain point destroys the possibility of the majority itself being a legitimate expression of the views of the society as a whole, because the society as a whole no longer has informational input into it to be able to adequately decide upon the issues before it. So I think we have to always think in terms of some balance of those two issues.

**Peter Bauer** I have much sympathy with Armen in focusing on such fundamentals as the number of people in jail or the number of victims of violence. But there is a major difficulty in this area. It is possible to have nobody in jail and yet for there to be a completely oppressed society, because nobody dares to rise against the rulers. The most effective naval blockade is one which never catches a ship because they are afraid of leaving port. The same applies to some extent to victims of violence. There are fewer victims of violence in East Germany than in the United States, but this does not mean it is a freer society.

There was once a society which operated by the unanimity rule. That was 17th and 18th century Poland, where parliamentary decisions had to be unanimous. The society failed to survive.

Finally, pure democracies have by no means always been tolerant. There are many examples to the contrary, from 5th century Athens to 20th century America.


**Assar Lindbeck** When we say that democracy means that everybody should be given the same weight in the political system, that can be interpreted many different ways. Suppose you have a society where 51 percent have the same opinion on all issues and 49 percent have their same opinion on all issues. Then you have two different voting procedures. One is that there is majority rule in every case, so that 51 percent decide on all issues in society. Another voting rule says that we let 51 percent decide in 51 percent of the issues, and the 49 percent in 49 percent of the issues. That is close to Mr. Friedman's lottery. You take a lottery on every issue with that weight: 51:49. That would mean that the 49 percent would have considerable influence on decision making in proportion to their numbers, instead of having 51 percent deciding *all* issues in society. Which system gives everybody the same weight in society? I think it is the latter rather than the former, which is one of many ways of saying that majority rule has very considerable drawbacks as a system of reflecting preferences.

# PART TWO

## CASE STUDIES IN THE RELATIONSHIP BETWEEN POLITICAL, ECONOMIC AND CIVIL FREEDOMS

# Chapter 4

# Economic, Civil, and Political Freedoms: The Cases of Singapore and Hong Kong

# Alvin Rabushka

## INTRODUCTION

A tale of two cities, Singapore and Hong Kong, is the opposite of Charles Dickens' *Bleak House*. Once upon a time, two islands stood barren, with nary a soul or house upon them. In Southeast Asia on the equator, Sir Thomas Stamford Raffles acquired the tropical island of Singapore in 1819 from Holland in exchange for Britain's territorial claims in the Dutch East Indies. He declared it a free port, setting in motion its history as an important trading centre. Captain Henry Elliot, twenty years later, seized Hong Kong from China to provide a secure base for British traders. Reflecting the laissez-faire sentiments of the day, he declared the island a free port, which developed as a trading emporium between East and West. Both colonies suffered severe wartime devastation under Japanese rule. Yet both rebounded, attaining levels of prosperity that are the envy of the developing world.

Singapore is a global city-state, which boldly implemented ambitious development policies and achieved remarkable economic growth with social stability. In the twenty years since it became an independent state in 1965, its per capita gross national product increased from \$470 to approximately \$6,800. With the exception of an economic contraction during 1985, Singapore generally maintained rapid economic growth, full employment, high productivity, and low inflation rates.

The British Crown Colony of Hong Kong was equally successful. Hong Kong represents the single best example of the market-economy model of development. Hong Kong overcame as many obstacles as any nation ever faced and received virtually no foreign aid in the process. Its land area is almost resourceless and consists largely of unproductive granitic rock formations. It suffers a population density that ranks it among the world's most overpopulated areas per square mile, and it is dependent on imports for its food, raw materials and all capital equipment. Located thousands of miles away from its most important markets, Hong Kong has not had full control over population movements across its borders; and it is ruled by a colonial government that critics regard as obsolete, antiquated, and inconsistent with the principles of independence, self-rule and human dignity.

Despite these formidable obstacles, the rate of growth of the Hong Kong economy was so rapid for so long that it came to have an almost certain inevitability. In 1948, per capita income stood at $180. Hong Kong's post-war transformation from a British trading post to an industrial economy was so dramatic that by 1985 per capita income surpassed $6,000, despite a severe economic shock during 1982-1984. In September 1982, China announced it would recover sovereignty over Hong Kong on July 1, 1997, when Britain's 99-year lease over Hong Kong's New Territories expires. The prospect that China intended to replace British rule sent the Colony's financial, stock, and property markets into a sharp tailspin, which reflected an initial loss of confidence in Hong Kong's future. Real growth recovered by 1984 after Hong Kong weathered a currency crisis, capital outflow, declining investment, eroding public finances, and all the uncertainties attending the transition to communist rule in 1997.

The outline of this paper is as follows. First I describe the general concepts of economic, civil and political freedoms as they are used in this paper. Then, I present brief accounts of each city-state. Starting from their historical backgrounds, I review the development of their economic, civil, and political systems. In the final section, I analyze the links between economic, civil, and political freedoms for these two cases.

## CONCEPTS AND MEASURES OF FREEDOM

For working purposes, the data published in the annual January-February issue of *Freedom House* supply clear rankings on civil liberties and political rights for most nations of the world. Countries are ranked on a seven-point scale from "most free," a score of 1, to "partly free," (3-5) to "not free," a score of 7.

Civil liberties encompass freedom of the press, court protection of the individual, free expression of personal opinion, and free choice in occupation, education, religion, residence, and so on. The opposite extreme is pervading fear, little independent expression even in private, and swift imprisonment and execution by a police state. In 1984, Singapore ranked 5 and Hong Kong ranked 2. Both Singapore and Hong Kong have sustained these exact ratings since 1975. It is important to note that Hong Kong, a British Crown Colony, is only one notch below the highest rating, whereas Singapore, an independent nation since 1965, is two notches from the bottom.

Political rights range from the presence of a fully competitive electoral process, to a limited role for opposition parties within a predominantly one-party state, to the complete absence of free elections, or the rule of despots unconstrained by public opinion or popular tradition. In 1984, Singapore ranked 4 and Hong Kong ranked 4. Compared with a decade earlier, Singapore improved one notch from 5 in 1982 and Hong Kong declined one notch from 3, the downgrading occurring in 1980. No explanation was given in the accompanying text to explain the reevaluation of Hong Kong's rating by the author. Since the competitive nature of the electoral process is the key to high scores on political rights, the election of an opposition leader to Singapore's parliament in December 1981 in a predominantly one-party state warrants some improvement in its ranking. However, colonial Hong Kong, which has seen a considerable expansion of elections throughout the 1980s to encompass the Urban Council, District Boards, rural Regional Councils, and even its previously fully-appointed Legislative Council, mysteriously fell in the ranks. Hong Kong deserves better, much better!

*Freedom House* provides no comparable concept, measure or ranking of economic freedoms that might be compared with civil liberties and political rights. A comparable treatment would require the analyst to develop a variety of indicators and assemble the requisite data to score countries on an overall measure of economic freedom.

A good approximation to the attributes of economic freedom appears in *Free to Choose*. In their best-seller, Milton and Rose Friedman propose adding an economic bill of rights to the American Constitution to preserve economic liberty.[1] Seven suggested amendments include: (1) a tax or spending limit on the federal share of national income; (2) no duties on imports or exports; (3) no wage and price controls; (4) no government-imposed occupational licensure; (5) all direct taxes must be assessed at a flat rate; (6) a money supply growth rule to insure sound money; and (7) an inflation-protection amendment. To these we might add such provisions as free movement of labour and capital, lack of exchange controls, proprietary rights, free entry and exit in every line of industry, and absence of state monopolies for procurement or distribution, some of which are implied in the Friedman bill.

## SINGAPORE

Singapore, "the Lion City," is an island, city-state economy, located on the equator.[2] About 77 percent of its 2.5 million people are Chinese; Malays constitute just under 15 percent and Indians just over 6 percent.[3] Its land area of 600 square kilometres is largely devoid of natural resources, and its people import the bulk of their food and raw materials. Singapore's major assets are a strategic location on the trade routes connecting Europe and Japan, an excellent harbour that does not require periodic desilting, a diligent workforce, and an honest, efficient government inherited from British colonial days.

Founded in 1819 by Sir Thomas Stamford Raffles, an entrepreneurial employee of the East India Company, Singapore soon became a well-known port and marketplace in Southeast Asia as well as the centre of British economic interests in the region. Raffles grafted a policy of economic liberalism onto a strategic location. By making Singapore a free port, he broke the Dutch trade monopoly in the region. Trade became the major economic activity, and British influence spread over the entire Malay peninsula.

For the next century-and-a-half, the island's rulers adhered to its founder's vision of making Singapore a great emporium resting on the Victorian doctrine of free trade. Successive colonial governors zealously nurtured the port, maintained a lean and efficient administration, and allowed merchants and bankers full scope for the exercise of their talents—a nineteenth century laissez-faire approach to economic affairs. Taxes were held to a minimum, and no harbour dues were levied as these could harm shipping and commerce. Indeed, voluntary contributions of private citizens, not government taxes, financed the construction of the island's first lighthouse. It was government policy to avoid monopolies and encourage competition to assure efficient business practices and low costs.

Politically, Singapore moved from a trading post under the control of the East India Company to a British Crown Colony in 1867. It was integrated into a broader political unit known as the Straits Settlements, which encompassed the British possessions of Penang and Malacca. It developed close economic ties with the nine states of peninsular Malaya that were under British influence. It adopted a financial system which pegged the Singapore dollar to the pound sterling, in which the local bank note issues enjoyed 100 percent backing in sterling. Its steady growth as a trading centre and home to British regional interests was interrupted when Japan occupied the strategic port during World War II. The British returned in 1946, but Singapore had a new status as a separate Crown Colony, since Penang and Malacca were joined into a broader Federation of Malaya.

Political independence was inevitable, and elections were first held in 1947. Singapore gradually moved to internal self-government in 1959 when Lee Kuan Yew, Singapore's first Prime Minister, and his People's Action Party (PAP) took control. The PAP attained full independence through a merger with Malaysia in 1963. However, this merger was shortlived. Singapore was expelled from Malaysia in 1965, when it became an independent, sovereign nation.

Apart from having to rehabilitate a war-ravaged economy, the immediate post-war years placed three major obstacles in Singapore's path to prosperity. First, a communist insurgency in Malaya between 1948 and 1960 spilled over into urban Singapore in the form of labour-union agitation. Labour unrest would complicate any plan to encourage industrialization. Political stability was a *sine qua non* of development. Second, as rising protectionism brought stagnation to entrepôt trade during the 1950s, unemployment threatened to become a serious domestic problem. Third, shortly after independence in 1965, Britain announced plans to withdraw its armed forces stationed in Singapore at an accelerated pace. Since British military spending accounted for almost 20 percent of the gross national product and 6 percent of employment, accelerated withdrawal threatened to create both a severe recession and a defence vacuum.

Lee Kuan Yew and the PAP proposed a political union with Malaysia, which would provide a good-sized domestic market for an industrial strategy of import substitution. Expulsion from the union with Malaysia in 1965, on political grounds by the government in Kuala Lumpur, destroyed the import-substitution strategy, since after 1965 Singapore-based goods faced a tariff wall throughout the rest of Malaysia. Producing for the smaller domestic market in Singapore alone could not generate enough new jobs. Factories which had been established with the hope of a larger market faced excess capacity. By the mid-1950s, the British had largely defeated the local communist insurgency in Malaya, thus restoring overall stability to the region. The PAP set about creating jobs through a policy of industrialization and shifted from exclusive reliance on the entrepôt trade that historically had been the foundation of the economy.

Independent Singapore inherited the free port and free-trade policies of its colonial past. Until the end of the 1950s, when entrepôt trade was the mainstay of the economy, the only major import and excise taxes were on petroleum, liquor, and tobacco, levied for revenue purposes. During the import-substitution phase of industrialization from 1959 through 1967, tariffs and quotas were imposed to protect nascent industries.

To assist local entrepreneurs and to stimulate the development of import-substituting activities, the government adopted legislation in 1959 exempting approved "pioneer industries" from the 40 percent company profits tax for five years and generous depreciation allowances. It temporarily abandoned the principles of free trade in favour of modest import tariffs and quotas. The government actively directed and participated in the economy. It created an Economic Development Board in 1961 to grant loans to approved companies and to take equity positions. The Board was also responsible for planning, construction, and operation of industrial estates.

External adversity provided a golden opportunity for Lee Kuan Yew and the PAP. The withdrawal of British military forces freed-up a large piece of land that the government converted into a major industrial estate, providing choice facilities to foreign investors. Deprivation of a common economic market with Malaysia forced a change in policy away from import substitution and toward manufacture for world markets. A candid internal assessment of the poor performance of highly protected "pioneer" industries, along with the recognition that import protectionism damaged the entrepôt trade and inhibited the development of new exports, reinforced the reality of a shrinking domestic market. The government also got control of the labour movement with restrictive legislation on labour activists and union activity.

### Economic Policy After Independence

After 1965, as a new, independent city-state with a sharply contracted domestic market, Singapore shifted quickly to the strategy of export-oriented industrialization. The government turned to already experienced foreign companies to invest and manufacture for export. Adding to the "pioneer status" legislation, companies were given tax incentives to export. Other measures permitted total foreign ownership of Singapore firms, free immigration of necessary business personnel and remittance of profits, no controls on capital movements, favourable tax provisions for research and development in high-technology industries, provision of readily-available factory sites accompanied by many amenities, and subsidies for manpower training programs. Singapore's government gave foreign and local businessmen a large measure of economic freedom.

To summarize, Singapore's economic policy adopted the most typical features of the capitalist system, including private ownership, Western commercial law, encouraging foreign and domestic investment, and, where possible, adhering to the practice of free competition to attain the fastest economic growth. Singapore's rulers emphasized the importance of economic production, making as much profit as possible, and only then to consider the problem of the distribution of wealth. Economic rewards were based largely on individual ability and performance.

## Labour Regulation

A second target of economic policy was a peaceful labour movement. To secure this aim, in 1966, the PAP enacted legislation that prohibited strikes unless approved by a majority of union members in secret ballot, required registration of all unions, and forbad noncitizens and criminals from working in union activities. Further legislation in 1968 placed the promotion, transfer, recruitment, retrenchment, and assignment of tasks of workers within the sole prerogative of management—these subjects were held to be outside the scope of labour-management negotiations. The Act also encouraged collective agreements of three to five years duration.

The results were spectacular. In 1961, 116 strikes cost Singapore 410,000 lost man-days of work. The communist grip on labour unions was broken in 1964. After 1968, only seven strikes erupted in the next three years. Days lost to industrial unrest fell to 1,011 in 1977 and completely disappeared in 1978.

In effect the government set up a system of wage nonbargaining. With acquiescent unions—35 Members of Parliament were placed in the National Trades Union Congress in 1979—wage levels are decreed annually on the recommendation of a tripartite National Wages Council (NWC) composed of employers, unions, and government representatives. The NWC was set up in 1972 to recommend orderly wage changes to prevent wages from rising too rapidly and, by pricing Singapore goods out of world markets, slow down investment and economic growth.

Until 1978, increases in productivity generally exceeded wage rises. In 1979, as part of a conscious policy to use labour more efficiently (given a labour shortage and stringent immigration controls), the government raised the average wage of a semi-skilled worker by 18 percent. Wages rose 19 percent in 1980 and 20 percent in 1981. The high-wage policy, which was supposed to remain in force for three years to make up for wages having lagged behind productivity in the 1970s, was continued right up to 1985, and ran well ahead of productivity increases. Finally, the economy turned sour in 1985. Singapore's official estimate of economic growth was -1.7 percent in 1985 and is projected at -2.0 percent for 1986.

Bad results required drastic measures. The response to a contracting economy, the first in Singapore's post-independence period, and an excessive wage-cost problem was a two-year freeze on wages as expressed by annual NWC guidelines.[4]

## Government Intervention

The laissez-faire policies of the colonial era gave way to a more activist and interventionist approach taken by the PAP government. Apart from severely curtailing the freedom of organized labour, the PAP government designed, directed, and participated in a bold, comprehensive industrialization programme. Earlier we noted the establishment of the Economic Development Board in 1961, which acted as the overall agency for economic development under the Ministry of Finance. The Board initiated projects and financed them in the form of loans and equity participation. It played a crucial role in the 1960s in the promotion of industrialization. The growth of manufacturing led to the creation of separate agencies during 1968-1969 for the management of industrial estates, financing of industrial development, promotion of industrial exports, and even provision of shipping services. These agencies are the Jurong Town Corporation, the Development Bank of Singapore, the International Trading Company, and the Neptune Orient line.

The government established a number of wholly owned and partially owned companies. The largest is Singapore Airlines. Other industries with substantial government ownership include trading, transportation, communications, finance, construction, shipbuilding and repairing, electronics, and engineering. By mid-1975, the government had equity participation in 52 enterprises, with a capital investment of $173 million.

Government equity investment must be kept in perspective. Total paid-up capital of foreign-controlled manufacturing firms reached $583 million by 1973; domestic equity capital stood at about one-third of that level. Total accumulated foreign investment in 1975 reached $1,426 million. The development of a manufacturing industry for export in Singapore occurred predominantly in the subsidiaries of foreign companies, which substantially exceeded the government's participation in industries and business enterprises.

In 1981, the government set up a high-powered investment corporation for the purpose of buying up or buying into high-technology western companies. Its operating fund, derived from Singapore's extensive foreign exchange reserves, was in the billions of dollars. At that time, Singapore's rulers envisaged an even greater role for the state sector in the island's economic future. By 1984 the government directly owned or controlled 450 companies and indirectly about 40 more through its statutory boards. Total paid-up capital of the 450 companies was $1.1 billion. Fixed assets were $8.1 billion, shareholders' funds totalled $2.9 billion, and turnover in these companies was $3.5 billion, equivalent to 24.6 percent of the 1983 gross domestic product.[5]

When the economic bubble burst in 1985, the government set up an economic committee under the direction of Prime Minister Lee Kuan Yew's son, Lee Hsien Loong. Its report, issued in 1986, recommended that Singapore reduce government regulation of business and excessive government-imposed costs. It blamed the island's economic malaise on high taxes and government intervention. The report stressed that individual entrepreneurship and private capital should be assigned the primary role in the development process over the corporate state and public capital in order to restore the economy to a high-growth path.

## Public Finance[6]

It has been the policy of Singapore's government to concentrate on trade rather than foreign aid. Accordingly, Singapore has no net foreign debt. External assets exceed liabilities.

Since independence, public spending has remained in a narrow range, usually below 25 percent of gross national product, despite a sharp increase in defence spending following the withdrawal of British forces.

On average, direct taxes (largely income and property taxes) supply one-third of government revenue, indirect taxes about one-sixth, the sale of government goods and services about 8 percent, and investment income and miscellaneous receipts about 12 percent, which represent earnings on Singapore's official surpluses, largely external assets.

Shortly after attaining internal self-government in 1959, Singapore's leaders stretched the top marginal income tax rate from 30 to 55 percent by 1961 on taxable income exceeding US$30,000. Since per capita income was below $1,000, only a handful of the population paid high rates. But Singapore's leaders remained conscious of the disincentive effects that would confront its citizens as growth pushed the middle class into high tax brackets. Accordingly, they raised the threshold for the top rate from $30,000 in 1977 to beyond $100,000 by 1977. In 1979 the government announced a series of rate reductions that slashed the top rate to 40 percent in 1985, which bites at a threshold exceeding $300,000, thus bringing the top marginal tax rate in line with the corporate rate. With per capita income of $6,800 in 1985, most Singaporeans faced an effective tax rate (disregarding personal allowances) of 10 percent.

Singapore also imposes a compulsory savings scheme—a tax—known as the Central Provident Fund (CPF), to which most employed residents of Singapore and all employers are subject. Established in 1955, the CPF initially imposed a 5 percent payroll tax on both employer and employee. The combined payroll tax rose, by 1980, to 37 percent, and reached the staggering sum of 50 percent by 1985. The sum is withheld and put into the national pension fund. The fund, in turn, invests its receipts in treasury securities, which are issued by, and the proceeds subsequently held by, the Monetary Authority of Singapore (MAS). Proceeds of these treasury-debt sales are then funneled into development expenditures and loans to statutory boards, but most is invested overseas.

Conceptually, CPF funds can be treated as public sector assets which are held by the MAS. In effect, the CPF acts as an arm of the MAS, withdrawing liquidity (via the payroll tax) from the domestic economy. Proceeds of government securities, "borrowed" from the CPF, are initially deposited with the MAS, which converts these funds into gold and foreign currencies, which appear as assets on the MAS balance sheet. In essence, the CPF is a mechanism for national savings that the government can direct into infrastructure, public housing, and external assets.

Individual contributions to the fund are credited with annual interest, typically exceeding the inflation rate but below the market rate of interest. Funds may be withdrawn before retirement to purchase an apartment in a government housing estate.

A declining economy in 1985 prompted the government to reduce the CPF rate for employers from 25 to 15 percent for two years in order to reduce wage costs.[7] It also announced reductions in both the corporate profits tax from 40 to 33 percent and the top individual marginal rate to 33 percent. The PAP has consciously sought to remove any tax disincentives to hard work. The property tax sector received a temporary fix instead of the permanent rate reduction from 30 to 16 percent that this distressed sector had sought. In general, post-1985 policy is concentrating on reducing fiscal surpluses, shifting savings to the private sector to encourage indigenous investment (much of Singapore's savings has been invested outside Singapore by the MAS), lowering income and payroll taxes, privatizing some public-sector businesses, removing regulatory rigidities, and giving greater play to market forces.

## Social Construction and Control[8]

The PAP government has remained extremely active in such social programmes as public housing, community development, and communications and education. When Singapore attained internal self-government in 1959, the PAP government accorded the housing problem top priority. It established the Housing Development Board (HDB) in 1960 to undertake large-scale public housing programmes, slum clearance and urban renewal. In 1975, reflecting Singapore's rising prosperity, the government set up another body known as the Housing and Urban Development Company (HUDC) to build apartments for middle-income groups. The government has willingly met the funding requests of the several housing boards for new construction.

The rentals and sale prices of HDB and HUDC units are heavily subsidized. HDB subsidies range from 44 percent for a three-room apartment to 27 percent for five-room units. Compared to private apartments, HUDC units are priced at a 50 percent discount. By March 1980, about two-thirds of Singapore's population lived in public housing estates. The government estimates that about 80-85 percent of the total population will live in high-rise public housing estates by 1992, when the urban redevelopment programme is completed. This will be a unique achievement for a non-communist country.

In addition, the Boards have the power to acquire compulsorily, through the Lands Acquisition Act of 1966, any private land it needs for housing development. Between 1960 and 1979, the government's share of land ownership rose from 44 percent to 67 percent. The government is also empowered to acquire lands to prevent speculation in the private property market. It typically pays below-market prices.[9]

Apart from public housing, the government has developed over 250 community centres. The PAP employs these centres as powerful channels for mobilizing mass participation in community development and support of government policies. The first centres were set up in the early 1950s when Singapore was still a British colony, but control over the community centres was decentralized. On obtaining power in 1959, the PAP disbanded all management committees of the centres and put all community organizations under the control of the Department of Social Welfare. In 1960, the PAP government enacted the People's Association Ordinance. The Prime Minister serves as chairman, and all management committees of community centres are recommended by Members of Parliament and appointed by the Prime Minister.

The PAP government has retained tight control of education and the mass media since 1959. It nationalized all schools and colleges in Singapore and put them under control of the Ministry of Education. All mass media are under the control or guidance of the government.

The PAP government has used the mass media, especially the press, radio and television, to promote and cultivate a national Singaporean identity out of the diverse Chinese, Malay, Indian, and Eurasian ethnic loyalties. Newspapers are privately owned, and are printed in English, Chinese, Malay, Tamil, and Malayalam. While reflecting the views of the public, the press generally supports government policies.

Government guidance and regulation of the press and other instruments of communication seriously encroaches on Western norms of press and speech freedom.[10] The PAP government believes that Singapore's unique social, cultural and political situation justifies the application of boundaries for the freedom of the press. Newspapers must renew their licences with the government every three years. While there is no formal censorship mechanism, the newspapers adopt a cautious approach and usually exercise self-censorship to make sure that their editorial policies are in line with national policies.

Self-censorship became customary after 1971, when the PAP government took a series of measures against the press. First, it arrested the four senior executives of *Nanyang Siang Pau*, one of the two largest Chinese dailies, on a charge of having launched a deliberate campaign to stir up Chinese racial emotions. It then took disciplinary measures against the managing editor of the *Eastern Sun*, one of the two largest English dailies, accusing him of receiving a start-up loan from communist sources, and subsequently closed down the paper. It later shut down the *Singapore Herald*, which was distinguished by its slightly more critical editorials on government policy. In 1980, the PAP government temporarily suspended permits for two Chinese newspapers, *Min Pao* and *Shin Min Daily*, until the publishers pledged in their appeals to modify their editorial policies.

Reported cases of self-censorship include withholding from circulation an issue of the *Far Eastern Economic Review* by its distributor in March 1977 for fear that some replies by the *Review*'s editor to certain charges by the Singapore government might constitute libel. Similarly, an issue of *Time* magazine in August 1977 contained 26 blacked-out words in a story regarding alleged government muzzling of the press in Singapore.

In general, the Newspaper and Printing Presses Act (1974) authorizes the government to grant and withdraw licences for the operation of printing presses in Singapore. A Board of Film Censors may ban films for such reasons as glorification of gangsterism, violence, crime, hippies, free love, promiscuity, homosexuality, lesbianism, incest, permissiveness, religious prejudice, racism, and political reasons. The Undesirable Publication Act (1967) prohibits the importation, sale or circulation of foreign publications considered contrary to the public interest, which includes those that may be politically, morally, religiously, or ethnically offensive.

The government fully controls and operates radio and television services, which, therefore, always respond to government calls for promoting national identity. Only one private cable broadcasting service, Rediffusion, is allowed to provide service. It used to receive a permit of ten years duration, but in 1980 was asked to renew its permit each year. Ostensibly the cabled broadcasting service tarried in switching from various Chinese dialects to Mandarin, which the government asserted jeopardized its national policy of promoting Mandarin.

## One-Party Dominance[11]

Under Lee Kuan Yew's leadership, the PAP government tolerated the existence, but not the effectiveness, of political competition. It explicitly withholds legal recognition from the communist party and parties associating with communists. In 1972, it extended its vigilance and scrutiny to all political parties on the grounds that no political party in Singapore may be used as a proxy by a foreign power to capture control of the country. The PAP shows no commitment to a competitive political system.

The PAP oligarchy has ruled with a benevolent hand. It has successfully delivered such political and economic goods as safety, law and order, and a rapid rise in living standards. It has, in Confucian terms, earned the "mandate of heaven." Its authoritarian, paternalistic style fits the notions of good government for people reared in the Chinese cultural tradition, who comprise three-quarters of the island's population. Confucianism stresses that good government should be based upon virtue and operate for the benefit of the people, as parents affectionately care for their children; in turn, the tradition emphasizes deference to authority and filial piety as the basis of superior-subordinate relations, which curbs tendencies to openly oppose or reject authority. The dominant one party system in Singapore is also congruent with Singapore's colonial heritage, which consisted of paternalistic British rule based on centralized authoritarian decision making and executive dominance from 1819 through 1959. Notions of democratic values and political liberalism rarely extended beyond a small number of politicized Western-educated intellectuals to the general public.

In October 1981, opposition Workers' Party leader J.B. Jeyeretnam broke the PAP's 13-year monopoly in parliament winning a by-election.[12] PAP leaders regarded his election as an aberration from their rightful political monopoly. However, the 13 percent swing against the PAP in the December 1984 general election, which returned two opposition candidates including Jeyeretnam, forced the party to take note that it was losing support, even though 77 PAP members won their contests. The televising of subsequent parliamentary debates, intended to show up the lone opposition duo, backfired. A majority of viewers polled in a newspaper survey in April 1985 revealed that 63 percent had negative feelings about PAP members. Critical letters began pouring into the newspapers, challenging government policies. The second generation of PAP leaders may have to earn its legitimacy.

## HONG KONG

Since its founding in 1841, and especially during the period of postwar British colonial rule, Hong Kong has been the world's closest approximation to a free-market, private-enterprise, capitalistic economic system.[13] Its residents have enjoyed the trading benefits of a free port, low taxes and limited government intervention in their economic and social affairs. But the British colony's post-war future was always under a cloud, regulated by the precise date of midnight, June 30, 1997—the moment Britain's 99-year lease on the New Territories (90 percent of the colony) expires. Novelist Han Suyin coined the phrase aptly describing Hong Kong as a "borrowed time, borrowed place," an entity with a perpetually uncertain future.

In 1982, Hong Kong's uncertain future leapt onto centre stage. Chinese leaders Deng Xiaoping and Zhao Ziyang firmly indicated to British prime minister, Mrs. Margaret Thatcher, during her September visit to Beijing, that China would reclaim sovereignty and administrative authority over Hong Kong on July 1, 1997. On December 19, 1984, after two years of intense negotiations, the British and Chinese governments signed a joint declaration that determined Hong Kong's political future. On July 1, 1997, Hong Kong will be reincorporated into mainland China as a Special Administrative Region. In return for the British transfer of sovereignty, China guaranteed in writing that Hong Kong would retain considerable autonomy; in particular, the territory's more than five million residents could retain their present social, economic, and legal systems for an additional 50 years through 2047.[14]

### Physical Setting, Population and Resources

Hong Kong lies inside the tropics on the Southeast coast of China, adjoining the province of Guangdong.[15] It consists of a small part of the Chinese mainland and a scattering of offshore islands, the most important of which is Hong Kong Island. By 1985, the total land area of the Colony was 1,067 square kilometres (about 410 square miles). Of the 1,067 square kilometres in the colony, 9 percent was used for farming and 74.7 percent was marginal unproductive land. Built-up urban and rural lands comprised the remaining 16.3 percent, within which most of Hong Kong's people lived and worked.[16]

Hong Kong remains one of the most densely populated places in the world.[17] The total population at the end of 1984 was 5,397,500, almost evenly balanced between males and females. The 1981 Census showed that 57 percent was born in Hong Kong; the other 43 percent was largely refugees and immigrants from other countries, mainly China. About 98 percent of the population was classified as Chinese on the basis of place of origin and language, most originating from Guangdong Province.

The British physically occupied Hong Kong in early 1841, well before the Sino-British Treaty of Nanking, signed on August 29, 1842, legally transferred sovereignty and administrative control to Her Majesty's Government.[18] By the end of 1841, the population of Hong Kong stood at about 15,000, of whom only a minority was foreigners. The great majority was Chinese people of the surrounding region, attracted to Hong Kong for its employment and commercial opportunities, despite the prevalence of tropical diseases. Captain Elliot, the de facto administrator of seized Hong Kong, announced that its Chinese residents would enjoy British protection, but would be governed by traditional law. Trade would be free of tariffs. Both economic and personal liberty were early fixtures of colonial Hong Kong.

The small Colony of Hong Kong almost entirely lacks natural resources. Its mineral wealth is negligible. Only one-seventh of its land is arable; the colony cannot, therefore, feed itself and throughout most of its history encountered difficulty in maintaining an adequate water supply, which it has remedied by building reservoirs and purchasing water from mainland China. Almost all industrial materials, capital goods, and the vast majority of foodstuffs are imported.

## Economic and Political History Since 1841

Hong Kong became a British possession in 1841 for the simple purpose of trade with China. Although the British dominated foreign trade with China since the end of the eighteenth century, conditions at Canton were unsatisfactory, reflecting the conflicting viewpoints of two different civilizations.[19]

The Chinese regarded themselves as highly civilized, with little need of foreign imports. They stringently restricted foreign traders to a clearly defined trading season, excluded family members from Chinese soil, confined the traders to a small area, forbade them from entering the city of Canton or learning Chinese, and arbitrarily varied shipping dues. Nonetheless the lucrative opium trade brought foreign free traders who hoped to get rich quickly. To stem the outflow of silver from China that financed opium imports, the Chinese emperor appointed Lin Zexu (Lin Tse-hsu) to stamp out the opium trade. He surrounded the foreign factories and compelled all foreign traders to turn over their stocks of opium. The British community retired to Macau, and then took refuge on board ships in Hong Kong harbour in summer 1839.

The British sent an expeditionary force in June 1840 to back their demands for a commercial treaty or the cession of a small island where they could live free from threats under the security of their own flag. Hostilities alternated with negotiations until the Treaty of Nanjing, signed on August 29, 1842, ceded Hong Kong Island to Britain in perpetuity. (China labelled this and subsequent treaties with Britain and other foreign powers "unequal" and therefore invalid in international law.) It also opened five Chinese ports for trade. A supplementary treaty in October 1843 granted Chinese subjects free access to Hong Kong Island for trading purposes.

Two subsequent treaties filled out the territory of British Hong Kong. The Convention of Peking in 1860, which terminated the Second Anglo-Chinese War (1856-58), ceded the Kowloon Peninsula, located directly across the harbour from Hong Kong Island, to Britain in perpetuity. The Sino-Japanese War of 1895 encouraged the British to augment their defensive position by demanding, and gaining control of, the territory north of Kowloon up to the Shum Chun River, and 235 adjacent islands. In accord with the terms in the Convention of Peking in 1898, China ceded sovereignty of these New Territories to Britain for a period of 99 years.

Colonial administration of Hong Kong followed normal British overseas practices, with a governor appointed from London assisted by nominated, not elected, Executive and Legislative Councils. British exclusivity in government gradually yielded to Chinese participation in both councils. On several occasions, local British residents pressed for self-government, but the home government rejected these demands fearing that a small European community might use self-government to take unfair advantage of the Chinese majority.

From its beginning, Hong Kong developed as an entrepôt free port, a mart and storehouse for goods in transit to Asia and the West.[20] This entrepôt activity diminished after World War II when the transition to an industrial economy took place.

Since World War II, manufacturing, largely export-oriented, light industries, became the mainstay of Hong Kong's economy, augmented by a myriad of servicing industries. Highly developed banking, insurance, and shipping systems created in the entrepôt era flourished in the 1960s, 1970s, and 1980s. In keeping with its free-port tradition, Hong Kong eschewed tariffs or other restrictions on the import of commercial goods.

## The Political Geography of Hong Kong

From the end of World War II through July 1982, Hong Kong enjoyed remarkable political and economic stability. Local Chinese did not clamour for democracy, a British-style welfare state, or political independence. Meanwhile, China resisted political encroachment on Hong Kong. What made these circumstances possible?

One answer is found in Hong Kong's political geography.[21] Hong Kong's prosperity served mainland China's developmental interests, largely through China's foreign exchange earnings arising from doing business in and with Hong Kong. Entrepreneurs from Britain and other countries benefitted from commerce in Hong Kong. Finally, the local residents, many refugees from China, found personal opportunity for economic improvement—life in Hong Kong was materially good. They did not clamour for more state intervention in their personal lives; many of them fled an oppressive communist government in order to obtain personal freedom in Hong Kong.

### China's Benefits from Hong Kong

Since the mid-1960s, receipts from Hong Kong, which ranged as high as $6 billion in 1983 alone, accounted for between 30-40 percent of China's total earnings of foreign exchange.[22] China supplied Hong Kong with about 20 percent of its imports, a wide range of inexpensive consumer goods, oil products, the bulk of its food imports, and annually increasing quantities of fresh water. It bought less in return, leaving a balance-of-trade surplus which helped finance China's development policies. In addition, Hong Kong was the clearing house for remittances to China. Local and overseas companies and individuals remitted to their relatives and business associates upwards of $100 million a year.

Hong Kong has the largest, deepest, and most modern port facilities along the China coast. It was an important redistribution centre for goods made in China to the outside world. Apart from quantifiable economic and financial benefits, Hong Kong provided China with indirect, but tangible, benefits in the form of access to Western technology and modes of business management, a convenient centre for trade contacts and financial negotiations, a training ground for thousands of Chinese technicians and service personnel, and a first-hand opportunity to observe the workings of a free market economy.

Finally, China is in the fourth millennium of its national history. Consolidating its power over the mainland and beginning the job of national economic reconstruction after 1949 were more important tasks for the communist leadership than recovering Hong Kong. The half century to 1997 is just the blink of an eye on China's time horizon. Why not let the British administration and people of Hong Kong develop the most modern city in Asia outside Japan? It would, sooner or later, fall into China's hands.

## Britain's Relationship to Hong Kong

Apart from a few scattered offshore, tax haven islands, and Gibraltar, Hong Kong became Britain's sole remaining major colony by the 1960s.

Local pressures on the British to hand over independence were missing in post-war Hong Kong. China ruled out national independence for Hong Kong as a feasible political option. China's leaders regarded sovereignty as indivisible. Too, a large proportion of Hong Kong residents were not Hong Kong born, but were refugees from the various provinces of China. Many of these refugees were politically acquiescent, seeking comfort and security; upon arriving in Hong Kong, they scrupulously disdained any form of political agitation. Besides, since most Hong Kong residents always presumed that their future would be determined by ministers in London and Beijing, there was little scope or point to local political activism. Therefore, most concentrated their efforts in economic, not political, activity.

In the nineteenth century, Hong Kong served as one of a string of British naval stations around the world that provided bunkering and repair facilities. By the 1980s, there was no British fleet in the Far East and the British base in Hong Kong became an isolated outpost.

Hong Kong provided Britain with modest economic benefits, which were concentrated in a handful of trading companies and individuals. Some funds flowed from Hong Kong to Britain in the form of pensions paid to retired Hong Kong civil servants living in Britain, dividends paid to British shareholders in Hong Kong firms, and payments for commercial facilities arranged through the City of London. British firms provided the railways and rapid transit carriages. The nationalized British Airways Corporation gained from Britain's authority to negotiate landing rights at Hong Kong's airport. Britain used its management of the Colony's external affairs to grant landing rights in Hong Kong in exchange for preferential foreign routes to British Airways. Finally, expatriate British civil servants serving in the Hong Kong government enjoyed a great deal of local respect and an especially comfortable standard of living.

## The Local People

To round off this tripod of consent, it remains to note that the vast majority of Hong Kong Chinese were content with British administration, despite any personal dislike of or racial aversion to "barbarians" or foreign rulers. While China convulsed in periodic political campaigns, post-war Hong Kong remained remarkably free of serious outbreaks of rioting, strikes or other forms of labour or political agitation. For most residents, Hong Kong was the only alternative to living on the Communist-ruled mainland. Too, life in Hong Kong was materially rewarding, with rapidly rising incomes. Finally, the Hong Kong government was exceptionally efficient. It housed nearly half the population in subsidized housing at below-market rents, provided a wide battery of medical and health services, and developed roads, communications, port facilities, waterworks, and public utilities at high levels, without high taxes.

## Historical Precedents of Economic and Fiscal Policy

Beginning with Captain Elliot's occupation of Hong Kong Island in 1841, the colonial government adhered to a set of free-market economic policies and conservative fiscal policies.[23] Hong Kong rigidly eschewed central planning, regulation of the private sector, budget deficits, high tax rates, industrial subsidies, costly labour regulations, and other instruments of state control. These policies were rooted in historical precedents of financial administration, a constitutional system of government, and the dogged application of an economic philosophy of nonintervention.

Hong Kong was a barren island with no large or established community entitled to political representation. It was established as a military, diplomatic, and trading station, not as a colonial settlement in the normal sense. For these purposes, the British Secretary of State for War and the Colonies imposed firm imperial control on the new colony. Self-government was never a feature of Hong Kong's development.

In practice, administrative absolutism meant that the colonial government did little more than maintain law and order, and raise taxes to pay for the cost of a modest civil establishment and necessary public works. Parliament instructed Hong Kong's governors to take from colonial resources all public expenditures except the salaries of only three principal officers in the colonial government. In 1855 the governor happily announced that Hong Kong had reached the objective of fiscal self-support, thus entrenching the doctrine and practice of balanced budgets.

Hong Kong, as a Crown Colony, was administered under the colonial regulations. The regulations date back to 1837 and serve as "directions to Governors for general guidance given by the Crown through the Secretary of State for the Colonies," especially in financial and administrative matters.[24] It was the responsibility of the Colonial Office to see that colonies did not incur debt and impose a charge on the British Treasury.[25]

Colonial Office policy and the colonial regulations which applied to Hong Kong reflected the prevalent economic theories of nineteenth-century Britain, which stressed the passive role of government in the economy. Private individuals and companies, not the government, were responsible for the creation and distribution of wealth.

The form and scope of the budget changed little since the granting of financial autonomy by Britain to Hong Kong in 1958. Nineteenth-century values of economic liberalism influenced official thinking and practice in post-war Hong Kong.

## Constitutional and Administrative Framework

Until September 1985, Hong Kong never had any form of representative democracy.[26] Administrative and executive authority lay in the hands of appointed civil servants whose personnel, at the higher levels, were largely recruited from the United Kingdom, though the pace of localization accelerated in the 1970s. Through the early 1980s, neither periodic elections nor public opinion polls guided or constrained the administrative decisions of these appointed officials. Hong Kong political activity took the form of decision making by appointed officials, sometimes within the administration, often in consultation with one of a myriad of official advisory committees, or, on occasion, by openly soliciting the public's views.

Constitutional authority for making policy was concentrated in the Governor, assisted, in practice, by his Executive Council. The Governor's powers were defined by the *Letters Patent and Royal Instructions to the Governor of Hong Kong*. As representative of the Queen, he was the head of government, and constitutionally accepted his instructions from the Secretary of State, though, in practice, instructions were rarely given.

As chief executive, the Governor held final responsibility for the administration of the Colony. He made laws by and with the advice and consent of the Legislative Council. In the execution of his duties, the *Royal*

*Instructions* stipulated that he shall consult with the Executive Council--his advisory body consisting of both *ex officio* members of government and other official and unofficial (non-government servants) persons appointed by the Secretary of State on the Governor's nomination. No provision existed for formal voting in the advisory body; the Governor sought to distill a consensus from the advice he was given and act on this advice unless he had overwhelming reasons for not doing so. The council met regularly, in confidence, and its proceedings were confidential, though many of its decisions were later announced.

The *Letters Patent* also set forth the constitutional foundations of the Governor's legislative authority. Clause VII stipulated that "The Governor, by and with the advice and consent of the Legislative Council, may make laws for the peace, order, and good government of the Colony." In the end of 1984, the Legislative Council consisted of the Governor as its presiding officer, three *ex officio* high public officials, and forty-three nominated, hand-picked members, of whom thirty were not civil servants. A clear majority of Legislative Councillors were drawn from the private sector.

In November 1984, the colonial government implemented a system of indirect elections to the Legislative Council.[27] Twelve members are selected by an electoral college comprised of members of various locally-elected bodies (District Boards, Urban Council, Regional Council). Another twelve are chosen by specific, functional constituencies. Of the 56 members of the Legislative Council, 24 are elected, 22 are appointed non-civil servants, and 10 are high ranking civil servants. *Ex officio* and nominated members still hold a clear majority. The first election under the completely new system of partially representative government was held in September 1985. The government also committed itself to a further review of representative tativetativetativetativegovernment in 1987 (though Beijing expressed dismay in late 1985 over the rapid pace of political reform).[28]

Decisions of the legislature are typically consensual, with an occasional holdout or two among the appointed unofficial members. The Legislative Council rarely withholds consent from legislation proposed by the official bureaucracy. Proceedings in the legislature rely heavily upon British parliamentary procedure in which the government proposes and the legislature disposes. The norm is that official motions are overwhelmingly accepted, although members often use the forum to speak on topics of personal or public interest.

In sum, the economic and fiscal policies of the Hong Kong government have been determined largely by the Governor and his high ranking subordinates, especially the Financial Secretary, who oversees the operations of the Finance, Monetary Affairs, Trade and Industry, and Economic Services Branches of the government. In addition to his responsibility for preparing the annual budget estimates, the Financial Secretary and his aides are heavily involved in wide-ranging activities that bear upon the fiscal health of government and the economic health of the Colony.

## The Legal System

Generally speaking, the law of Hong Kong follows that of England and Wales; the common law and rules of equity were in force in Hong Kong through 1985 so far as they were applicable to the circumstances of Hong Kong.[29] On occasion, laws were made to apply to Hong Kong by order of Her Majesty in Council, as expressed by Article IX of the *Letters Patent*. In practice, this was largely confined to matters which affect Hong Kong's international position, such as civil aviation treaties. Local legislation, closely modelled on British or Commonwealth country statutes, augmented the common law. Cases from Commonwealth countries and the United States were quoted in the courts and considered with respect. The Hong Kong courts applied a doctrine of binding precedent similar to that adopted by English Courts. Appeals from Hong Kong courts could be lodged with the Privy Council in England, whose decisions were binding on Hong Kong courts. In short, Hong Kong residents enjoyed fundamental human rights protected under the rule of law.

## Economic Policy and Performance

The performance of the colony over the last thirty-five years owes much to the minimum of interference with the free play of market forces. A low top 17 percent tax rate on individual earnings and 18.5 percent on corporations, and the lack of any capital gains tax, encourages risk-taking and hard work. The absence of tariffs and other restrictions on trade, including capital movements, makes investment in Hong Kong very attractive.

In the early stages of its industrialization, real gross domestic product grew about seven percent per year from 1948 to 1960. Between 1961 and 1980, real GDP rose 9 percent per year. As large numbers of countries stagnated in the early 1980s due to a worldwide recession, Hong Kong managed to sustain a real annual average growth rate of 7.6 percent between 1979-1984 (despite both a serious credit crunch in 1982 following an overheated property boom and an economic confidence shattering political crisis that accompanied China's announcement in September 1982 that it would takeover Hong Kong in 1997).

A steadily rising stream of industrial exports fueled Hong Kong's rapid economic growth. Exports increased by 9.4 percent a year in real terms during the 1970s. In constant terms, the value of total exports doubled between 1981 and 1984; in volume terms, domestic exports grew at an annual average rate of 9.6 percent between 1979-1984.

During the 1970's, productivity (measured by output per work-hour) increased eight percent per year at the same time hours worked per worker fell two percent per year; thus Hong Kong's labour force produced more while working fewer hours. Since the oil-reduced recession of 1974, the unemployment rate has fallen beneath three percent and the economy has worked at a full employment level despite an inflow of several hundred thousand immigrants and refugees. From the late 1950s until the mid-1970s, real wages more than doubled, and have continued to rise in the last decade.

Capital formation (savings as a share of GDP) has exceeded 20 percent throughout the 1960s and 1970s. Hong Kong's industrial transformation occurred without foreign aid or special concessions to overseas investors.

What factors have fueled Hong Kong's outstanding economic success? The answers can be found in the territory's liberal economic policies and its prudent, conservative fiscal policies.

Economic affairs in Hong Kong are conducted in an environment of free enterprise. Since 1841, government policy has dictated a hands-off approach toward the private sector, one that is well suited to Hong Kong's exposed and dependent economic and political situation. Due to its small and open nature, the economy of Hong Kong is very vulnerable to external factors, and government action to offset unfavorable external factors is often of limited effectiveness. The government holds the view that the allocation of resources in the economy is most efficient if left to market forces. Nor has the government tried to dictate the structural development of the economy.

Hong Kong's economy can be described as a free-enterprise system. It enjoys a tax structure with low rates that provides incentives for workers to work and for entrepreneurs to invest. Both workers and entrepreneurs are highly motivated, given that all individuals have equal opportunity to get rich if they work hard or succeed. The primary role of the government is to provide the necessary infrastructure together with a stable legal and administrative framework conducive to economic growth and prosperity. The infrastructure includes a modern and efficient seaport in which is located the world's third largest container port, a centrally-located airport with a computerized cargo terminal, and excellent world-wide communications. There are no import tariffs, and revenue duties are levied only on tobacco, alcoholic liquors, methyl alcohol, some hydrocarbon oils, and the first registration of motor vehicles.

Apart from providing the necessary infrastructure, either directly or through cooperation with privately owned public utility companies and autonomous bodies, the government neither protects nor subsidizes manufacturers. It normally intervenes only in response to the pressure of social needs. The philosophy that underlies government in Hong Kong can be summed up in a few short phrases: law and order, minimum interference in private affairs, and the creation of an environment conducive to profitable investment. Regulatory economic controls are held to a minimum, no restrictions are placed on the movement of capital, and the few direct economic services provided by government are operated on a commercial basis.

Hong Kong is a completely free market in money. No barriers restrict exchange between the Hong Kong dollar and other currencies. Indeed the ever-increasing funds that were attracted to Hong Kong banks helped finance industrial development and have made Hong Kong today a major financial centre. The colony's currency, the Hong Kong dollar, is linked to the U.S. dollar at a fixed rate of HK$7.80 to US$1, which means that the new issue of Hong Kong bank notes must be backed by equivalent U.S. dollar reserves.[30] Hong Kong residents who hold Hong Kong dollar banknotes thus effectively conduct their business in U.S. dollars one step removed, since they can convert their local currency into U.S. currency at a guaranteed fixed rate. Hong Kong public officials can only create new local money after first acquiring U.S. dollars to back the issue of local notes either through a balance of trade surplus or capital inflows from abroad.

It is a general principle of Hong Kong's economic and tax policy not to discriminate between residents and non-residents. On this principle, overseas investors may fully own local factories.

Hong Kong is a duty-free port and allows the entry and exit of most raw materials, consumer goods and commodities, with only a registration charge. The absence of tariffs and exchange controls means that Hong Kong manufacturers can supply both domestic and foreign markets on the basis of least-cost production.

The government of Hong Kong does not impede the setting up of private business enterprise. Free entry is permitted and encouraged into almost every line of production. Legal formalities to set up business are few and inexpensive. Except for land grants from the mid-1970s to land-intensive industries that inject new technology into the economy, no protection or government assistance is traditionally given to manufacturing industries, utilities, service industries, or private citizens. No attempt is made to distort factor prices in favour of any particular type of development. Market forces are allowed to shape the economy, and industries that lobby for protection from the competitive forces of the market place are fiercely resisted. As a result, Hong Kong enjoys among the most modern factory facilities in the world.

Hong Kong does not impose a statutory minimum wage. Earnings of industrial workers fluctuate with overall economic activity. Loyalties to firms are less important then salary and fringe benefits and thus workers respond quickly and rationally to market opportunities. Trade unions play little part in setting wages or working conditions. Labour is highly mobile between industries and trades, with little restrictions owing to rigid craft demarcation or entry protected by trade unions. The result of a free market in labour, which accompanies a free market in business and investment, is that most of Hong Kong's work force is fully employed and enjoys steadily rising wages.

In spending only what it can afford, the Hong Kong government is, by worldwide standards, unique. Except for a small number of tropical paradise tax havens, no other government so intently holds expenditure within means. Its standard rates of tax on earnings and profits (a maximum rate of 18.5 percent on business profits and 17 percent on salaries and interest) is the lowest in the industrial world and its official government reserves are the largest in proportion to any year's expenditure.

The official view in Hong Kong is that a low rate tax system facilitates rapid economic growth, which, in turn, yields sufficient tax revenues to finance essential public services. Personal allowances are extremely generous. A family of four does not pay income tax unless it earns more than US$11,000. Indeed, in the 1982 tax year, only 218,000 salaried taxpayers of a total population exceeding 5 million paid any income tax in the 1982 tax year. Moreover, 13,000 salaried taxpayers, about 6 percent of the total number in the salaried tax net, contributed over half the total yields from the salaries tax, despite the low rate.

Hong Kong developed extensive housing, education, health, and other social and community services through low rates of taxation, with virtually no need to resort to borrowing. Budgetary policy is virtually unique in Hong Kong. In thirty-two of the last thirty-five years through 1982, the budget ended the year in surplus and interest earnings on the accumulated surplus is sufficient to pay for the territory's police force. Moreover, these surpluses accrued after charging most capital expenditure against current revenue.

Government spending and public-sector employment are closely monitored to guarantee that the rate of growth of the public sector does not outpace that of the private sector. This is to insure that the public sector, which has a natural tendency to grow over time, does not crowd out the private sector to the detriment of Hong Kong's external competitiveness. In recent years, government spending as a share of GDP ranged from 13 to 19 percent, but the financial authorities are watchful to prevent the share from surpassing the critical 20 percent threshold. Between 1982 and 1986, government's share of GDP declined from 19 to 16 percent, as the Financial Secretary tightened the government's belt in response to the political crisis of the early 1980s.

How did the common worker fare under this system? The evidence on post-war income distribution suggests that the 70 percent of the population in the third through the ninth deciles gained the greatest share of the increase in national income. Low-paid unskilled workers benefitted most from the rapid increase in employment opportunities. The well-being of the poorest 20 percent showed dramatic improvement: By 1976, their average household income reached US$1,300, which surpassed the poverty index of all Asian countries. Under a low-tax regime, rising income translates fully into greater purchasing power and a higher standard of living for lower income families.

## Hong Kong's Future?

Hong Kong's future came into open concern on July 18, 1982, when a local newspaper story reported an announcement from Beijing that China definitely intended to reclaim sovereignty over the whole of Hong Kong by 1997, when Britain's 99-year lease on the New Territories expires. Any hopes of the status quo of British rule continuing into the twenty-first century permanently ended when Chinese leader Deng Xiaoping personally conveyed this statement of official Chinese policy to Mrs. Margaret Thatcher, the British prime minister, during her September 1982 visit to Beijing.

Although the worldwide recession hit Hong Kong's exporters earlier in 1982, reinforcing the economic slowdown produced by a monetary contraction, Beijing's summer announcement shattered political confidence in Hong Kong's economic future. Despite promises by Chinese authorities that Hong Kong's free-wheeling economy would not be integrated into China's socialistic, state-directed system, the stock, property, and foreign exchange markets fell sharply. The Hong Kong economy remained on shaky ground throughout a string of Sino-British negotiations over the future of Hong Kong, which were held from September 1982 through September 1984. The Financial Secretary presided over three successive budget deficits, raised the top corporate and individual tax rates two percentage points, entered the local credit markets for the first time to borrow HK$1 billion, and drew down a major chunk of Hong Kong's vaunted fiscal reserves. Land values stagnated. The stock exchanges did not recover until July 1984, when the outlines of an apparent agreement came into focus. Despite a strong recovery in export orders throughout 1983 and 1984, new investment in plant and equipment failed to materialize for the first time in Hong Kong's post-war history. Many investors lacked confidence that Chinese authorities would preserve the free market economic system of Hong Kong after 1997, and began to transfer resources out of the colony.

On September 26, 1984, the British and Chinese governments initialled the draft agreement on the future of Hong Kong, which was ratified by both sides in 1985. Beijing would recover sovereignty and administrative authority over the entire territory of Hong Kong, but China promised Hong Kong a high degree of autonomy in all matters save foreign affairs and defence. (The enforcement of this agreement after 1997 depends on China's goodwill, not Britain's presence.) Hong Kong would retain its social and economic systems, including rights of person, free speech, press, assembly, association, travel, movement, correspondence, strike, choice of occupation, academic research, religion, and private ownership of property. (These same rights are stipulated in China's own constitution, but have been routinely disregarded by the mainland's Communist rulers.) Hong Kong would remain a free port, a separate customs territory, maintain its own convertible, fully-backed currency, run its own public finances (remitting no taxes to China), issue its own travel documents, and operate its own police force. These policies would be stipulated in a Basic Law (constitution) of Hong Kong, which would become a Special Administrative Region of China, and would remain unchanged for 50 years. The underlying idea is Deng Xiaoping's concept of "one country, two systems [socialism and capitalism]."

Only time will tell if Hong Kong successfully retains its free-market economy, high growth rate, and personal liberties under the rule of law just before and after 1997. Estimates of annual capital outflow in both 1985 and 1986 are in the neighbourhood of $2.5 billion, suggesting that Hong Kong's better-heeled residents are taking few chances.

## SUMMARY AND CONCLUSION

Singapore and Hong Kong arose in virtually identical nineteenth-century circumstances—as free port, free trading city-states under British colonial rule. Against the backdrop of centuries-long imperial dynastic traditions, British rule introduced private property, civil liberties, and a general concern for individual rights into East and Southeast Asia.

It is worth noting that the Chinese language had no word for individual freedom before the twentieth century. In 1911 Sun Yat-sen's followers overthrew the decaying Qing dynasty and set about creating a Western-style constitutional democracy. This was the first time that the concept of individual freedom played a role in over four millennia of China's history. Thus Singapore and Hong Kong offered their residents freedom and opportunity absent in neighbouring lands.

In 1985, the two city-states have markedly diverged. In Singapore, one man, Lee Kuan Yew, and one political organization, the People's Action Party, have exercised virtually unchallenged power since gaining independence from Britain. Although they have assigned to private enterprise primary responsibility for the creation and distribution of wealth, the PAP government consciously abandoned the laissez-faire practices of its colonial past. The government established a large number of state-owned corporations and became the Republic's primary landowner and landlord. On the political front, the PAP effectively suppressed all political opposition and muted its media critics. The "Singapore model" generated high growth until its high-wage policy of the 1980s not only braked, but reversed, the course of economic progress. Back-to-back years of economic contraction brought calls for renewed emphasis on private enterprise and a diminished role for the state in Singapore's economy.

How will economic, political, and civil freedoms fare in Singapore's future? The PAP government appears ready to enhance economic freedom, has shown somewhat more tolerance to its political opposition in the 1980s, and may ultimately tolerate a greater measure of free expression. But as of 1986, Singapore affords its citizens a much greater measure of economic liberty than of political or civil rights.

In 1986, Hong Kong's economic, political, and civil institutions were still readily traceable to its 1841 founding: a free market economy, colonial rule, and legal protection of individual rights, including freedom of speech, press, travel, employment, and so forth. Apart from the normal ups and downs of international business cycles, the one serious blip in Hong Kong's sustained post-war economic progress occurred in 1982-1984 after Chinese leaders announced in 1982 that they would recover sovereignty and exercise administrative authority over the territory by 1997.

The clock is counting down on British Hong Kong. At the stroke of midnight on June 30, 1997, the five yellow stars on red flag of the People's Republic of China will be raised at Government House and the Union Jack will be lowered, folded up, and put away for good. Of course, the outlines of post-1997 political organization in Hong Kong will be in place well before 1997 as Britain prepares for an orderly withdrawal. Since the Sino-British Joint Declaration does not permit any expatriate to hold the post of department head in the government of the Special Administrative Region of Hong Kong after 1997, apart from the Governor and perhaps one or two high-ranking aides, most Western faces will be gone by the early 1990s.

China has promised in writing a high degree of autonomy to Hong Kong. It said that Hong Kong's people can retain their economic, political, and social systems for 50 years until 2047. But will China's guarantees be durable? For their part, the British are trying to reform the Colony's political structure in the direction of greater local representation. If Hong Kong's residents are to govern themselves, they require local institutions by which they can retain autonomy. Some analysts argue that representative institutions, including direct election of all members of the legislature, may be the only effective means of building the broad-based support on which Hong Kong's post-1997 leaders can resist mainland China's blandishments—a curious political twist. If the autocratic, but benevolent, colonial structure remains intact until 1997, China will inherit a mechanism whose virtually unconstrained authoritarian legal powers are no longer moderated by British traditions of individual rights and gaining the consent of the governed.

## NOTES

1. Milton Friedman and Rose Friedman, "The Tide is Turning," *Free to Choose* (New York: Harcourt Brace Jovanovich, Inc., 1980), Chapter 10.

2. For a comprehensive history of Singapore from its founding until the mid-1970s, see Mary Turnbull, *History of Singapore 1819-1975* (Singapore: Oxford University Press, 1975). For a cross section of development issues, see Peter S.J. Chen, ed., *Singapore: Development Policies and Trends* (Singapore: Oxford University Press, 1983). An overview of Singapore is presented in the government's official annual report entitled *Singapore 1984*, published by the Information Division, Ministry of Culture. On more concrete topics of economic development see Lee Soo Ann, *Singapore Goes Transnational* (Singapore: Eastern Universities Press, 1977); Goh Keng Swee, *The Practice of Economic Growth* (Singapore: Federal Publications, 1977); and Theodore Geiger, *Tales of Two City-States: The Developmental Progress of Hong Kong and Singapore* (Washington, D.C.: National Planning Association, 1973).

3. Many newly independent countries have adopted xenophobic policies, expelling long-time foreign residents and traders. In contrast, Singapore welcomes its foreign community. The official line, stated in the government's annual report, is that "this foreign community is an important segment of the population because of its valuable contributions to the country's economy." See *Singapore 1984*, p. 4.

4. *Far Eastern Economic Review*, March 27, 1986, p. 73.

5. *Far Eastern Economic Review*, July 25, 1985, pp. 68-69.

6. For details on Singapore's public finances see the Singapore Yearbook, Singapore's annual budget documents, and the annual report of the Board of Commissioners of Currency. Thoughtful accounts of the Monetary Authority of Singapore, the currency system, the Central Provident Fund, and the links to the budget are found in *The Financial Structure of Singapore* (Singapore: Monetary Authority, June 1980); Tan Chee Huat, *Financial Institutions in Singapore* (Singapore: Singapore University Press, 1978); and John R. Hewson, "Monetary Policy and the Asian Dollar Market," in *Papers on Monetary Economics* (Singapore: Singapore University Press for the Monetary Authority of Singapore, 1981), pp. 165-194.

7. *Far Eastern Economic Review*, March 27, 1986, pp. 72-79.

8.  See Peter S.J. Chen, "Singapore's Development Strategies: A Model for Rapid Growth," in Peter S.J. Chen, ed., *Singapore: Development Policies and Trends*, pp. 13-20.

9.  During 1979 and 1980, the press reported a large number of appeals lodged against government compulsory purchases in which the transaction prices were 20 percent below the value claimed by the owners and assessed by chartered land valuers.

10. Eddie C.Y. Kuo, "Communication Policy and National Development," in Peter S.J. Chen, ed., *Singapore: Development Policies and Trends*, pp. 268-281.

11. See Chan Heng Chee, *The Dynamics of One Party Dominance: The PAP at the Grass-roots* (Singapore: Singapore University Press, 1976) for an account of how the People's Action Party came to exercise virtually unchallenged hegemony of Singapore politics.

12. *Far Eastern Economic Review*, July 11, 1985, pp. 34-37.

13. The material in this section draws from two books I have written on Hong Kong. See *Value for Money: The Hong Kong Budgetary Process* (Stanford: Hoover Press, 1976) and *Hong Kong: A Study in Economic Freedom* (Chicago: University of Chicago Press, 1979). The first volume analyzed policy-making and budgetary practice within the Hong Kong government. The second presented a comprehensive treatment of politics and business in Hong Kong, showing the structure of the Colony's free market economy and documenting its remarkable economic growth.

14. For a detailed account of the negotiations, the issues, and their resolution, see Bruce Bueno de Mesquita, David Newman and Alvin Rabushka, *Forecasting Political Events: The Future of Hong Kong* (New Haven and London: Yale University Press, 1985).

15. Valuable descriptive material and statistics on Hong Kong are published in an annual report, of which the most recent edition used is *Hong Kong 1985: A Review of 1984* (Hong Kong: Government Printer, 1985). A convenient source of recent data is the *Hong Kong Monthly Digest of Statistics* (Hong Kong: Census and Statistics Department).

16. Ibid., p. 117.

17. Ibid., pp. 284-285.

18. For an excellent political history of the founding and early years of Hong Kong, see G.B. Endacott, *Government and People in Hong*

*Kong* (Hong Kong: Hong Kong University Press, 1964). A summary treatment appears in *Hong Kong 1985*, pp. 291-299.

19. *Hong Kong 1985*, pp. 292-293.

20. This section draws from Alvin Rabushka, *Hong Kong: A Study in Economic Freedom*, pp. 16-20.

21. Alvin Rabushka, *Hong Kong: A Study in Economic Freedom*, pp. 20-29. See also Norman J. Miners, *The Government and Politics of Hong Kong* (Hong Kong: Oxford University Press, 1975), pp. 1-46.

22. Derived from *Hong Kong Monthly Digest of Statistics*, November 1985, Tables 5.4 and 5.5, pp. 24-25. For a comprehensive review of the economic interdependence of China and Hong Kong, see A.J. Youngson, ed., *China and Hong Kong: The Economic Nexus* (Hong Kong: Oxford University Press, 1983), *passim*.

23. This section is summarized from Alvin Rabushka, *Value for Money*, pp. 12-37.

24. Sir Charles Jeffries, *The Colonial Office* (London: George Allen & Unwin Ltd., 1956), pp. 106-107.

25. See Brian L. Blakeley, *The Colonial Office, 1968-1892* (Durham: Duke University Press, 1972), pp. 135-149. The regulations that applied in early Hong Kong were *Rules and Regulations for Her Majesty's Colonial Service* (London: Her Majesty's Stationery Office, 1843).

26. See Alvin Rabushka, *Value for Money*, pp. 38-82. See also *Hong Kong 1985*, pp. 294-295.

27. "White Paper: The Further Development of Representative Government in Hong Kong," November 1984.

28. Emily Lau and Philip Bowring, "Laying down the law," *Far Eastern Economic Review*, December 5, 1985, pp. 12-15. Xu Jiatun, director of Xinhua news agency (China's unofficial mission in Hong Kong), in an unprecedented local press conference on November 21, 1985, implicitly accused Britain of "having a tendency to deviate from the joint declaration." He also stated that the political system of the Special Administrative Region of Hong Kong was China's business and would be clearly stated in the Basic Law. Some Hong Kong residents interpreted Xu's remarks as calling for a halt to all political reforms until 1990, when the Basic Law comes into being.

29. *Hong Kong 1985*, pp. 63-69.

30. The architect of Hong Kong's fixed U.S. dollar exchange rate system is John G. Greenwood, an economist with G.T. Management (Asia) Ltd. in Hong Kong. Over the years he has published a series of articles describing the shortcomings that existed in Hong Kong's floating exchange rate system during 1974-1983 and feasible reforms in a journal he edits, *Asian Monetary Monitor*. The most important articles are "Hong Kong's Financial Crisis—History, Analysis, Prescription," *Asian Monetary Monitor* 6, no. 6 (November-December 1982), pp. 2-69; "How to Rescue the HK$: Three Practical Proposals," *AMM* 7, no. 5 (September-October 1983), pp. 11-39; "The Stabilization of the Hong Kong Dollar," *AMM* 7, no. 6 (November-December 1983), pp. 9-37; and "The Operation of the New Exchange Rate Mechanism," *AMM* 8, no. 1 (January-February 1984), pp. 2-12.

# Discussion

## Edited by Michael A. Walker

**Alvin Rabushka** Both Hong Kong and Singapore have a number of common origins which I think are worth keeping in mind, although there are also some dissimilarities, and there is always going to be a problem as we get deeper and deeper into the personalities and idiosyncracies in history in any given case. The salient common points that one wants to keep in mind are that both territories started as virtually uninhabited islands, both territories had superimposed upon them external systems of political and economic organization. They had colonial-type systems and laissez-faire free trade economies imposed on them. Neither tried substantially to disrupt or alter the indigenous cultures of either the Malay or Chinese populations. And finally, of course, both populations are heavily Chinese; in the case of Hong Kong, 98 percent, and in the case of Singapore it came to be about 75 percent.

The next thing I want to talk to you about is the word "freedom." In Chinese the word "freedom," *zi you*, consists of two characters, and what is important about this word is that it didn't exist until the 20th century. In fact, the Chinese had to manufacture a word. And why did they get into this business? In the 19th century they were overrun by the West, were whipped by the British in the Opium Wars, and the Western powers developed their spheres of influence. China's leaders decided that Chinese culture was still superior to all other cultures, but Chinese science, Chinese technology, Chinese military capability, and the Chinese economy were not. And maybe, just maybe, in trying to learn from the West to modernize and make China independent and strong, you needed to borrow the political systems in addition to their economies, their military machines, and their technologies. In borrowing the political systems you needed the structures of governments, like presidents, legislatures and judiciaries, and you needed the language with which to talk about them. So this word "freedom," and individual liberty, keeps cropping up. From the beginning of China's recorded history there were no such words. So they had to manufacture this word *zi you*, "freedom," which actually means "to move oneself or self-movement." To a Chinese who has been raised, educated and brought up in traditional language and culture, the word is not self-movement so much as what it means in a cultural context: selfish, greedy, putting oneself ahead of family, community, and village. It is very instructive to examine liberty in the latest dictionary put out five or six years ago by the People's Republic of China. One definition refers to something like the freedom of speech, assembly and other rights as guaranteed in the constitution, which of course isn't worth the paper it is printed on; another notion of liberty as defined here is the petty bourgeoisie's aversion to discipline; and there is another one called "Capitalist tendencies to run wild." This is what the Mainland Chinese communists mean by "freedom." But if you look at the pre-communists, what you find is that there is a heavy emphasis on selfishness in the dictionary, as opposed to village, clan, commune, province, country, emperor, and so forth.

It shouldn't, therefore, surprise you that the Chinese imported an American, Professor Willoughby, to write a constitution in 1911, after the revolution. That constitution didn't last very long. Yuan Shihkai who was the succeeding general dissolved it, declared himself monarch, re-established the old imperial system, and as fate would have it he died because he misbehaved. But in any case, you never really got, in this creation of freedoms, while they are in the constitution—and also in the constitution of Taiwan, by the way—any sense of what these words mean. But when the British brought them to Singapore and brought them to Hong Kong, they were predicated upon a common law tradition. They were predicated upon a parliamentary system. They were predicated upon a Manchester liberal notion of the economy. And the British imposed these on the indigenous people, set up systems of property rights, and over a period of time began to increasingly educate them. So to say you are a Westernized Chinese means that you hold to the common law tradition. And to say you are a Westernized Chinese in Hong Kong who is a little bit nervous about 1997 and the absorption of Hong Kong into the People's Republic of China is to say you are a little worried about the rule of law giving way once again to the rule of man, and the loss of your individual liberties. Because articles 51 and 54 in the Chinese constitution allows the suspension of rights in articles 28 through 50 in the interest of the state or in the interest of national security.

Now let me just make a comparative observation about the two. While their early histories were quite similar economically, politically and socially, upon independence Singapore decided to go the import substitution route but was smart enough to scrap it quickly and return to an export-oriented free trade system, with a somewhat activist government; that is, there are some state-owned corporations, but as a total share of the national assets and national income they are not terribly consequential. They have a conservative fiscal policy. They have had a very sound monetary policy. But they are very heavy handed in social controls, and quite rightly end up with a very low civil liberties score of 5 on the Freedom House scale, and I think that is basically correct. They end up with a political freedom scale of about 4, and that's okay, or maybe a touch on the generous side. With economic freedom, a score of 2 is maybe what I would give them, if there were a 7-point scale.

Turning to Hong Kong, which never really departed from its original 1841 philosophy of economic liberalism, fiscal conservatism, free trade and a generally non-interventionist government, the civil liberties score is 2, which is probably right, or 2-plus or 1-minus. From time to time there have been occasional odd intrusions on it, but by and large, as an individual, and for those of us who have spent a lot of time in Hong Kong, one feels no less free in Hong Kong than one does in the United States on a civil liberties dimension. In terms of economic liberty, surely it is the number one with the star on the top. Nobody's close to being in second place. There is a big gap with whoever is number two in the world. And while it is not perfect by the theory of competitive markets, it is so much closer that anybody else has a long way to go to catch up.

Finally, political freedom. Here the Freedom House score is 4. (By the way, there was some earlier confusion. They do publish an ancillary list of dependent territories; it just wasn't in the paper.) One juggles and compares Singapore at 4 and Hong Kong at 4. Large numbers of Chinese from Singapore tell me they think they feel freer in Hong Kong, even though Hong Kong is not a country and therefore one cannot vote on one's rights. Whereas in Singapore, while one can, one really isn't exercising any freedom of vote in a one-party state highly controlled, where the opposition may be in jail if they are a little too outspoken.

The final thought I want to offer you is a curious irony, a paradox. That is, I think that many of us see Hong Kong as having been able to have a long-run view of the future and being free from day-to-day electoral pressures, being relatively free from interest group lobbying; the government's been able to put in place and maintain a steady regime of economic liberalism, fiscal conservatism and low tax rates, and the departures from that are minor and inconsequential over the long run. Therefore, anybody's been able to take a long-run view subject to the China factor. And the China factor has now materialized, and the long-run view is shrinking by a year every year—namely, 1997 is the deadline of British rule in Hong Kong.

This whole aversion to democracy in Hong Kong, which is something that might have interfered with its economic freedoms, now becomes possibly the only mechanism to preserve it. By that I mean that there has to be a buffer between the people of Hong Kong and the government in mainland China. That buffer has, for 140 years, been the British. The British are going. And while the Chinese have promised a great deal of autonomy and

50 years of maintaining their social, economic and political systems unchanged, what is the enforcement mechanism for that? The international treaty is no enforcement mechanism at all. It's not even a treaty; it's simply a joint declaration. The enforcement mechanism, it appears, has to be some sense of internal buffer with which local people can resist the blandishments emanating from Beijing. And it may just be that some form of locally elected representative institutions will provide local people some rallying point around which they can in fact resist bureaucratic rule from across the border. It may be a very weak buffer, but it may be perhaps the only buffer. So that these economic freedoms that have pretty much remained intact, apart from Japanese occupation, since 1841 may now depend upon some form of democratic evolution.

**Alan Walters** A most interesting question emerges from this paper. Why did Hong Kong and Singapore so successfully resist the tide of dirigisme and socialism which swamped both economic advance and civilised progress in so many other, for the most part ex-colonial, countries? As Rabushka points out, they had no natural advantages of plentiful resources, like their neighbours Malaysia or Thailand. On the contrary, poor Hong Kong had to cope with continual waves of penniless, illiterate and often disease-ridden migrants on an inhospitable, densely populated peninsular and island rock.

This puzzle has led to the suggestion that economic progress is spurred by the *absence* of natural resources, and that this is the main explanation for the success of the four little dragons as well as Japan, Israel and the many wealthy mercantile city states of Northern Europe from the 15th to the 19th century. But, apart from the anomaly of embracing the idea that nothing is better than something, this cannot be adduced as a necessary reason for the rejection of socialism and a highly regulated economy. There are many resource-poor states that have embraced socialism or communism; perhaps Albania is the most notorious example.

It is, however, possible to argue that the availability of resources and the rents that are derived from them does provide a fertile ground for statism. The appropriation of the rents through political activity does divert effort from producing goods and services. At least Hong Kong and Singapore were spared this temptation.

I suggest that the main reason is to be found in the colonial history. From the work of Peter Bauer and Basil Yamey we know that in Britain's African colonies, until the 1930s the ambient administrative system was very similar to that which obtains today in Hong Kong. The colonial administration provided a stable monetary system, usually a currency board, law and order, and the basic infrastructure for transport, elementary education and health. Government bore only lightly on economic activity; taxes were low and there was substantial economic freedom.

This benign administration changed in the 1930s. Ideas of socialism took root in Britain during the 1930s. Statism, syndicalism and communism became fashionable at the great universities, particularly Cambridge and Oxford, and soon infected the civil service. The upper echelons of the colonial office, particularly under the leadership of Sir Andrew Cohen, head of the African Department at the Colonial Office and Lord Mc-Pherson, who eventually became head of the Colonial Office, readily embraced the role of more government economic ventures and more regulation and controls. They found sympathetic ears from Labour Colonial secretaries and, perhaps more surprisingly, from Conservative Secretaries who believed in big business and were contemptuous of small peasants.

Such notions were readily implanted in the colonies during the last half of the 1930s, with all the paraphernalia of marketing boards to regulate prices (and swell the coffers of the rulers), controls on production and wages, et cetera. During World War II such colonies were harnessed to the controlled war economy and later to the post-war regulated systems. The apparatus of a socialist state, with all its deadly potential, was bequeathed by the dying colonial administration to the new rulers.

Why did not Hong Kong and Singapore succumb to this socialization? One reason is that both were ports and entrepôts rather than sources of food or raw materials or of manufactures before 1950. As Rabushka points out, they were established initially to secure free ports and so the regulatory apparatus of a socialist system would soon have eliminated their livelihood. A distinguished official in the Foreign and Commonwealth Office has suggested that the great British trading companies, such as Swires and Hutchinsons, put considerable pressure on the Colonial Office to retain the free market system in Hong Kong. (I find this rather difficult to credit. Most business pressure seems to be in the form of trying to secure and protect monopoly positions.) One cannot, therefore, put too much faith in this rationalization for the relative immunity of Hong Kong and Singapore. It would not be difficult to imagine a civil servant arguing that the entrepôt trade was too fragile a basis for Hong Kong development and that what was really required was the establishment of a manufacturing base, which, according to the contemporary ideas of development, would require tariff protection, government sponsorship, control or even ownership.

Perhaps one of the reasons for the rejection of such socialist development was the fact that the colonial office, and later the foreign and commonwealth office, regarded Hong Kong as ultimately part of China.

Unlike the colonies of Africa and Asia, Hong Kong was merely a small chip off a big country, and was always considered to be a temporary ward of the colonial office until 1997. Ironically there was thought to be little of a future for Hong Kong except as a port for China. And who could forecast what would happen to that vast country riven with civil strife and social upheaval? Hong Kong was regarded as a backwater of the colonies.

Perhaps this was aided by the fact that both Hong Kong and Malaysia (including Singapore) were occupied and devastated by the Japanese during the war. They were never part of the regulated war economy of the United Kingdom. (Perhaps that is also the explanation for the fact that Malaysia also substantially eschewed socialism in its post-war development.) Furthermore, by the time the turmoil in the Far East had subsided, Singapore, Malaysia and Hong Kong had had ample time to observe communism in practice. The bloody insurgency in Malaysia and Singapore was suppressed but the fight against the conspiratorial communist party, as it sought to undermine the fragile period of early independence, continued through into the 1960s. Similarly the haven of freedom and prosperity in Hong Kong contrasted sharply with the repression and degradation on the mainland.

The real puzzle is that Hong Kong, and for its colonial period, Singapore, enjoyed one of the most efficient governments in the third world, yet that government was appointed by a foreign office and metropolitan government riddled with the ideology of socialist planning—perhaps one of the most inefficient governments of the industrialised nations. (Harry Johnson once suggested that the best solution to Britain's economic problem was to swap governments with Hong Kong.) The governors and civil servants appointed by the foreign and commonwealth office were committed to the principles of small government and free private enterprise and trade.

I suppose that in part the anomaly is explained by the traditional (British) colonial form of government known as indirect rule, particularly with respect to the Straits Settlement (later Malaysia and Singapore). Indirect rule enabled the colonial administrators to exercise oversight of an indigenous system of local government by the traditional rulers (mainly Malays). But the colonial authorities insisted on the basic framework of English law covering trade, commercial arrangements and the protection of property. The colonial (later the foreign and commonwealth) office appeared to choose its administrators carefully so that they would fit well in the ambient system of unobtrusive government. (No doubt many will remember Sir Sydney Caine as a superb financial secretary in Malaysia before he became Director of LSE.)

In Hong Kong, however, there was no indirect rule of the kind practised in Nigeria or Kenya or Malaysia. British law obtained throughout. The chief officers were appointed by the Colonial Office. The British colonial authorities, nevertheless, managed to place the appropriate Manchester liberals in all the senior offices of the colony. But this selectivity must have been reinforced by the fact of the great success of Hong Kong and Singapore, and of course to a lesser extent Malaya. Demonstrably, small government worked well in contrast to the mainland with the Kuomintang chaos of 1946-49, and the turmoil and degeneration after 1957.[1] Hong Kong's unrivalled performance was the ultimate reason that it retained its economic system. It would be unwise, however, to presume that such continued success, so confidently expected, will ensure that the economic and governmental system remains in place. The benign colonial administration was, like the colony itself, an odd and beautiful anachronism in a socialist sea.

**Walter Block**   I wanted to thank Alvin for a very interesting and informative piece, but as is my wont I come not to praise but to criticize. I have three very small criticisms. The first amounts only perhaps to a typographical error. On page 2 he mentions in the sentence: "It suffers a population density that ranks it among the world's most overpopulated areas per square mile." Now I would substitute for "overpopulated" "highly populated." I don't like that word "overpopulated." It just seems to me that it is very antithetical to human rights, properly understood, to suppose that there can be too many people. I was having a discussion, before I came here, with a person who has eleven children and who is making a claim that we have overpopulation. I asked him which of his children he wished were never born. He was aghast at that, just as I am aghast by the concept of overpopulation. I don't think there is overpopulation anywhere; there can only be highly concentrated population.

I also would take issue on page 5 with the list of rules in this economic bill of rights. Rule 6: "A money supply growth rule to ensure sound money." In my view, to argue by analogy, the best relationship between church and state is one of complete separation. And the same goes for the relationship between education and state; it should be one of complete separation. Likewise for the relationship between money and state, it too should be one of complete separation. I don't think that the Feds can be trusted to apply a 3-5 percent rule, or anything else. I think the best thing to do is repeal the Fed root and branch; just disband it. Instead, we could have a free market money, whatever it is—gold, platinum, or competing monies or what have you. But I certainly would be reluctant to accept a money supply rule because it implies the continued existence of a Central Bank.

The third point is on page 42 where it says that Hong Kong has a completely free market in money. Yet in that paragraph we learn that Hong Kong public officials can only create new local money after first acquiring U.S. dollars to back them up. Well, if the U.S. is not a completely free market in money, and Hong Kong is dependent upon the U.S., then Hong Kong can certainly not have a free market in money, based on government fiat currency.

**Gordon Tullock**  First, with respect to this business of how it remained free, I happen to have been a vice consul in Hong Kong during the latter part of the Labour government, and I can tell you that they pretended vigorously that they were a welfare state. The annual report said they had the same rules as England. They had lots of social welfare officers, and so forth. And, as a matter of fact, they did, except that the appropriations were such that they could deal with perhaps one-half of one percent of the population. I always suspected that one-half of one percent paid for its privileges, because another aspect of the government was that it was thoroughly corrupt—at least the junior English people. I don't know if the higher-ups were, but I do know one of my Chinese friends who came over from Macao by writing a letter to the Governor himself—they both happened to have been in the same college in England. He was invited for dinner and the Governor said, "Now, why did you bother to use a letter instead of paying the usual fee?"

With respect to overpopulation, you have to remember, the population is there because they can't get out. It is not that they are there voluntarily. They left Communist China voluntarily, but they are not staying in Hong Kong voluntarily.

Finally, with respect to democratization, I regard that as waving a red flag before a bull. There is nothing that the Chinese government wants less than a demonstration that genuine democracy can work anywhere within its area. As it happens, it is, of course, a violation of the joint agreement, because the joint agreement says they will retain the same situation for the next fifty years, and the democratization has occurred after that joint agreement. So I would deduce that one way or another Hong Kong is going to be part of China with some odd, decorative, special characteristics within three or four years of 1997, provided it makes 1997.

**Brian Kantor** A Chinese person was asked about the relative performance of a particular governor, and the answer he got was, "Well, he was very good, but there were mudslides..." In other words, he was held responsible for what we would call "acts of God."

There is one feature of Hong Kong's economic life that has escaped attention and shouldn't have done, and I think you would remove the asterisk from the 1 if you thought about it. Hong Kong appears very densely populated in parts. There are areas of Hong Kong, particularly some of the islands, where in fact there are almost no people at all. Lantau, which is only a half mile away, is rural bliss, there are few people there. There are parts of Hong Kong Island itself which are quite sylvan. And you ask yourself why, and then you discover the answer: The Hong Kong government is the only developer of land. There is only one land developer; there is a monopoly of land development. And the revenues from long lease sales, 99-year lease sales, go straight into the budget. So, whereas Hong Kong is lightly taxed in the usual sense, in fact what they get away with in the form of lower taxation they suffer in the form of unnaturally high rents, because the supply of land for development purposes is artificially restricted. I think that is an important limitation on market forces. Hong Kong would in fact have developed much less densely if there had been free access to the land development market.

Also in Hong Kong there is serious regulation of utilities. All the utilities—the telephone company is government, the utility companies, some of the transport—are regulated by officials according to what are known as "schemes of control," and they don't make an awful lot of economic sense.

So, if you ask yourself where Hong Kong succeeds economically, I think that one real advantage there is minimal interference with imports or exports. That is an enormous advantage. The other one, I think, is in the labour market. There is really minimum interference in the labour market. Also, I think what is of particular advantage to Hong Kong right now, given the uncertainty about 1997, is freedom from exchange control. That, I think, is very important in helping Hong Kong at the moment, because it enables the people who live there to diversify their portfolios while outside investors from the rest of the world who are willing to take a gamble perhaps on Hong Kong are freely able to do so. So I think that is very important to them at the moment.

**Raymond Gastil** I wanted to make two points. One relates to the Survey of Freedom, and that is that Hong Kong makes a good example of the attempt of the Survey to actually look at the behaviour of factors in a situation rather than to have any definite categories which are given points. In the case of Hong Kong, the reason why I gave it as high a political rating as it received, over a long period of years, was because I knew that the people in Hong Kong were there largely because they didn't want to be in China. So I knew that in Hong Kong, unlike many other colonies that the Survey dealt with, there was really no question about whether the people wanted British rule or didn't want British rule. The fact that the British were ruling it, without much local supervision over that, really wasn't as important as those facts in defining Hong Kong.

More recently, in the last couple of years, because of the reasons that Alvin mentioned, Hong Kong has tried to develop legislative institutions which will introduce—and they are doing it very slowly—an element of democracy into the situation, because the British have, without Hong Kong agreeing to it, made an agreement with China by which the society is essentially being given over to the tender mercies of Communist China. In effect, the British have reduced the rights of the Hong Kong people politically at least as much as they have increased it by granting these legislative institutions. So I am just saying that is a good example of a judgement that doesn't fit the standard rules for judging political rights.

I thought this was one of the most interesting papers, but I am not clear what the point is supposed to be, and that is something that maybe you will comment on later. The point I drew from it—as I did from some of the other papers—was that perhaps we can come up with some ideas of the limits of the positive effect of political and civil liberties on economic development. In other words, there is probably an optimum point for these freedoms in relation to economic development, and once you go beyond that point you may have a declining relationship. That is a suggestion that comes to me, at least, but maybe you have other conclusions.

**Herbert Grubel** I spent last fall in Singapore and studied the origins of its economic miracle. The story I encountered is much the same as that told by Alan Walters about Hong Kong.

However, one fundamental characteristic of the developments in Singapore remains a puzzle to me. Lee Kuan Yew was educated in Cambridge and there undoubtedly was exposed to all of the powerful and then current ideas about the merits and feasibility of social democracy and the welfare state. When he took office as prime minister of Singapore, he and his government were subjected to strong pressures to initiate a broad system of social security. One Singapore minister of the period is fond of telling a story about delegations from the International Labour Office in Geneva. These delegations would come regularly to his office and insisted that the government of Singapore was severely remiss in its duty by not initiating modern social welfare programmes. The minister became tired of these visits and was able to stop them only after he announced that he would toss the delegation out of the window of his office.

Given the intellectual and political spirit of the 1950s and 1960s and the educational background of Singapore's leaders, the puzzle is why and how they resisted the resultant pressures for the creation of a welfare state in Singapore. Kernial Sandhu of the Institute of Southeast Asian Studies in Singapore and John Wheatly of the Committee for Social Thought of the University of Chicago are in the process of editing a volume of essays to be titled *Managing Success—Singapore*. In it this puzzle will be addressed.

A tentative answer to the puzzle found in these essays suggests the following. On the one hand, the government was run by a party which maintained all of the outward ideological commitment and internal organizational structure of a party strongly committed to socialist ideals. To this day, the ruling party is known as the People's Action Party. On the other hand, the policies of the party were set by leaders, including Lee Kuan Yew, who had seen the adverse consequences of a ruthless Marxist organization in operation during the turbulent years after the end of the Japanese occupation. But this is really only a partial answer. Why did these leaders not take up the positions of power and the opportunity "to do good" that the Marxist system would have provided them and that so many leaders in other developing countries found impossible to resist? I have no answers to this question and wonder whether anyone here has any.

**Michael Parkin**   The thing that really puzzles me about these two examples is not the thing that really puzzles Alan, although Alan's real puzzle is a real puzzle. The real puzzle arises from the other side of the political marketplace. We spent a lot of time in the last number of years trying to develop an ingenious theory of how come we get such bad governments and how come we get such big governments. These theories usually run— at least those that seem plausible—in terms of the political process being a process in which there are rents that are being created that someone sees as being proper to exploit, and to invest their resources in that rent-grabbing rather than wealth creating activity.

Now, I always found those explanations very appealing, and they make a lot of sense, in explaining things that I have seen in most countries of the world. But then I come to these odd-ball cases, and the question arises, what is it about them that makes them different? Why is it that the rents that are there are not being grabbed, and in the process, wealth being dissipated in the same way that seems to be occurring in other places? So my puzzle is not why did Lee Kuan Yew do that things that he did, but why did he get into power, and how was he able to stay in power, when there were so clearly incentives for others to remove him, and do, by their standards, a better job for themselves but a worse job for the people? And why in particular these two cases? Why Hong Kong and why Singapore? Have there not been elements that have emerged, probably in the 1940s I would think would have been the time when it ought to have happened, before the really clear example of the People's Republic was there? But why did these countries manage to stay as placid and secure as they did at that time? It seems to me a major puzzle. And if there is a simple answer, or an answer, it would help a great deal to shed an important light on these other theories as to why we see the growth of rent-grabbing governments in other places.

**Gordon Tullock** The answer to why Lee Kuan Yew stayed in power is simple: He has efficient secret police. (Laughter)

Now, I will turn to other matters. In particular, I would like to elaborate a little bit on something that Brian said. What he said was perfectly correct. But I don't think most of you understood it, and it does show that the Hong Kong government civil servants sometimes make ghastly mistakes. Their method of financing a large part of the Hong Kong government is to sell a small part of this empty land every year at auction; that is, you pay a large "purchase" fee in return for a 99-year lease at a very low rental. They will tell you they can't sell it all because they have to save it for future generations, and this is as idiotic a revenue-raising method as I can name. From Peter Bauer's work I deduce that they did this in Malaya for a while, too. As far as I know these are the only two places in the world that follow this particular feeble-minded approach to real estate. This is a government which in many other respects is extremely efficient, but this is their principal source of revenue.

**Douglass North** I am going to add to what Gordon said and what Brian said, because I think we may very well have overdone our praising of Hong Kong and so on. Hong Kong has also had, in addition to its controlled lands, rent controls since 1921. That's a long time—a long time before most places in the world had rent control. It has persisted with it all through these years, as my former colleague, Steve Chung, has written about very eloquently. So I think we could overdo it.

**Alan Walters** Yes, I think it is overdone in many ways. I do think it's wrong, for instance, for Brian to say there are substantial regulations of utilities. The bus system is one of the best in the world. The public light buses came in, and were allowed to come in, run by gangsters initially, but they worked well. They were immensely popular. They were eventually legitimized and became an essential part of the system. All Hong Kong buses are private. The public light buses are not regulated with respect to the fares. It is one of the few major cities in the world where the fares are not regulated. Nor is entry regulated; entry is free.

On the other points that were made, it is true that rent control was instituted in 1921. But now rent control is largely a cipher. It has disappeared, and the process of key money and all the rest of it is gone. Of course, it only applied to existing buildings and not to new ones. So, there was much demolition and reconstruction. Hence you got big turnover of buildings and a great deal of waste as a consequence.

I would also like to come back to another point which I think it is necessary to make. It was suggested that one of the reasons why they retained such a degree of freedom and didn't go in for rent seeking was because (this was suggested, incidentally, by a foreign office official) the colonial government in Hong Kong, and to a lesser extent in Singapore, was dominated by the Swires and the Hutchinsons—the big merchant firms who wanted free trade. That's the first time I have heard of a merchant firm wanting free trade. Normally they are rent-seeking operators of the first water and constantly pressing for exclusive rights, and so on. If you read the history of the Swires, you find they were desperately trying to get special consideration. For reasons which are not clear, the foreign office didn't want any part of it.

**Alvin Rabushka** There are a lot of points here that are matters of fact and some matters of theory and some matters of interest. Let me deal first with this business of why Hong Kong and Singapore didn't succumb to the socialist road or the interventionist road.

Let me begin by telling you a little story. In about 1971 a new governor arrived on the scene in Hong Kong, Sir Murray MacLehose who was the first professional diplomat ever appointed to be governor of Hong Kong. Up until that time, it had been colonial service types. He worked for a different master, the foreign office, and he thought that Hong Kong was really a municipality as he saw it from his foreign office perspective. He decided that he would try to ratchet up, as hard as he could and as quickly as he could, social spending. His plans were ground to a halt by the world recession and the oil crisis of '73-'74. Then the Hong Kong economy rebounded in '75, more rapidly than any other economy in the world, and grew over the next six years at the highest rate of any economy in the world. And in part because the adjustment mechanism had been so quick, real wages had fallen, returns to capital had increased, the economy became more efficient and more competitive. Meanwhile, the financial secretary was summoned to London and he was told that he had two choices: he could either quit or he could increase social spending significantly. Well, he didn't like this, and his basic position on this was: no, I am not going to do that, and I guess you may have to fire me but I would be careful about that because if you do that and lose the confidence of the local business community you are not going to get very far.

Now, what in fact had happened was that all through the '50s, '60s and early '70s the British were trying to decolonize. They forgot about Hong Kong—just plain forgot about it—and woke up in 1970 and discovered they had a colony left. It was the only big one they had, and it was about time they started meddling and interfering. They didn't like limited government, and they didn't like the lack of a welfare state. They didn't like the repudiation of labour policies, and they tried to do something about it. The one attempt to do something about it didn't succeed, and so Hong Kong has been allowed to go off on its merry way.

Now, aiding and abetting that all along has been the fact that China was not prepared to ever tolerate an independent third government in China. So the development of anything remotely resembling institutions of political independence would have been nipped off in the bud. Therefore competing, entrepreneurial, rent-seeking political groups would not have been allowed to play the game even if the British wanted to let them play. The Chinese wouldn't have let them play that game.

In the case of Singapore, I think the answer is much simpler and much easier. It turned out that the import substitution scheme Lee Kuan Yew proposed, following conventional learnings he might have picked up in England and elsewhere and that the rest of the world followed, worked out perfectly fine on paper so long as Singapore was part of the Federation of Malaysia. But in 1963 when Singapore was rudely expelled one day, and they woke up to find that they were this little island with a population of two million, the notion of having a hinterland and a bigger market collapsed, and so they quickly discovered that they had to go the export route. They did it; other countries that had similar situations didn't.

**Tibor Machan** In these various equations, I would like to know where, if anywhere, the fact of very little military preparation, financing and so on figures in. I don't know if anywhere. But I would just like to know, because it seems as if very often the existence of a military industrial complex serves as an excuse for rent-taking and makes opportunities that are horrendous.

Second, did someone in Hong Kong read Henry George?

**Alvin Rabushka** Everybody's got that wrong, but I will answer later.

**Ingemar Stahl** As I understand the discussion, the major thing about Hong Kong and Singapore may be their free trade policies. What are the political prerequisites or conditions for keeping a free trade policy once you have started it? I think that is the crucial point. This type of free trade could be put on the Freedom House list as a kind of civil right—I should have the right to enter into trade with anybody inside or outside my country. If that were a dominant part of civil rights, I think that would give a very good correlation between GDP per capita and that specific type of civil right. It is important to reformulate part of free trade as civil rights in the sense that you should have the right to enter into trade with anybody inside or outside your country without interference from the government.

Another thing which I think is important in these city-states is that there have been no pressure groups from declining industries. There are obviously no agricultural organizations trying to preserve high food prices and trying to stop imports of food, for very obvious reasons. Can it be that the answer to many of our questions can be found in an explanation framework that there were no pressure groups from the declining industries?

The final question would be, do we have any observations whatsoever of countries which have been changing from a protective policy to a free trade policy? Are there any on this list of 165 observations where we have this type of policy change? It is one thing to preserve a free trade status, another thing to go from a protective status to a free trade status. Hong Kong and Singapore are unique countries in the way that they have preserved free trade, and we can discuss the political prerequisites for that. But do we have any observations of countries which have been highly protective and have changed to free trade states?

**Assar Lindbeck** To answer Ingemar's last question, many countries have been studied. There are many studies by the World Bank, Ann Krueger and others. They usually get much higher growth rates, for instance, for those countries. There are a dozen or so countries which started with import substitution policies in the fifties and switched to an export-oriented strategy. Bella Belasas has written about them.

Was your question what we know about civil liberties in those countries?

**Ingemar Stahl** No, the political prerequisites or conditions for changing that type of policy.

**Assar Lindbeck** No, maybe they have not studied the political prerequisites. They have just noted that some countries have switched. I think it is usually small countries because import substitution policies start to give declining returns much faster in a small country than in a large country. In India you can pursue import substitution with much less cost than in Hong Kong and Singapore. I think the smallness of these nations is one explanation of why they have abandoned import substitution. It is much more expensive for a small country, like Sweden, for that matter.

**Peter Bauer** Did not Britain and France shift occasionally from a protectionist stance in the 19th century? The repeal of the Corn Laws and the Colsden-Chevalier Treaty of 1860 seem examples.

I would like now to ask some questions rather than making new points. First, does the joint declaration of 1985 make any substantial difference to the prospects in Hong Kong? The People's Republic of China could have taken Hong Kong at any time since 1950. Does not what will happen to Hong Kong depend on the play of political forces in the People's Republic of China? Perhaps Alvin, Gordon or Brian could comment on this.

Second, does the joint declaration cover only the New Territories or does it apply also to Hong Kong Island and to Kowloon?

Third, does the Hong Kong government sell the land simply to the highest bidder or does it take into account the use to which the land will be put? Before the war in the British colonies of S.E. Asia the government, when giving out public land for private use, set different terms for land in accordance with the use to which it was being put, including the different commodities produced on it. Perhaps people would enlighten me on these subjects.

**Brian Kantor** Alan raised the point about bus riding. I don't want to go into any great detail, but I understand there was a strike of taxi or ordinary bus service, and so they allowed this new entrant into the market. But anyway, they all seem to charge the same fees, and taxis are regulated and all seem to charge the same fees. The point, I think, about this is that the closer one looks at these countries, the more one appreciates how, in fact, regulated they are. That comes as something of a shock. They are not exemplars of free market economies. The forced saving scheme in Singapore—a huge proportion of the GNP was being forced, and where was it going? It was going through government channels into foreign investment. Yet Singapore, of course, has done very, very well, despite the distorted capital market. In fact, you find distortion or relative underdevelopment of the capital markets everywhere. In Hong Kong itself—the banking system is heavily licenced, heavily regulated. While I was there in August, the first money market fund was established in competition with the banking system. But there was a restriction—the minimum investment was fairly high.

You turn to Taiwan, and Taiwan has achieved spectacular growth rates and yet it has what one must call a highly interventionist policy. They are saving at the rate of over 30 percent of their GDP. They are investing at the rate of only about 18 percent. All the difference is going into foreign exchange reserves held by the Central Bank. It is holding over $2000 of foreign exchanges per capita. The second or third largest stock anywhere is held by Taiwan. The banking system is underdeveloped because it is restricted, because the post office savings bank is safe so all the savings go through the post office bank, through the government financing government enterprises and things like that.

So one looks for explanations other than, perhaps, what one would be inclined to, I think. They are not notably free, although it is clear that in all these countries there is an intense endeavour and ability to improve economic status through hard work, through saving. That energy there, which you will notice, is so impressive. And I think in all those countries, you really have a first generation of Chinese who are really escaping subsistence. They have some margin. They have been able to put some margin between them and disaster, and they are enthusiastic about those kinds of opportunities which they didn't have before. It's just that ability to cope with the disasters that befell their fathers and grandfathers, and the institutions that allow them to strive and improve their economic state.

**Herbert Grubel** I support Brian's statement. The government of Singapore has a large involvement in productive enterprises. As a result of the current economic crisis in that country this involvement is under study. The ownership of some prominent, large enterprises like shipyards and Singapore Airlines is well known. On the other hand, as I found out at a seminar at the University of Singapore, there is no official record of the magnitude of public ownership of small- and medium-sized enterprises. It is only known that there are many of these and that most were started under a programme of support for technologically advanced business.

Milton Friedman has often noted the tendency of autocratic governments to become increasingly repressive as they attempt to cover up past mistakes in economic management. The existence of the large publicly owned sector in Singapore raises the interesting question of why such a process of repression has not taken place. One reason is almost certainly that the country has enjoyed a solid 20 years of growth averaging 10 percent annually. Everything, including the management of mistakes, is easier under these circumstances.

However, there appears to be more to the story. The current crisis involves negative real economic growth rates. It is severe by international standards and certainly in the light of the preceding years' performance. It is due to a very large extent to errors made in economic policy, most notably pay increases suggested and implicitly mandated by an official Wages Council. There have also been unreasonably high increases in taxation.

The interesting fact is that the policies adopted for dealing with the crisis are almost exactly those which market-oriented economists would prescribe. Real wage rates, taxes and government spending have been lowered and a programme for the privatization of publicly owned enterprises is under way. What is it in the make-up of the Singapore leadership that gives them this resilience? Is it the same characteristic that made for resistance to the introduction of modern welfare programmes that I discussed earlier?

**Alvin Rabushka** I want to mention what I said at the very outset, which is that Hong Kong, point by point, represents a significant departure from the pure textbook theory of absolutely perfectly competitive markets running every sector of the economy. Having said that, however, nobody else even comes close. So on that relative standard, it's a number one asterisk asterisk. (Singapore is maybe a two or a one minus.) There is a little regulation, okay. But compared to everybody else, it's a bastion of liberalism across the board in almost every respect, whether it is free entry, free movement of prices, free trade, free labour, free capital, free immigration or free whatever it is. It is just so far beyond in its total approach. If we were a symposium of Hong Kong economists and political scientists, we could roundly condemn all the intrusions and interventions, but against the other 161 countries it just smells and looks very, very good.

Singapore doesn't smell and look quite so good, but it is certainly terrific when we have nailed down the best ten of the lot. I think we want to remember that, and keep that in perspective.

Let me answer some quick joint declaration questions, just to get the facts off the board and then turn to land, unless I run out of time. The joint declaration says that there shall be a legislature constituted by elections.

They didn't pre-empt how that should be. The Chinese have their views on that, which they have tried to make clear, and they have pretty much constrained how far the British can go on this. This is a continuing point of controversy, and my guess is that it has probably gone about as far as it can go. But there is some concern by local people that it would be desirable to take it a bit further.

In terms of the other joint declaration questions that Peter raised, the real joint declaration was bargaining not about 1997 but about 1984. What I think they set up was a notion that the British were going to stay in charge. There would be an orderly colonial government until 1997, so there would be another business cycle or two to make some money. God knows what's coming in 1997.

With the time horizon shrinking fifteen years and counting down the loan date, the sense was that people were getting very nervous, and the investment picture was going to contract very sharply. So they cut a deal that basically gave them another decade. I don't know that it makes any difference after 1997, but it has bought the rest of this decade and that may be the ultimate. By the year 2010 we may look back and say, what did the joint declaration do? And the answer would be, it bought ten years in the mid-80s and early '90s. And it may not have done much more.

The agreement does cover all 408 square miles: Hong Kong, Kowloon, and the new territories—all of it. The British originally held to separate, but the Chinese rejected that position. In the end, the British compromised.

Finally, land sales. With the rare exception of the late '70s, land sales constituted a relatively small proportion of revenue, never more than 8, 9 or 10 percent. It was not significant. It only got significant in the 1978-81 period when it hit 20 to 25 percent due to the inflationary boom and the money supply boom. If the government is collecting and spending on the order of 16 percent of GNP out of taxes, and land sales are generating something on the order of 10 percent of that on average, you are talking about 1.6 percent of the national income being collected that way. The mix between direct and indirect taxes is not far from fifty-fifty.

I think far too much emphasis is placed on the land as a fiscal device. It is simply not all that important. In fact, given the historical surplus position of the government, they never really needed that money. Why have they been selling it? Out of historical convention the Crown owned all the land, and because it has always been a Crown colony the Crown continued to own all the land. They would have had to change the convention which they didn't feel was necessary. I have had this argument with a number of Hong Kong government officials, and I have come around to their view that it just would not have made terribly much difference in the greater scheme of things whether all the land were privatized at one time or whether it was auctioned off, as it was, to the highest bidder.

**Alan Walters** Just a comment on the transportation system. It is one of the best and freest transport systems in all the countries. Again, I think Alvin's point is that, relatively, it scores on many of these things. I must say on the banking side, too, it is a very free banking system. How else could it be the third biggest capital market in the world? If the banking system were tied up, it wouldn't be so. It is very big. The success mocks the position that it's severely regulated.

**Raymond Gastil** Listening to this discussion, it appears to me that the emphasis on institutional questions may miss the point: there are often other kinds of explanations which are quite sufficient. I can think of three that come together. One is that during periods of world trade—and you all are much more familiar with this than I am—city-states comparable to the ones we are talking about here were very successful when trade was active. I am thinking of places like Venice and Athens and, at other times, the Netherlands and Amsterdam. The situation was propitious for them.

Another thing we've talked about is the fact that the Sinic area peoples —Chinese, Japanese, Korean—are exceptionally successful right now and, of course, that fits into this and adds a cultural explanation.

The third thing, which we talked about earlier, are the refugee peoples. Think about the Cubans who have come to Miami or the Jews and Hungarians and so forth who came to New York in other periods. In these cities we have a very large percentage of "special" populations who have been gathered in from other places and who, for one reason or another, couldn't succeed as well there as in this place. They make a very special and, I would say, a rather superior population compared with surrounding areas that gives them special advantages. It adds a selective definition. I bring these up as alternative explanations.

**Assar Lindbeck** I would like to reinforce Alvin's point that it is very dangerous to look at only one country. You will find hundreds and thousands of interventions if you put a looking-glass to one country. To get the real perspective, you have to compare it to other countries. Look at the studies that have been done on international trade in recent years by Krueger and others. Most developing countries have an enormous number of regulations. You need licences for import, export, building, and often even for production and output. There are regulations for capital markets and often effective tariffs of 100, 150, or even 500 percent with enormous primeval import substitution relative to exports.

If you look at Hong Kong and Singapore in that perspective, they are completely different animals. You don't have 100 or 200 percent tariffs on different goods. You don't have permits for import and export and production and everything else. Even Taiwan and South Korea have come out as relatively free trade-oriented countries in these studies compared to India and some African countries, or practically any country in the developing world, because they don't have those several hundred percent effective tariffs on imports. We make this mistake often, and I think it is very dangerous. We look carefully at one country and say that free trade is a myth because we found hundreds of interventions, but comparison with other countries is necessary to get the perspective.

**Tibor Machan** I would like to go back to the military question. What about the absence of a major military necessity in Singapore and Hong Kong?

**Alvin Rabushka** The percentage of GNP in Hong Kong spent on defence is about equal to Denmark. I use that number to make the point. Three-quarters is borne by Hong Kong taxpayers and one-quarter by the British. By the way, most of this defence is designed to keep Chinese refugees from inundating Hong Kong rather than actually defending Hong Kong against an invasion of the military.

Singapore has a higher percentage, but even within the total Singapore budget you are looking at a relatively small public sector. So long as 80-85 percent of resources are in private hands, you are going to get an efficient economy.

**Gordon Tullock** One final item with respect to the defence of Hong Kong. For a long time there was always an American carrier off shore. With the gradual reduction of the strength of the American Navy I think this ceased to be true, but carriers aren't very conspicuous. The Chinese may not have known it was gone for quite some time after it disappeared.

**Herbert Grubel** I wish to return to the case of Singapore to illustrate how it is possible to have economic management while at the same time retaining important freedoms.

First, the government of Singapore used the market and prices to deal with what were perceived to be market failures. For example, to limit traffic congestion on the small and densely populated island, the government did not use non-market devices to ration the numbers of cars. Instead, it exploited the existence of a downward sloping demand curve and raised domestic prices. But it did so not by the imposition of import tariffs, which would have encouraged the development of an inefficient domestic automobile industry. Instead, it imposed an excise tax. More innovative and widely discussed is the government's system of charging special user fees for automobiles in specified areas and times of potential congestion.

Second, the government has maintained very high standards of honesty. The manager of a local brewery recently sent the prime minister a case of beer that was part of a small lot brewed on the occasion of one of the firm's anniversaries. He received a personal letter of thanks from Lee Kuan Yew. Enclosed with the letter was a cheque in payment for the beer.

Third, the government has used its autocratic powers to ensure that integrity is maintained in certain areas other than economic management. According to a sociologist at the University of Singapore, the independence of the judiciary and the universal accessibility of the educational system are two such areas considered to be absolutely crucial for the maintenance of the system's legitimacy. In recent years there have been widely publicized disputes between the government and the media which have, in one instance, led to severe penalties on the publishers of the *Asian Wall Street Journal*. According to this sociologist's interpretation, all of these disputes have involved what the government considers to be inaccurate reports about corruption in such crucial areas of government legitimacy. A story in the *Asian Wall Street Journal* had alleged that the judiciary was in the pocket of the government.

These insights about the operation of the Singapore government suggest to me that paternalism can be successful if it is limited in scope and managed carefully and with personal integrity. This, of course, leaves open the question of why the government of Singapore has been so successful while so many others around the world and in history have not.

**Alvin Rabushka** I will conclude with two stories. First, in 1981 I was in Sri Lanka and very much interested in the electoral transformation of 1978 and the pursuit of more market-oriented policies and did the rounds of the Treasury. I reflected that the financial minister there often quoted Hayek, von Mises, Friedman and other luminaries in his budget speeches. I said, "Did you read these books and guides and that is how you decided to adopt these policies?"

He said, "No. He's a literate man, and he likes to spice them up with quotations from *Free to Choose*. But the truth of the matter is," he said, "after 30 years of failure and watching 30 years of success in Singapore, we decided they did it right, we did it wrong. So from now on we're going to try to do what they do."

They send all their people to Singapore for training. Lee Kuan Yew has become close friends with Julius Jayewardere. In effect, when your shops are empty, your cars don't work, and the economy has ground to a halt, you look around where things work. They work in Taiwan, in Singapore and in Korea, and Singapore was the closest. So that is how they got into the Singapore model in Sri Lanka.

Now, a little story of incentives in both Hong Kong and Singapore, and why they seem to respond correctly to incentives. I had a conversation recently with two retired former financial secretaries in Hong Kong. In Hong Kong's constitutional and legal system the financial secretary, by prerogative, has one hundred percent say over tax and policy. He virtually doesn't have to consult anybody in the government, although he usually confers with the governor first. The view of the financial secretary is very simple: if things go right, the economy gets credit, but if things go bad, he gets the blame. He learned from a study of Hong Kong history that interference in the economy over the years tends to make things go bad, and you get the blame. So if you want to survive, get ahead, and do well, leave things alone. That's the incentive to which Hong Kong economic policymakers respond. Open economies really turn things sour in a hurry when you intervene.

That lesson isn't lost on Lee Kuan Yew, but his incentive is a little different. It's much more traditionally Chinese; he is worried about maintaining the mandate of Heaven. How does he lose the mandate of Heaven?—if things go sour. So in a sense, honest government, keep the economy growing, and you keep the mandate of Heaven.

The economy ground to a halt in 1984 and 1985. It slowed down, and they're worried about losing the mandate of Heaven. Create a commission with the son, cut tax rates on social insurance, cut tax rates on personal income, try to liberalize here and there, have a freer financial sector—Why?—to sustain the economic growth that would once again give you back the mandate of Heaven.

Remember, that mandate of Heaven in Singapore, unlike mainland China and elsewhere, is predicated upon the common law of British traditions—private property rights, a free trade system and so forth. So one can see that there are incentives.

I will conclude my remarks. I still don't have the answer to the question Alan Walters raised, and that is, why is it when they proceeded to depart from the tried and true colonial policy and things went bad, and one could have forecast they would go bad, that they departed from the policies and doomed themselves? What was a great, thriving, prosperous, free port is no more, and the suicidal instincts that so many followed were not followed in these other places.

**Alan Walters** There is something that has not been raised with regard to some of the seemingly trivial civil freedoms that are abrogated in Singapore. For instance, the government "discouraged" people with long hair. They also regard even mild forms of pornography as illegal. Much of this is very much concerned with the perception of the government of Singapore that Western standards over the past 30 years have declined.

When Lee Kuan Yew reviews British society in particular, and Western society generally, he observes a rapid decline of standards—a rapid decline of, for instance, a respect for reality and truth; certainly, declining respect for religion and declining respect for parents—all the encroachments of the welfare state, too.

They limit the civil freedoms which normally would be imported from the West because the West has gone wrong. There is some basis for their belief; the standards of the West have declined in many respects.

**Walter Block** We are engaged in a war of ideas, and words are the ammunition in a war of ideas. As George Orwell told us: he who controls words has an advantage in this war of ideas.

There are two people around this table who have played a great role in trying to save certain words for us. Milton Friedman, with the word "liberal," has insisted time and time again that we try to keep this word for ourselves and not let it go by the boards. And certainly Peter Bauer, with "foreign aid," has objected strenuously again and again, eloquently and passionately, that "foreign aid" is pejorative and implies that these government to government financial transfers, to use his terminology, are benevolent and succeed in their task.

I would like to put in a plea with regard to another phrase that has been used around this room. I don't like the concept "rent seeking." As far as I am concerned, "rent" is an ancient and honourable tradition, part of the free enterprise system. Rent is a contract between consenting adults, and there is nothing evil or vicious or depraved about rent. Yet, when we use the phrase "rent seeking" and apply it to what we do, we demean the word "rent" and lose its meaning. Let's call it "booty seeking" or "theft seeking" or "loot seeking" or something else of this sort to distinguish it from legitimate forms of "rent seeking." I am trying to save the word "rent" from this association with what is really, in effect, theft. So I put in a plea that we try to adopt this usage.

**Gordon Tullock**   Although I claim to have invented the concept, I am happy to say the title, "rent seeking," was invented by Ann Krueger. I take this as evidence that we should try to keep women out of scholarship. I have always told foreigners that they shouldn't translate it directly; they should try to find some other word for it. It is very hard to get it out of the language once it is in. Bhagwati has been pushing "dup"—directly unproductive. I encourage him, but I don't think he will succeed.

**Tibor Machan**   When I use the term "rent seeking" I put it in quotation marks for just those reasons. But we might as well add "transfer payments." What are transfer payments or "redistributing wealth," as if you just did a very neutral thing. I know I am going to draw some ire from some people, but unfortunately I think the attempt to keep economics entirely positive and to give scientific or value-neutral terms to things like theft have led to this. We now have this artificial language to talk about things which in most ordinary, civilized societies are normatively discussed. What will murder be called in the positive economics language? I don't know. There is an enormous vocabulary of jargon which arises out of this, and you may have an enormously complicated and long-lasting fight on your hands.

**Michael Parkin**   I don't think I am engaged in a battle of ideas. I think I am engaged in a process of trying to understand the world and figure out why things happen the way they do. I find that the language I use in that process is secondary, but it is useful to have words that have some clear meaning.

This word "rent" means the gains from economic interaction, the gains from trade or rents which someone will always seek to maximize. The two parties to the trade will always have an incentive to try to grab the biggest part of the gain from the trade for themselves. There will always be third parties, that in some cases may be governments, that will have some incentive to try to siphon off some of that gain that might accrue to one of the sides. So it seems very natural to use the word "rent" to describe the thing that all people seek when they seek to interact with each other and to make gains from that economic interaction. I don't think of this as having any kind of moral overtones in either direction.

**Milton Friedman** I was just making fun at Walter's wanting to get a neutral term for theft.

**Walter Block** I do not seek a neutral term to describe theft. On the contrary, I want to insist that we call theft, theft. My complaint is that we keep calling theft or loot seeking, rent seeking. Why impugn a perfectly good concept like "rent" by linking it with theft?

I agree with Michael that most of the people around this table or at least I, not wanting to speak for anyone else, am engaged not only in a war of ideas but also in another task. We also function as scientific positive economists attempting to understand economic reality. I think most of us wear two hats in this regard. But whichever hat we are wearing, we ought to save as many words from pejorativism as possible.

I certainly agree with Tibor that there are more words than "rent seeking." It is just that "rent seeking" has been used here continually. Certainly, we could add to the list of endangered words "transfer payments" or "redistribution" or "tax expenditures," which is another favourite of mine. I would part company with those who say rent is just trade between two people, each one trying to get more of the gains from trade. This is true in a limited sense, but "rent seeking" is different from ordinary commercial activity. We have to distinguish between the economic process of production and the political process of trying to grab or steal what other people have produced. This is not a normative economic distinction only; it is also part of positive economic analysis to distinguish between voluntary trade on the one hand and the machinations that occur through the political process. These are very distinct from trading a wristwatch for a pencil, for example.

**Peter Bauer** Is it not the case that the term "rent" has a strict technical meaning in economics, namely a payment in excess of the supply price?

**Michael Parkin** I agree, he is right. The word has a very precise meaning. But whenever there is trade between two parties, there is going to be a gain from that trade. It is always going to be in the interest of one or the other or, indeed, both of those parties to seek to put that trade through at a price that benefits and advantages one of the parties. That is always going to be a feature of economizing behaviour. The fact that people seek to do the best they can for themselves means that they will seek to buy for the lowest possible price. It is part of the economizing activity. To say that there is some good "rent seeking" and some bad "rent seeking" seems to me to miss the point.

Economizing is doing the best you can with a scarce resource, for yourself. That is what economizing is.

**Assar Lindbeck**  The term "rent seeking" as used by Ann Krueger and others is, of course, the idea that private agents get privileges or monopolies from governments, for instance, to get licences for import/export which they can exploit in the market in various ways. That is a gain you can get which is not related to productive effort but to good contacts and bargaining with government for privileges and monopoly positions. I think that is what the term "rent seeking" means in Ann Krueger's terminology. Every licence has a rent. If you get the licence free, you can sell it in the market or use it in other ways and get the profit on it. That is the way she used it, and I think that is a very useful term.

**Milton Friedman**  I just want to go along Peter and Assar's line. In point of fact, the use of "rent seeking" in that way is consistent with the technical economic definition of it, because all of these are cases in which somebody is being given the possibility of selling something at a higher price than the supply price. It is a difference between that higher price and the supply price that is what people seek—that is the "rent" they are trying to get. So I don't think there is any contradiction between the use of "rent" in that "rent seeking" way and the technical economic definition of it.

Perhaps we ought to solve the problem by calling it "quasi-rent seeking," on the grounds that these privileges are eroded over time and therefore it is only a temporary excess of demand price over supply price.

**NOTE**

1. Even at the end of the "eight good years" in 1957 the consumption per capita in China was still some 11 to 13 percent below that of 1933. See Colin Clark, "Economic Development in Communist China," *Jnl of Pol. Ec.*, April 1976, pp. 239-264.

# Chapter 5

# Black Africa: Free or Oppressed?

## Lord Bauer

### The Price of Freedom

*Liberty, what crimes are committed in thy name.*[1]

Post colonial Africa is termed liberated, free. Yet millions in Black Africa live under mass coercion and lawlessness undreamt of in the 1920s and '30s, indeed under conditions harsher than at any time since slavery. Since the 1960s, hundreds of thousands, possibly millions, perished through government action or in civil wars, or amidst the collapse of order brought about by government policies, and millions have been forcibly uprooted.

I shall examine this tragic and paradoxical situation and its background, largely with reference to British Colonial Africa, primarily West Africa. Somewhat similar developments took place elsewhere in Africa, though the change was less abrupt because before the war personal freedom, especially economic freedom, was greater in British Colonial Africa than elsewhere.

### Restrictions of Colonial Rule

The people of a colony are politically unfree in a clearly defined sense. They do not have a say in government. They do not participate directly in the political process beyond the municipal, village or tribal level, though they may have a large measure of freedom of speech and information. How objectionable the population regards such alien rule depends on such factors as the characteristics and activities of the government, on the ethnic and cultural homogeneity of the population, and on the expectations of different groups about successor governments.

For various reasons the great majority of the population did not find the British colonial rule in Africa particularly irksome. For the first time in centuries, perhaps in history, their lives and property were safe. Slave trading and tribal warfare had been suppressed. Taxation was light. The population of most colonies was heterogeneous. In Nigeria, for instance, there were, as there still are, some four or five major tribal groups and at least sixty different tribes, a diversity which dilutes the concept of alien rule. The vast majority of ordinary people knew little of politics beyond the village or tribal level and had never known elective government. Their concerns were with their families, with raising and marketing their crops, and with tending their animals. Like most people, they were much more interested in not being misgoverned than they were in self-government. For these reasons the population at large did not much question colonial rule. Adverse economic changes, such as a fall in export prices or higher taxes, elicited outbreaks of discontent with little or no political thrust.

There did, however, emerge in the 1930s numerically small but articulate groups resentful of colonial rule and hostile to it. They were Western educated or westernised people, some of whom began to be heard in politics, in schools and colleges, the media, and in commerce. They were vocal, and they also had contacts with their opposite numbers in the West.

They resented colonial rule, partly because it was alien but also because it denied them the power, status and money they hoped for under an independent government.

### Reversal of the Principles of Colonial Rule

Until the late 1930s, modern British colonial rule in Africa was guided by clearly recognised principles. These were: limited government, especially in economic life; acceptance of traditional leaders and local councils as representatives of African opinion and interests; and their gradual evolution and reform towards independence.

Limited government, open economies, and maintenance of traditional authorities made colonial rule widely acceptable, which in turn made government relatively easy and inexpensive. In such conditions public affairs vex no man, as Dr. Johnson observed.

Between the 1930s and decolonisation in the 1950s and '60s, the guiding principles of British colonial rule were abruptly reversed. In both the political and the economic spheres, one set of principles was replaced by their exact opposite.

As heirs designate of British rule, traditional rulers and councils were replaced by recently urbanised, articulate, literate or partly literate westernised people, notably politicians, teachers, journalists, lawyers and their allies in commerce. Gradual modernisation and reform of traditional authorities and institutions was to be replaced by early introduction of mass democracy interpreted as universal suffrage, a concept previously wholly unknown in Black Africa.

This abrupt reversal of political direction took place in the 1940s and '50s under the impact of such forces as the emergence of U.S. interest in Africa and the influence of Fabian socialism in the British Civil Service, as well as in politics, academia and the media.

The mass of the population in the African colonies did not press for these political changes and was indeed largely unaware of them. And those who were aware of them did not like what they saw. This was recognised with unexpected candour by Obafemi Awolowo, a prominent Nigerian politician of the early post-war period:

> Given a choice from among white officials, Chiefs and educated Nigerians as the principal rulers of the country, the illiterate man today would exercise his preference for the three in the order in which they are named. He is convinced, and he has reasons to be, that he can always get better treatment from the white man than he could hope to get from the Chiefs and the educated elements.[2]

The illiterate man, in the context synonymous with the ordinary man, was, however, not given a choice.

## Introduction of Economic Controls

The other main guiding principle of colonial rule, limited government, especially in economic life, was similarly reversed at about the same time. It was replaced by a system of close economic controls; without these the political changes may not have issued in the far-reaching and lasting consequences which I shall note later.

Over most of British Africa the establishment and extension of such economic controls began in the late 1930s and gained momentum in the war and early post-war years, a momentum which continued until independence and beyond. By the eve of independence, these economies were largely state-controlled. The controls and their instruments included state monopoly of major branches of industry and commerce, notably in the import and export trade, including comprehensive monopoly over agricultural exports; numerous state-owned and operated enterprises, often with monopoly power; licensing of commercial and industrial activity; comprehensive control over international transactions; ethnic quotas in employment and in the allocation of licences; price controls and prescription of minimum wages; large-scale support for co-operative societies, in effect, extensions of government departments.

Such controls place the economic opportunities and even the livelihood of people, outside subsistence agriculture, at the mercy of the government and its agents. This was particularly evident in the operation of agricultural export monopolies (marketing boards), which, by virtue of their sole right to purchase and ship these products, could impose a ceiling on producer incomes.

The war and its immediate aftermath did much to promote these controls by lending spurious plausibility to the need for them, even when they were quite irrelevant to the war or were even contrary to their declared purposes. This applied notably to the most far-reaching of these measures, state export monopoly over all major crops.

The principal controls were introduced because they appealed to dirigiste civil servants whose power and status they enhanced; to some British politicians; and to some influential commercial interests, both expatriate and African. They also accorded with the ideology of the terminal period of colonialism in Africa.

The departing colonialists thus bequeathed to their successors the ready-made framework of economic totalitarianism. The incoming African rulers welcomed the controls because these gave them a close grip over their subjects which enabled the rulers to pursue more effectively their personal and political purposes. They extended the controls whenever they could. As we shall see, the West has helped them to do so.

### Economic Controls Increase the Power of African Governments

Some results of the controls which I have recited are familiar: divorce of output from demand; raising of costs through quotas and restriction of entry; creation of contrived scarcities with the resulting divorce of prices from the opportunity cost of resources; and emergence of privileged incomes and windfalls unrelated to productive performance.

Certain characteristics of the African scene reinforce or compound these results. The pronounced ethnic, tribal and geographical differences in human, physical and financial resources increase the economic costs of controls. Again, the controls obstruct emergence from subsistence agriculture and keep many people in poverty and backwardness. The absence of effective price control at the retail level both increases the windfalls and privileged incomes and makes them evident and even measurable.

The controls bequeathed to the independent African governments, and extended and reinforced by them, have endowed the rulers with pervasive power over the economic and even physical survival of their subjects. In these conditions the stakes in the struggle for power increase very greatly. People's energies and resources, especially those of alert and ambitious people, are diverted from productive economic activity to the political arena, sometimes from choice, but often from necessity. Who has the government becomes a matter of overriding concern. This sequence promotes and exacerbates political tension and conflict, especially so in the multi-racial and multi-tribal countries of Black Africa. One of the results is the emergence of centrifugal forces and of armed conflict which in turn invites forcible suppression.

The rulers in Black Africa are largely articulate, recently urbanised people as are their allies in the politicised military. There are wide differences in political and military effectiveness between these rulers and the unorganised, inarticulate and illiterate rural people. This difference affects the way political power is exercised, including the operation of controls, the method of taxation, and the pattern of public spending.

The primary interest of the rulers is to maintain themselves in power and to extend it as much as possible. For this purpose they reward their supporters and enfeeble their actual or potential rivals and opponents. Therefore, they try to reduce their subjects to an undifferentiated malleable mass by removing all social and economic distinctions among them.

In the pursuit of their overriding objectives, the rulers are unconcerned with the hardships they inflict. Recurrent examples include large-scale maltreatment of their subjects, often but by no means always ethnic or tribal minorities, maltreatment extending to officially perpetrated, encouraged or tolerated killings and massacres; coercive transfer of population, including enforced herding of people into so-called socialist villages, often mere sites; suppression of private trade; forced collectivisation and other forms of confiscation. These policies have often been reported in the Western press, including newspapers notably sympathetic to the new African governments, such as the *Washington Post, The New York Times, The Times* (London), and the *Financial Times*.

In recent decades in Africa, despotism and lawlessness have gone hand in hand. Economic controls have provoked and exacerbated conflict. Preoccupation with these controls has diverted the resources and attentions of governments from the basic task of protecting lives and legitimate property. Indeed, over wide areas of Black Africa, the governments themselves have destroyed public security. Large-scale maltreatment of their subjects by the rulers extending to massacres, killings and forcible removement of people from their homes to distant regions and the breakdown of public security have inflicted massive hardship on millions of Black Africans. Persistent fear for their lives and property has become the lot of millions.

It is sometimes thought that the situation in Black Africa represents a reversion to pre-colonial tribal conflicts. The analogy is incomplete. The traditional chiefs often ruled capriciously and brutally. But within the confines of their tribes, at any rate, they were usually constrained by tribal councils, by custom and by fear of deposition. They were much closer to their people than are the contemporary rulers. Nor did they possess such physical and financial resources as do the contemporary despots. These resources have all too often been augmented by the West, a matter to which I shall shortly return.

Nor are the African governments elective. Governments change not through elections, but through coup, civil war, or the death of the ruler. (Dr. Nyerere has resigned as President of Tanzania but remains President of its sole party in which power is vested.)

## Some Results of Economic Controls

The oft-noted pervasive corruption in Black Africa does not inhere in the African character. Nor does it inhere in the extended family, though this system facilitates the spread of corruption which originates in other government involvement in the economy which underwent a rapid and large-scale extension in Africa after World War II. Under some of the controls, corruption became practically inescapable. Two major economic controls, state monopoly over agricultural exports and import licensing, throw into relief the operation of economic control in Africa.

State monopoly over agricultural exports in British Africa was introduced first in British West Africa (the marketing boards) and subsequently extended to East Africa and elsewhere. Restrictive licensing of traders and processors, on the other hand, was first introduced in the 1930s in East Africa and subsequently spread to West Africa. Such spread of control was the result of centralised decision making in a dirigiste climate at high echelons both in London and in the colonies. This was accompanied by the diminution of the status and influence of provincial commissioners and district officers closer to the grass roots.

The West African marketing boards were established during the war and put on a permanent footing in the early post-war years. The British government documents announcing these measures incorporated categoric assurances that the boards would on no account serve as instruments of taxation. They would act as agents and trustees for producers by means of short-term, intra-seasonal, price stabilisation. These assurances were promptly broken.

From their inception to the early 1960s (when some of the boards ceased to publish accounts), many hundreds of millions of pounds were withheld from West African producers by the boards directly and through other taxes made possible by this system. This extremely heavy taxation operated both in the terminal years of colonial rule and continued after independence. It represented taxation at rates far higher than those borne by other groups with comparable incomes in West Africa.

As a result of the operation of the marketing boards, hundreds of millions of pounds came to be handled by people who previously had thought in terms of only very modest sums. They had little experience of government or sympathy for the majority of the people. The marketing board system was also inherently corrupt in that its operation was unrelated to its declared purposes and also clearly violated formal official undertakings. In any case, the primary loyalties of the politicians and civil servants who controlled the boards were to their families, relatives, friends and political allies, not to the abstract concept of the public welfare of large and heterogeneous countries. Understandably, and even inescapably, they used the system in their own political and personal interests and those of their families and allies.

The funds which accrued to the boards and the governments through the operation of the state export monopolies were spent in accordance with the priorities of the rulers. Large-scale political and personal favours, military spending, prestige projects, expensive government buildings, heavily subsidised industrial or commercial ventures (many of them complete failures), and loss-making co-operatives had been prominent among these priorities, to some extent already in the late colonial period and more so since independence. In Ghana, for instance, the Nkrumah Government rapidly dissipated the large reserves of the export monopolies inherited from the Colonial Government, spent the cocoa revenues and was bankrupt after several years of acute shortage of consumer goods in the country.

In their early years the operation of the marketing boards reflected the personal and political interests and inclinations first of the British civil servants and to some extent also the influence of the trading firms. Subsequently, they served the purposes of African politicians and administrators and those of their agents and allies. Neither the British civil servants, nor the politicians and administrators in control of the boards, ever had to pay much heed to their unorganised and largely inarticulate constituents or subjects.

In Black Africa there is generally no effective price control at the retail level. In its absence the allocation of an import licence or of a controlled commodity at a price below the market clearing level produces a windfall the size of which is readily ascertainable. This generates a scramble for licences and controlled supplies. Extensive corruption becomes inescapable: the bribe serves as a rationing device and as a partial return of a gift. The windfalls which accompany specific controls also set up and exacerbate political conflict, especially in multi-ethnic societies.

Such results of the controls are examples of the interaction of the familiar variables of economic theory, such as prices and quantities, with factors treated as parameters, such as the political climate or the extent of the exchange economy. This type of interaction deserves closer attention in economics, especially in development economics, than it often receives.

## Western Aid Reinforces Totalitarian Rule

Western politicians, civil servants, academics, people in the media and businessmen bear a distinct responsibility for the widely prevalent despotism, lawlessness and corruption in Black Africa.

The controls introduced in the last years of colonial rule politicised economic life and intensified the struggle for political power. This result was much reinforced and extended by massive official aid to the new governments. This aid has enabled them to pursue, for years on end, barbarous policies which also entailed extremely damaging economic results. Thus it was Western aid which enabled Dr. Nyerere to continue so long with forcible collectivisation, with the forcing of millions of people into socialist villages, with suppression of trade. Dr. Nyerere not only received massive Western aid, but was held up by Western spokesmen, notably including Mr. McNamara, as an example to be followed by other African rulers. The critical role of Western aid in the political survival of Dr. Nyerere has been freely acknowledged by his Western admirers.

The totalitarian rule of a number of other African despots, including Nkrumah, among others, was for long shored up by Western economic aid. Sustained large-scale Western aid to the Government of Ethiopia has certainly been of great assistance to that Marxist-Leninist dictatorship and may well have been indispensable for its survival. Official Western aid to that government has been in place since the mid-seventies and it still continues on a large scale. Over this period the government pursued all the damaging policies listed in section 4 above, which in turn were largely behind the several civil wars still (as of June 1986) being waged in Ethiopia.

The West also provided military assistance to despotic rulers. British military and financial aid enabled Obote of Uganda in 1966 to destroy the widely popular Kabaka and his many supporters and to establish his dictatorship. When the Tanzanian army mutinied in the 1960s, Britain provided the troops requested by Dr. Nyerere to enable him to stay in power. President Mobutu of Zaire also owes his survival to Western military and economic support.

Without aid, African rulers might well have decided to rely on less economic control and on less large-scale brutality. They might have had to rely more on market forces. African experience contradicts rather than supports the currently much canvassed idea that official aid could be used to bribe the recipients into more market-oriented policies. The opposite outcome is much more probable. Closely controlled economies serve the purpose of the new rulers in Africa; they will abandon close economic control only if they are forced to do so by the danger of a breakdown. If they are rescued, they will not abandon it even though they may pay lip service to private initiative. It is therefore not surprising that advocates of so-called policy-oriented aid have already begun to warn that it would be politically unwise to ask recipients to liberalise more than a small part of their economies.

Western academics, media men and businessmen have also helped along the politicisation of life in Africa. The special interest groups behind the marketing board system and the import controls included both civil servants and merchants. State economic monopoly was welcomed by academics who also provided the stream of insubstantial and inconsistent rationalisations for the special taxation of the producers. Western academics have persistently supported both so-called development planning in Africa and official aid, and the linking of aid to the adoption of comprehensive planning. Comprehensive planning, i.e., extensive state economic control and official aid, have been the two principal policy proposals of modern mainstream development economics.

Since the war, both academics and the media in the West have widely supported African governments, however coercive and brutal, as long as they could be labelled progressive. This label has come to carry a set of distinct connotations: distrust of the market system, personal freedom, private enterprise, private property and individual farming; pursuit of politically organised egalitarianism; and rejection of traditional rulers, even if freely accepted by the population. Hostility to the West is also often part of this syndrome.

Both academics and people in the media have often rationalised or excused totalitarian policies as necessary for economic progress and for nation building. These policies have patently obstructed economic advance and emergence from poverty. The advocates of nation building regard people as bricks rather than as human beings, bricks to be manipulated at will for the purposes of the rulers. Far from building nations, throughout Africa such policies have engendered large-scale violent conflict and generated centrifugal forces.

Nkrumah enjoined African politicians first to seek the political kingdom because, if they attained that, all else would be added unto them. The support of the West has been indispensable for the success of this quest. The results and rewards of attaining the political kingdom have much exceeded expectations. For this outcome too, the West is largely responsible.

## Misconceptions and Misuse of Language

Liberty, Sir Isaiah Berlin wrote in 1958, was a concept so porous that there was practically no interpretation it was capable of resisting. The confused identification of the sovereignty of African governments with the freedom of Africans is an example.

Discourse on African matters has come to be vitiated by misconceptions and misuse of language. Blacks in South Africa are supposed to be enslaved. Yet large numbers of Blacks from all over Africa travel long distances to get there.

Indeed, public discourse on African freedom confirms that the world language of the late 20th century is not English. It is Newspeak.

# NOTES

1.  Mme Roland, quoted by Lamartine, *Histoire des Girondins*, Oxford Dictionary of Quotations, 1964, p. 408.

2.  Obafemi Awolowo: Path to Nigerian freedom, quoted in Frederick Pedler, *Currents of West African History, 1940-78*, London, 1979, p. 265.

# Discussion

## Edited by Michael A. Walker

**Michael Walker** As a moderator must be seen to be impartial, I won't in any way attempt to shape the discussions as they are ongoing. However, I have spoken to several people and made a survey of opinion, and it appears that the invisible hand is not pushing us in the direction that a lot of people would like to see the discussions going. Therefore, simply by way of salting or seeding the ground, I ask that we direct our comments or investigation toward the structures of government or the forms of allocation of property rights that are most likely to lead to the enhancement of freedom rather than unduly focusing on issues which may be peripheral to that. I ask that you bear that focus in mind in thinking of how to address the papers this morning.

There have been several attempts—Armen Alchian and Al Harberger and, to some extent, Doug North—to push us in this direction, but we have to some extent avoided it. I hope we can pull the discussion back to focus on these issues of property rights.

**Voice** You are infringing on our freedom. I stick up for freedom of speech.

**Michael Walker** This is why I say it is a matter of planting seeds. I will now once again don the mantle of the impartial moderator, famous for his moderation, and simply stand down.

The first paper of this morning is "Black Africa: Free or Oppressed?" by Lord Bauer, and the first comment on this paper will be provided by Brian Kantor.

**Brian Kantor** I want to take up one major issue arising out of Lord Bauer's paper and that is the influence of limited government on land use and its effects on the productivity of land. As Lord Bauer has told us, the British policy was to accept traditional leaders and local councils and hope that they would evolve gradually towards independence.

These policies of indirect rule entrenched customary land usage which, of course, was anything but a system of individual property rights. It was a system of common land usage and, of course, common land usage doesn't encourage the most productive use of that land. In fact, it strongly discourages it.

I have circulated a discussion of the effects of these policies on South Africa and Africa generally in which I refer to the work by Herbert Frankel in his paper called "The Tyranny of Economic Paternalism in Africa: A Study of Frontier Mentality." He contrasts the British policies with what might have been the effects of a more active involvement, and the replacement of traditional land use rights with private property. One of the critics of the British policies was one of the governors of the Cape, Sir George Grey, who, Frankel suggests,

> placed his finger on the Achilles heel, not only of South Africa but also of subsequent British colonial policy elsewhere in Africa, which advocated the isolation of the natives in large areas in which they were administered under systems of indirect rule and were supposed to be left to work out their own destiny. The reasons for their policies were not by any means merely humanitarian; they were adopted largely for administrative convenience and to save expense.

And then Frankel argued that

> looking back from the vantage point of our own times, it is clear that the root cause of the economic backwardness of various African territories, as well as the Native areas in the Union, lies in the failure to modify customary control of land occupation and tenure, which has prevented the emergence of land use and ownership compatible with modern forms of commercialized production in a money economy. The failure to make of the land a viable factor of production has condemned the peoples on it to eke out a precarious subsistence.

The South African government, regrettably, of course, built its own policies of separate development on the existence of these tribal areas and the authority of traditional leadership. Of course, these policies of separate development justified restrictions on the migration of Blacks out of these areas to the towns and, in fact, was the ideological justification for apartheid which, of course, you all recognize has served South Africa particularly badly.

These policies, incidentally, have recently been abandoned. It is interesting that the South African government has abandoned the policies of separate development which proved so impractical but, in fact, justified much abuse of freedom in South Africa, particularly economic freedom.

So, from the advantage of hindsight, I think it is a great pity that, in fact, the traditional land use system in South Africa wasn't overwhelmed or abandoned a long time ago. Something better might have been put in its place. Of course, one might hope also for something better than the kind of African government so clearly described by Lord Bauer.

One of the issues that emerges, of course, is what kind of African government could one expect in South Africa? Could one hope for something better, and has the experience of Black Africa influenced perceptions of what constitutes good government in South Africa? The most recent experience of Black takeover from whites, in Zimbabwe, is perhaps the most important one. The results, I think, have not been totally disastrous. The whites in Zimbabwe are tolerated, and a fairly large number of them still remain—less than half the number that were there, say, fifteen years ago. But Zimbabwe is not by any means a model society. It could easily degenerate further. In fact, there is very little encouragement provided there of the kinds of economic freedoms enjoyed in, say, Southeast Asia. Certainly, Southeast Asia hasn't influenced Zimbabwe. The experience of other African countries doesn't seem to have made much of a difference for Zimbabwe.

In South Africa, of course, the likely alternative government—and I will explain why it is likely—is the African National Congress. The ANC operates and thinks very much in the modern African tradition. Its views of government, the proper authority of central government, what government should be doing, how it should operate, appear very much within what has become the mainstream African approach. The African National Congress is powerful and is the likely alternative government in due course, because it has established its international acceptability. The leadership of the alternative government of South Africa, as of Zimbabwe and other African countries, will be anointed in the United Nations in the international arena. The ANC has played that card very skillfully. At this point in time, any government other than the ANC would be totally unacceptable to the international community. This, of course, gives the ANC itself enormous authority and power which is quite possibly unrepresentative of opinion in South Africa itself, including Black South Africa. So the competition, the constituency that matters, is in part very much outside rather than inside South Africa.

The experience and the lessons that Africa may have to teach Black South Africans would seem to be unimportant because the influence of that experience via the opinions of Black South Africans may not count for very much. It may not count for very much at all in that the ANC has managed to obtain for itself this power outside of South Africa.

One would have hoped that the experience of Africa, the failures of Africa, would have influenced perceptions of what constitutes good government *inside* South Africa among Black South Africans. The problem is that this experience, as yet, is unlikely to be very influential over the outcomes in South Africa.

**Raymond Gastil** I was very interested in Peter's discussion of the history of Africa and all the types of things they had done or shouldn't have done that led to the present situation. But in reading through what is going on in Africa in the Survey year after year, one gets more and more depressed and is struck primarily by the uniformity of the data, whether it be in relation to societies that are almost all rural or societies that have important urban sections, whether it be societies with a British background or a French background, or Italian, or Portuguese, or the United States, whether it be countries that have been aided a great deal by the West, or countries that are largely ignored, whether it be countries that are heterogeneous, as many of them are with very different tribes, or relatively homogeneous like Somalia, for example.

It seems to me that a lot of the explanation has to somehow lie outside these particularities of historical experience. I am not going to say exactly what those are, but I think they must lie to some extent in a lack of development of a basis for the kind of modern life and state-organized societies that have succeeded. The features that make it very difficult to move in the modern world, either politically or economically, should be examined in a broader framework.

**Walter Block** I would like to read two sentences from Peter's paper:

> Preoccupation with these controls has diverted the resources and attention of government from the basic task of protecting lives and legitimate property. Indeed, over wide areas of Black Africa, the governments themselves have destroyed public security.

In my view, if we had approached the governments of South Africa with an open mind and with no preconception, we would never say that "preoccupation with these controls has diverted the resources and attentions of government from the basic task of protecting lives," because the basic function of these governments is *not* to protect lives or property or anything of that sort. It is to engage in kleptocracy or robbery or what have you.

I think a value-free social science approach towards these governments would identify them clearly for what they are. They are not groups that have been diverted from the main goal of protecting anything. They are working very efficiently at what they want to do, which is to take advantage of and brutalize their population.

I see corruption in these cases as a positive. Corruption is only a negative if what the corruption is a reaction against is a positive. But it is patently clear—certainly from Peter's analysis—that what these African governments are giving us is the very opposite of what we would desire. Therefore, the corruption is a positive.


**Gordon Tullock** First, the normal situation of the human race has been to live under a despotism of one sort or another, usually quasi-hereditary—it isn't perfectly hereditary, but quasi-hereditary—which is pretty obviously run primarily for the benefit of the people at the top. They have charitable impulses like the rest of us, and they do nice things, but basically they are selfish. On the whole, this form of government (although I don't regard it as ideal) hasn't worked out too badly. It seems to me, on the whole, if we look at Africa what we should hope for is to move them up to the level of the ordinary autocracy.

The ideal autocracy would run a very efficient economy and tax it heavily in order to maximize returns. I mentioned to you that I have just finished a book on autocracy, and as far as I can see there are almost none that actually do this. It is not very obvious why not. But there are a lot of them that come closer to it than the average African autocracy. They do give reasonable service to their citizens. They don't like crime because it lowers taxes and they don't like foreign invasion because it lowers taxes and they don't like disease because it lowers taxes, so they give reasonable service. If we have realistic goals in Africa, it seems to me that what we should be doing is trying to improve the security of the present dictators.

In Zaire the road system has collapsed because they simply haven't wasted resources rebuilding it, because Mobuto doesn't know if he is going to be around two years from now. But if you give them a longer range point of view, it increases their security. The way you do that is to teach them how to run a secret police. Secondly, try to see if they can't be motivated to just improve efficiency. Their methods of taxing imports and exports by these boards you are talking about is a very inferior way of getting money out of imports and exports. It does get it, but it is not by any means the best way.

Now all of this would in fact mean that the average citizen of an African country would be a lot freer than he is now. It is a long, long way from an ideal system, but I think it also is a more realistic goal than to suggest that we try to democratize them.

**Herbert Grubel** I wonder whether Lord Bauer or Brian could tell us a little bit about the experiment of the Ciskei. I feel that this is a most encouraging development and, for the concerns of this conference, I think it is of special interest. As you may know, the Free Market Foundation in South Africa has persuaded the government of the Ciskei to try the kinds of experiments that would really allow us to see the effect of establishing certain freedoms on economic and civil development. I wonder whether it is being carried through and what the effects have been thus far.

I also wonder whether there is any speculation, Brian, as to what the ANC might do with this experiment, if they were to take over.

**Michael Walker** Herb, this is really introducing a second subject. Before we go on to that, may I ask if there is anybody who would like to follow Gordon's point on the relationship between the permanency of government or the effects of the property rights the government feels itself to be party to, before we go on to that particular subject.

**Assar Lindbeck** Commenting on the discussions so far, when I go to conferences (which I do not do very often) they are usually economic theory conferences with the young people. At those conferences the topic is usually optimization models for governments, and the role I play is to point out the limitations of those models, considering not only lack of information but all the elasticities that are supposed to be in those formulas, and also the unrealistic assumptions about targets of government, pointing out the self-serving elements of government behaviour, the short time horizons of governments, et cetera.

But at this conference, I think I should take the opposite position because there is a one-sidedness in the other direction by many of us here, in particular by Walter Block, who assumes that governments are just like large-scale thieves. I think this is an equally one-sided view of governments.

I see politicians as rather mixed figures. They certainly have an overwhelming target to stay in government, to seize power, to enjoy power. But many of them, at least those I have met in my life, also have other objectives. Like us, they would like the standard of living to increase for the people in the country where they live. And some of them even want to provide freedom of choice for people, even if that often does not rank very highly. But I think high living standards and services for people are very usual targets among politicians.

We should avoid this very unbalanced, one-sidedness of dealing with politicians as thieves because that makes the analysis less intelligent than necessary. I think a much more realistic approach is to deal with politicians as very mixed figures operating in systems where survival often forces them to very short-sighted behaviour rather than to start by assuming they are just thieves.

**Peter Bauer**  I find it difficult to accept that these rulers have pursued extreme policies because of short time horizons. Nyerere has been in power in Tanzania for 23 years, Mangistu in Ethiopia for 12 years. I don't think their policies can be explained by the myth about the short time horizon forces.

**Assar Lindbeck**  It's an expectation calculation, how long do they expect to be in power? But I think your point is still valid.

**Svetozar Pejovich**  On the time horizon, I don't think it is important how long one leader is in power in order to judge the influence of the time horizon. Tito was in power for almost 40 years. I think it is the dynasty that is important. If you think in terms of a dynasty, like the Romanoffs in Russia or the British, it doesn't matter how long the leader expects to live because he knows his children will take over from him. I think you can argue that dynasty and constitutional governments do not differ much. They both have the same time horizon—perpetuity. The longer they're around the more they are perceived to be the same. And I will also say that resistance to any structural innovation is the same. So, if we want to discuss time horizon, I think the relevant issue is dynasty, not the life expectancy of a single leader.

**Tibor Machan**  Once again I want to come in because, in a sense, I would like to defend the integrity, intelligibility and nobility of libertarianism against the wildness of Walter Block. First of all, I want to say that it is a myth to think that Walter Block is advocating anarchism. He is advocating something that is a government, but he has renamed it. He now calls it a "defence agency" or your "protection agency" or whatever, but its function is exactly the same as the government's.

The difference is supposed to be that this "thing" is operating in a market. But here is where the major category mistake enters. Markets already presuppose a legal framework which is supposed to be overseen by some sort of a law of government, something like a referee in a tennis game. The players can't also be the referees. It just makes a mistake of analysis to treat governments, in that sense, as competitors—as IBM is a competitor with Data Processing Corporation. So whatever it is that Walter Block will substitute for this thing called government, even though he sounds as if he is eliminating the thieves, he is going to introduce another gang that is just as susceptible to thievery as the government that he has now wiped out by redefinition.

So, in effect, what we ought to look at is whether governments (or whatever you want to call them) can do their jobs better. I think Peter Bauer is on the right track to stress that many of these governments have gone off the course of what their job description is, and the task is to establish institutions and pressures on them which re-establish that course. Referees at tennis games, as John McEnroe will tell you, can be terribly corrupt and inefficient and stupid and so on. Yet, even he doesn't advocate their elimination. He simply advocates that they be more competent at the task they are doing.

Similarly, I think Peter Bauer is on the right track to advocate that these governments be devised in such a way that they can do their protection of the rights of individuals and get out of all the other business they are involved in.

**Douglass North** I want to make three points that appear on the surface to be unrelated, but I hope to bring them together.

The first point is that, certainly, as an economic historian and in all the work I have done, one of the things I am impressed with is that time matters in the world. It matters in the sense that we don't observe the development of stable political systems producing stable property rights emerging overnight anywhere. I think that is terribly important, because we are asking something like that to happen in a place like Africa, where we are going in overnight and attempting to get tribal people to produce something that took four or five hundred years for us to produce in the Western world, and we didn't even do it very well when we did it. But we still managed to do well enough to produce something like stable rights in the system.

The second point I want to make, which is related even if it doesn't look like it, is that there is a very interesting book by a woman anthropologist named Elizabeth Colson called *Tradition and Contract*. She lived amongst tribal groups in Zambia for 35 years and traced them through tribal groups with no state all the way on through colonial groups to independence. What she attempts to do is look at the kinds of contracts they evolved in this process. In effect, it is a mini-story of the evolution of property rights.

What she observed when there was no state is not surprising and, indeed, has been written about by Evans Pritchard and a number of other anthropologists, and that is that the threat of the feud dominated the way in which trade took place. Family groups traded with other family groups. Contracting between these parties was usually honest. If one party welshed on the deal the other party would not necessarily do you in but would do a member of your family in, so the family imposed discipline on the trading groups. It's a long story, but there is a long literature by Evans Pritchard and other anthropologists looking at the threat of the feud as a way by which one evolved some form of stable contracting amongst parties that had no state.

She then sees the time when British judges came into Africa, and this fits with what Peter was saying. The Africans adopted this very readily and very quickly because it made for surer contracting between parties and much less threat of having a feud or somebody putting witchcraft on you. So there was real acceptance of this process. It was a big step in Africa moving from a system with no state to one in which the state played a minimal but very effective role in guaranteeing contracting and bringing parties to justice who did each other in.

Now, in the third state, when you get independence, of course she sees this all breaking down, and Africans really having no way to reassemble and structure rights in the new system.

It seems to me that that is where we are. What bothers me about this conference—I said it at breakfast this morning—is that we are not trying to model the way political systems evolve, or how they evolve, in a way that will allow us to understand what this process is. As far as I know, the best books on Africa that attempt to do this are by Bob Bates in *Markets and States in Tropical Africa* or *Political Economy in Tropical Africa*. Both books attempt to look at how the political process evolved after independence that produced things like marketing boards and the process by which urban groups have come to tyrannize very scattered and very diffuse rural electorates in the system. All of this, at least, is an attempt to analyse, which gets us somewhere. I think that is what we have to do if we are going to make any sense out of this process and, therefore, try to make a positive step toward improvement.

**Walter Block** On this point, Gordon's implications and mine are at sharp variance. He wants to increase or introduce secret police and more efficiency in their operation. He wants to promote their security and increase their tenure. It seems to me that if Godzilla were in charge, Gordon would be advocating that he be fed more virgins.

If I understand it correctly, Steve proposes that we have a dynasty for these people. It seems to me, as Peter has shown, that these governments are among the most vicious, depraved and brutal on the face of the earth, at least today. My view would be to lessen their power, not to increase their power.

As to Assar, he misconstrues me slightly. I did not say governments are large-scale thieves; I said governments are large-scale thieves that are legitimized—a big difference.

As for Tibor, I would like to recommend two books that make this case a lot clearer. One is *The Machinery of Freedom* by David Friedman, and the other is *For A New Liberty* by Murray Rothbard. These make the libertarian case a lot clearer. It has nothing to do with referees, particularly. It has to do with the initiation of violence and a monopoly of defensive services. There is no justification for a coercive monopoly. Certainly the referee function is one that could be produced by slightly less bloodthirsty people than these dictators in Africa.

**Alan Walters** I think Gordon's model is a little extreme. The model of West Africa, particularly, is one of a number of profit maximizing monopolies. You see this in Ghana, for instance, where there are managed exchange rates and state marketing boards fix prices to maximize the revenue of the government. The thing that limits such expropriation is the ability of people to escape from the state exactions. What one should do is to limit the ability of the government to exploit, not increase their efficiency. I disagree there entirely with Gordon.

You want to increase the ease with which people escape such exploitation. This has brought a discipline on the government of Ghana. Much of their cocoa was going across the border and being shipped out through other countries. Smuggling *out* took place on a massive scale. What we ought to do is *not* improve the border policing but increase the likelihood of smuggling and the ability of people to escape.

Also, I think Peter is entirely right in stressing how important it was that the colonial governments of pre-1930 gave rise to property rights which were defined and defended. In Ghana there was massive development of peasant agriculture. The erosion later was associated with a very important phenomenon. Hitherto it was colonial government, and then it became, vaguely—and I think this argument was put by Brian Kantor—more internationalism.

Now we come to the stage where internationalism is so important an issue in Africa, primarily through the agency of aid but other measures too, that we see the spectre of Africans having neglected all their infrastructures so it's wasting away. The roads in Africa amount to 10 billions of dollars—often provided by aid—and were allowed to rot. But they know very well that they will be bailed out. The West will return and rebuild all these roads.

The governments look as if they are behaving like children, but they are not. They know very well that this money will flow in to recompense them for all the expense of putting their infrastructure right. So the internationalization is, in my view, very important in the drift from colonies to independence to internationalism along with the pervasive effect of knowing very well that they can tap the Western taxpayer.

The restoration of property rights issue is very important. They have all been eroded by this mixture of deprivation by their rulers, the inability of the people to escape, and the belief that they will be bailed out anyway by the international community.

**Gordon Tullock** An example is Germany before the unification in which you had a set of well established, highly efficient, very small despotisms. It appears to have given very good government as far as we can tell. I don't read German, and the people who prepared the study are idealists, so I am not sure if that is an accurate account.

**Alvin Rabushka** Yesterday, Alan Walters raised the question of why did Hong Kong and Singapore do it differently, and why did everybody else make a botch of it? He gave a very good account of it. I wanted to narrate a conversation I had in Britain last month with some recently retired high level civil servants of the Hong Kong government. I said, "Why did you do it right, and why did Africa do it wrong?" Here is the thrust of the remarks, because I think you will find it quite interesting.

In the first case, the independence proceedings were done much too quickly. The upshot of them being done much too quickly was that the proper process of localization, whereby a trained civil service could have emerged to learn from their colonial overlords, never occurred. So instead you put people into positions of economic and financial power whose actual experience and competence was at very low levels. This was compounded by the immediate rush of the international community to proffer upon them substantial amounts of money in exchange for following the policy recommendations. Thus, they got pressured into, as it were, all kinds of public sector enterprises which they had no business getting into but which were foisted upon them and then forever sustained by these international agencies.

They got heavily dependent on external loan finance rather than beginning with a view that might have been the view of the colonial governments of the pre-World War II period that would have been much more inclined to follow free trade, export-oriented policies.

Finally, they were victimized by a whole host of tribal pressures. The colonial process of independence foisted upon them one man one vote or, as they would say in Africa, one election once. In this system of government you had to get into this war of outbidding, in terms of what you did with the public sector resources available at your disposal for your own tribal unit. In retrospect, his view would have been that what you needed to do was stretch out, train, localize and keep the door shut to external aid. That would have produced a different pattern. Recolonizing, I think, is a touch out of the question.

Alan also partly stole my thunder because I had been sitting here going back through the roster of 104 countries I have tried to learn something about. In Africa one can enumerate only five, really, that by World Bank figures have turned in remarkable economic growth records. The two best—head and shoulders; nobody's even close—are Swaziland and Botswana. Swaziland is committed, by the way, to a principle of free enterprise. The king overthrew the constitution there because he didn't like it and re-established a royal monarchy. This seems to have been pretty good for a long-term commitment to free enterprise. Also, the private sector is pretty much run by South African settlers, and the same thing is true in Botswana. These two countries really have adopted intelligent, free market policies. Botswana runs a legitimate democracy, by and large, which is rather interesting. It scores high on political rights and civil liberties, and scores terrific in economic freedom. They all go hand-in-glove in Botswana.

As you pointed out quite rightly, the Ivory Coast is de facto, with a hundred thousand Frenchmen still within the French colonial ambit. Here the president is president for life, so the political freedom score would be quite low, but civil liberties are quite high. They have an open immigration policy. There are almost a million Africans from surrounding countries who freely work in the area.

With Gabon, which is oil-rich, and then Cameroon, these are the five countries. That's all there really are in terms of the high performers. I think they fall within one or another of these frameworks, which explains why.

**Brian Kantor** I think we should try to re-emphasize the international nature of Africa. The world intervened in Africa, and I think in some sense it didn't intervene enough at an early stage to force Western-type property rights. To this day, if you ask yourself how governments have come into being in Africa and how are they initially established—and this is the point I made earlier—the international community really appoints the new governments of Africa. Unfortunately, I think, the kinds of new governments that are acceptable to the international community, at *this* stage, given its nature, are not likely to do the right sorts of things for economic or political freedom. That is the reality.

Just one other point. I would echo Gordon's remarks. You have something of the classic dilemma in Africa at the moment. You want order, and perhaps only governments can bring order, that is, security of life and property. Yet, those governments that are capable of establishing order— efficient governments—are, unfortunately, likely to be effective also in interfering in their economy. That is the dilemma you face. If you have to chose between life and interventionist-type policies, I think you would probably prefer to have security of life. I think that *is* the dilemma of Africa. Efficient autocracy in places like Uganda would be very high on everybody's list.

**Tibor Machan** Doug North asked a very interesting question. Last spring I was lecturing in Italy, Belgium and Austria, and almost everywhere similar questions were asked—the old Leninist question: "What is to be done?" Unfortunately, I can only suggest an answer of another famous Marxist, Mao: "Let a hundred flowers bloom." After having thought about this for not a short time, I don't believe there is any mechanical way in which these things can be accomplished. I don't think there is a structure. I don't think certain kinds of engineering approaches that are desirable and desired by a lot of people can be realized here.

It is an extremely contextually circumscribed situation. Intellectuals have to do one thing, and if you are a politician, another thing, and if you are a bureaucrat, another thing, and if you are a teacher, another thing, and if you are a businessperson, another thing. If your values are this—and it is a big "if"—then you see a situation in which you can have an impact and you have to devise what that impact is. It sounds terribly mundane, but perhaps some of these things *are* mundane.

The only way to bring about these kinds of things is with the kind of activity Lord Bauer is engaged in—writing about it, trying to analyse it, giving analyses and information to the people who are closer and closer and closer to the situation. Conferences like this *are* productive, despite the fact that tomorrow morning at nine o'clock nothing much gets done as a result of them. But maybe a few things will be produced by the people sitting around here that will then reach that level where one who is very interested in practical consequences can point to it and say: "You see? This has happened."

I don't think we need to be so pessimistic, just because at this stage of the process it is mostly talk and there is no straightforward mechanical device by which to institute some of the good ideas and, therefore, it's all going to remain at this level. I do not believe that. I don't know if this is going to be regarded as addressing the point, but I believe it is the only answer you can give: contextual application of your ideas to the situation over which you have some impact.

**Raymond Gastil** I agree with Tibor on that very modest approach to the subject. But I wanted to comment on a couple of points that Brian made. One, it seems to me that the property rights argument may be right to some extent. Yet, if you look at India, for example—a country that has largely been left in a traditional property rights system as far as most of India is concerned—certainly in my terms it is vastly superior to Africa. Perhaps property rights is not a sufficient explanation.

The other point was the international appointing of governments, which is a point Brian made a couple of times. I think that is vastly overstated. Even France, which is much more inclined to interfere in this kind of thing than is, say, Britain, has tended in the last few years to give up in many cases and just accept whoever comes along. The current leaders in Chad are not particularly what France would choose, but they just pick up the pieces and wait for the next one.

**Peter Bauer** I find it very hard to follow Brian Kantor's dilemma here. He says that efficient autocracy is necessary in Africa to secure life and property, that autocratic government is apt to interfere in economic life. I think this is a false dilemma. The autocracies of Black Africa since World War II have not secured life and property but have massively interfered in people's lives. In Tanzania, Dr. Nyerere's government has collectivized land, expropriated property, and forcibly herded many millions of people into distant villages. On the other hand, the pre-war British colonial administrations were autocratic but did not interfere in people's lives. Today, Hong Kong is perhaps the freest economy in the world, but the government is non-elective.

**Douglass North** I wanted to reply to Tibor, because I disagree with him strongly. Most of us around this table are economists, and we have evolved some very sophisticated modellings of the economic process. We have moved from there to study property rights, and we have even evolved some models to analyse this part of it. Now you say that when it comes to looking at the political process, we can't do it. I don't believe that.

There is a guy on my left here who started *Public Choice*, and I think that while he may have led it astray—probably did!—nevertheless we have made a beginning in trying to model something that we have to get at if we are going to get at these issues. I don't think they are insoluble; I think they are analysable. Some parts of them may be more difficult to analyse because they move us from analysing how people in the self-interest models behave politically, but some of it also gets us into norms of behaviour and things that we understand very little about. But to say that we can't do anything about it is a counsel of despair, and I don't agree with it at all.

**Milton Friedman** I just want to come to Brian's defence against Raymond by citing a particular example of what he means by internationalization. So far as I understand it, Gatsha Buthelezi has more internal support within Africa than either Bishop Tutu or Reverend Boesak. Yet it is almost inconceivable that he could end up as the alternative government, simply because the American intellectual community does not regard him as a credible representative. Because he is consistently downplayed on the news and so on, it is taken for granted that when you want to get the view of a representative African you go to Tutu, you do not go to Buthelezi. I think that is a very simple example of the kind of thing Brian has in mind.

**Michael Walker** We are now going to go to Herb's point on the Ciskei.

**Herbert Grubel** A very interesting experiment in the Ciskei is relevant to our concern over the extent to which freedom supports economic development. I wonder whether people who are specialists in African affairs can tell us a little bit about how this experiment has gone recently.

**Brian Kantor** Leon Louw and his Free Market Foundation succeeded in persuading the government of Ciskei to adopt policies encouraging economic freedom. He succeeded where we have failed—others, like myself, have failed to persuade the South African government to move in that direction. So here you have a case of quite successful persuasion; that is, a government looking for growth found certain ideas about how you achieve that growth through deregulation and low tax rates—the usual range of policies that one understands encourages growth. That government accepted those recommendations and implemented them. I think there are good results. I can't give you figures off the cuff that would indicate the degree to which it is helping. Yesterday we heard about transport activity in Hong Kong. Certainly, the deregulation of transport in the Ciskei has led to a huge increase in the number of participants in that particular market, and transport is a very good place to enter a modern economy as an owner of capital. I think it is working very well. In fact, it is working so well that the South African government is concerned about losses of tax revenue and the tax haven nature of the Ciskei. So, in that sense I think it is clearly working.

Going back to your earlier point, Ciskei is vulnerable because it is based upon a traditional structure out of the traditional leadership which the South African government entrenched. If the ANC came into power in South Africa, they would conquer Ciskei and integrate it again into South Africa at large. So the continued success of Ciskei depends upon the continued survival of the South African government. It is completely dependent for its security on the South African government.

**Gordon Tullock** I have one very brief remark about Leon Louw's activities there. He has firmly carried out one-half of my advice; that is, try to make them efficient economically. Unfortunately, as far as I can see, he is trying to undermine their domestic security. He says he hasn't been very successful in producing freedom of a political nature there, and I think he hasn't. But he is certainly trying. It is not just conquest from outside that that place has to worry about; it is also an internal uprising which leads to the kind of government you are getting in the rest of Africa. Every citizen is better off with the current traditional regime firmly entrenched, although, as you know, it has had difficulty. I think the chief of secret police is now a refugee in another part of South Africa.

**Walter Block** First, I wanted to correct Herb who said that this was a right-wing organization. Leon Louw is not a right-winger; he is a libertarian.

Secondly, there are eleven homelands in South Africa. When the Ciskei experiment started, Ciskei had the lowest growth rate. By any statistical measure they were the worst off; it was just a barren wasteland. Now, with a low flat tax of 15 percent, which starts at a very high rand amount so most people don't pay any tax and the rest pay 15 percent flat tax, and there are no controls, no marketing boards, Ciskei has become the Hong Kong of

Africa. It now has the highest growth rate of all the homelands. It went from the lowest to the highest very quickly, so that is one objective criteria.

The danger now is that there is a great immigration—everyone wants to live in Ciskei to take advantage of the freedoms. This is similar to what is happening to South Africa as a whole, with blacks pouring in from these bordering countries to South Africa. This despite the presumed horrors of that country.

I am a little disappointed that I didn't find Ciskei in the Freedom House analysis. I found Transkei but not Ciskei, and I would urge that Ciskei be put in and highlighted and spotlighted. I think this is a beacon for all of us on South Africa, and I am very happy with what's going on there.

**Tibor Machan**  The Ciskei incidents and the subsequent developments, for example, are being written up in *Reason*, very prominently, as a major story. It's getting to be known across the country here. I wonder what sort of systematic principles are exhibited in this kind of "how do we get from here to there" such that we could learn from it? Let's follow Doug's recommendation and learn from this. What is being exhibited here, so that theoretical economic analysis can benefit from it? Here is a test case. What are the principles that are at work here? A guy like Leon Louw reads some books, starts a foundation, presses on, influences government, that influence gets around, people in Napa Valley discuss it and then they go away to the World Bank and mention it and so on. How would you model this? That is what I would like to know.

**Herbert Grubel**  The Ciskei experience is like the results of a laboratory experiment in the natural sciences. That is what makes it such an interesting object of study. There is widespread agreement on the proposition that over-regulation and over-government leads to stagnation. But no one has set out deliberately to design policies for stagnation. All of our evidence on the relationship involves inferences and counter-factual questions. We have here one of the few occasions in history where a programme of policies is designed to achieve clearly stated objectives. Moreover, the policies were designed with the help of a blueprint which was drawn up by economists who believe in the power of markets, prices and incentives. I for one am most eager to learn the outcome of the experiment. Once we have this knowledge, we can build models to learn what was done right and what went wrong.

I have a question for Brian. One of the most important obstacles to economic development in the Ciskei has been the inability of individuals to sell land. This policy has evolved from a tribal tradition and has been in effect for a long time. It has been hailed by some as a superb system of social insurance since it leaves the option of working this land as a last resort in times of emergency. It has also resulted in the holding of extremely small parcels, many of which have been combined in large areas of fallow land without fences that is treated as a huge commons. Land that is farmed suffers from the application of inefficient methods. One of the recommendations of the Swart Commission for reform of the Ciskei has been that individuals be granted permission to sell and buy land. This recommendation has been approved by the tribal chiefs of the Ciskei. Has this policy been put into effect?

**Brian Kantor** I would say probably not. My impression is that the land tenure system has really not been addressed comprehensively. On the fringes there are experiments with alternative tenure arrangements, particularly under irrigation schemes and the like, but fundamentally the land still remains under traditional use. Therefore, the development that will take place will not take place on the land. It won't be the development of land; it will be other kinds of development.

In the Indian story, a vast proportion of Indians continued to live on the land. So the more productive use of land is really an essential requirement for development. Doug made the point that it took Europe 400 years before the land was enclosed. In Africa the land has *not* been enclosed, except on the fringes. Perhaps Peter Bauer will tell us more about the origins of plantation developments in West Africa. There are plantations in Africa, obviously, but the vast bulk of land remains under common use.

**Alvin Rabushka** Nothing fails like failure. I had in my office not too many weeks ago a delegation of advisors on economic policy to the prime ministers of eight French-speaking African countries that included Guinea, Mauritius, Chad, Niger, Zaire, and a couple of other basket-cases. After a discussion of David Stockman's book, which they had all been reading while they were travelling, we got into a discussion of developmental policies. By and large, what they all said was (a) their countries were complete basket-cases and they knew it; and (b) the prospect that the international community was going to be less generous (which they anticipated) meant they were going to have to be more responsible for their own resources. Therefore, they were quite interested to discuss policies and proposals that would make them more successful.

Finally, there has been a remarkable intellectual transformation. The supply-side revolution has basically converted the World Bank and the

IMF, although there is still going to be some inertia and resistance. If you read the last three annual reports of the World Bank, all they talk about is pricing, markets, privatization, de-nationalization and so forth. It is quite clear that the intellectual struggle is totally won in the case of African development, but it may take 10, 20 or 30 years to mop-up and get rid of this structure of interests that has developed out of the past policy.

So, I would say that, when Gastil does his survey in 20 years, there is a very strong probability Africa's economic freedom will score considerably higher and, if my own analysis is right, they will look better in the other dimensions as well.

**Assar Lindbeck** It is true that both in the World Bank and the IMF sympathies for the liberal market developments strategy has increased. Having had contacts with the World Bank in the last few years, I would say that the gain of the market-oriented paradigm is a thin layer of people who happen to be in charge just now. The bulk of the bureaucracy has not really accepted this approach. If those who are now in charge of this market-oriented paradigm disappear or fail, the planners can very easily come back.

**Michael Parkin** A point which Rabushka made a factual basis for a little while ago can be made with a different emphasis. As Rabushka pointed out, there is one independent nation in Black Africa on the Freedom House list that is free, and that is Botswana. It also is a country that is apparently doing very well in economic terms. I wonder whether Peter perhaps should have taken some notice of this particular case as an exception—as something that provides variety and a way of getting a measure of what has to happen in a Black African country for it to be different and stand out and follow a different and freer road.

I also wonder whether there is some lesson to be learned from those experiences we were talking about yesterday about how success stories get mimicked. Why it is that countries are increasingly looking at the experiences of Hong Kong and Singapore, for example, and trying to find ways of adapting what they see there. Is there anything we can learn by this more constructive approach of first of all studying the success stories against the failures in a comparative setting that tells us that something more promising can be achieved in Africa?

**Ingemar Stahl** Yesterday, we discussed the influence of the previous colonial powers on differentials in development between Latin America and North America. Now we are talking about Africa as an aggregate, although we can see that they have a British, French, German, Belgian, Portuguese and to a small extent Spanish background of colonial powers. This is more a question to Peter and Doug: could you come to terms with this model, or does colonial history play any role in this case?

**Brian Kantor**  Just a point about Botswana. It has one big advantage. It is a one tribe, one language country. It is a vast area, but actually most of the development is taking place contiguous with South Africa. It has a customs union agreement with South Africa and is part of the South African market. The major developments there are mineral developments financed by De Beers. They have been very encouraging to foreign capital. I think those are some of the ingredients of their economic and political success.

Swaziland also has the advantage of one tribe—a kind of unity which many other African countries just don't have.

**Michael Walker**  Peter, would you like to wrap up?

**Peter Bauer**  To begin with the most substantive point raised by Brian. He said that the British reliance on traditional authorities, which in turn favoured communal tenure of land, has been responsible for much of African poverty and stagnation. This certainly doesn't tally with experience in East and West Africa. There are three million acres under cocoa in British West Africa, with every tree owned and operated by Africans. The same is true for ground nuts, cola nuts, and coffee. This doesn't quite tally with Herbert Frankel's analysis and Brian's, which I accept in connection with the native reserves in South Africa. It doesn't explain the situation in British colonial Africa.

In fact, the development in West Africa was epitomized by Allan Mac-Phee, a British economic historian, as a super-imposition of the 20th century A.D. on the 20th century B.C. This was not stagnation.

Now, I am not sure that Assar had me in mind when referring to politicians simply as gangsters or thieves. That is not at all the thrust of my paper.

**Assar Lindbeck**  No, I didn't say that.

**Peter Bauer**  I see. I tried to show how the interaction of ideology and incentive systems has brought about the present situation in a particular cultural background or climate. I think chance also played a major role.

We ought sometime also to address the question of how the ANC, Tutu and Tambo have come to be recognized by the so-called international community as representatives of African opinion, much as Nyerere and Nkrumah were. I think it is common ground between Brian and myself that this is an inappropriate choice.

There is no such thing as the international community. There are certain articulate groups writing for a self-styled quality press, and they have a great deal of influence in the contemporary climate. How this has come about in the last 40 or 50 years is of much interest and importance.

There is an oft-quoted passage in Keynes' *General Theory* to the effect that in the long run the world is governed by little else but the ideas of political philosophers and economists. That is supposed to be the *only* thing on which Hayek and Keynes agreed. If Keynes' opinion were true, the world would have been on a free trade basis for the last 200 years because economists have very largely been free traders for 200 years. We ought to pay much more attention to the interaction of ideas, interest groups, and cultural factors.

Keynes' passage totally ignores the influence of religious leaders and military commanders. It cannot be denied that Christ, Mohammed and the Buddha had some influence on affairs in the long run, as did Alexander the Great, Julius Caesar, Napoleon and other military leaders.

I want to comment on something that Brian said—that things were not so bad in Zimbabwe; there are still quite a lot of whites left. Of course, they are still there, but over half of them have left. Zimbabwe looks very much like a totalitarian regime. If you ask the Ndebele you may get a rather critical opinion about Mugabe's rule.

The mimicking or imitative effect of success stories like Hong Kong and Singapore can be easily overrated. Sri Lanka, where the policies are very different from Singapore and Hong Kong, may have moved slightly towards a market economy. This has come about largely as a result of the bankruptcy of previous policies. A more market-oriented economy is more likely to result from a breakdown of a closely controlled economy than it is from trying to prod a government with grants and subsidized loans.

# Chapter 6

# Capitalism and Freedom in Latin America

## Ramon P. Diaz

This paper addresses the question of why the Latin South within the Western Hemisphere has fared so differently from the English-speaking North, over both economic and political affairs.

When the Latin-American Republics became independent in the early nineteenth century, to many they seemed called to outstanding destinies, quite comparable to those of the former English colonies. Adam Smith, looking at them before independence, believed that their wealth of natural resources would largely offset the handicap resulting from the inferiority of Spain and Portugal as metropolitan powers. "In a fertile soil and happy climate," ran his sanguine appraisal of their prospects, "the great abundance and cheapness of land, a circumstance common to all new colonies, is, it seems, so great an advantage as to compensate many defects in civil government."[1] About a hundred years later (and little over a century ago) Lord Acton expressed views quite as optimistic as Smith's, and as George Canning's had been in the 1820s, when England recognized the sovereign status of the former Spanish dependencies. Quoting George IV's Foreign Minister to the effect that his support of Latin American emancipation had "called a new world into existence to redress the balance of the old," Acton wrote that, although "it [was] still generally believed that in point of political and material success [the new countries contrasted] much to their disadvantage with the North American Republic...[by 1868] in the greater part of South American this [was] no longer true, for in several of those vast communities population and trade [were] growing at a rate that [exceeded] that of the Union."[2]

It might be pointed out that the latter part of Acton's comparison left out the political side. Perhaps it was just ellipsis, and it was being tacitly assumed that political improvement would follow in the wake of material progress.

Not all observers agreed. Alexis de Tocqueville, writing in the 1830s, downplayed the role of natural resources. Yes, he admitted, nowhere in the world could one find "more fertile wildernesses, greater rivers, and more untouched and inexhaustible riches than in South America." "Nevertheless," he bluntly interposed, "South America cannot maintain a democracy." And he dealt quite as tersely with the economic half of the comparison: "Other nations in America," he commented, "have the same opportunity for prosperity as the Anglo-Americans,...and these nations are wretched."[3]

And, of course, it was Tocqueville who was right—the benefit of hindsight allows us to speak confidently—and the others wrong. The Latin American Republics may have been called to prosperity and the rule of law, but they missed the appointments. Whether there will be another chance is a different matter, with which I will come to grips before I am through.

## The Latin American Economies in the World Context

That Latin America would have disappointed Canning, and reaffirmed Tocqueville in his skepticism, does not require proof, but I will provide some illustrations.

Table 1 summarizes an array of economic indicators laid out in a well-known textbook. The figures remind us that very close to one half of the earth's population live in conditions of unspeakable poverty. Two hundred and sixty dollars per head a year implies degrees of penury which we find hard to imagine. Moreover—something the table fails to show—the economies of the first class are growing very slowly in comparison to their populations. At the growth rate that they recorded during the '60s and '70s—a better time for economic development than the '80s are proving to be—they will take 58 years for their *per capita* GNPs to become twice as large, and that would only amount to a pitiful $520. Within this appalling class we find only one Latin American country, Haiti, quite unlike the others, furthermore, in most other respects as well.

The bulk of the Latin American population[4] live in the middle-income group of countries. This still means poverty, by the standards of most people, but of a different kind. Moreover, average growth in the sample period would lead the per capita income to multiply by two—should it be kept up—in 20 years.

On the other hand, even if Latin America's level of poverty is not quite of the tragic kind, even if the two variables in the table that proxy for quality of life—adult literacy and life expectation at birth—suggest that Latin America does better in that connection than regarding measurable income, that is not this paper's subject. What the table says about the point in question is that Latin America on the one hand, and the United States and Canada on the other, may live in the same hemisphere geographically speaking, but economically they live worlds apart.

The table also shows Latin America growing significantly faster than the United States, although more slowly than the industrial market economies, and just barely ahead of Canada's speed. Should these trends linger on, Latin America would catch up with the United States in a century and a half. I suppose hardly anyone would attach any meaning to that kind of an approach. We cannot reason as if growth rates were tangible objects, instead of the summation of a large number of varying forces. What is significant is that a country that has achieved a high level of economic development has at the same time shown that it has possessed certain virtues, without which sustained growth is impossible—virtues of stamina, creativity, stability, resourcefulness in the face of change or challenge— virtues that one day may depart from a given society, and the next day may settle down in the midst of another, but by and large have to do with the more enduring features of their cultural make-ups. Latin America has yet to prove that it has acquired these virtues. A fairly good growth record kept for two decades, *by itself*, affords no decisive evidence. The United States may have lost them, in spite of its having possessed them in eminent degree, but a lull in its advance is far from conclusive proof.

*Superlative* ability to grow, on the other hand, even if maintained for as little as a couple of decades, carries with it a lot of credibility. This is the case of the Southeast Asian countries. Table 2 lists the economies in that region, and in Latin America, that grew at annual rates of 4 percent or more on the average during the 20-year sample period. The two regions are similar in size of population (Latin America roughly 10 percent larger). The comparison shows that Southeast Asia outperformed Latin America by quite a lot.[5]

When one looks at the records of the economies listed on Table 2 one is generally impressed. One's skepticism at official growth statistics tends to melt down. One tends to recognize in them the sort of drive that elsewhere has materially changed living conditions, the sort of qualities that at different times have distinguished England and the United States, Germany and Japan. Well, all this in Latin America is largely concentrated in its Portuguese-speaking area. Abstracting Brazil, the region's growth rate for the relevant period reduces to a lackluster 2.4 p.c. It hardly seems that the Spanish-speaking Americans (outside the U.S.!) have already found the way out of their troubles.

The picture darkens further if we inspect it from the angle of specific economic difficulties. We then see the Latin American economies assailed by the twin foes of inflation and the foreign debt.

The author's insistence in comparing Latin America to Southeast Asia, now again in Table 3, might perhaps be objected to as unfair, Southeast Asia being admittedly too well-behaved a region to serve as an unbiased term of reference. The author admits this readily, but would in his turn point out that his starting point, the Smith-Canning-Acton great expectations regarding Latin America, justifies his criterion: Latin America was cut out to withhold comparison with the United States and Canada, let alone the Far East.

And then, does Table 3 not bring out with tremendous power the Latin American frustration? Does it not instantly explode all the exogenous-forces theories, or devil theories if you prefer, of the Latin American indebtedness?

The exogenous forces, I hasten to record, were real enough. William Cline has worked out an interesting appraisal of the effects of four different shocks to oil-importing LDCs. The high price of oil is reckoned to have cost them $260 bn between 1974 and '82; high real interest rates (above the 1961-80 average) are supposed to have meant $41 bn; the influence of lower commodity prices and export volumes, both due to the world-wide recession, is assessed at $100 bn; $401 bn in all, whereas the corresponding debt between 1972 and '82 had risen by $482 bn.[6] However, as Cline does not fail to point out, domestic policies, including reaction to the external shocks, were highly instrumental to bring about the debt crisis. And it is in this respect that the Latin American countries' debt profile stands out into the unmistakable individuality that Table 3 portrays. "Brazil," Cline writes, "...after the first oil shock,...consciously followed a high-risk strategy of pursuing high growth based on rapid accumulation of external debt. The resulting legacy of large debt proved to be an oppressive burden when the international economy weakened and exports declined instead of continuing their earlier rapid growth." Argentina, still according to Cline, incurred gross overvaluation of its currency by trying to combat inflation through the tabular exchange-rate system, eliciting high imports and discouraging exports, and was ineffectual at adjusting the ensuing disequilibrium, allowed inflation to get out of control in 1981, and topped everything by getting itself into the South Atlantic war. In the cases of Venezuela and Mexico, but also in those of other Latin American countries, "policies led," in the words of the same author, "to large capital flight abroad." Cline further writes:

> The basic flaw was maintenance of an overvalued exchange rate on a fully convertible basis, combined with domestic interest rate policy that failed to provide sufficient attraction to retain capital domestically. As a consequence, in 1982 the decline in Venezuela's official external assets reached over $8 billion, although on current account, its deficit was only $2.2 billion. Similarly in Mexico errors and omissions showed outflows of $8.4 billion in 1981 and $6.6 billion in 1982, and short-term capital outflows added $2.1 billion in 1982, for total capital flight of $17 billion. In Argentina, in 1980 and 1981 errors and omissions and short-term capital outflows registered total capital flight of $11.2 billion. Thus recent capital flight has contributed nearly one third of total debt in both Venezuela and Argentina, and approximately one fifth in Mexico.[7]

There is a missing link in the above-outlined scenario. The running down of the central bank's assets (or running up of its liabilities) absorbs money. There must have been one source in every case that kept the public well supplied, despite the public's permanent swapping of domestic currency for the central bank's international reserves. And most certainly, that inexhaustible source was the fiscal deficit. "In Mexico," Cline informs us, "the government...allowed budget deficit to surge to 16.5 percent of GNP in 1982 when the upcoming presidential election made the authorities reluctant to carry out effective budget-cutting measures."[8]

In other countries in the area the fiscal deficit was of comparable size. When the limits of foreign indebtedness were reached, other methods of deficit financing became mandatory. Convertibility at fixed or crawling parities had to be discontinued, and currency floating or, more frequently, exchange controls, often in combination with fast-sliding parities, instituted in its place. In short, inflation replaced debt expansion as the key financing expedient.

By referring again to Table 3 the reader may grasp the singularity of Argentina's debt situation. It should be no surprise to him or her that as soon as the country's creditworthiness collapsed in 1981-82, the Argentinean inflation reached levels that even in Latin America were unprecedented.[9] Table 4 records them.

These data tell us of the tremendous acceleration of the price growth, particularly since the second half of 1984. In the first 15 days of June 1985, producer prices zoomed at 3200 percent (annualized rate), and many observers found they had to revert to the long-unused word *hyperinflation* to describe a phenomenon that looked headed for the complete demonetization of the Argentinean currency.

The story told by Table 4 ends on an encouraging note—the last two lines bespeak a successful shock treatment of inflation. Moreover the Austral Plan, as this campaign has come to be known, despite its paraphernalia of price controls, was centered around President Alfonsin's solemn commitment not to print any more unbacked currency. So after all Argentina might have a new start, just like Germany did in 1923. But... yes, there is a but, and it could be couched thus—but...we are in Latin America!

And, in Latin America, remedies never go deep enough, never get to the roots of the evil. The Germans in 1923 went all the way to hyperinflation, and then all the way back to stability. Theirs was an exhibition in German thoroughness. Argentina's stopping just short of hyperinflation, and just clinging to the ledge of the precipice, has been a show of Latin American brinkmanship.

Thomas Sargent has lately laid down with great clarity what the essence of the 1923 German anti-inflationary policy was. "The government," he has written, "moved to balance the budget by taking a series of deliberate, permanent actions to raise taxes and eliminate expenditures." Then, quoting J.P. Young, he reports that, by a decree dated October 27, 1923, the number of civil servants was cut by one fourth; all temporary employees were to be discharged; all those aged 65 or more were to be retired; the railroads discharged 120,000 men in 1923 and 60,000 more the next year; the Post Office reduced its payroll by 65,000; and the Reichsbank itself, now that the days of hectic, round-the-clock money printing were over, started cutting down its staff.[10]

Not so in Argentina. The bureaucratic fat also there awaited the surgeon's scalpel, lest it would suffocate the patient. Instead of which the Argentinean government has come up with a diet. In Argentina not one civil servant has been touched. Their real wage has been allowed to dwindle some 30 p.c. A few new taxes have been instituted but, more than anything regarding revenue, real tax collections have benefited from the lower inflation. And the authorities have been able to borrow more locally, given the Argentineans' new readiness to hold securities denominated in local currency. But their success, which is far from complete, as the table shows, is also felt by most to be precarious. Structurally nothing has changed. The bureaucratic burden that began by pushing the country into a huge foreign debt, and went on to make it stumble to the brink of hyperinflation, is still intact. The core of the Austral Plan, after one year's enforcement, still consists of the initial psychological shock—the Argentinean inflation is down from four digits to two, largely because the people believed that the Austral Plan, to them essentially incomprehensible, somehow would work. Like the Baron of Munchhausen, the Argentinean government has freed itself from the quicksands by pulling at its own bootstraps.

But the essential facts remain, and the same applies to Brazil, who followed suit with its Cruzado Plan, and to Mexico, who is about to contribute a new specimen—the Aztec Plan—to the collection. We are not about to witness the happy ending of a horror story. We are just out of the theatre for an intermission. And then the show, with its triad of blood-curdling ingredients—deficit, debt, and inflation—will be resumed, God knows for how long.

Hardly the context within which we are likely to see Latin America finally keep its long-deferred appointment with prosperity.

## A Political Survey

The Western Hemisphere may be properly said to be the hemisphere of democracy. The Northern half is where democracy started. The Southern half is where democracy is most talked about.

This author is aware of the fact that democracy as a subject for speaking and writing has not been quite neglected in the North. Still, the sway it holds over the South's political discourse must be unparalleled. This is more clearly understood as soon as it is realized that in Latin America the word *libertad* is used invariably as synonymous of *democracia*. A country is free if its citizens have free access to the poll booths. If the elected authorities then make all the other decisions for them, still they are free. Free to choose? Yes—candidates.

A glossary of essential political terms within the Latin American context must have entries for two more words: sovereignty and revolution.

*Democracy* is a word with a small ration nucleus and emotional connotations that are both vast and intense. Sovereignty seems to be devoid of the rational core altogether. If the IMF subjects its financial assistance to certain conditions, the country applying for help has had its sovereignty impaired. If foreigners buy land—perhaps a hangover from Mexico's Texan experience—sovereignty suffers. If you suggest that a country's gold stock, that lies totally idle while substantial interest charges accrue on its foreign debt, should be sold, you are overruled for having ignored the role of sovereignty. This author has been accused of treason to the national sovereignty for proposing that the central bank should be shut down and people allowed to import and use whatever currency suited their whims.

The fact that people would then contemplate the effigy of foreign, instead of national, heroes on their money was widely held to be sovereignty-offensive. As I was driving to my office this morning I heard someone state, vis-a-vis the alleged privilege of foreign public-works contractors in local tenders, that sovereignty was at stake. Semantically, the word does not seem to exist. When its sound activates the ear drums, the connection with the spine appears to be direct, leaving the brain clean out of the circuit.

*Revolution* does have a clear meaning. It refers to drastic political change, something like the French Revolution, the infinitely prestigious paradigm. And then, of course, it has its thick emotional coating. Revolutions are good. *All* revolutions, that is. Results are sometimes good, sometimes bad. When they are bad, then the revolution has been betrayed. Anti-communists believe that Stalin fouled up the Russian revolution, or even Lenin did, if they hold stronger views. And so did Fidel Castro, and the Sandinistas. If by a conservative we are to understand someone who shares Burke's dislike of the French-style revolutions, then there are no conservatives in Latin America. By the way, the word *conservative* is still in use in some countries in the region to designate political parties; in most it is just a term of abuse.

This essential glossary can be turned into a cultural *vade mecum* by just pointing to the conceptual omissions that loom largest in the region's political discourse and by making one or two remarks about political education in the schools.

In the first place, I should mention that the Latin American's concept of the state has no conspicuous place for the judiciary. For a Latin American the making of laws is everything; their enforcement, nothing. The region produces a great many lawyers, but very few of the more competent or ambitious would contemplate joining the bench. They would much rather sit in congress, where a type of advocacy more suited to their talents—attaching more weight to eloquence and less to learning—is prevalent. Judges tend to stand much lower socially than in the Anglo-Saxon countries. Court-houses tend to be depressingly poor. Proceedings tend to be lengthy and dominated by red tape. Since as a rule there are no juries, only very rarely has the ordinary citizen any kind of contact with judicial affairs.

Perhaps in this connection Latin Americans are merely being consistent with their love of democracy. When Tocqueville came to America in 1831 he found the aristocratic ingredient in the society's otherwise democratic disposition "at the bar or the bench." "The courts," he wrote, "are the most obvious organs through which the legal body influences democracy." He had already placed on record his belief that "the prestige accorded to lawyers are now the strongest barriers against the faults of democracy."

And a little further on: "There is hardly a political question in the United States which does not sooner or later turn into a judicial one. Consequently the language of everyday party-political controversy has to be borrowed from legal phraseology and conceptions. As most public men are...lawyers, they apply their legal habits and turn of mind to the conduct of affairs." And he rounds off his vision of the aristocratic influence of the courts tempering the democratic inclination of society by adding: "Juries make all classes familiar with this."[11]

So it is perhaps in order that a society whose heart is turned wholly toward democracy should allot a lowly place to men who owe their authority more to their own qualifications than to the favour of electors or the preferment of those that the electors have placed in high office.

In the second place, the Latin American society diverges from its Anglo-Saxon neighbour on account of the reduced estimation that it places on the institution of property. This feature is more clearly visible from a historical perspective. A prominent Latin American, who was destined to be one of the pioneers of the idea of independence from the Iberian colonies—Francisco de Miranda—visited the United States in 1783-4. In the diary he left of this tour, he commends the workings of the courts, deplores the lack of brilliance of the legislative assemblies, and, quoting Montesquieu to the effect that the foundation of a democracy must be virtue, laments that North Americans attached so little weight to virtue, and so much to property, in allotting power and influence.[12] It is transparent that Miranda was disappointed at finding that the legislatures, both at federal and state levels, were essentially assemblies of property owners, with essentially business-oriented interests, instead of men of sensitivity, bent on rewarding merit and succouring need. I imagine that, had this visitor had access at the time machine and visited Congress in the twentieth century, he would have found its climate more congenial. But, although one of degree, the difference still stands. Property owners, or tax payers, have never been openly represented in Latin American parliaments, while they have always been a significant constituency, albeit often a minority one, in the United States.

From the angle of political theory, it might be said that Latin American democracy has sought its inspiration very much in Rousseau, and very little in Locke.

Finally—last but not least—I believe there is an important difference between North and South regarding political education. It has to do with the concept of the state that Latin American children imbibe in schools, particularly—again—the emotional coating with which the substantial core is thickly covered. It has to do with the role of national heroes in the system of values that Latin Americans build up during their young days.

A visitor to any Latin American town is bound to be struck by the number of men celebrated in bronze and marble in public places, generally on horseback, almost invariably in uniform. By leafing through the school history textbooks, he would learn that these men form a hierarchy, and that those on the top echelons are openly proffered to the children as the proper objects of a quasi-religious cult. Perhaps it could be said—even further—that they are treated as incarnations of a godlike entity, the Nation. The Greek city-states and their pantheons of gods and goddesses is the closest analogy that history can offer. Through the veneration of these heroes, children are taught that selfless service to the Nation, in uniform and on horseback, with a view to make it larger and more powerful, is the supreme calling for a human being. And that uncritical devotion is the proper attitude with which to consider their relationship to the State and its affairs.

The difference between South and North may be again one of degree, but I believe it to be pronounced.

Allow me to sum up the politico-cultural portrait of a Latin American. He or she believes that democracy is the *summum bonum*, that sovereignty is sacrosanct, that progress proceeds through revolutions, that the two powers of the state are the executive and the legislative, that property has to do with the seamy side of human nature, and that his particular republic has a claim to his undivided, uncritical loyalty.

And now let us inquire how the communities made up of such men and women have fared in history, particularly in the direction of freedom, or the rule of law, still from the same North-South comparative viewpoint.

The differences do not take long in making themselves manifest—they start at the very beginning, with the emancipation process. The Anglo-American colonies declared for independence because they had a grievance against the English Crown; the Spanish-American, because they perceived that the Spanish Crown lacked the power to enforce its sovereign rights.

When around 1810 the South rose against their Spanish authorities Ferdinand VII had been deposed by Napoleon, who had installed his brother Joseph on the Spanish throne. The Latin American rebellion adopted the appearance of a legitimist movement, in support of Ferdinand, on the same lines as a large faction of the Spanish army had revolted against the French, with strong popular support, in what the Spanish called their War of Independence.

A casual observer might conclude, therefore, that one and the same independence war was being fought on the two sides of the Atlantic. Behind the legitimist facade, however, the Spanish Americans were interpreting the word independence in quite a different meaning. What set them on the war path was the perception that Joseph Bonaparte had too much on his hands, with the Spanish and Portuguese uprisings and the presence of an English Army under Wellington on the Peninsula, to send reinforcements to its American garrisons. There is ample evidence that this was so, but the matter became transparent when Ferdinand recovered the Spanish Crown, and his transatlantic subjects showed themselves less than enthusiastic about returning to the fold, in fact were prepared to fight for the preservation of their newly won autonomy, with the help of Mr. Canning and the English Foreign Office first, and President Monroe's opportune doctrine later.

It is true that the Latin Americans could have invoked the harsh, monopoly-ridden, economic treatment that their metropolis dispensed them, in comparison to England and its colonies, as Adam Smith had pointed out.[13] Under Carlos III (Ferdinand's grandfather) some liberalization of the obnoxious trade restrictions to which the colonies were submitted had begun, but grounds for complaint certainly existed. It is true also that self-government in most cases brought along free trade, and the consequent encouragement to material progress. It remains to be factual that the Latin-American independence wars were not fought over these issues. What seems significant, furthermore, from the point of view that this paper determines, are the political effects of the specific forces that wrought Latin American emancipation on its subsequent development.

It seems fair to classify those forces as centrifugal. All empires generate them. While the centre remains powerful, they are neutralized. Once the centre weakens, the empire exploded into many pieces. This happened to the Roman Empire in the fifth century; and to the Spanish Empire essentially the same thing happened in the nineteenth century.

This, in part, accounted for the political fragmentation of Latin America, while the Union to the North held firm, although, of course, the much larger size of the former at independence time surely contributed. Thus also the enormous difficulty of carrying out any integration project to fruition in Latin America is made less intriguing. The Central-American Common Market, that everybody saw destined to succeed, scuttled after just a rough soccer game; LAFTA abandoned after an extension of the original period— in its turn identical to that set by the Treaty of Rome for the EEC's customs union—with two-thirds of the targets unhit; the Andean Pact no longer even talked about. These failures are puzzling, quite unlike any other results of integration projects executed elsewhere in the western world, such as the EEC's customs union and common market, or the *Zollverein* in the nineteenth century. The idea of centrifugal forces kept operative under the surface of brotherly solidarity therefore seems useful as a safeguard against total bewilderment.

The concept of centrifugal forces has the disadvantage of being a metaphor. It would be desirable to have something more objective and less fanciful instead. An economist might be tempted to hazard a utility-maximizing model for this purpose, in which the elites in the different regions were the maximizers, and the holding of power was a major utility-generating variable. The plurality of regional maximands would constrain one another, and would ensure the plurality of political units. One essential feature would be the absence of significant variables in the objective functions that worked toward social cohesion, like the purpose of preserving a unitary rule of law over the territory common to all the agents. Another relevant feature would be that the men likely to hold political power in their own hands—say, the men in uniform and on horseback—were a very high proportion of the elites, and those whose utility came from other sources, say business success, or just money, were correspondingly few.

But through the concept of centrifugal forces, despite its lack of scientific rigour, easier communication can probably be achieved. There is another dark spot over Latin America that this idea can help illuminate. I mean the area of territorial conflicts between Latin American states. It is well known that in the late 1970s a war between Argentina and Chile over a couple of islets in the Beagle Channel was only very narrowly avoided. El Salvador and Honduras actually had their war, not long ago. Paraguay and Bolivia, Chile, Peru and Bolivia, and Argentina and Brazil are other examples of belligerent confrontations. But this is not all. Reciprocal territorial claims are still alive, and plentifully so. Bolivia and Peru have them against Chile, Ecuador has them against Peru, Mexico and Guatemala have border delimitation problems, and so have Venezuela and Colombia, Uruguay and Brazil, Peru and Brazil. In some cases—fortunately not in all—military spending by these capital-hungry countries is strongly influenced by their antagonism. All along, in the meantime, the protestations of brotherly love and solid endless flow. Yes, centrifugal forces are an indispensable idea.

## What Happened after Independence?

The new states needed constitutions, and it could come as no surprise to anyone that they inspired themselves largely in the constitution that their prosperous neighbour to the North had adopted. Nor could it be thought astonishing that the results in fact of charters almost exactly equal in law differed fundamentally.

There was a shrewd observer, for whom it did not take long to grasp this, nor to associate the deep cleavage to the dual nature of the law, made up of letter and spirit, like human beings are said to be composed of body and soul, and to the varying difficulty of duplicating one and the other ingredients. Back in the 1830s Tocqueville wrote:

> The Mexicans, wishing to establish a federal system, took the federal Constitution of their Anglo-American neighbours as a model, and copied it almost completely. But when they borrowed the letter of the law, they could not at the same time transfer the spirit that gave it life...In fact, at present Mexico is constantly shifting from anarchy to military despotism, and from military despotism to anarchy.[14]

And this cyclical pattern of anarchy and despotism has lingered on throughout the region. Anarchy stimulating the hunger for order, causing the pendulum to swing, but, alas! all the way to despotism; despotism whetting the appetite for freedom, causing the pendulum to swing back, but, for some reason, all the way to anarchy; and so on and so forth; only despotism and anarchy assuming different garbs as time goes on and places change. For example, inflation, strikes and other labour-union-inspired methods of disrupting order make up the threatening profile of anarchy in Uruguay's horizon today, just after twelve years of military dictatorship, whereas in the previous anarchical period urban guerrillas played the leading role.

The cycles in the region are not synchronous. While this author grew up in a mildly anarchical Uruguay that thought itself the model democracy, the Caribbean was a dictatorial lake. At the time, the South of the South looked down on the North of the South and whispered jokes about banana republics while out loud protesting their solidarity to the enslaved peoples. Later the pattern was reversed.

Besides cycles there seem to be trends, or the political equivalent of the Kondratieff long cycles. Lloyd Reynolds believes he can detect *turning points* that are not just inflections on a cyclical curve, but the initiation of long-run, *intensive-growth* trends for the eight largest Latin American economies, that he includes in a study of "third-world" economic growth.[15]

Reynolds writes:

> In Latin America, independence was in most countries followed by a prolonged period of recurring civil wars, lasting as late as 1876 in Mexico and 1885 in Colombia. The turning point usually dates from the emergence at long last of a stable government able to exercise effective control of the country for an extended period.[16]

For Argentina, Reynolds sees the turning point in 1860, and it is certainly true that Argentina had fabulous growth in the next seventy years. The other River Plate country, Uruguay, too small to make Reynolds' sample, would have probably shown its turning point somewhat earlier, in the early 1850s. By the 1860s Uruguay's economy was growing at fantastic rates. Between 1864 and '68 several variables, like foreign trade, tax receipts, postal deliveries (in physical units) more than doubled (in real terms). Immigration was causing the population to grow at over 4 percent annually.[17] And roughly the same was happening in Argentina. Moreover, there was nothing about either country that would induce an observer to use the expressions "third world" or "underdeveloped" to describe them. At the time they were usually referred to as *young* countries, like Canada, Australia, or New Zealand, by which their high ratio of land and other natural resources to population was alluded. I would like to revert to my earlier quotation of Lord Acton, to the effect that several Latin American economies were growing at rates that exceeded those of the Union; at the time of his writing (1868) the River Plate countries at least seemed to bear him out. What is particularly relevant to my subject, both countries were practising capitalism after the Western paradigm and had achieved reasonable standards of freedom. They had very open economies, both commercially and financially, in which government intervention was small and predictable, and they had sound money. Uruguay in fact had never had any official currency. It practised free banking, and private banks issued bank notes convertible into gold.

My point in having focused on the River Plate in the 1860s is the idea that one turning point, however suitable it may be for Reynolds' specific purposes, fails to meet my own. I am dealing with capitalism and freedom in Latin America and I find that in the 1860s or, say, one hundred years ago, both capitalism and freedom were not doing badly over large areas of the region. And I could certainly say nothing similar today. One century ago a high-calibre observer like Lord Acton was implicitly extrapolating certain trends unfolding before his eyes to forecast that the South would eventually turn into something quite like the North. Today a similar view would be hard to find. The great riddle that Latin America poses is not that it is taking so long in reaching take-off speed. After all one in six of Reynolds' sample have not made their turning points yet. The riddle is that, after reaching something that could be perceived as *the turning point*, Latin America failed to stay on the course that seemed to follow naturally therefrom. Their difficulties do not have to do with backwardness, they have to do with instability.

## Why?

It is foolish, before the image of a country's failure regarding material prosperity and effectiveness of the rule of law, to stand in bewilderment, like Oedipus before the Sphinx. The answer may lie just in the utter simplicity of Milton Friedman's dictum in *Capitalism and Freedom*—"the typical state of mankind is tyranny, servitude, and misery."[18] Development theorists err when they indulge in so much hand wringing before some economies' inability to grow. They should concentrate on the handful of countries that succeeded in establishing the institutional structure that we call the rule of law, after which material prosperity flowed naturally in, and inquire, day in and day out, how on earth they achieved that unbelievable wonder—to constrain those in power, those who wield the sword, to act within the prescriptions of abstract law, and set them to abide, while in bright uniforms and on horseback, by the rulings of old men in black robes.

If Latin America's case calls for more than our repeating Friedman's dictum, it is because its countries were so close to joining the exclusive club of the prosperous and free. Adam Smith and Canning thought them eminently eligible for membership. Acton believed that some were already in and, in fact, so they were. But then they opted out, and *why* they did is a problem that seems genuine.

Allow me to go back to the skeptic in my sample of illustrious observers. Tocqueville attributed Anglo-American success to "their laws and *mores*." He wrote:

> Other nations in America have the same opportunities for prosperity as the Anglo-Americans, but not their laws and *mores*, and these nations are wretched. So the laws and *mores* of the Anglo-Americans are the particular and predominant causes, which I have been seeking, of their greatness.[19]

By *mores* he understood "habits, opinions, usages and beliefs." He recalls that the imitation of the United States' Constitution had failed, South of the Rio Grande, to duplicate the North's economic and political success, and concludes that *mores* are paramount as explanatory factors.[20]

Tocqueville speaks as if *mores* could be set up, transferred, or adopted, at will. "[Anglo] Americans," he concludes, "have shown that we need not despair of regulating democracy by means of laws and *mores*."[21] Laws, he has already pointed out, can be copied, but only the letter of the law is thus transferred. To infuse the spirit of the law is more difficult. Surely what Tocqueville refers to sometimes as the *spirit of the law*, and sometimes as *mores*, are one and the same thing.

Nowadays, we tend to call it culture. The root of the difference between North and South is cultural. Any bridging of the gap has to involve cultural change. And to bring that off is far from easy.

It would be wrong to say that what Latin America is in need of is sound economic policy. Up to a point economic policy can be improved from the outside, by persuasion and pressure, like the IMF often does. But exogenous policy changes are also flitting policy changes. *Cherches le naturel, il revient au gallop*, the french say, and they are almost right. Not quite right, though, because the word *naturel* in this context is based on the dichotomy of Greek origin and enduring reception between *natural* on one side and *artificial* or *conventional* on the other; while there is a third class of entities that the dichotomy misses out, as Hayek has explained.[22] In the dichotomy *natural* stands for everything that is clearly independent of men's actions, and *artificial* for what is the intended effect of men's actions. The third class includes all the effects of men's actions that are the results of "human actions but not of human design."[23]

The difference between North and South is not *natural*. It is not geographical; it is not ethnical.[24] It is, at the same time, not the intended result of men's actions. There are, it is true, parts of Latin America where the revolution-issued governments have chosen to dissociate their communities from both capitalism and freedom. But they are as yet only a small minority (even if a growing one). Most governments and influential parties pay lip-service to private enterprise, and as for political freedom, they proclaim themselves its most ardent devotees. And yet, political freedom is precarious, and imperfect at the best of times, and private enterprise is frustrated and impeded to yield the fruit that it is capable of bearing, indeed that it has borne generously in the past, in several parts of the South.

The trouble lies, therefore, in the depth of cultural undercurrents, where light does not penetrate easily, where deliberate manipulation defies the resources of social engineers.

### What Could Be Done?

Culture is not immovable. If allowed, it will travel. It can be changed from the inside, perhaps even in the desired direction. But there is no simple way of achieving success. Beliefs and prejudices are deeply ingrained in consciousness. Apart from which there are always vested interests with a stake in the existing arrangements, ready to resist change.

By concluding that the root of the problem is cultural, and not natural, however, we at least know that we do not have to sit and wait until a lucky cosmic ray hits a Latin American chromosome, and brings about a favourable mutation. Cultural mutations you can strive for.

Economic policy is not at the root of the problem, but some economic policies can help. That is very particularly the case with policies that promote commercial and financial openness.

On the contrary, nothing could be more damaging than intensifying the tendency to economic seclusion that the region incurred after World War II, largely due to the influence of ECLA's Raul Prebisch and his theory of the declining long-run terms of trade of primary producing countries.[25] The renewed danger that this seclusion might be intensified now comes from the financial side, and the mushrooming recommendations that Latin American countries repudiate their international obligations or—what is not materially different—submit them to unilaterally-determined constraints, after Peruvian President Alan Garcia's decision to limit servicing of his country's foreign debt to ten percent of its exports.

International economic relations are highly effective at bringing about cultural diffusion, by penalizing attitudes contrary to generally accepted practices and discipline, and, conversely, rewarding performance attuned to international standards.

Back in the early 1950s several Latin American countries cut themselves off from that fabulous engine of growth that foreign trade was again to become, once again, in the next two decades, by foolishly raising tariffs and other barriers to trade. Now it is being suggested that they cut themselves off from the world capital market as well. The necessarily finite burden of debt servicing, again foolishly, is implicitly assumed to justify forever relinquishing the international sources of investment financing. But that is not all. Isolated economies can do as they please over all matters. The world has no carrot or stick to entice or coerce economic agents in Albania. Theirs is a country enjoying superlative sovereignty. If this is what Latin Americans really want, they should call their creditors and tell them to jump in the ocean.

On the contrary, everything that Latin Americans do to promote their international competitivity and creditworthiness is bound to foster a cumulative strengthening of prosperity and freedom.

Then, of course, there is education. Education is the number-one method of promoting cultural change, only it presents a serious difficulty in the form of a vicious circle—who educates the educator?

The first thing in this connection seems to be to realize that a system of state schools is likely to become subservient to a quasi-religious cult of the state and its pantheon of heroes. With a method of education vouchers, on the other hand, even if there are no guarantees that it will change the countries' outlook and values, because of the vicious-circle nature of the difficulty, the possibility of a return to rationality at least becomes feasible.

And then, finally, there is leadership. Leadership that can manifest itself in all walks of life. By and large, this must have been the principal variable accounting for cultural change in the history of mankind. Unfortunately, its random component must be very strong. So when one gets to this point one is really just wishing Latin America, after such hard times, a streak of good luck. It could certainly use it.

Table 1
Basic Indicators of the World Economy

| | Population millions, 1980 | Per Capita GNP | | Adult Literacy %, 1977 | Life Expectancy at Birth, years, 1980 |
| --- | --- | --- | --- | --- | --- |
| | | Dollars, 1980 | Average Annual Growth %, 1960-80 | | |
| **Low Income Economies** | **2,160.9** | **260** | **1.2** | **50** | **57** |
| within which:    Haiti | 5.0 | 270 | 0.5 | 23 | 53 |
| **Middle-Income Economies** | **1,138.8** | **1,400** | **3.8** | **65** | **60** |
| Within which    Latin America (a) | 314.1 | 1,890 | 3.5 | 74 | 63 |
| **Industrial Market Economies** | **714.4** | **10,320** | **3.6** | **99** | **74** |
| Within which:    United States | 227.7 | 11,360 | 2.3 | 99 | 74 |
| Canada | 23.9 | 10,130 | 3.3 | 99 | 74 |
| **High Income Oil Exporters** | **14.4** | **12,630** | **6.3** | **25** | **57** |
| **Soviet-Block Economies** | **353.3** | **4,640** | **4.2** | **100** | **71** |
| **Total World** | **4,381.8** | **2,590** | **2.5** | **66** | **62** |

(a) Fourteen republics: Costa Rica, Cuba, Paraguay and Uruguay not included.

Source: Fischer & Dornbusch

## Table 2

### The Success Stories

Fast-growing Countries in Latin America and Southeast Asia, 1960-80

| | Population (mm.) | Average Growth Rate (%) |
|---|---|---|
| **Southeast Asia** | **253.2** | **4.7** |
| | | |
| Indonesia | 146.6 | 4.0 |
| Thailand | 47.0 | 4.7 |
| South Korea | 38.2 | 7.0 |
| Malaysia | 13.9 | 4.3 |
| Hong Kong | 5.1 | 6.8 |
| Singapore | 2.4 | 7.5 |
| | | |
| **Latin America** | **126.7** | **5.1** |
| | | |
| Brazil | 118.7 | 5.1 |
| Ecuador | 8.0 | 4.5 |

Source: Fischer & Dornbusch

## Table 3

### Debt Owed to Industrial-Country Banks by Latin American and East-Asian Countries, June 1982

| | Debt (billion dollars) | Debt per Capita (dollars) | Debt Service as % of Goods & Service Exports | Debt Servicing Disruption in 1982-83** |
|---|---|---|---|---|
| Mexico | 64.4 | 920 | 58.5 | yes |
| Brazil | 55.3 | 470 | 87.1 | yes |
| Venezuela | 27.2 | 1,830 | 20.7 | yes |
| Argentina | 25.3 | 910 | 102.9 | yes |
| Colombia | 5.5 | 210 | 23.9 | no |
| Peru | 5.2 | 299 | 53.4 | yes |
| **Regional total/average** | **182.9** | **660** | **66.5*** | |

Percentage of debt disruption  97

| | | | | |
|---|---|---|---|---|
| South Korea | 20.0 | 520 | 21.1 | no |
| Philippines | 11.4 | 230 | 36.1 | no |
| Indonesia | 8.2 | 60 | 11.3 | no |
| Malaysia | 5.3 | 380 | 5.0 | no |
| **Regional total/average** | **44.9** | **180** | **21.2*** | |

Percentage of debt disruption  0

\* Weighted average of debt-service to exports ratio computed by using *debt* as weights.

\*\* "Debt-servicing disruption" alludes to a discontinuity of any sort in debt-servicing during the sample period.

Source: Cline, p. 35.

Table 4

## Price Inflation in Argentina

| | | Percent Increase, Annualized | |
|---|---|---|---|
| | | Consumer Prices | Producer Prices |
| 1983: | 1st half | 312 | 276 |
| | 2nd half | 590 | 595 |
| 1984: | 1st half | 571 | 543 |
| | 2nd half | 826 | 720 |
| 1985: | 1st half | 1530 | 1900 |
| | 2nd half | 44.5 | 7.38 |
| 1986: | Jan-May | 53.2 | 20.6 |

Source: INDEC, Argentina

## NOTES

1. Smith, Bk 1, Ch XI, Pt III.

2. Acton, pp. 214-5.

3. Tocqueville, pp. 306-7.

4. The sample reflected on Table 1 contains approximately 95 p.c. of the total population.

5. Despite which Latin America's per capita GNP was still over twice the South-East Asian by 1980. Incidentally, the East-Asian land availability per head was about one hectare, Latin America's almost six. This would have given Adam Smith a bit of a shock.

6. Cline, pp. 20-6.

7. Cline, pp. 26-7.

8. Ibid.

9. Only Bolivia surpassed, more or less simultaneously, Argentina's record.

10. Sargent, pp. 83-4.

11. Tocqueville, pp. 263-70.

12. Miranda, vol. 1, p. 22; vol. 2, pp. 118-20.

13. Smith, Bk. IV, Ch. VII, Pt. 11.

14. Tocqueville, p. 165.

15. Reynolds, p. 958. Reynolds defines *intensive growth* as "capacity to produce rising appreciably faster than population" (p. 943).

16. Reynolds, p. 964.

17. I have dealt with this period of the Uruguayan economy elsewhere: Diaz (1985), p. 33.

18. Friedman, p. 9.

19. Tocqueville, p. 307.

20. Tocqueville, pp. 307-8.

21. Tocqueville, p. 311.

22. Hayek, p. 180.

23. Hayek, ibid.

24. The North Americans differ from large areas of the South in that their ethical background is quite independent from the continent's native populations. But the same applies to the River Plate, and to some extent to Chile also, and the River Plate and Chile have come to look more and more like the rest of Latin America. This simple fact exempts me from the rather difficult task—although, as I believe, feasible—of attempting proof that the difference is not ethical, or racial, or natural, after all.

25. I have dealt with this theory at some length in Diaz (1973), Chapter 2. Uruguay's catastrophic results for having heeded ECLA's advice despite its tiny size I have dealt with in Diaz (1984 and 1985).

# REFERENCES

Acton, John E.E.D. (Lord) "The Rise and Fall of the Mexican Empire" (1868) in Acton, *Essays in the Liberal Interpretation of History*. The University of Chicago Press, 1967.

Cline, William R. *International Debt and the Stability of the World Economy*. Institute for International Economies, 1973.

Diaz, Ramon P. *The Long-Run Terms of Trade of Primary-Producing Countries*. The International Institute for Economic Research, 1973.

"Uruguay's Erratic Growth" in Arnold C. Harberger (ed.) *World Economic Growth*. Institute for Contemporary Studies, San Francisco, 1984.

"Small must be open" in the Wilson Center Latin American Program (ed.) *Uruguay and Democracy*. (So far only a Spanish-language edition has appeared: Ediciones de la Banda Oriental, 1985.)

Fischer, Stanley and Dornbusch, Rudiger. *Economics*. McGraw-Hill International Book Company, 1983.

Friedman, Milton. *Capitalism and Freedom*. University of Chicago Press, 1962.

Hayek, Friedrich A. von. "Dr. Bernard Mandeville" (1978) in Chiaki Nishiyama and Kurt R. Leube *The Essence of Hayek*. Hoover Institute Press, 1984.

Miranda, Francisco de. *The Diary of Francisco Miranda's Tour of the United States*. Hispanic Society of America, New York, 1928.

Reynolds, Lloyd G. "The Spread of Economic Growth in the Third World" in Journal of Economic Literature, vol. XXI (September, 1983), pp. 941-80.

Sargent, Thomas J. "The Ends of Four Big Inflations" in Robert E. Hall (ed.) *Inflation: Causes and Effects*. The University of Chicago Press, 1982.

Smith, Adam. *The Wealth of Nations*. Cannan Edition. The University of Chicago Press, 1976.

Tocqueville, Alexis de. *Democracy in America*. Translated by George Lawrence. Edited by J.P. Mayer. Anchor Books, 1969.

# Discussion

## Edited by Michael A. Walker

**Michael Walker**  Ramon Diaz has some opening remarks, and then Arnold Harberger will comment on the paper.

**Ramon Diaz**  I would like to comment on Latin America in the context of the discussion we have been having so far. A number of success and failure stories have been emerging, and I think Southeast Asia—Hong Kong primarily—is very much a success story. I would propose to have Latin America counted as a great failure story. I think Africa, which could not be termed a success, elicits less surprise than Latin America.

At its inception, Latin America was considered a land of promise, and for a time it worked well. We have a totally different problem from the African one. When we asked ourselves what might be done, we were confronted with a situation in which nothing good, or very little good, has happened. In the case of Latin America, we find a set of countries that were doing perfectly well in the 19th century, at least some of them, and then declined. In Southeast Asia in Hong Kong we find civic freedoms and the rule of law. We don't find political freedom as a general feature. It is a fact in Japan. It is not in Hong Kong, in the sense that it is a colony. Hong Kong is a very special situation.

In Latin America we find a wealth of natural resources we don't find in Southeast Asia. This was considered very relevant by observers in the 18th century—Adam Smith, in particular, and later by Lord Acton. This is something in common with the United States. Another thing in common stems from the fact that Latin America adopted institutions that at least superficially looked like those of the United States. I think we have to bear in mind a complication. When Latin American countries became independent they had two paradigms, the American and the French one, and two philosophies of the state—the Lockean one that had shaped the American Constitution and Rousseau's that had been extremely influential in France. And the two lived side by side in the history of Latin America in a dialectical way and to a large extent in a state of confusion.

In the course of Douglass' paper we became conscious of the difference between densely populated countries in Latin America, which also occur in Africa, and very sparsely populated ones, as in the United States and in the River Plate. But we don't see a big difference as time goes on. Countries that had a sparse native population do better at the beginning, but then we see them converge and get more and more like the others, as though a cultural factor was becoming dominant.

We have mentioned the instability of the River Plate, Argentina in particular, when it was a success story. I could refer to the case of my own tiny country that clearly has to be an open economy more than a bigger economy. It was doing marvellously well in the 1870s and 1880s, and towards the end of the 1880s it began adopting protectionist policies. Why? I really don't know. The arguments given in support of these policies were totally contrary to fact. Supporters of these policies invoked the need of creating jobs, but at the time we were receiving a tremendous influx of immigration attracted by excellent job opportunities.

The philosophy of populism was very readily bought in Argentina and in Peru whenever it was presented. I think that there are cultural undercurrents that have been dominant and prevalent in this respect. It is the Rousseaunian conception that the state, to which individuals resigned all their rights, will provide all the good things.

We have talked about democracy and majority rule. From a Latin American perspective, I want to stress that democracy is more than majority rule. I would like to stress that liberal democracies of the West have the rule of law and, particularly, an independent and competent judiciary, an expedient judiciary. Latin American countries don't, and we are tremendously at fault in having failed to produce this.

The extremely interesting question that Tibor was asking is: what could be done? I think there is nothing but to preach, to explain, to get more people to understand and particularly to press for policies of openness. Those are the great dispensers of discipline.

My country, which had done very well and was one of the high income countries of the world in per capita terms, closed itself and declined steadily. There was nothing to show that things were going badly. With an open economy, I think your mistakes show much more quickly. I think openness will make for better development of institutions that will ensure property rights and promote investment.

**Arnold Harberger** I have known Ramon Diaz for a long time, and I have come to have a very high respect and regard for his erudition and opinions. I very much appreciated his paper.

To explain the lack of economic development in Latin America is difficult, particularly since, as we have pointed out earlier, some episodes of good economic progress indeed have taken place. I wrote down a list of things that I find different in Latin America. The role of the state, which Ramon emphasized, is certainly a lot higher. It is a more unified and commanding state than we have in the United States and Western Europe. The role of the military is very different from that here—much more interventionist and feeling themselves somehow responsible for how things go. The role of the Church, obviously, has been very great in Latin America throughout history, although it has varied and there have been a lot of anticlerical movements too—but very different from North America. The role of business has been very different.

I am thinking of these as a hierarchy with the state on top, the military, then the Church. So pretty far down in the scheme comes business. Business is often too much hand-in-hand with the government, and the rest of the time it is being stepped on. It seems to me that very rarely is business just going about *doing business* as it is in this part of the world.

Last, I would say education has had a low priority in Latin America compared with North America and Western Europe. It has been unfortunate that there has been relatively little upward social mobility in Latin America, which I think is part of the reason why populist and romanticist notions catch on.

Autocracy is an old story, as Gordon has pointed out, and it is old in Latin America. But the expanding role of the state is new. It is new worldwide, and I think it has taken some roots in ideas. I know of only two cases in Latin America of a contracting role of the state: one is Uruguay in the period after 1974, when friends of free markets were in charge of the Uruguayan economic policy; the other is Chile, when other friends of free markets were running *that* economic policy. By the way, the Chilean reduction in the role of the state entailed eliminating 150,000 government jobs, which in the United States would be equivalent to eliminating three million jobs. So you can see something of the task that faces a lot of these countries if they are going to seriously reduce government's role.

Now, military government is no guarantee. This is part of our dilemma. The best eras of economic policy in recent time in Latin America have largely been under military governments: the Brazilian miracle; the Uruguayan miracle, turning around a quarter century of stagnation; the Chilean mini-miracle, and perhaps a second mini-miracle now in progress in Chile; Guatemala, definitely in the 1960s and early 1970s; and maybe Nicaragua even in that period (I'm not so sure about that case, but I think they had a good growth rate anyway). The really good performances that were *not* military governments are Mexico in the period 1955 to 1972, when they had two profoundly valuable people, Rodrigo Gomez and Antonio Ortiz Mena, running the show for 17 years. These two men produced more growth and more stability in Mexico with no oil than Mexico had later with all the oil but no Rodrigo Gomez. You figure that one out.

In Latin America, unfortunately, there is a predilection to romanticism. There is a tremendous, incredible vulnerability to demagogy—that is our great enemy in Latin America. There has been a tremendous development of mythologies in the intellectual communities in the universities and in the press—nationalist, protectionist, distributive mythologies.

Self-pity is almost a continental attribute vis-a-vis self-reliance. Asians think self-reliance in any situation in which you put them. Anything that happens to them was done by fate, and they respond positively to try to get out of the dilemma. Latin Americans are forever explaining that somebody else did it to them; they didn't do it to themselves. They are not thinking, how can I climb out? The military governments are best at leading them to think their way out of that, but it is a terrible dilemma for us as freedom-loving individuals. How do we cope with that dilemma? Eighty percent of the time we see something we like in government policy it comes from a kind of government we don't approve of as a political system. This dilemma of freedom versus autocracy is present in Latin America.

I go to East Asia and I admire them, but I think their autocracy is much tougher than the Latin one. But somehow it doesn't strike us, or our press representatives, or our people as so bad, because they come out of a different tradition where that is a more natural course of events. So I don't really know how we should react. I think the big challenge for us to think about in Latin America, and ultimately the linchpin for what's going to happen, is how can one reduce the size of the state?

I am just going to tell one final story. I worked for the government of Panama in the Planning Ministry for more than ten years, helping with economic policy, happily, in a good period. We had quarters behind the Presidency of the Republic, with a galvanized roof that sometimes leaked and a floor that had holes in it. Gradually we got carpet on the floor, the leaks were patched in the roof, and a couple of things were added. When Nicky Barletta was minister, there were two cars in the whole Ministry of Planning—an old Mercury that the Minister himself drove, and one car with one driver that everyone else could go around in if they needed to for some official business. I went back in 1984 on two or three occasions. The same ministry was now housed in a five-storey, gleaming white building. There were 80 cars and 80 drivers. There was a raft of secretaries in the front of the office where I was working, all reading novels or talking to their boyfriends on the telephone. I would want somebody to place a call, and I would come to the secretary closest to me, and she would look up from her book and say, "Why me?" Now that vision of government—as having to give people jobs, people having the right to those jobs, the idea of productivity absolutely disappearing, and people asking why you are putting upon them when you ask them to do one little thing that is productive—has proliferated more through Latin America than many people are aware. When I say you have to cut the size of the state, I really mean it, and I am referring to this kind of thing which is endemic in many, many parts of Latin America. It is the true danger as far as I can see.

**Milton Friedman** I wanted to expand a footnote which Ramon Diaz has in his paper that has to do with the reference to Adam Smith. In discussing it with Rose's brother, Aaron Director, who is a great admirer and expert on Adam Smith, he points out that there is a very significant difference between the statements Adam Smith made about North and South America. With respect to North America, he said it was both prosperous now but it also will continue to rise in prosperity. He said, if it remained part of the Empire, the capital of the British Empire would move over to the other side of the world because it was already more prosperous and would become increasingly so—a remarkably accurate prediction.

On the other hand, with respect to Latin America he made the statement that they had lots of natural resources and it is possible that they would be able to overcome the bad features of their institutions, but he never made any predictions that they would.

**Walter Block** I wanted to get back to Tibor's question of what is to be done. I certainly agree with Arnold that reducing the size of the state is the best thing, although I would say that second best is reducing the productivity of the people in the state. I like the idea of secretaries not doing anything, because mainly what they do in these five-storey buildings is to make it impossible for the private sector to work. So if we have to have a public sector, let's be happy that they talk to their boyfriends or whatever.

What can be done? I think reducing the size of the state is the key. Given our discussion of Ciskei, my question is, can we have a Ciskei here? And my answer is, not really. I regard Leon Louw as similar to the way Milton Friedman described George Washington—unique and accidental. Leon is articulate, personable, charismatic, and I think it would be hard to replace him.

Ramon mentioned the Lockean theory, and one of the things I would like to put on the table in this regard is the question of land reform. It seems to me that the discussion of South American and Latin American development is missing an integral point without this concept. As I understand it, there are three views on land reform in the South American situation: the socialist, the libertarian and the conservative. The socialist advocates land reform from rich to poor. The libertarian advocates land reform from the thief to the victim of the thief or, given that the thievery took place many years ago, from the children of the thieves to the children of the victims. Whereas, the conservatives derisively dismiss all notions of land reform. They say we should not have any land reform at all. It's too complicated; we'd have to go back to the year one; it's impossible.

Another argument against land reform on the part of the conservatives is that it is not in the interests of these people; they would be better off not advocating land reform and to just have a free market from now on. This is a confusion of positive and normative economics as I see it, because both can be true. That is, it may well be that the peasants would be better off if they completely forgot about all notions of land reform (positive economics) and also that they are morally entitled to land reform (normative economics), however unwise it would be for them to press on this issue, and just concentrate on bringing about a free market. As well, if you look at this issue from the point of view of the peasants who have had their land stolen, or their grandfathers who had their land stolen, they see two main viewpoints. The socialists want to give them land reform. They want to give them their property because in many cases the two go together; namely, that the theft was from the poor to the rich. From the viewpoint of the average peasant, it is the socialist who is advocating private property rights, and it's the conservative who is opposing private property rights. So, the peasant says to himself, if socialism is in favour of private property rights, I am a socialist.

**Gordon Tullock** These Indians never owned that land; the Inca owned it. They can't have had anything stolen if they never had it.

The other thing I want to say does deal with the Indian. In South America there is a very favourable development which is called "Ranchitos" in Caracas, "Favelas" in Brazil, and so forth. A lot of land is owned by the government in South America. The government is careless about protecting it, and people move in and set up a settlement. The government fights, and after 20 years the government gives up. So, in essence, they have it. But during the period that this is going on, you are going to have self-governing small communities which, to all intents and purposes, are illegal. Hence, they are not under very much state control. In the western part, the former Inca empire, they are perfectly clearly carrying on the tradition of village self-government which the Indian tribes had before. I think they are the most promising thing we see in South America.

Strictly speaking, you don't have them in the southern cone because you don't have this particular class. In fact, Argentina and Uruguay and Chile had a radically different history from the rest of Spanish-speaking South America.

But I think we have a very promising development popping up there which may—particularly if the government is prevented from totally strangling it, which of course it tries to do—lead to the development of a significant open economy. Certainly it is open right now within the ranchitos running up the sides of the hills in Caracas. They are building their own roads, putting in their own utilities and so forth. But they are also resisting payment of much taxes or paying any attention to government regulations.

**Lindsay Wright**  I want to bring up a new point. I agree with Ramon's description of the growth of the state and his comment that it is a fairly recent development—certainly, since the 1930s under Vargas in Brazil, the state has taken on a new character that it didn't have before that time. But I was surprised that he didn't mention the contribution of a corporatist ideology to state expansion. Under Spanish colonialism there was a transfer and adoption, by native populations of the Iberian-Catholic tradition, of an organic society in which the state played a large role in structuring state/society relationships from above. This phenomenon is different from that which some claim is occurring in Western Europe where state/society relationships are being structured more by societal interest groups. In the Latin American context, I think it is difficult for democracy to survive, even though a number of countries have recently returned to democratic forms of government. Given the continuation of that corporatist ideology, it will be difficult not only for democracy to survive but for the state to be reduced. In this case, I would agree with Walter that reduction of the state's role in controlling and organizing interest groups and associations, unions, business and professional groups is problematic and a great limit to political freedom as well as economic freedom. Perhaps Doug's analysis of institutional development would benefit from an examination of the ordering of state/society relationships from above.

**Ramon Diaz**  On Lindsay's point, I'd like to say that one of the best reasons for optimism in Latin America is the fact that during the early 20th century you have to remember that the homelands of that part of the world—France, Spain, Portugal, Italy—were also very unstable democracies with many interruptions in democratic processes, if they had them at all. We now have a solid group of fairly successful democratic regimes with predictable legal systems and so on, in a sense that we never had before. It seems to me that Latin American countries that have always looked to these countries may now be in a much more favourable position for authentic and predictable progress in the future.

**Assar Lindbeck** The corporatist nature of some Latin American societies strikes me as interesting and important. Certainly the Peron regime appeared to be a fascist-influenced corporatist state. Let me ask two questions of those who know something of this. The first one is, what is the main difference between the corporatist in Latin America and in Europe? In Northern Europe, Norway, Sweden, Denmark, and perhaps Germany, you have strong, organized interest groups, particularly labour markets. But other groups like homeowners and pensioners also have their own organizations in some European countries. Austria has this kind of coalition between government and unions and to some extent business also. What is the main difference between the corporatist in Western Europe and in Latin America?

Secondly, I understand that one country tried to destroy the corporatist in Latin America; namely, Chile and the Pinochet government. They tried to create a more atomistic society. Big corporate structures and interest groups in society can be a protection for the individual against a strong state. Some of those who have criticized the Chilean experiment say that this shield from the state provided by big organizations was removed by the Pinochet regime. How do you look at those things?

**Brian Kantor** The Austrian experience in corporatism is an interesting one. Corporatism there has been perfectly consistent with rapid economic growth. The difference, of course, is the degree of openness to international trade. Austria has a common market with Germany, so the room for inefficient economic policies is really very limited.

So it comes back to the point that Ramon raised about the importance of openness. If you can hold your economy open, it will have to be efficient. But, of course, people in different countries may not choose to remain open. I think that is really the issue: why do some countries as opposed to others choose greater degrees—it's always a question of degree—of openness? The pressures to close are important everywhere. They are very important in South Africa, Australia, the U.S. and in Southeast Asia as well, in Taiwan and Thailand. They all have degrees of protection, yet restraining the populist appeal of protectionist policies is so important.

**Walter Block** I hate to be a pest or a gadfly, but I don't see why we have to call this phenomenon "corporatism." Robert Hesson of the Hoover Institute wrote a marvellous book in defence of the corporation. I think we can call it fascism or statism or something else. Why are we giving up this word "corporation"? It is part and parcel of the free enterprise system, and I can't see why we should conflate this economic fascism with the corporation. It is true that some corporations get involved in that, but it is certainly not intrinsic to the nature of corporations.

**Assar Lindbeck** The word doesn't come from there. You are mixing terminology.

**Lindsay Wright** "Corporatism" actually has nothing to do with corporations, as you are referring to them in terms of business enterprises. It actually refers to corporate groups; meaning, in the traditional sense of the word, any group that is organized to pursue its interests.

**Assar Lindbeck** Producers mainly.

**Lindsay Wright** Traditionally it referred to guilds. In the newer terminology now used, it has a broader meaning including business groups, labour groups, certainly those involved in production, but other societal interest groups as well.

I disagree with what Assar said about corporatist institutions providing protection for the individual against the state. What has happened in Latin America is that corporatist institutions have been given monopoly representation by the state; in effect they are simply extensions of the state and, in my view, don't provide extra protection for the individual against the state.

**Arnold Harberger** Responding a bit to the corporate and corporatist issue and to what Assar was asking about Chile, I think we can identify two free market experiments that took place in Chile. One of them was prior to the general collapse in 1982. Sergio de Castro in Chile, whom many of you know, was the intellectual leader of that. I know him extremely well, he is a very good friend of mine, and it *is* his way of thinking. He says, you have to take action first, then let people live with it for a while, and only then expect them to approve. That was his whole way. In the early days of those reforms, I used to come to his office and say, "Tejo, what new friends have you made since the last time, and who are your friends?" By the time it ended, the only friends he could name were the exporters. Then came the dramatic appreciation of the real exchange rate, and there went the exporters, so that there were no friends at all. Some time after de Castro there was an interlude where a new minister, Luis Escobar, tried to hark back to the ad hoc policies of the 1950s or early '60s. Happily, the Chilean business community in particular recognized that this was no path to follow.

The present minister, Herman Buechi, is much more artful, and he probably learned the lesson from the earlier experience. He seems genuinely to be cultivating the different interest groups in society without giving up very much. It is a great art, if you know how to do it, to hand small bones out and maintain the general structure of economic policy. That's what happened, and I really do agree with what Assar said. It is an atomistic principle of economic policy that is being pursued.

**Ramon Diaz** Latin America is big. It is probably not as heterogeneous as Africa, but it is big. For instance, about land reform without going into the issue, the word "peasant" is not interpretable in Uruguay/Argentina. There is no one who considers himself a peasant. There are no landless peasants. The ranches are huge, very capital-intensive, and they employ very little labour. No one has ever been deprived of ownership of land.

I am not an expert on what happens in the densely populated countries of Middle America and other places with large Indian populations, but I hear that Mexico has really wrecked its possibilities of developing agriculture through land reform. What I hear about the land reform that has been imposed, largely through the State Department's offices to El Salvador, is more or less the same. And about corporate or guild socialism, we have nothing of that. Our interventionism has been French oriented; it is based on a conception of the state as a benevolent dispensator of goods. It has nothing to do with Catholic social theory. It was brought in by a strongly anti-clerical party. The Church simply does not play any part at all. There are lobbies, of course, but this is common to all countries.

**Peter Bauer** The discussion of land reform seems to me to be both overblown and confused. In much of Latin America, as in Asia and Africa, millions of extremely poor people live in areas where uncultivated land is a free good. There is, nevertheless, agitation for the expropriation and redistribution of cultivated land on which effort and money have been spent to make it valuable. Who will not welcome a gift of valuable assets?

If redistribution of wealth and income is thought desirable, why should this take the form of the confiscation and redistribution of one particular form of asset rather than proceed on the basis of differences in wealth and income?

**Tibor Machan** Just a couple of things on land reform. We were talking about economic freedom and the other freedoms—civil rights and political liberties and so on. I am not sure that the ideal land reform here doesn't really capture a lot of other things such as some conception of justice. If our doctrine of economic freedom doesn't in some way accommodate a basically felt need for justice, either on the part of the people who are actually in those societies or on the part of the people who presume to talk for those societies, then I think economic freedom is doomed. I think the notion that peasants never owned the land, even if that is true, is irrelevant. Suppose you chop off my hand, and I go into court and get money from you. I never owned that money. But we are not literalists here; we are compensating for an evil that they perceive had been done.

I think it is a myth to believe that somehow everything has been hunky-dory, and that major segments of the populations in many of these societies haven't been mistreated. They know they have been mistreated, and they feel they have been mistreated. However much we want to be positivist economists, this value judgement on their part has to be accommodated *somehow* lest we lose the battle completely.

My point is that a compensatory or restitutionalist political approach is absolutely indispensable. The question is how to make it so that it is indeed accommodating to criteria of justice. Obviously, we ought not to just randomly distribute wealth and goods and services and whatever is of value and desired by people. That is not what I have in mind. But to ignore these claims does indeed fall smack into the hands of market critics who pretend to rectify these matters. I don't think they rectify it, but they make a hell of a big claim about going about rectification. If we dismiss the notion of rectification outright, as Gordon Tullock's remarks seem to suggest, I think we are doomed. This directly relates to the notion of the relationship between economic freedom and those other goods with which we are concerned at this conference.

**Milton Friedman** For Tibor's information, I want to quote from my great teacher, Frank Knight, who used to say over and over again, "What's really going to ruin this world is a search for justice." He is right. If you take justice as your objective, you can be sure you are going to end up with a totalitarian dictatorial state. Justice has to be a by-product, or it will never be achieved.

**Gordon Tullock**   Actually, Tibor and I have been going on about this for quite some time. He feels more strongly about it than I do. Nevertheless, firstly I was responding to his statement that the land had been stolen from these people. Politically, there is frequently much to be said for impoverishing certain people for the benefit of others, if the people you are going to impoverish are going to be permanently removed from power. So I don't rule it out.

But the problem with justice is, unfortunately, that different people think different things are just. The really bloody wars in history have been between people, both of whom are convinced that they are right. I am not going to say that you will not eventually invent a legal system or an argument for a justice which will become something that everyone will believe in. But I do say that right now there is very little agreement as to what is just. Khoemeni, you must remember, is a very just man; he just has different ideas of justice than I do.


**Arnold Harberger**   I think Tibor has a point. I don't feel the same way he does concerning land reform, but I feel that in some sense the myth of equal opportunity is a necessary piece of a good free market system. In the United States, men born in shacks have ended up in the White House. Many others from like origins have ended up on Wall Street and in our universities. It is a commonplace event with us.

In contrast, I have been going to Chile since 1955, and I don't know of a single member of the Union Club in Santiago who was born of landless labourer stock. Not one in thirty years, and I have been on the lookout for these people. The carbineros, who are the police force, are made up of two groups—the officers come from one social group; the men come from another social group—and it has always been that way.

To get into the university, you have to pass exams. The university is virtually free, but—and this is true broadly in Latin America—to get good secondary schooling you have to go private. The people who can afford good private secondary schools are the wealthy and the middle classes. So the poor people have to send their kids to schools that don't prepare them adequately to take the exams to get into university. In each country there are some good secondary schools, and they provide some filtration for the children of the poor. But it is small relative to the size of the population, and I think it is a tremendously important aspect that has to be surmounted. Mexico has done quite well in surmounting it. Panama too, for that matter.

**Walter Block** I would like to talk about land reform also, but first just a brief word on the corporatist issue. It might or might not be correct etymologically, but certainly as a public relations endeavour everyone assumes, as I do, that corporatism has something to do with corporations. Further, Lindsay Wright maintains that this word means a group that is organized to pursue its interests. To this Assar stresses that it is mainly a corporate group that is involved. But what is so wrong with a corporate group organizing to pursue its interests? I maintain that there is nothing intrinsically wrong with this at all. So, whether it is "corporation" or "(producer) co-operation," this can be a legitimate activity. Why denigrate it?

On the land reform question, we have a whole continent that we are in danger of losing, and people like Milton Friedman and Gordon Tullock and, if I interpret him correctly, Peter Bauer as well, are proposing in effect a banner which says "down with justice." This is my interpretation of the statement, "What's going to ruin the world is a search for justice," and my interpretation of Gordon's view that since there is very little agreement, we should oppose it. How do you expect to win the hearts and minds of the people of South America and get them to rally under the banner of "down with justice" or "ignore justice" or "don't search for justice" or anything of that sort?

As for Peter's claim that all this land is a free good, I don't know what the Conquistadores were doing there then. If land was such a free good and there were surpluses, why did anyone have to conquer anyone? We have a question of fact and of value; it is not *only* a question of fact. If Milton, Gordon and Peter were convinced of the fact, they would take the same view anyway that the search for justice is going to ruin the world and it is Khoemeni-ish and it will be bloodthirsty. I think there is a great value difference here on the land question and the justice question and between me and the supposed value-free positive economists who are making very normative claims about justice and injustice.

**Tibor Machan** If we are having problems with the meaning of the term "justice," I submit we surely have problems with the meaning of the word "freedom." If we cannot endorse justice because of its ambiguity and its multifaceted interpretation throughout the world, we have to follow suit with the concept of freedom. Marxists interpret freedom differently; T.H. Green interpreted freedom differently. There are numerous different usages of the concept freedom. Roosevelt interpreted it in a most insidious way and so forth. I don't find that to be a great argument. If subjectivism is supposed to be our ruling "metatheory," you might as well forget talking about anything.

The second point is that the land reform issue is, for me, simply a symbol. Obviously, in some areas it has no bearing.

Finally, justice is a more substantive issue for us. I think the concept of economic liberty is an ingredient of the broader classical liberal concept of justice. In fact, justice is supposed to be secured, in a classical liberal framework, by first securing liberty for all. This is one of the roads to justice. There are other ingredients to justice, but one way, for example, that you treat a person justly in classical liberal theory is by not depriving him of his liberty without due process. That is an ingredient of justice. If, as Frank Knight argues, the pursuit of justice has gotten us into very bad trouble, then I would submit that the pursuit of liberty is also going to get us into a lot of trouble because liberty is a necessary though not a sufficient condition of justice as conceived within the liberal philosophical framework.

**Peter Bauer** I want to address Al's comments with a brief reference to what Tibor has just said.

Al emphasized the importance of equality of opportunity, which he said was absent in much of Latin America. Equality of opportunity is often an ambiguous idea. Normally, it refers to an open society, one in which there is *carriere ouverte aux talents*. In this sense, equality of opportunity results in differences in income and wealth, which reflect differences in people's attitudes and motivations. The poor in such a society are often thought to be oppressed simply because they are less well off than others. This is so both in the West and in less-developed countries. The Malaysian government imposes strict ethnic quotas against the Chinese because they have greatly outdistanced the Malays in spite of preferential official treatment of Malays since colonial times.

I am sceptical about the significance of secondary education and of class differences as factors behind economic differences. Many people in Latin America have become rich even though they had little or no formal education. Academics are particularly apt to over-estimate the economic benefits of formal education. Current ideas about human capital formation may have contributed to this. Capital should refer to accumulated fruits of the investment of resources. It is not sensible to use the term simply to describe aptitudes and motivations. What was the human capital of the very poor, illiterate, unskilled coolies who flooded into British Malaya in their hundreds of thousands between 1880 and 1930 and who transformed the economy of that country? Absence of formal education is entirely compatible with material success.

Nor are differences in social class necessarily correlated with differences in wealth, much less are they causally related. They are certainly not so related in S.E. Asia or in much of Europe. I know that the class structure does not present a major obstacle to economic advance in Britain, and I doubt whether it does so in Latin America.

**Milton Friedman** I want to come back to this justice versus freedom thing, because we don't want to make this an empty play on words. We don't want to beg the question. If freedom means anything, it is incompatible with justice, if justice means anything.

If we are going to have a defensible definition of freedom, as I see it freedom fundamentally means the absence of physical coercion. Justice means that people get what they deserve. But somebody has to decide what they deserve and what is appropriate to them. So, the underlying basis for Frank Knight's comment—which may be a smart crack, but which had a very strong basis in a very deep analysis of society—is precisely that the attempt to achieve justice will destroy a free society because it pits people with different conceptions of what other people deserve, one against the other, and Khoemeni is a perfect example of that. You have that over and over again. Now, if you take freedom as your fundamental objective, equality of opportunity, in the sense in which Al was discussing it, becomes part of the concept of freedom. People are free to use their own resources in whatever way they wish, so long as they don't interfere with the freedom of anybody else to do the same thing. That is not the same as justice. If you insist on making justice a component of freedom, I think you are emptying both concepts of meaning.

**Douglass North** I want to point out to Tibor that his comments that have generated all of this heat are in direct contradiction to the earlier comment he and I made in the exchange on which he had no body of theory that he wanted to use. Now, suddenly he has implicitly got some theory about how justice is playing a major role, therefore there is implicitly a theory in it. I wanted to remind you that you have actually done that.

I want to talk about justice in a different way, Milton. I agree with what you are saying, but to ignore as a part of the modelling process its effect upon human behaviour is to make a big mistake. May I suggest, again, that you all go back and read the theoretical parts of the paper I wrote for this conference. In talking about norms of behaviour, it is explicitly concerned about the degree to which people will overcome the free rider problem and that that is a negatively sloped function in which the higher the price you pay for your conviction the less these things count. But the function shifts and if you pay low prices, ideologies or your views about justice, fairness and so on play enormous roles in the world. I tried to say that over and over again in the paper, and it doesn't seem to have had much effect on you. It *does* play a big part, and if we structure institutions in such a way that people at low cost can express these convictions of justice and fairness, whatever they are, they play a big part. That is what we are trying to model in this process of trying to understand how institutions work. So justice plays a role. I agree with your point, but I don't want to ignore justice because, in terms of people's perceptions, the institutional structure may very well make it have a big role in what happens.

**Arnold Harberger** In trying to judge societies and countries in a reasonable way, I have come to think much more in terms of generations than in years or quinquennia. I think economic progress is well measured when we see the children of one generation living a lot better than their parents did. I think that is easily measured, and it is one of the things that we should do in a more serious way in economics and in the social sciences.

I think equality of opportunity is distinct from economic progress as such, because you could have progress with each caste in an Indian system going up but nobody changing deciles, so to speak. Natural social mobility entails churning; people from higher deciles drift down and lower deciles drift up. In Brazil I once supervised a wonderful thesis that dealt with only a five-year period using income tax declarations arranged according to deciles. The typical person who was in a given decile at the end of that five-year period had been two deciles below at the beginning. Similarly, the persons who were in a given place in the beginning, fell two deciles by the end. I felt this was a wonderfully positive statement about the upper reaches of Brazilian society, that this was really happening.

**Peter Bauer** That seems to contradict what you said before about social rigidity.

**Arnold Harberger** I was talking about Chile in particular.

**Peter Bauer** I see. The situation you just described completely pertains to Malaysia, for example. I thought it contradicted what you said before. But perhaps what you just said applies to Brazil, but not to Chile, though I am surprised that this should be so.

**Assar Lindbeck** I would like to comment on Milton's justice. I think Milton is throwing out the baby with the bathwater here. There are some concepts of justice that are extremely important for modern civilization, not only as myth but also as reality. I think most of us would agree about the importance of justice in the sense of equality in relation to the legal system—that people are treated in an equal way by the law. We talked about legal justice, and I don't think Milton would like to throw that baby out with the bathwater.

What you are worried about is the concept of justice as translated to the distribution of wealth. We should make the classical distinction between equality of opportunity versus equality of results. I think you would also accept the idea about justice in the sense of equality of opportunity in starting points in life. But here we come to a real dilemma, because the starting point in life of one generation is often the result of the outcome of the previous generation. If you have a society where different families have accumulated different amounts of wealth during a few centuries, then baby A and baby B are born in different dynasties, so to speak, one with zero and one with much wealth. What is the difference between opportunity of outcome and manipulation results? That depends on how we look at the institution of inheritance. Is inheritance something completely sacred that society should never intervene in, even if it would mean that 99 percent of all wealth is held by 1 percent of a population?

I don't find it unreasonable to intervene in the distribution of wealth in a society where it is completely reckless, as I think it was in Nicaragua during Samosa's regime, if I understand it correctly. Whereas, in a wealthy state of the Western European kind, I would be less willing to intervene in the distribution of wealth as accumulated over the centuries because of the cost of doing that. Also, the benefits would be much smaller than to intervene in Samosa's Nicaragua. So I think a more balanced view about justice could be defended.

**Alan Walters** Discussing this problem of justice, I thought we normally took the view that we could not agree on the ultimate sharing out of wealth or anything of the sort. It is impossible. I quite agree with Milton there.

What we can agree on, however, is some sort of rules or procedures. That's what we see coming in this theory of justice. I think societies can agree on rules and procedures for resolving issues of this kind.

The equality of opportunity is a very slippery fish indeed. When you try to grasp it, it slips away from you. What opportunity? Do we dare penalize natural talent?

I find the argument that Al used quite nerve-wracking, because of his emphasis on formal education. Many of the formal education systems in Latin American countries are products of the state. You *have* to get a Ph.D. or an M.A. to get *this* job. Consequently, they have a degree of state corruption built into them. You find entirely different attitudes, for instance, in Hong Kong. It is much more varied and not dominated by the state at all, as it is in many Latin American countries. I think what Peter says is substantially consistent with all my observations. Formal education and achievement—although most of us have a formal education, so we hate to admit it—are not highly correlated, except in academic work, of course. Lady Bracknall had the appropriate view when she said, "There is far too much education in the world, but fortunately most of it has no effect whatsoever."

**Walter Block** I would like to take issue with Assar's statement which equates justice and intervention in the distribution of income. In my view, that is just "Robin Hoodism." A critique of inheritance is just an attack on giving people gifts, and I think people have a right to give other people gifts if they own the property in question.

I want to concentrate my main criticism on Milton Friedman's equation of freedom and the absence of coercion. He misses a crucial point. It is not the absence of coercion; it's the absence of initiatory coercion. To say that it is just plain old absence of coercion is fundamentally conservative in the worst sense. The banner here would not be "down with justice" but "whatever is, is right" or "the status quo for us."

Take, for example, the case of slavery. When we had slavery in the United States this was a clear case of injustice because those slaves, in justice, owned their own bodies. The only way their ownership rights over their own bodies could be alienated from them was by using coercion. Those people who did not want any coercion or any force to be used, were upholding an unjust system, were upholding the status quo. Suppose Marcos, right before he was forced to abdicate, declared that he was the owner of the whole country. According to the Friedman view of the absence of coercion, no one would have the right to overturn his ownership of the entire Philippines. He would then collect rent instead of taxes. The point is that it is the absence of initiatory coercion that is of relevance, and how you determine whether it is initiatory or defensive depends upon who owns the property.

**Milton Friedman** I think we ought to get rid of straw men. Walter has a great preference for straw men.

**Brian Kantor** I thought it would be helpful to introduce notions of end-state use of justice and process. One might regard the process as being just, as being fair, without regard to what happens at the end, without any view of what is a desirable outcome. If the process is fair, you can approve of it. So the question raised by Walter is, where do you start this process? At what historical point in time? Clearly, people acquiring wealth by theft is not a fair process and you wouldn't want to protect them. But when did the theft occur? How far back in history do you go to exercise retribution? I think that is the real problem. Unless one can legitimize the status quo, it becomes very difficult to go forward.

Take the example of slavery. The way out of slavery was surely through compensation not through expropriation of wealth in the form of slaves. Similarly, perhaps an appropriate way to think about how you go forward is through a process of compensation. If you can make a change and compensate the loser—and I think you should compensate him—then there is room for improvement. There is room for negotiating your way out of an impasse which the status quo may have imposed.

When you remove rent control, shouldn't you compensate the existing tenants? You shouldn't have introduced rent control right at the beginning. But once you have done it, how do you get out of it? Those are the ways I like to think about the issue.

**Raymond Gastil** The last few speakers have actually made the point I want to make. It basically boils down to this. There are many different ways in which one can support the proposition that freedom and justice go together and are not antithetical at all. The only way in which one would understand Milton's position, as I see it, is to have a very specialized definition of justice, referring to a redistributive philosophy which says you go into a situation with no history and no past. You then decide these people seem to be less well off than those, so you start dividing things up differently. I think we might be able to agree on the problem with that approach. There are so many *other* senses of justice, and a number of those have already been brought out.

**Herbert Grubel** I find the discussions of justice, equality of opportunity and all this very interesting, but I thought this session was concerned with

Latin America and the experience of freedom and how it affected all kinds of other things.

I would also like to support Doug North's suggestion that perhaps we can be a little bit more systematic in our discussion. I would like to ask Ramon Diaz and Arnold Harberger whether they have any hypotheses about the origin of romanticism in Latin America. Does it have something to do with the openness of the economy in the educational system, statism, or the class system, to mention just some of the ideas that have been introduced in earlier discussion? How important is romanticism in explaining the development of Latin America? Can it explain the different experiences of the Latin American countries and permit any generalizations about why some did better than others?

**Ramon Diaz** I think romanticism, education and statism are closely related to one another, as one would have expected. I think a Rousseaunian concept of the state is at play. I think nationalism is at play through education. In my paper I developed and stressed the idea that each country has its pantheon of heroes, and children are taught to think about their own countries in a different way from other objects. They are not taught to think of their own countries in a rational way; idols are proposed to them.

**Herbert Grubel** Why?

**Ramon Diaz** This, I don't know. It is a philosophical current, inherited perhaps from Spain, but to me that is a datum. I really don't know how it evolved or why the Anglo Saxons had a much more rational attitude.

**Herbert Grubel** The Church?

**Ramon Diaz** No, I don't think the Church does that. Actually, the idolization of heroes—the liberators you see on horseback in bronze all over the place—is anticlerical. They represent a religion that is in collision with the traditional Christian religion.

**Herbert Grubel** If we don't know, we can't really do anything then.

**Ramon Diaz** No. We can try to instill reason where there isn't any, try to explain, try to move the discourse from a plane of irrationality onto a plane of rationality.

**Voice** You want to tear down the statues.

**Arnold Harberger** I think what Herb was asking for has one answer in that every society of whatever kind tries to transmit some essence of itself from one generation to another. We see the roots of these various things at different points in the past. You ask: why is it there now? That is the society now, and it is transmitting its values as religious families transmit their faith to their children and as some intellectual families transmit their beliefs. It is just social values being passed on.

**Tibor Machan** I can't let Doug's remark go by, because I hate contradicting myself. I don't have anything against theory, but I do question whether *formulas* can be had in connection with all problems. My suspicion is that some of the theoreticians around this table and around a certain profession, including certain versions of the neo-classical economic school, are looking for formulas by which to have changes instituted. That doesn't mean that someone who doesn't look for formulas doesn't want *explanatory* schemes.

Obviously, I am very interested in theory to explain value judgements, the facts, even to anticipate the future, but I may not agree with a theory that demands, for example, utter predictability in all facets of human life. I suspect—and granted, this is a very large topic—you and I differ on this. That is why you are looking for a certain kind of structural approach, and I am not looking for that kind of structural approach.

Another point is that just as we have a difference between political/legal justice and moral justice (of the sort among friends and members of the family and so forth), so we have legal and political freedom. We do not mean by "freedom," when we use it in classical liberal circles, the "freedom" that people use when they say they are "free" of a headache, for example. So I am talking about procedural legal justice in the non end-state sense that Nozick made prominent.

Finally, as far as opportunity is concerned, as a refugee, I wanted to come to America because of a certain kind of equal opportunity. Not an equal economic starting point, but equal opportunity in the sense that wherever I ended up economically, no one had the right to come in and stop me from moving on. In that I was equal to everybody else, or at least as equal as anywhere in Western civilization or in the world where that was possible. Now that is an equal opportunity that is very much cherishable without having to buy into some crazy notion of equal opportunity meaning that you start at the same point. So I think it is perfectly possible to say that justice requires *that* kind of equal opportunity—no one has the authority to stand above you and hold you down. It doesn't mean that you have to start with the same heart, the same eyes, the same height, the same wealth, the same grandparents, the same whatever.

**Milton Friedman** I just want to say that there is another straw man being thrown around. There is nobody in the world who really argues that you have to have perfect predictability or that you can have perfect predictability of anything. It is just a straw man.

I want to say one more thing along Doug North's line. I agree with his position, and I want to recommend to everybody what I think is the most perceptive statement of that position and that is Ed Banfield's book on *The Moral Basis of a Backward Society*, which exactly makes your point, I think, extremely well.

**Ingemar Stahl** Just a few words on Lindbeck's theory of acquisition and justice. When we discuss economic freedom, I think the relationship between the state and the individual is a basic thing. There are very good reasons not to accept wealth taxation. That raises a time consistency problem immediately, and taxation can be retroactive. In a declaration of economic rights, a basic rule would be that taxes should always be on returns.

Inheritance taxes create a specific problem in the sense that there is an obvious transfer from one person to another. There is also a practical problem. If I give some better genes to my children by marrying a nicer girl, how do we treat that from the taxation point of view? Kurt Vonnegut has a very nice short essay about how these problems could be solved; we would turn to some ridiculous forms of taxation. So it seems, especially in a society where most of the property is transferred between generations— genetically within the family rather than land or liquid assets—that we would have very good reasons for giving up inheritance or gift taxation.

**Walter Block** I wanted to reply to Brian on the two points he made about compensation, and how far back do you go in determining property rights. In terms of compensation, I think we have to distinguish between justice and political feasibility. Now, with justice it is clear that the people we compensate for rent control are landlords not tenants, although it might be that the only politically feasible way to get rid of rent control is to compensate the tenant, but that is a different question. It is the same thing with slavery. The people you compensate are the slaves, not the slave owners, although political feasibility or reducing debts due to war might indicate the other alternative.

As to how far back you go, the libertarian theories I espouse indicate that you go as far back as there is proof. If there is proof that the property was stolen, then no matter how far back it was—there is no statute of limitations in justice—you make the appropriate changes. If there is no proof, then you can't. Then you go to Milton Friedman's view of no coercion and assume that the status quo is correct. It is an entirely intellectually coherent system. It is not a straw man whatsoever, and it can't be derisively dismissed. It has to be confronted.

**Michael Parkin**  I was provoked by Brian's suggestion that it was helpful to distinguish between process and end-state theories of justice, and equally provoked by the latest remark that it is. I used to think it was helpful, but I no longer think it is a helpful distinction.

There will still be arguments about justice, whichever way you approach it, simply because we can visualize the end-state consequences of any particular process. So there will always be an argument as to whether this process or that process is the appropriate process. The essence of the justice dispute is the distributive dispute. It is about who gets the stuff. There is simply no solution that all people can agree to. Therefore, it is as Milton says—a pointless concept to build into our philosophical discussion. Brian's examples were all examples of Pareto improvements. If there is a Pareto improvement to be had, the prediction is that you will have it. You will find some way of making side payments such that the Pareto improvement will occur. That doesn't somehow overcome the distribution issue.

Now it is true that we think we can see many things in the world that are bad and that can be improved upon in a Pareto sense. I'd take the position that they are technologically not available. They are simply not in the feasible set, and we have misdefined what is Pareto and what isn't.

**Tibor Machan**  On this notion of end-state versus procedural justice, the objection that there will always be the possibility of visualizing the end-state of a certain process is an interesting one. I think one has to come to terms with it. It has in fact been advanced against Nozick, for example, by David Norton in his book *Personal Destinies*. But the objection that there will always be debate on the meaning of justice, on what is just and what is not just, I have never understood. There is always a debate about *everything*. I have never heard of anything there is no debate about. There are nearly 300 versions of Marxism. There are as many versions of classical liberals, and there are utterly too many versions of liberty. I have just not been able to see the point when people say, with liberty we are safe but with justice we are not. It's not true.

**Brian Kantor** I'm sorry, Walter was right. When you remove rent control, you are harming tenants and favouring landlords who have a windfall gain, so you really have to "buy off" the tenants at that point in time if you hope to succeed politically. I think there is an issue of political art here that Al raised. Just because we haven't done it in the past—and this is in reply to Michael—doesn't mean that there isn't a possibility of innovation. A politician may come up with a scheme for compensation that satisfies the existing interests and promotes economic efficiency. We, as people who involve ourselves in economic policy issues, should think about such schemes. It may help progress a lot.

**Ramon Diaz** I think the answer to what we need in Latin America is to have cultural change, and that is a very difficult thing to do. Education is the obvious way, if we could control it in the right direction, but that is not easy. Leadership?—we may be lucky. That's a chance.

What I am concerned about at this meeting, particularly in connection with Latin America, is that we have the idea that distribution was important, and not about Africa and not about the Far East. Something about Latin America has caused the view that it is important to distribute there. Let me tell you my frank conviction that it isn't so. Peasants or rural workers will be a lot better off when agriculture is more productive, and the last thing we want to do is to distribute it. Actually, what we do is tax agriculture very often through export taxes and through tariffs imposed on imports, principally. This is what causes a lot of poverty, apart from policies of the more developed countries as well—a common agricultural policy and things like that. But certainly distribution of property and income will not be a solution. We want to grow. We want to achieve secure property rights from all investment and increase productivity. That has been the source of progress in the centre of the West; it will also be in the periphery.

# Chapter 7

# Political and Economic Freedom in the Welfare State: Some Basic Concepts Applied to the Case of Sweden

## Ingemar Stahl

### Introduction

When I first was asked to present this paper I was quite ignorant of how little of good theory economists really have when it comes to a basic analysis of an almost socio-philosophical character of freedom, rights, liberty, rules, et cetera in society. Few of the words mentioned here will be found in the indices of standard textbooks in economics. We all, however, use the words frequently in our daily argumentation. But what scientific background have we got for our everyday conversation?

Ambiguity or perhaps deliberate obscurity rules in this area. The Swedish prime minister recently claimed that economic *and* political freedom were increased when government expenditures and taxes were increased for social welfare purposes. More decisions were then to be made in "democratic order" (i.e., by a majority decision rule), and economic freedom was increased in the case of sickness, old age, unemployment, et cetera. The price paid was a smaller post-tax choice set, that on the average is compensated for by a larger post-subsidy choice set. Economic freedom might, following the argument, be decreased for some but increased for a majority. The potential or actual coercion that follows from a majority decision is often neglected.

But how should economists as social scientists argue in a discussion about political and economic freedom? We have no simple measure stating that economic freedom has increased by x percent or that political and civil freedom has decreased by y percent in the same way as we talk about changes in the GNP. We have not even got a common ordinal scale for metering freedom or liberty. Most of the economists' measures are taken from the market, where quantification is simple: Prices and exchanged commodities are easily metered. Although many economists (including myself) believe that economics has something to do with relations (mainly exchanges) between individuals in a system of social order, almost all our measurements refer to flows and stocks of commodities. Only on rare occasions do we deal *directly* with relations between individuals.

A starting point for a discussion about freedom must, however, be an analysis of *relations* between individuals or groups of individuals. It is rather meaningless to ask if Robinson Crusoe was free or not, at least not until Friday when his relatives appear on the island. Freedom of speech does not seem to be an important human right until there is at least one listener. Although many of us support the idea that an "exchange" paradigm is more important for the development of economic science than a traditional "optimization cum equilibrium" paradigm, we have little to offer when it comes to hard analysis of social and economic relationships. Recent contract and property rights theory is far behind the logical and mathematical refinements that characterize present-day general equilibrium theory. It is also interesting to compare on one side the large space devoted to show the correspondence between preference logic and utility functions as a description of individual choices with, on the other side, the almost complete neglect of analysis of more complicated but equally important concepts like (private) property rights which can be found in the theoretical standard works (e.g., Debreu 1959, or Arrow-Hahn 1971).

Property rights can be taken as an example of the type of analysis that will be used in this paper. In the standard textbook it seems as if "ownership" is a relation between an individual and a physical object: Smith owns a piece of land. In a more sophisticated analysis ownership is regarded as a relationship between individuals (for examples, see many of the articles in Furubotn-Pejovich). Ownership then means that Smith can exclude other persons—but perhaps not all persons—from entering or using the land. We will in the following say that Smith has a right or a *claim* that another person should not use the land. For a full definition of a claim we need a certain action, say, entering the land or picking rare orchids on the land. According to Swedish common law, the right-of-way principle will in general mean that an "owner" does not have a claim that other persons should not walk on his property. In general we have to define a claim as existing or not existing for a pair of individuals $(P_i, P_j)$ with regard to a certain action $(A_k)$.

For a full description of the "claim" aspect of property rights or ownership we need a full matrix describing if a certain person has a claim or not for a certain action against other persons. A claim might be valid against some persons but not against other persons; e.g., members of the police force or officials.

But we can also talk about Smith's *freedom* (liberty, privilege) to enter his own land. But when it comes to picking rare flowers Smith might be denied this possibility, say, by nature preservation legislation. A third aspect is if Smith can transfer his "ownership" or title to the land to other persons. This aspect could be called legal *power* or competence. If Smith is a Swedish citizen with land in Sweden he will in general be denied the right to sell his property to non-Swedish citizens. For some types of land there will be more restrictions regarding potential buyers; agricultural land and forests can only be transferred to relatives or to persons accepted by land authorities.

A fourth aspect is if Smith's ownership (or perhaps only some aspects of his ownership) can be changed or altered by another person (or by authorities). This will be called the *immunity* aspect of ownership. New legislation might thus change some of the actions that Smith is allowed to perform on land under his title. According to Swedish law, the government can change or prohibit actions on the land without compensation (say, changing town planning restrictions regarding number of storeys or density of new buildings on the land). The land owner thus lacks immunity with regard to certain actions performed by the government. (As will be obvious later, immunity is in general an aspect which is of importance in the relationships between individuals and the government.) However, according to the basic "rights" in the Swedish constitution, a final transfer of title can only take place with compensation from the government. But property rights can be diluted to the point where economic compensation for government expropriation becomes a token.

We have heard four words—claim, freedom, power and immunity—used to characterize different aspects of property rights. These are also the four words used by Hohfeld in his pathbreaking essay on what he thought to be "the lowest common denominators of the law" (Hohfeld, 1913). In this paper Hohfeld's concepts will be used with some minor changes proposed by some Swedish scientists emanating from jurisprudence and philosophy. The main reason for using this conceptual framework is completely eclectic. In the property rights literature or in the economic analysis of contracts, rights, rules, et cetera, I have seen no coherent conceptual framework. Even Hohfeld's analysis seems to be neglected or unknown. Neither Rawls nor Nozick and Buchanan, as leading representatives of a school of "neo-contractarians," are using this type of analysis (however, Nozick mentions Hohfeld *en passant* in a footnote). None of the three has elaborated his own theory of rights, and they are all using "rights" in rather ambiguous ways and making no distinction between, for example, the freedom (liberty) aspect and the immunity aspect.

In the next section Hohfeld's concepts will be presented in a more complete way with some of the additions proposed by recent research in jurisprudence. The section that then follows contains a short discussion of some of the basic types of contracts that are of importance for an analysis of "economic and political freedom." To a certain point it is possible to make a connection between the basic type of contracts and Hohfeld's concepts. Finally, follows a part of the paper where the concepts developed are applied in a discussion of some features in a highly mature "welfare state" like Sweden.

## Basic Concepts of "Rights"

A simple conclusion from the previous discussion of property rights is that ownership is not a simple atomic concept but can be seen as a bundle of different characteristics. To say that a person has a "right" generally means that he has a complex aggregate of claims, liberties, powers and immunities with regard to other persons or groups of persons. In the elaboration of a classification scheme of "rights," the following points are important:

1.  "Rights" should be regarded as relations between two parties.
2.  Different "rights" can be regarded as bundles or aggregates of more basic concepts.
3.  There are logical relations between the basic concepts.

The first point has been illustrated by the example of property right: One important aspect is the legal possibility of excluding other persons from using the object of ownership. In a more general setting, rights, liberties and freedom can be regarded as relationships. Often rights are not formulated in this way, but a simple example from the UN declaration of rights can illustrate how a reformulation can be made.

Article 9 reads: "No one shall be subjected to arbitrary arrest, detention or exile." A possible reformulation could then be (for the "arrest" part of the sentence):

> For all individuals x and all states y such that x finds himself in the country y and is not suspected of having committed a crime

| x has versus y | (parties involved) |
| a "right" | (legal relation) |
| that x is not arrested by y | (action concerned or state of affair; Kanger, 1984) |

As this example shows, declarations of rights to a large degree consist of relationships between individuals (or individual citizens) and the state, and of rights in which the immunity aspect is important. But modern declarations of rights are also strongly influenced by the ideology of the welfare states as, for example, in Article 26:1 in the UN declaration of rights:

Everyone has the right to education. Education shall be free, at least in the elementary...stages. Elementary education shall be compulsory...

This Article will then mean:

For all individuals x and all states y such that x is an inhabitant of y

x has versus y
a "right" that x is given free elementary education
y has versus x
a "right" that x participates in education.

The first type of right is obviously of the claim type. The second is a negation of x's liberty to abstain from the education. A possible interpretation is a claim from the state versus x. From this Article will also follow that y has tax claim on other citizens or on x at another stage of life.

An important part of Hohfeld's analysis is that the different types of "rights" stand in definite logical relationships to each other. If a landowner has a claim that a person should not enter his land, this also means that the other person has a duty (or obligation) not to enter the land. As soon as there is a claim from x versus y there will be a "correlative" duty from y versus x. In the language of deontic logic a claim from x means that y *shall do* or shall perform a certain act.

As shown later, Hohfeld's concept of liberty (freedom or privilege) is logically not clear. It might mean either that x may act in a certain way or that x may refrain from acting (Kanger, 1966; Lindahl, 1977). We will however not go into further detail in this intricate issue; for our purposes it is sufficient to note that liberty stresses that certain acts *may* be performed. It is an absence of duty and can thus be regarded as the opposite of a duty. The correlative—usually called "no-right"—has been shown to create some minor problems with the internal logic and shall not be explained here.

In the same way there will be correlative and opposite pairs with regard to power and immunity. The correlative of power is liability, and the correlative of immunity is disability. If x has an immunity versus the state with regard to changes of the legal character of some parts of what constitutes ownership, the state has a corresponding or correlative disability. But disability is also the opposite of power as liability is the opposite of immunity.

If right - duty - liberty - no-right can be used for describing legal positions the other quartet is mainly aimed at describing legal changes. The figure below shows how the four concepts in each group are connected:

| Positions | | | Change | | |
|---|---|---|---|---|---|
| right | c | duty | power | c | liability |
| o ↕ | ↔ | o ↕ | o ↕ | ↔ | o ↕ |
| no-right | ↔ c | liberty | disability | ↔ c | immunity |

o = opposite concepts; c = correlated concepts

The concepts proposed by Hohfeld as a kind of legal "quarks" have been analysed and refined with the use of deontic logic, i.e., the logic of sentences based on "shall do" and "may do" (see Lindahl 1977; Talja 1980). But for our more modest purposes it is sufficient to bring in some of the basic distinctions originally made by Hohfeld, who used more of intuition and a judicial hunch than of formal logic. His arguments are also in a legal research tradition as they are based on analysis of a large number of cases.

## Basic Types of Contracts

In the previous section the aim was to find some concepts of legal rights that can be building-stones for different types of contracts. In this section some basic types of contracts will be characterized. Hopefully most of the contracts of economic importance will belong to one or another of the types here mentioned.

The first type of contract is a general type of ownership or *exclusion rights*: x can exclude y. As has already been discussed, property rights are really a bundle or an aggregate of more basic rights.

Another type of contract or relationship is *voluntary exchange*, a quid pro quo type of relationship. Most of economic theory is about this type of relationship between a seller and a buyer, but in most cases the relationship is never made explicit as most transactions are thought of as taking place in an anonymous market. (When we talk about markets do we not really mean firms specializing in transaction? Should not "between firms" or "within firms" be substituted for "markets" or "hierarchies"?)

A third type of relationship is between *principal and agent*. This type of relation was described by Hohfeld as "the grant of legal powers to the so-called agent, and the creation of correlative liabilities in the principal." In the economic context the study of principal-agent relations has mainly concentrated on the potential conflict of interests.

As our fourth type of relation or contract we will take a *patron-client* relation. In an extreme case this will be a master-slave relationship. The basic idea is that the client has given up some rights which have been taken over by the patron. An employment contract has more features of a patron-client relation than an ordinary exchange contract, although duties and corresponding claims are specified in both cases.

A fifth and more complicated relation is the formation of an *association*; individuals x, y and z form together a new subject s. The basic contract (or the constitution when it comes to the state) has, among many other things, to specify a decision rule with which the interests of the participants are transformed into actions by the association.

In a modern society every individual will have contractual relations with many other individuals. They are members of the state, of the county and the local community, to mention some important political and compulsory associations. They belong to different trade unions or other interest groups with voluntary membership.

But a membership in an association usually also means establishment of principal-agent and patron-client relations. The voter is a principal, his representative member of parliament (or the local community council) his agent. But the MP is, in his turn, a principal in relation to the public administration. In the next step the administration may play a patron role against the original voter, who now is a client; the unemployed votes for an MP who controls the budget and the rules of the unemployment insurance system (working on behalf of the political part of the government) which in its turn unilaterally but according to rules or statutes can determine how much unemployment benefits shall be paid out to the original but unemployed voter.

The emergence of these types of rather complex chains of relations may be a typical feature of a welfare state in which government programmes have taken over the role of private insurance; a simple exchange relationship between a provider of insurance or health care and a customer on a voluntary basis has been transformed into a chain of relations of a partly very complex nature and involving explicit or implicit coercion. We have just mentioned one side of the coin; the other is a similar complex chain for determining the taxes that have to be paid for the services provided.

We will not go into detail here in a description of the different relations society's members are involved in. It may be sufficient to observe that a very dense network of contractual relations will probably create a stability for society.

### An Application: The Swedish Case

Sweden is an extreme case of the modern welfare state. At present the size of the public sector (consumption, investments and transfers) is roughly equal to 65 percent of GDP, compared with less than 40 percent for the United States. Although the growth rate has slowed down considerably since 1970, Sweden still has a per capita GDP placing her at one of the top positions in the wealth league. To many economists a large public sector would mean a decrease in economic "freedom." It is not equally obvious that a large government sector will mean a corresponding increase in political "freedom." Only if one is a supporter of an extreme majority rule doctrine would this be true. The extreme case would be that all social states had to be ranked by a majority principle and that there were no areas of complete privateness.

The size of the public sector is an indication that government compared with a classical constitutional market economy is involved in many areas where most of the services provided are of strictly private character. Although all formal rules of the democratic game are followed, an extreme case of the Swedish type means that coercion might be large. The question an economist would ask would be: How much of the public sector would be left if we adopted a rule of (almost) unanimity of the Wicksellian type? A partial answer to this question might be given by the Finnish neighbour using a rule of qualified majority for taxes and expenditures and with a public sector share of GDP of a little more than 40 percent.

Instead of discussing in terms of political, economic and civil freedom, we will try to apply some of the concepts developed earlier to indicate some specific features in the contractual structures of the welfare state.

The most important association is, of course, the state. The basic social contract will then be the constitution. The present Swedish constitution was changed in 1970 in the direction of what could be called a super-democratic constitution with few obstacles for quick decision making in the political field. One-chamber system with elections every third year creates a momentum in the political sphere. The powers given to government are virtually unrestricted. Except for some almost classical civil rights of the immunity type (freedom of speech and organisation, etc.), there are only two immunities in the economic field (expropriation of real estate can only be made after compensation and a clause against retroactive taxation, that has been morally violated twice). In principle, government could increase taxes to 100 percent.

As has been discussed earlier, the extension of government into fields that could be managed by private markets drastically changes the complete contract structure. In the private market we have a duty to pay for services and a claim to get them but also a liberty to change between different producers. In the welfare state this liberty (or power) has disappeared, and there is no direct correspondence between the individual claims of services and the state's claim of tax payments in the individual case.

State ownership in the usual sense of the word is rather insignificant in the manufacturing sector. One could perhaps even think about a tacit agreement, a kind of supra-contract between the political sector and the industry, similar to the concordats between state and church in many countries. The content of this concordat would then be that government accepts and morally supports a viable and internationally competitive industrial sector with virtually free entry and no or rather low protection or direct financial support (except for some years after 1976 with some disastrous results). Restrictions on private property rights or direct government ownership are mainly limited to domestic sectors and especially the tax-financed service sectors.

The Swedish economy is an open economy with few regulations. There are still some regulations regarding free capital movements. In the rights context this means that the power and liberty aspects are strong in this sector of the economy but they are weak in other parts of the economy. There are few restrictions against free entry in the industrial sector, while at the same time restrictions limiting individual liberty and power apply to the domestic sectors. I am free to start a factory and sell industrial commodities to everybody inside or outside the country, but I am not allowed to start a school without government approval. Even if freedom of speech and expression is guaranteed (an immunity type of right), I have no right to start a radio or TV station (lack of power or liberty). I have a claim versus the government that it should provide me with health care, schools for my children and long-term care for my parents. But I have little choice in selecting the provider, and it might even be difficult to start a fee-paying private alternative.

Are there any simple explanations of this duality in the economic structure: a highly capitalistic export-oriented sector and domestic sectors like health, housing, education and culture dominated by a doctrine of social welfarism? One possible answer might be that different international agreements put restrictions on what governments can do. By such agreements a government can commit itself to a free trade policy and thus create an immunity against pressure groups on the domestic scene. There are few or no similar commitment alternatives for non-traded commodities. The immunity against political interventions in the export sectors are thus not guaranteed by the domestic legal framework but through mutual international agreements.

But remember how difficult things can be if we use ambiguous concepts. In everyday language a government signing an international agreement on free trade gives up some "economic freedom," i.e., the liberties and powers to do unwise things on the domestic scene. At the same time the export industries gain some "economic freedom," i.e., they acquire a certain amount of immunity against involvement of domestic politicians.

New developments in institutional economics, mainly in the public choice field and in the law and economics field (property rights analysis and contract theory), have increased our understanding of how economies work far beyond the incomplete understanding we get from the institutionless neo-classical analysis. But it may be a very hard way before us. The attempt in this paper to bring in some basic concepts from the theory of jurisprudence should be seen as research in progress. It is a test that easily can fail, and it seems at present difficult to navigate an easy route between the oversimplification of the traditional usage of rights and freedom terminology and the still complicated introduction of new but more defined concepts of different types of rights.

**A Short Bibliographical Note**

In this paper a number of articles and books from jurisprudence and philosophy have been referred to. As this field is not so well known, some short comments might be necessary.

The basic articles by Wesley Newcomb Hohfeld (first at Stanford University, then at Yale University) are:

Some Fundamental Legal Conceptions as Applied in Judicial Reasoning, *Yale Law Journal*, Vol. 23 (1913) and Vol. 26 (1917). Together with an introduction by Walter Wheeler Cook in *Yale Law Review*, Vol. 28 (1919) the articles have been reprinted many times in a volume of Hohfeld's collected works. A recent version was printed in 1964 by Yale University Press.

The Swedish development of Hohfeld's system using the deontic logic originally developed by George Wright has been presented in the following article and monographs:

Kanger, S. and Kanger, H. (1966) Rights and parliamentarism, *Theoria*, Vol. 32, pp. 85-115.

Lindahl, L. (1977) *Position and Change: A Study in Law and Logic*, Synthese Library, Vol. 112.

Kanger, H. (1984) *Human Rights in the UN Declaration*, Uppsala.

# Discussion

## Edited by Michael A. Walker

**Assar Lindbeck**  It is a fact, I guess, that it is always easier to express yourself with your own classification system and your own terminology. Therefore, when I read this paper, I was not fully convinced that I should shift to this terminology rather than the terminology I am familiar with from previous years.

What I find particularly interesting in Ingemar's paper is the principal-agent system, wherein a rather simple contract between two parties—for instance, between an individual and an insurance company—is replaced by a complicated chain of principal-agent relationships.

Also, I think his discussion of the Swedish economy as a two-sector economy is close to the point, although I would like to modify it a little. It is not really the export sector versus the rest of the economy. The government is really monopolizing or intervening in specific types of services —which I'll come to later—while other services are in the private sector without very much government intervention.

I would like to make a different classification here, and fill it with forms immediately. When I think about individual freedom of choice in the welfare state, I tend to think of three aspects: first, freedom of choice; second, predictability of the effects of choice; and third, civil liberties.

In certain respects, welfare state policies have *increased* individual freedom of choice. Take the example of government guarantees of loans for students. (As a matter of fact, that's a reform Ingemar Stahl was advisor to 20 years ago.) I think that increases the freedom of choice of many individuals because it creates a market that did not exist otherwise because it is very difficult to borrow with human capital as collateral. If governments give guarantees on those types of loans, poor people are given an option to study, which they did not have before.

Some people, moreover, argue that social security systems have been created to compensate for market imperfections, in the sense that moral hazard or adverse selection prevents private markets for insurance from arising to some extent. If that argument is correct, you have another example of a reform that in some sense increases the options of the individual because it creates a market that did not exist before. Of course, by the compulsory nature of the system, as Ingemar points out, that is certainly a reduction in the freedom of choice for those who could get private insurance anyway.

It is easy to think of welfare state policies that reduce freedom of choice. Let me just briefly mention three types. The first one is distortions of freedom of choice by taxes and subsidies. Suppose that you have a 100 percent marginal income tax rate; it would be impossible for the individual to change his own money income by his own effort. I think everybody would agree that that would be a very severe restriction of his freedom of choice between leisure and income. But that also means that if the marginal tax is 90 percent or 60 percent or even 50 percent, there is a limitation of freedom of choice. In that sense, the conventional economic concept of distortion is really very closely related to reduction of freedom of choice. You could also say it is related to the property rights idea. An individual has certain human capital he can use for leisure or income. The marginal tax rates expropriate part of the return on this human capital, so his freedom of choice is reduced.

The average tax rate is also important here. Suppose you have a very high *average* tax rate and the individual gets non-marketable service in kind in compensation—like health care, education, child care and old age care. That means many individuals will simply be forced to supply much more labour in the market than otherwise to get what they regard as a decent level of consumption. This is very relevant for the Swedish case, because if you pay tax rates that on the margin are about 70 percent in Sweden, as it is for the average citizen with all taxes included, you get lots of services in kind. As a matter of fact, for most families with two children it is impossible for one parent to stay at home; both really have to work in the labour market. So the freedom of choice between looking after your own kids or sending them to a day care centre is eliminated. If a university professor or a colonel has two children, he comes below the poverty limit in the system in Sweden. If he applies for social welfare, then the answer is that his wife should work. So there you have a very clear case where freedom of choice has been reduced, not by the marginal tax but by the high *average* rate combined with transfers in kind. That was the distortion part.

The next part is very obvious, and that is public monopolies. It is not really necessary in a welfare state to create public monopolies because you could have different types of voucher systems as suggested by Milton and others. But, in fact, welfare states tend to create monopolies for day care, old-age care and education. The reason is not clear. It could be that politicians want to control not the income distribution in general but the distribution of specific goods and the quality of those goods. Maybe some politicians enjoy power in general. This is another example where welfare state policy logically would not require public monopolies but, in fact, in many countries they tend to occur.

Public control in radio and television is another example. As Ingemar pointed out in the paper, it is really amazing that private ownership of newspapers is regarded as completely necessary for a pluralistic, open society like Sweden, but the same persons are completely against breaking up the public monopoly of radio and television. If Gutenberg's innovation were made today, it would certainly be argued that printing presses are too important to be in private hands in the same way as television in our country. So the second part is public monopolies.

The two previously mentioned limitations on individual choice imply that either markets are distorted or you have monopolies. However, the individual is allowed to say whether or not he wants the service at the distorted prices. The third type of limitation of freedom of choice is related to price regulations that create excess demands and queues. It is obvious that rent control has that effect. People cannot get what they want. There is a limitation of freedom of choice in the sense that they would like to have one consumption factor but they cannot get it, and they are rationed by the authorities or through informal rationing.

You have the same thing in the public sector. Public monopolies usually do not charge market clearing prices but set low prices and then ration the goods instead. There you get what I would call a "frustration effect"—not being able to consume what you would at existing relative prices. There might be something deeper here, too, namely that people might value the act of choosing as such. Suppose you have price control and everybody in that system gets exactly the consumption bundle they would choose in the equilibrium market. Still, you could argue that people will be very frustrated and feel that their freedom of choice has been abolished simply because the act of choosing has been eliminated from the system.

The second aspect I want to talk about is predictability of the consequence of choice. Because taxes and subsidies and interventions create problems, governments have to change the rules all the time. They can never predict how people will react, so you get a chain of changes and new rules to compensate for the effect of the previous policy interventions—all the time, in an infinite chain. That means rule instability, and it is very difficult to know what the effect of what you are doing will be. I don't know how to classify this in terms of liberty or choice. It means that you are formally free to choose, but you have no idea what the consequence of your choice will be because the rule might change the next morning.

Another consequence is that when politicians see that the individual is ahead of the state in innovating adjustments, there is a strong temptation to make the rules so vague that the administration or the courts can make any interpretation they like. You have very strong tendencies in that direction. In Sweden we call them "general clauses." If you act against the intentions of government, the government can make your decision non-operative. That is also a development that reduces predictability.

My final point is regarding the vagueness of rules. If you have very vague rules, the administration and the courts will have a great deal of discretion. So you move from a system ruled by law to one ruled more by discretion. The public authorities in each individual case decide what shall be done. This very personal power which bureaucrats have over individuals is a problem with regard to civil liberties. This tends to expand because of the necessity to introduce more controls over individual behaviour because of the incentives for tax evasion, benefit fraud, et cetera.

I don't think welfare states have gone very far in intervening against civil liberties, but there is a slight drift in that direction. For instance, a number of years ago the authorities asked individuals to fill in a form where one question, directed toward unmarried or divorced women with children, was: "How many nights a month does your previous husband or your boyfriend spend in your house?" Of course, the mass media were outraged over it. As long as you have a free press that protects civil liberties, I think those types of intrusions on civil liberties will be rather vigorously fought in societies with pluralistic political systems.

Instead of intrusion in civil liberties, I think it is more likely that societies of Sweden's type will get a lot of slack in administration of these benefits—people can get benefits even if they are not entitled to them. It is a trade-off between slack rules and control. Depending on the type of political system, you will get more or less of one thing.

Control has gone furthest in Sweden in the tax system. For instance, small, one-man enterprises in particular have a problem because if they do business with other small enterprises they can be forced to pay the taxes for the others too. The law requires them to check that the others are paying all their taxes on transactions—sales taxes, payroll taxes, et cetera. But we can get insurance against that now; the private sector now has an insurance system for this type of "new risk" that the government has created in the system.

**Gordon Tullock** I have a question, and I think it is sort of a by-product of something you said at the beginning. You remarked about loaning money to university students. I have always rather admired the Swedish system on this, on the grounds that it is much better than ours. Unfortunately, that is not very strong praise. Is it indeed true that they charge reasonable interest and then collect the loans?

**Assar Lindbeck**  Zero real terms.

**Gordon Tullock**  And do they collect the loans?

**Assar Lindbeck**  Yes, they do. It is a problem with foreign students; they come in and then leave the country sometimes.

**Gordon Tullock**  It is certainly better than providing the subsidized education that we do, in any event, even if the subsidy is only on interest.

**Raymond Gastil**  A number of people at this conference have suggested that we should put more emphasis on economic rights such as freedom of choice, property and so on, in our Survey. Assar has convinced me that I am glad we didn't choose freedom of choice as a basic right. Ingemar's discussion gets us a little bit down the road towards understanding what a property right might look like as a basic right. He reminds us it is a bundle of rights, and I am reminded of the fact that in this case, as in so many cases in the real world, there is no country in which all aspects of property rights as he defines them exist in general, and there are very few countries where some aspects of property rights as he discussed them do not exist. So it is always a mixed system, but I thought it was a helpful classification.

There is one statement on page 13 that illustrates a point of view or way of thinking about majority rule that I have felt existed in a number of people in this group, and while I feel I am speaking into the wind, I will nevertheless make another intervention in this regard. The sentence starts:

> To many economists a large public sector would mean a decrease in economic freedom. It is not equally obvious that a large government sector will mean a corresponding increase in political freedom. Only if one is a supporter of an extreme majority rule doctrine would this be true. The extreme case would be that all social states had to be ranked by a majority principle and that there were no areas of complete privateness.

To me, that discussion of majority rule is just odd. In the first place, you say that it is not equally obvious that a large government sector will mean a corresponding increase in political freedom. As far as I can see, it has no relationship to that subject. When you talk about majority rule, you are talking about something that a population *can* do by exercising its political rights. You are not saying anything about what it *will* do. So it *could* decide not to have any welfare state at all, or it could decide to have a quite developed welfare state. Extreme majority principle or not, I see no way in which just invoking a majority principle gets us to a society in which there is no area of complete privateness. I just make the suggestion that my understanding of majority rule doesn't accord with this.

**Gordon Tullock** Once again I want to argue that aggregating preferences does not necessarily require that you use majority rule. It isn't a terribly good rule. But it is true that once you have decided to aggregate preferences and enforce the results of the preferences on other people, anything can happen. Majority rule is rather likely to lead to a lot of oddities. I have to emphasize only "rather likely," because the United States spent the whole 19th century under a very majoritarian system, and there was no expansion of the state during that period as a percentage of general income. But it is indeed true that majority rule has a tendency in any event to interfere in various places—the log rolling, special interest groups and so forth do occur. I would like a voting system that has somewhat less tendency to have that happen.

Many people think majority rule is what democracy means and, of course, they have a right to define words as they wish. What I want is a system which is in fact basically under control of the populace, and there are many, many voting rules that work better than majority rule for that purpose.

**Ingemar Stahl** The intention I had by this phrase—and it might not be quite clear—is a reference to the discussion by Amortia Simm on the impossibility of what is called "liberal preaching." The idea is that in an extreme case in welfare state economics there are ideas that can describe every socialist state. I might be able to read *Lady Chatterley's Lover* in one state and not in another. I think many politicians, even in the Swedish case, think it is better—we would get more democracy, they would say—if more decisions are majority decisions. That is why I am against it. I am opposed to the idea that they get more democracy, "more political freedom" as some people would say, if we put more and more decisions under majority rule. I am opposed to that idea because I believe in the unanimity rule.

On another point, the difference between my way of discussing it and Assar's way is that Assar is immediately going to the choice set. Freedom can then be defined as the size of the choice set.

**Assar Lindbeck** And its properties in general.

**Ingemar Stahl** Yes, but you can't say "properties in general." What I wanted to indicate by the first eight pages in my paper is that if we are going to have a discussion of rights—property rights, contracts—we have to look upon the relation structure which is very important. I might have failed a little bit there. Some of these ideas are extremely difficult, and I don't really know if they can be applied generally. For example, the choice set is determined in a very liberal world without any state interference. Then, using my terminology, we would say that I have a claim on government that they should provide me with free health care. There is a corresponding duty for the government to provide me with health care. But at the same time there is a claim from the government on me that I shall pay tax. The choice set is exactly the same as before. So you can't define freedom from the size of the choice set.

You have to go into the relation structure; that is, how many contracts, claims, immunities, et cetera you have against the state. It might be easier if you think it's only the relationship between me and the state that matters. But as in the Swedish case, we should broaden this because many of these freedoms and rights are against other types of institutions like trade unions and pressure groups. If you go to medieval society—and I guess Douglass knows much more about this—you really have to be careful to speak about rights and the relationships between different institutions and different persons. You don't need to mention very much about relations if it is just between you and the state. In a completely totalitarian state that might be true. But the more complex the state is and the more different pressure groups there are, the more we have to stress the relation and the contract structure, because they may differ very much between different persons or the relationships might change between different sub-sets of persons.

**Svetozar Pejovich** Suppose that only people who have high school degrees or only those whose wealth is $100,000 or more have the right to vote, would you still be against the majority rule?

**Gordon Tullock** I would not regard it as optimal, even with those restrictions. By the way, you will find discussions of this kind of thing in the formal literature. If I may answer this, in a way it means that the outcome is more informed. But any restriction of the total number of voters means the outcome is more informed, because by increasing the weight of the vote you increase the likelihood...

**Assar Lindbeck** But there is a difference. If you give the right to vote to school graduates, then it is more informed. If you give it to those with $100,000 or more in wealth, you are simply giving the right to vote to those who have more at stake in protecting the status quo.

**Gordon Tullock** There is a disadvantage, which is that the small group has a strong motive to cheat.

**Voice** I want to go back to the matter of Assar's freedom of choice approach, and it seems to me that Ingemar is correct. As I heard it, Assar was equating freedom of choice with what I thought was almost a Pareto-improved situation. He was saying, if the state by doing something can make people better off, then that is the same thing as extending the freedom of choice. That's how I heard the examples. The loans for students would be a case in point. That would be a case in which things would be made better if the loans paid for the full cost of the education not just for support, and if the rate of interest reflected the opportunity cost of the funds and the cost of collecting them and the probability of default and so on. Then I could see that there would be an improvement in that case.

There would be other cases that go the other way. Assar suggested that public monopolies were perhaps a source of reduction in freedom of choice; that might in general be so. As a matter of fact, you could imagine situations in which it would be possible to have marginal cost pricing on some natural monopoly product that might not get organized that way if it was not provided by the state.

To be succinct, the basic idea that freedom of choice is the same thing as a Pareto improvement came across to me. I would like some clarification, perhaps, that Assar doesn't have that in mind. And secondly, examples to illustrate.

**Assar Lindbeck** I am not sure that I can give a satisfactory answer, but what I tried to do was to start with a more common sense approach that is easy to fill with empirical observations. What I want Doug to do is discuss the welfare state consequences for freedom of choice, which means that I would concentrate from the beginning on how interventions of the state influence freedom of choice. Then I thought, and I still believe, that it is very reasonable to say that if the marginal tax rate is 100 percent, an individual is not able to choose between leisure and income—he's stuck. I think that is a good starting point. Then say it is 90 percent, then his freedom of choice is very limited. Then you say that Pareto improvement is very much related to increased freedom of choice. I have nothing against that interpretation. What's wrong with that? Increasing the freedom of choice in the sense that the set will increase will often lead to a Pareto improvement. Still, I think it is very useful to define this as something that changes the freedom of choice.

I would say the same thing when you have price controls. Public authorities start to ration goods, and individuals still cannot decide for themselves if they are going to use their income to consume more goods. I think it is very reasonable in connection with common sense to say that the individual's freedom of choice between beef and apartments has been reduced by rent control. I am not going to give up common sense because, first of all, common sense makes sense, and secondly, it is not very common.

**Ingemar Stahl** There is no difference between Assar and me when it comes to giving a description of the Swedish case in everyday language; I agree on most points. In this paper I tried to be a little more careful when it came to discussing what rights and structures and contracts might be. Take an extreme example here. In my terminology, I have the liberty or power to use one special field for my sheep, and everybody has that power and liberty. I can use it, you can use it, everybody can use it. It is complete freedom, because everybody has this choice set. There would be immediate conflict.

Most of us would then say that it is better that I have a claim right on the land and you have a duty not to trespass on that land with your sheep. That is a restriction of freedom which is very good for many reasons because it defines property rights. So we have to be a little bit careful here when we talk about the choice set for everybody as a definition of freedom. This is still an open question, but I think we have to go through the hard work of contractual structures of society. My idea is that when we look at the contractual structure of the welfare state, it is like a network with many bonds between individuals and institutions. It becomes a very stable system where there are very few liberties in the sense of powers that can change your position. The type of topological idea I have is a society where all of these attributes are linked to each other with so many different contractual structures that it becomes extremely rigid. But that is a way of looking at it.

When it comes to descriptions, there is no difference between you and me. But this is the start of a research programme, and I think we have to be very careful when we use these words. We have to go far, far deeper than we were doing earlier to look at the contract structures and the rights structures. The idea I have here is that taking some of the research work from jurisprudence might help us a little bit. It is still a question. I am not quite sure that it is a good way, but we have to try it to see if it works. If it doesn't work, it was an impasse. There are many impasses in scientific work.

**Milton Friedman** I want to go in a very different direction. I want to get back to some common sense and ask about some features of the welfare state that I think some of us are curious about. I have two in particular that I want to talk about, but I am only going to talk about one at the moment and that is the underground economy. One of the effects, obviously, as you were saying before, of the conflict between civil liberties and the widening of administrative regulation is that you either have slackness or reduction in civil liberties.

One of the ways that comes out is in the fact that people engage in illegal transactions among themselves. I remember some eight or ten years ago when we were in Sweden being told by some people there about cases of architects trading architectural services for dental services and similarly strange barter arrangements like that. I understood that there was widespread evasion of taxes via payment in cash as opposed to cheque. They called it "off the books."

This is purely an inquiry for information from both these gentlemen who are knowledgeable about this. Number one, what has been happening to the extent of that activity over a period of time? And second, how important do they estimate it to be in a sort of broad way? I'm not asking for an Ed Feige estimate of the percentage of the underground economy as a numerical value, but just your own conceptions of how important and significant it is and how much it limits what government is able to do.

**Ingemar Stahl** Every foreign opinion about the Swedish underground sector is exaggerated for two good reasons. One is that the control apparatus of the state is enormous in the sense that our social security numbers are used everywhere—on income accounts, on bank accounts, et cetera. As soon as one part of a transaction is controlled, the other part will also be controlled. That system, instead of sales tax, also has some self-controlling features, so you could say that tax administration is extremely skillful in Sweden. There are the service sectors, but remember that many of these, such as day care centres, are in the public sector. There is no way to do it in the underground sector.

I think the most important effect of taxation is that Swedes are working for themselves, not exploiting the possibilities of exchange. So we are getting back to a kind of do-it-yourself attitude. There may be more losses because of the lack of trade with everybody doing things themselves. And, of course, with high marginal tax rates you can only exploit productivity differentials where you have them six times in favour or against yourself. We don't look for differentials where it is just twice. That is why we don't have a private service sector; that's the do-it-yourself sector in Sweden. There are a lot of possible exchanges which do not take place where there are reasonable but not large productivity differentials between the trading partners.

**Assar Lindbeck**  Some 85 percent of the labour force work as employees. To the extent that they work for the government or in large firms, the possibilities for tax cheating in their ordinary activities are extremely small. The main area where you have cheating is in small enterprises in the service sector. The restaurant sector is probably at least 50 percent in the black sector.

There have been attempts at estimates, using various types of figures, for instance, government sampling studies in different branches. One of Ingemar's colleagues came up with between 4 and 8 percent of GNP, which probably is a more reasonable figure than Feige's 30 percent, which used a rather reckless method. I think he used currency circulation figures, and that is influenced by so many other things that it is not very reliable.

Two things happen here. One is that honesty becomes very expensive in the system, and there is a reduction in general morale. Twenty years ago people never boasted at the lunch or dinner table that they were cheating on taxes; they do that today. Also, of course, there is a substitution effect in favour not only of tax cheating but also of activities where tax cheating is easier than in other areas, such as drug peddling and things like that.

The biggest effect is perhaps what Ingemar said a little about, and that is the division of labour between families and markets and the government. Earlier, the family was in charge of personal services—it took care of the kids, the sick, and the old—whereas now these services are in the market. Now, a high marginal tax rate means that it is really impossible to buy services in the market with things or services produced in the household. The expansion of public services for individuals, like child care and old age care, rests with the government. Personal services are provided by government institutions, while households are taking care of *things* rather than human beings. We used to think that families were the natural units to take care of people, but now government is doing that. To me that is the most dramatic effect of the welfare state.

**Milton Friedman** I just want to pursue this two steps further. Number one, you didn't mention the extent to which you have a black market in rent control in housing. And I am just asking the question, is that an issue or not? The second thing is what you say about family seems to me more general. Every socialist regards the family as the primary enemy of the state, and almost every socialist measure is designed to reduce the role of the family. What you are saying is that the Swedish socialists have been very effective in doing that.

**Assar Lindbeck** Yes, in an interview some time ago I said that in Sweden we have not socialized production firms but socialized households instead. That is what I meant by that. It is household income, and the services which earlier were pursued by households, that are now done by the government.

There are two very large areas of black market activity. In spite of public day care centres, the system is not complete because it is so extraordinarily expensive. It costs some $10,000 per child, so only 40 percent of families get their children in public day care centres. Much of the rest is in the private sector with people taking care of other families' kids. That is not reported, and tax authorities never clamp down on that. So there you have a considerable sector.

It's quite true that you have rent control, and that means that contracts on apartments are sold regularly. Nowadays, that's mainly in the big cities. There has been so much house building in Sweden in the last 20 years that you have a pronounced excess demand rate only in the very big cities now. Isn't that true, Ingemar?

**Ingemar Stahl** Yes, in the two largest.

**Assar Lindbeck** Stockholm and Goteborg, there you have it. Having children myself, the expression I often hear when kids are working is that they work "stainless." Taxes are "stains," and if you work stainless that means you work in a sector where you don't pay taxes. That shows you the attitude among young people; they don't think it is immoral, anyway. Some people regard the politicians who created the tax system as more immoral than those who break the rules.

**Voice** I want to respond to Mr. Friedman's statement about the family and socialism. A study was made by a group of sociologists not so long ago saying that in the Soviet Union the family was a much stronger unit than in the United States. What Milton is saying is true, because at the same time that we had that strong unit, kids are encouraged to speak out about their parents behind their backs and to send them to gulags. The problem with our sociologists is that they simply report what they see; they don't know how to interpret it. There is strength in some ways, but at the same time confidence, trust and loyalty are totally broken.

**Peter Bauer** In considering the impact of the welfare state on the family we need to draw a number of distinctions. For example, we need to distinguish between redistribution of income and redistribution of responsibility between individuals and families on one hand and the government and its agents on the other hand. The two types of redistribution are quite different. I think redistribution of responsibility is a far-reaching effect of the welfare state.

**Ingemar Stahl** I think one could formulate a dilemma or a "catch 22" for the welfare state. If you ask people, why don't you go to the opera or why don't you buy that service or that service, they would say, I can't do it because although my gross income is not that small my net income is so small that I can't afford it. Then you might ask, if you can't afford it, why do you pay so much in taxes?—because we require all these services from the government. It is a vicious circle. I think this process can explain the growth of the welfare state.

We mentioned two things regarding the underground economy. The first was that in the controlled state the controls are very tough. The second is the do-it-yourself economy, and I forgot to mention the fringe benefits. When you have a marginal tax rate of 85 percent, you have to be very careful to put your expenses on the expense account and regard them as an input cost in the firm. You don't put it down as your own consumption but as an input cost. If you go to a Swedish hotel desk in the morning, people will always try to get the newspaper on the bill because it is six times more expensive to pay for it yourself. If you go to some countries, it is extremely difficult to get a receipt from a taxi driver. The first thing a Swedish taxi driver will offer you is a receipt. You can even trade in receipts. The fringe benefits economy is extremely difficult to estimate. There are some indications, however. For example, Swedish offices are in general much nicer than American offices. We will have a nice carpet in the office, but we can't afford it at home.

**Assar Lindbeck** And two Swedes at this conference. (Laughter)

**Alan Walters** Peter made a point that I thought was rather minimized by Assar and Ingemar. This issue about the responsibility chain changes things dramatically, and I will give you an illustration. The health service in Britain is primarily organized for the doctors on behalf of the doctors—in fact, not just the doctors, but the super doctors called consultants—a very small group. The whole structure of care is both constrained and distorted. For instance, if you want a hernia operation in Britain, you probably have to wait four or five years, because the consultants are not interested in hernia operations. They are more interested in things where they can come to distinguished conferences such as this. Consequently the whole structure is distorted and corrupted. Education is another typical case. The Inner London Education Authority, for instance, which is the biggest education authority, is corrupt in every sense. An enormous amount of money is spent—roughly twice the expenditure per pupil as anywhere else in the country. The whole structure of education is dominated by the providers who are organized by left wing...

**Voice** University of California faculty. (Laughter)

**Alan Walters** You probably *do* teach those things.

Not only has education been a failure in the sense that the kids can't read and write—not just that—but their minds are substantially distorted by preaching of the naturalness of homosexuality, of anti-white racism, of the irrelevance of much of the normal moral code. These politicized groups of providers manipulate education for their own ends. By dint of their contacts and infiltrations into the various power groups, extremists become the dominant teachers of the welfare state.

It is very difficult for the press and the normal organs of a democratic society to root out this corruption. One of the ways that was suggested for education was to get parent power back into the schools. This is extremely difficult in Britain.

**Raymond Gastil** Let me just suggest that from the point of view of the Survey, I have noticed that Sweden seems quite different perhaps from other similar welfare states such as Norway, Denmark, and the Netherlands, particularly in regard to the family. We brought up the family a minute ago, and there seems to be some evidence that the percentage of children that are taken over by the Swedish social services and taken away from their parents is several times greater than in those other countries. So I just wanted to point out that there are some real differences between welfare states that otherwise would seem to be very similar.

**Herbert Grubel** This is a brief technical point. When the state provides services which previously were provided by the household, one important effect is an upward bias in the estimate of national income growth. This happens when the supply of government child care induces women to cease the production of child care in the home and instead to supply their services in the market. One can perceive that the state supply of child care occurs with the labour which becomes available by the entry of the women in the market. There is no net gain in output except to the extent that there are economies in the public as against the private production of child care or that the productivity of women is raised by specialization. But since child care in the home is not recorded in the national income accounts and government provided child care is, the main effect of the government supply of services is an increase in the statistics of national income.

I also have a question for our experts from Sweden. To what extent are the people of Sweden aware of the costs of the welfare state that we have been discussing, lower real income and loss of freedoms? Is the subject discussed in the media and by politicians?

**Milton Friedman** I was going to raise an issue which we can't go into here. I am always astounded in the United States, let alone other countries, that everywhere I see waste and yet everywhere I see a high standard of life. The problem is, how do I reconcile these two? Is it really true that if we used our resources efficiently we could have three times the standard of life we have now, because I think we are wasting an enormous amount of resources in all these various ways. The same thing is true here, the same thing is true in Sweden.

I was going to ask our Swedish experts to what extent they believe that the change in the conduct of the welfare state has led to a reduction in the standard of life below what it otherwise would be. By standard of life I don't mean the numerically calculated statistical GDP, because I agree with Herb. I think that is very much distorted in a society like Sweden, when you count government services at cost and you don't have a decent way of indexing it for inflation and so on. So I am really asking for a different kind of impression—a more qualitative, intuitive impression—than I am for a statistical survey.

**Brian Kantor** I would like to return to the point I raised the other day in terms of how the system affects the economic outcomes and therefore the dangers in the welfare state for democratic processes. I am getting a strong impression here—and I would like our friends from Sweden to answer this question or confirm my impression—of a great big merry-go-round. The people are putting in taxes and taking out pretty much in proportion. When colonels and university professors are paying very high average tax rates and are on welfare, what are the redistribution effects of that system? It doesn't seem to me as if there is very much redistribution—enormous amounts of efficiency losses, but not redistribution.

**Assar Lindbeck** Quantifications have been done by the moderate cost of public funds approach, which is really that instead of Harberger triangles you get Harberger parallelograms because you start from a distorted situation. The best studies indicate that if you look at the choice between work in the home and work in the market, the growth rate would have been cut down from 3 to 2 percent during the last 15 years—these are Ingemar Honsenschultz Steward's figures.

I should say one word about what we call "cross-holding" in the system. It is true that the gross flows are much larger than net changes, but you have to consider that much of the welfare state is really redistribution over the life cycle of individuals. You get money when you are young and go to school; you pay net to the system when you are between 30 and 60; and then you get it back later on. Which means that the redistribution of wealth is much, much smaller than the redistribution of yearly income.

The redistribution effect on yearly income is extremely large. In an article in *European Economic Review* two years ago, I showed the difference between the income redistribution of factor income, disposable income, and per capita disposable income. It's a fantastic difference. If you take the highest decile to the second decile, for instance, it is 160 to 1 factor income; disposable per capita income is about 2 to 1. But, you see, that is because that statistic is on yearly income. If you take a life income, the redistributions are much smaller.

**Ingemar Stahl** In a description of the welfare state and its internal dynamics, I would prefer to use a paradigm of the prisoner's dilemma, in the sense that everybody is playing in the wrong field here because they believe everybody else is trying to make claims on the welfare state. Until now we have not been able to come to the conference table for a kind of disarmament of the welfare state. With this type of decentralized behaviour of different pressure groups, every group will continue to pressure for more from the welfare state under the assumption that the other groups are also doing it?

**Assar Lindbeck** And all the others pay.

**Ingemar Stahl** Yes. But that is part of the prisoner's dilemma.

Some consequences of the welfare state have to do with the rights question, and I have mentioned that before. If you have an all-encompassing social welfare or social security system, people are not responsible and there will be a moral hazard problem. This creates a control problem for government. Our colleagues from the benefit/cost calculation-oriented departments always support different types of measures for government control in the lives of the citizens. If you go to a Swedish hospital, it would say: "belongs to the County Council of Stockholm." You don't know if it's the dress the patient has on or if it even might be the patient himself.

The Swedish law system is a typical statutory law system and not a common law system. This means that it is extremely difficult to get compensation, say, in a torte of negligence. In the court they would say you have already gotten it through the social security system. You can't claim compensation again. This means that another type of moral hazard is created in the system.

I think some of these issues should be pursued a little bit more, because these are aspects of the social welfare state that are really not well studied.

# Chapter 8

## Freedom, Property Rights and Innovation in Socialism*

## Svetozar Pejovich

### Background Notes

Economists have long been concerned with the neoclassical efficiency paradigm. Given initial endowments and preference functions, exchange moves resources from lower- to higher-valued uses. In a private-property, free-market economy all resource use opportunities are exploited, and allocative efficiency can be conceptualized. The wealth of nations is maximized when people have the right to choose. Methodological individualism combined with contractual freedom and private property provides important insights into social problems that stem from scarcity, generates refutable predictions, and explains a wide class of economic events. The neoclassical price takers' model represents an ideal of allocative efficiency against which many people judge economic performance. To earn respectability, alternative institutional structures must demonstrate similar outcomes. In this mode, *the entrepreneur is a passive agent who directs production in accordance with the consumer preference.*

Instead of remaining a benchmark against which to judge the consequenes of different institutional arrangements, the price-takers' model has become a guide for policy. Laws and regulations have been enacted under a pretense of enhancing market competition. SEC, FTC, FCC and many other institutions have been formed to assure the economy of a price-takers'

*I want to thank Armen Alchian, Steve Wiggins and the participants of the 13th Interlaken Seminar on Analysis and Ideology for many valuable comments. The Lynde and Harry Bradley Foundation and the Texas Educational Association research grants are gratefully acknowledged.

competitive environment. Yet, the concept of perfect competition is a poor vehicle for understanding various competitive strategies, institutional structures and organizational forms. Moreover, the assumptions of private ownership in resources and zero transaction costs leave outside the scope of neoclassical analysis cases whose market solutions are inconsistent with the marginal equivalencies for the general optimum, as well as cases that arise from the existence of various types of property structures.

Given their assumptions of private ownership in resources and zero transaction costs, neoclassical economists have developed a powerful apparatus for discussing *some* economic issues. However, analytical tools such as demand, supply and investment schedules have frequently been used to analyse social and economic issues in a non-private property, non-market environment. The problem is that the incentive effects of private property rights embodied in those analytical tools are not operative under alternative institutional arrangements. A mechanical transfer of neoclassical analytical concepts from a free market economy to a non-market environment is surely misleading. For example, Lange and Mises initiated a technically impeccable debate on the issue: Could the Soviet (planned) economy simulate the price-takers' results? This and other similar debates are examples of academic resources being wasted on wrong questions.

In response to those limitations of the standard theory of production and exchange, a significant body of literature has grown up around the central idea that property rights matter in two ways. First, property rights are a major determinant of incentive structures. Thus, property rights influence economic behaviour in specific and predictable ways. Second, new property rights develop and existing ones are modified in response to economic change. The emphasis on the interconnectedness of institutional arrangements and economic behaviour alleviates some limitations of neoclassical economic analysis. Importantly, the property rights approach has shifted the focus of economic analysis away from "toy" issues and toward substantive analytical problems that have direct bearing on policy.

Let us go back to the Lange-Mises debate. To assume that the Soviet manager will seek to maximize the firm's profit upon being told to do so is like assuming that a three-year-old will stop eating sweets when told to. Substantive questions are: What is the Soviet manager's survival trait? What is the penalty-reward system? What is the cost of monitoring the manager's behaviour? What does the manager gain from pursuing planned objectives? "To publish a set of rules asking the state enterprises to behave 'as if' they were profit maximizing entrepreneurs in competitive industry ignores the actual personal motivations faced by these men" (Brittan, 1980).

The property rights literature has applied economic analysis fruitfully to many diverse problems. Viewing the firm as a set of contracts among factors of production has not only improved our understanding of its *intra-organizational* processes but has improved our comprehension of economic processes in general. The area of comparative economic systems has taken on an analytical content. Instead of just recording and interpreting Soviet economic performance ex-post, we can deduce it ex-ante from the effects of Soviet property rights structure on economic behaviour. The allocative efficiency of the labour-managed firm has been investigated rather extensively. A paper by Jensen and Meckling (1979) highlights this endeavour to evaluate the concept of self-management. The property rights literature has been able to anticipate recent economic problems in Yugoslavia (Pejovich, 1976). It also explains why current stabilization policies in Yugoslavia are not going to work as intended (Pejovich, 1986). The Yugoslav experience having failed to vindicate the concept of self-management, new "Oscar Langes" have begun to surface. Their common purpose is to salvage the idea of labour participation in the management of business firms (Rutterman, 1984; Sternham, 1984). Friedman defined the issue as: "It forces [socialist and pro-socialist intellectuals] to try to estimate what the results would have been in a free market and therefore to take into account relevant considerations in achieving efficient production" (Friedman, 1984). Alchian and Meckling keep reminding us that the property issue is why the survival of such an "efficient" institution depends on a bloody revolution, a dictatorship, a monopoly in the market for organizational forms, or all of the above.

The property rights literature has made a major contribution to better understanding of the allocative effects of different institutional structures. It has, however, done little to improve our understanding of the *expansion of choices.*

## The Expansion of Choices

A theory of economic change should discuss the following issues: (i) How are new choices introduced and evaluated in the system? (ii) What is the effect of different property rights on the expansion of choices? (iii) Can the development of new property rights be deduced from economic change?

The basis for those questions arises from the fact that people prefer a wider to a narrower range of choice. A disruption of the prevailing equilibrium (and a reduction in economic efficiency) may be compensated by the expansion of choices. The entrepreneur (innovator) then becomes an active agent in the system, while the consumer gets to *judge* entrepreneurial decisions.

One set of institutions may be superior to another set not because it happens to be more efficient in terms of the neoclassical maximization paradigm, but because it encourages the flow of innovation with the expansion of the new opportunity set (Buchanan, 1985). The central issue is the effect of alternative institutional arrangements on the flow of innovation.

Neoclassical economics has appreciated the importance of innovation. It has treated innovation as a deliberate element of firm strategy (Nelson and Winter, 1977; Rosenberg, 1976; David, 1974). It has explored the effects on innovation of risk, uncertainty and R & D (Kamien and Schwartz, 1982; Klein, 1977). The effects of the distribution of firms by size, concentration ratios and market shares has been looked into by many writers, including Abernathy and Utterback (1978) and Boylan (1977).

However, the neoclassical view of the firm as the unit of analysis (which ignores behavioural effects of the intra-firm relationships) and the narrowness of its maximization paradigm (which assumes the firm's choice set to be given) have made innovation an external phenomenon. Once innovation is made, the "given" set of choices is adjusted to embrace it. That is, neoclassical analysis deals with innovation *after* it is introduced into the system.

Innovation *is* the pursuit of economic gain. It is characterized as an expansion of the firm's choice set. In that sense, the neoclassical maximization and growth paradigm is analytically narrow—it means more *of the same*. Innovation expands the meaning of economic development into the expansion of choices. It disrupts prevailing relationships and brings about a discrete jump from the old to a qualitatively new situation. Innovation has two interdependent social functions: It alters the economy and offsets the law of diminishing returns. An important *economic* issue is how to appropriately enable people to attempt to innovate.

Innovation is complex. For the purpose of analysis it could be broken down into: the freedom to innovate, the ability to innovate, the incentive to innovate, the implementation of innovation, and the evaluation of innovation.

The paper is an inquiry into the relationship between freedom, property rights and the flow of innovation in socialism.[1] The line of reasoning in the paper is exampled by reference to the Yugoslav economy. Relative to other East European states, the Yugoslav economic system is most interesting for a study of socialism.[2] Yugoslav institutions are supposed to simulate the production efficiency of capitalism while preserving the socialist character of the economy. They have been operative for several decades. Thus, their performance can be evaluated. Moreover, the concept of self-management has strong followings in the West.

### Freedom to Innovate

Innovation means doing something that is new. It could be the development of a new good, the opening up of a new market, a new source of supply, a new method of production, or a new way of organizing activity. At the firm's level, innovation is primarily technological (NSF, 1983). Technology, broadly defined, includes physical objects, human capital and physical production methods. That is, technology embodies the prevailing knowledge. However, the growth of knowledge is unpredictable, and that contributes to the unpredictability of innovation.

The innovator translates knowledge into new choices. The unit of analysis is then the innovator rather than innovation itself. Innovation is a consequence of the innovator's perception about the applicability of knowledge, willingness to accept the risk and uncertainty associated with doing something new, and ability to see the innovation through (as innovation unfolds many people have to say "yes"). The innovator must possess such traits as ingenuity, optimism, stubbornness, perseverance, and imagination. Moreover, potential innovators are difficult to identify ex-ante. The growth of knowledge being unpredictable means that specific innovations cannot be planned in advance. One cannot simply decide to have one innovation each month. In a nutshell, innovation is individualistic in its origin and social in its consequences.

However, we should be able to identify and influence some specific objective conditions that are conducive for carrying out innovation. One such objective condition is the freedom to innovate.

The prevailing property rights in society determine who has the right to acquire and determine uses of resources (e.g. who can innovate). Property rights also define constraints on the rights to use resources. In a private-property economy all individuals are allowed to innovate, while the right to contract private-property rights to resources lowers the cost of identifying the value of resources in alternative uses.

The Yugoslav system of self-management reached its maturity during the 1965-73 period. Even during this period the government kept the basic constitutional requirement: To share in the firm's residual, Yugoslav workers must combine their current labour with the firm's physical assets. The employees can neither sell their rights in the residual nor enjoy them when they quit. A Yugoslav economist is quoted saying: "If the workers really owned the firm, they would sell off their shares and then we wouldn't have socialism anymore" (Beloff, 1985, p. 251).

The property rights analysis has demonstrated that the Yugoslav system of self-management is inefficient (Jensen and Meckling, 1979), predicted the emergence of serious problems such as inflation, unemployment and liquidity crisis (Pejovich, 1976), and suggested that the Yugoslav government will have to choose between creating capital markets or reintroducing bureaucratic controls (Furubotn and Pejovich, 1974).

The Yugoslav government made its choice in 1974. The Constitution of 1974 and the Law of Associated Labour of 1976 modified and redefined institutional structures in Yugoslavia. *De jure*, the 1974 reform strengthened and expanded the system of self-management. *De facto*, the government took the economy back toward a greater reliance on political and bureaucratic controls. To accomplish this dual effect of *more* self-management and *more* controls, the government made the employees' property rights assignments both cumbersome and vague.[3]

The pool of those who can acquire and use resources in Yugoslavia is for all practical purposes restricted to the working collective.[4] The term "working collective" is important here. The employees of the firm cannot, as individuals, acquire private property to productive resources. Only the working collective as a whole can do so through its Workers' Council (WC). An employee who perceives an opportunity for innovation must convince the WC about his idea. Convincing and persuading the WC is quite a task. The WC reflects the composition of the firm's labour force. The firm's management is *not* represented on the WC. The members receive no extra compensation, have no staff support to help them understand the issues, and they continue to work at their regular jobs; that is, they do not receive on-the-job training to be business leaders. Yet, the WC must approve or reject all major investment, financial and other internal decisions that may affect the firm. To have to get a group of people with diverse attitudes toward risk, different incentives, different technical knowledge, limited business experience and different age distribution to comprehend and approve a *novelty* must certainly impede the flow of innovation.

Until 1974, the firm's director was in the best position to get his ideas through the Workers' Council. The director was the Council's employee, but he was also its business expert. The director was the person in the firm who could best formulate the alternatives and identify their expected consequences for the WC. The director's evaluation of the alternatives, his method of presentation, and personality traits had considerable influence on the WC's decision. Members of the Council also knew that it was in their self-interest to go along with the director and vote for his favourite projects. They knew that once they were off the WC, the director could reward them by better (or worse) paying jobs in the firm, send them abroad, and ignore shirking.

Predictably, the mangers' power, influence and prestige grew steadily during the 1965-73 period. Party cadres soon were threatened by this "new" class. True, managerial jobs, like all other important positions, were filled by the Party network. However, the prevailing property relations pushed the Yugoslav manager into a position of influence that was neither anticipated nor welcomed by the party leadership. Managers were becoming independent decision makers, true captains of the economy, and also quite rich (Bajt, 1972). The case against the managers was put as the technocrats vs. the people. Two aspects of the institutional reform after this period are relevant here: (i) the atomization of business firms, and (ii) the transformation of Yugoslavia into a contractual society.

In the mid-1970s, the Yugoslav government made a fundamental change in the organization of business firms. Three new legal categories were introduced: (i) *Associated labour* refers to the whole set of economic activities that combine current labour with capital goods. Only those Yugoslavs who work with capital goods can participate in self-management decisions. (ii) *Organization of associated labour* (OAL) refers to a self-managed organization. It is what we usually call a firm in the economic sector and an institution in the non-economic sector. I will continue to use the word "firm" to refer to this organization. (iii) *Basic organization of associated labour* (BOAL) identified work units, plants and departments. BOAL is the *fundamental*, lowest level, economic unit in Yugoslavia today. The law says that employees must form a BOAL whenever the results of their joint labour (e.g. teamwork) can be measured in value terms either in the market or within the firm. The BOAL's "employees" elect their own Workers' Council who, in turn, appoints the BOAL's director. The BOAL's residual, which differs from one BOAL to another in the same firm, is appropriated and allocated by the BOAL's collective. (Obviously, the classic intra-firm pricing conflict has to arise.)

Each BOAL sends representatives to the firm's Workers' Council, which, in turn, appoints the firm's director. BOALs within a firm negotiate written contracts among themselves. These contracts specify their mutual rights and obligations, composition of decision-making bodies, criteria for the distribution of income, assignments of costs of law suits, coordination of production schedules, etc. Negotiations between BOALs within a firm are real, long and often sharp (Beloff, 1985, p. 229).

The firm's powers are only delegated powers, and the firm's income is set according to contractual contributions of its own BOALs. These conditions reduced the firm director's power, prestige ·and influence by the mid-1980s. The atomization of the Yugoslav firm created many new (and costly) problems. For example, the Yugoslav railroad system has been broken down into 350 separate BOALs with as many new managers.

Basically, the 1974 reform curbed the influence of market forces on the allocation of resources. The government avoided returning the economy to a system of administrative controls. Instead, it created a *sui-generis* contractual society which has turned out to be (perhaps inevitably) a mix of *more* self-management and *less* freedom. As we said, BOALs negotiated contracts among themselves. Institutions and firms in related activities negotiate contracts. These contracts specify the pooling of resources, criteria for the distribution of earnings and other business issues. Self-management agreements, as those contracts are called, are combined into social contracts. Besides business firms and institutions, labour unions, trade associations, political groups and government bureaus participate in negotiating social contracts. Regional social contracts are combined into social contracts for a province, republics and finally the social contract for Yugoslavia. Provision of welfare, health, education, arts, and other services is negotiated between the suppliers of those services (e.g. hospitals, pharmacies, ambulances) and those who demand them (firms, institutions and trade groups on behalf of their members). On top of this structure of contracts we find a new self-management bureaucracy (self-management associations, public agencies, committees of interest and trade groups).

Contractual agreements among all those groups encompass economic life in Yugoslavia. Working from the bottom upward, contractual agreements are supposed to reflect preference functions of the working people. In practice, the party leadership formulates economic guidelines which the party apparatus is supposed to plug in at each level of negotiations.[5]

The atomization of productive units and the system of contracts have attenuated the workers' rights in their respective firms. The atomization has broken the firm into small groups moved by their own self-interest. The system of contracts has brought back, in a roundabout way, the administrative controls. And, above all BOALs, firms and contractual agreements is the new self-management bureaucracy. It runs the systems on behalf of those who are supposed to have the right to govern it. S. Kraiger, a revolutionary turned economist, made the following comment about this new bureaucracy: "Every single reform we recommend needs a market. But the operations of the market would only destroy the power of the ruling body.

And it is the Rubicon, which those in office do not wish to cross" (*Danas*, 8/1982, p. 2).

I now summarize my perceived effects of property rights in Yugoslavia on the freedom to innovate. The working collective still represents the pool of those who can innovate. However, the number of people who have to say "yes" as innovation unfolds has risen significantly since 1974. The government has, in effect, collectivized the phenomenon which, by its very nature, depends on the individual, the personality traits, and the system of incentives. Today, a Yugoslav worker with an idea for innovation has to persuade the BOAL's Workers' Council, then the firm's Workers' Council, and finally the self-management bureaucracy. The BOAL's director has to deal with his own Workers' Council, the firm's Workers' Council and the self-management bureaucracy. The firm's director must get all BOALs on his side. In comparison with a private-property, free-market economy, the Yugoslav system of self-management has (i) reduced the number of people who are free to acquire and use resources, and (ii) collectivized the activity by requiring more people to agree on the wisdom of some proposed innovative effort.

### Ability to Innovate

It is important that we do not confuse freedom with power (Jensen and Meckling, 1985). Freedom to acquire resources is one thing, the power to actually get them is another. The ability to acquire an asset does depend on the buyer having enough resources to pay for it, and the seller having a bundle of rights in the asset that he is willing to transfer at a price the buyer is willing to pay.

Suppose that the working collective of a Yugoslav firm approves its director's proposal to implement a technological innovation. The issue is: Does the Yugoslav financial system enhance the innovator's ability to carry out innovation?

In a capitalist economy, financial markets match the demand for resources with the supply of resources at prices which reflect contractual agreements on various issues, including risks. The fewer imposed regulations in the financial markets the better they will respond to the innovators.

State ownership in capital and the collective's attenuated property rights in the residual limit the scope of financial markets in Yugoslavia. The supply of private venture capital in Yugoslavia is insignificant. Some private wealth exists in Yugoslavia, but property rights preclude this source of income from being used to finance innovations. Foreign capital has dried up. Inter-firm markets for undistributed profits is virtually nonexistent; incentive structures discourage business collectives from lending funds to other collectives. Thus, the Yugoslav collective has two major sources of funds: the firm's own residual and bank credit. The former is not a promising source of investable funds. There are simply too many claims against it. About 70 percent of the residual is usually allocated into the collective's wage fund. The collective consumption is financed from the residual. The law requires that a percentage of the residual be set aside as reserves. Bank credit is then left as the most important source of financing innovation in Yugoslavia. The collective's ability to carry out innovation depends on the organization of the banking system.

The rate of interest in Yugoslavia demanded by the banks is set below its market clearing price, with a resultant "insatiable" demand for bank credit. A collective seeking funds is not given a choice to compete for bank credit by offering to pay more than the official rate of interest. Financial markets in Yugoslavia do not bring the borrower and the supplier of bank credit together to negotiate a mutually acceptable price.

Banks in Yugoslavia are operated by the managers of the firms which are also their *chief borrowers*. To form a bank, management of several firms get together and negotiate a contract. They have to satisfy many legal provisions including (non-refundable) contributions to the bank's credit fund. Once the bank is approved, the founders govern the bank, appoint the bank director and other officers, appropriate the residual (the residual does not belong to the bank's collective), and appoint the credit committee. The last point is important here. The representatives of business firms which "own" the bank replace bank officers as the allocators of funds. With the bank's rate of interest held below the market clearing level, the evaluation of credit applications must be expected to reflect the committee's subjective preference and their respective firms' self-interest.

Let us review the ability to innovate in Yugoslavia. First, the major source of innovation financing is bank credit. Second, prices in financial markets are not market clearing prices. Third, bank credit is allocated by the committee representing business firms which (i) appropriate the bank's residual, and (ii) are its chief borrowers. A novelty (that is a *risky* venture) is not a likely winner in competition for funds that are sold below the market price. In other words, the prevailing property rights in Yugoslavia tend to reduce the innovator's (i.e., the collective's) ability to innovate.

### Incentives to Innovate

The act of innovation, being a non-routine action, usually entails a relatively high degree of risk and uncertainty about its outcome. The innovator must be given sufficient incentives for the risk he takes. An effective way of providing an innovator with sufficient incentives is to assure him that he or someone has the right to appropriate the gains from innovation. In a capitalist economy, the right of ownership and contractual freedom offers greater rewards and hence incentives to accept the risk and uncertainty associated with innovation. The gains come from the market acceptance of innovation.

In discussing the effects of the Yugoslav property rights structures on the flow of innovation in Yugoslavia, it is necessary to ask: (i) Does the innovator have the incentive to accept the risk and uncertainty associated with innovations, and (ii) does anyone else have incentive to provide the innovator with the resources to attempt innovation?

*The Yugoslav property rights structures preclude the capitalization of the future benefits of a successful innovation into their present market value.* This immensely important proposition has several behavioural implications.

(i)   The collective captures some of the benefits of innovation in *the form of higher wages.* Given the employees' time horizon, i.e., the expected length of employment by the firm, the collective members' incentives are to approve innovation that shifts income forward and/or postpones costs. That is, the collective members have incentives to seek innovation that increases the near-term cash flow. This incentive is quite restrictive. It may rule out some economical innovations because the benefits extend too far beyond the collective members' time horizon.

(ii)  The expected length of life of innovation affects the collective's incentive to approve the innovator's idea. If the expected life of innovation exceeds the collective's time horizon, the employees will have less incentive to approve a novelty. Again, some potentially profitable projects may be turned down for the wrong reasons.

(iii) A worker who comes up with a successful innovation *shares* the benefits with other members of the collective. Even if the innovator gets a cash prize or periodic payments, he will capture for himself only a small fraction of the total gain from innovation. Moreover, an innovator who leaves the enterprise before the life of innovation ends forfeits all the future benefits from innovation to those workers who remain with the firm.

(iv)  The prevailing property rights in Yugoslavia reduce the director's incentive to innovate. In the West the manager-innovator captures the benefits in the market for managers. The present value of his future earnings goes up. A successful innovation in Yugoslavia does not reward the manager-innovator. The costs of information about the manager's performance are much higher in the markets without private ownership. Thus, the Yugoslav director has less incentive to accept the risk associated with innovation.

(v)  The innovator (the collective) has incentives to seek a loan that bunches benefits within the collective's time horizon and, hopefully, extends its amortization to future workers. At the same time, the credit committee of the bank (representing the firms which "own" the bank's residual) has incentives to grant those loans whose interest payments over *their* time horizon are assured.

## Freedom, Innovation and the Yugoslav Economic System

Innovation is a very individual phenomenon. It depends on the individual perceptions of the applicability of knowledge, attitudes toward the risk and ingenuity in putting things together in a new way. Innovation cannot be predicted, planned, or ordered to happen. The suppliers of innovations are difficult to identify *ex-ante*. The community's potential for economic development could be deduced from the analysis of the effects of its institutions on the ingredients of innovation such as the freedom to acquire resources, incentives to try out new things and the ability to secure economic power to finance a novelty.

Economic development does not depend only on the savings-investment relationship, the availability of resources, or the "equilibrium path." Economic development depends primarily on institutional arrangements that increase the right of people to innovate, enhance the individual's incentives to innovate, and provide a subsequent evaluation of innovation. That is, an essential problem of economic development is the freedom to search for and adapt a set of social institutions within which opportunities and incentives for innovation are enhanced. The emergence of economic freedom in Eastern Europe (and elsewhere) should be related to changes in property rights and their behavioural effects. A theory of economic change that links freedom, institutions and innovation will fill an important void in neoclassical analysis.

The system of "self-management" in Yugoslavia has constrained both the firm's efficiency as well as the innovator's freedom and ability to expand the set of choices. Co-determination in Germany seems to be going the same way (Watrin, 1985). The Hungarian situation is still fluid and difficult to evaluate analytically. In general, property rights assignments associated with labour participation in the management of business firms reduce the number of potential innovators, their power (ability) to innovate, and incentives to innovate.

A casual visitor would have noticed a remarkable difference between the quality of life in Yugoslavia in the early 1970s and the early 1980s. It is not to say that the situation in the 1970s was great. It was only not nearly so bad as it is today. Stores were cleaner, supplies looked better, employees were more alert (especially when the manager was around), and in sidewalk cafes stories were told about business deals. Inflation, liquidity problems, unemployment were all alive and well. Yet, the system provided room for business leadership. Today, Yugoslav stores are poorly kept and badly supplied with goods. People seem sour and resigned.

Economic numbers support casual observations. The rate of unemployment increased from 8 percent to 15 percent. Counting 700,000 Yugoslavs in Western Europe, unemployment is about 20 percent. Quality of labour input per employed worker has been falling by 1.5 percent per year (Bajt, 1983). This problem of "unemployed employed" has been attributed to laxities in the organization of production and plain shirking by workers. The average rate of taxation by inflation in Yugoslavia is now about 70-80 percent of the money stock. The rate of economic growth has been negative; the average real income of Yugoslav workers has been declining by about 7 percent per year. A Yugoslav sociologist calculated that between 1982 and 1984 the number of hours required to buy a pair of shoes had doubled (Beloff, 1985, p. 234).

The paper has two conclusions. Self-management in Yugoslavia has *collectivized* innovation and *alienated* the innovator from its results. More generally, economic superiority of capitalism over all the various types of socialism does not arise from the neoclassical efficiency test. Superior economic performance of capitalism should be attributed to the fact that socialism collectivizes and hinders innovations.

The time has come to ask a general question: Is the principle of state ownership in resources—whether it takes the form of the Soviet administrative planning, or the Hungarian "privatization" or the Yugoslav system of self-management—so incompatible with the basic rules of human behaviour that it could never work? Whatever the answer, it is intellectual madness to continue to contend that the system is inherently virtuous.

## Other Issues

Two critical issues have been left out of this paper. They are the implementation of innovation and the evaluation of innovation. The former should analyse the effects of alternative property rights on the flow of innovation from their inception to the final integration into the economy. A recent study has estimated that the speed of implementation of innovation in the USA and West Germany is more than twice that in the USSR (Marten and Young, 1979). The evaluation of innovation is important. To introduce a novelty into the system does not necessarily make the people better off. To say that innovation is risky means that it often does and indeed will fail. In a capitalist society, people in the market evaluate innovation and their judgement is quickly incorporated into relative prices and affects the innovator's wealth. In socialist economies the evaluation of innovation is done by a much more ambiguous procedure.

## NOTES

1. Property rights are defined as behavioural relations among men that arise from the existence of resources and pertain to their use. For the purpose of this paper, freedom means that changes in property rights are (or could be) triggered by the interaction between the prevailing institutions and man's search for ways of achieving more utility.

2. The Yugoslav system's basic characteristics are: (i) The state owns capital goods held by the business firms (it makes some people feel better to call it *social* ownership). This preserves the character of socialism and reflects the ruling elite's dogmatism. (ii) Employees govern their respective firms through Workers' Councils, the highest organs of management. This is what sets the Yugoslav system apart. Workers are supposed to control allocation of resources. (iii) Employees own returns from their firms' capital. Workers' Councils decide how to allocate profit between firms' wage funds, reinvestments of earnings, and other uses of funds. (iv) Major sources of investment funds are retained profits and bank credit. In Yugoslavia, investment decisions have been transferred from economic planners to firms, banks and Workers' Councils. (v) Plants within each firm, institutions and firms in related activities, as well as groups bound together through common interests (e.g. firms, chambers, trade unions) negotiate contracts for polling resources, criteria for the distribution of profits between wages and other funds, and other matters. These are called self-management agreements. Self-management agreements encompass the entire economic life of Yugoslavia. They aren't voluntary, but mandated by law, with basic terms often stipulated in advance. Within those constraints (i.e., controls) contractual terms are negotiated among participants.

3. I believe that it could be demonstrated that more self-management inevitably leads to more contracts.

4. The right of private ownership is limited to a very few assets and has many economic and political constraints.

5. The leadership does not necessarily get its way in each and every instance. As orders travel down from the top they tend to get attenuated. Party members frequently face the problem of their loyalty to the party on the one hand and self-interest within their economic units on the other.

## REFERENCES

Abernathy, W. and J. Utterback. "Patterns of Industrial Innovation," *Technology Review*, 1978, pp. 40-47.

Bajt, A. "Economic Growth in Yugoslavia," CESES Conference, Florence, 1983.

Beloff, N. *Tito's Flawed Legacy*, London: Victor Gollancz, 1985, p. 251.

Boylan, M. "The Sources of Technological Innovations," in B. Gold (ed.), *Research, Technological Change, and Economic Analysis*, Lexington: Lexington Books, 1977.

Brittan, S. "Hayek, the New Right and the Crisis of Social Democracy," *Encounter*, January 1980, p. 38.

Buchanan, J. Comments on H. Albert's paper, "Is Socialism Inevitable?" Symposium on Socialism, Interlaken, 1985.

David, P. *Technical Change, Innovation and Economic Growth*, Cambridge: Cambridge University Press, 1984.

Friedman, M. *Market and Plan*, London, CRCE, 1984, p. 13.

Furubotn, E. and S. Pejovich. "Property Rights, Economic Decentralization, and the Evolution of the Yugoslav Firm, 1965-1972," *Journal of Law and Economics*, 1974, pp. 275-302.

Furubotn, E. and S. Pejovich. "The Soviet Manager and Innovation," in E. Furubotn and S. Pejovich (eds.), *The Economics of Property Rights*, Cambridge: Ballinger Co., 1974, pp. 203-216.

Jensen, M. and W. Meckling. "Human Rights and the Meaning of Freedom," Liberty Fund Conference on Freedom, 1985.

Jensen, M. and W. Meckling. "Rights and Production Functions," *Journal of Business*, 1979, pp. 469-506.

Kamien, M. and N. Schwartz. *Market Structures and Innovation*, Cambridge: Cambridge University Press, 1982.

Klein, B. *Dynamic Economics*, Cambridge: Harvard University Press, 1977.

Nelson, R. and S. Winter. "In Search of a Useful Theory of Innovation," *Research Policy*, 1977, pp. 36-76.

Pejovich, S. "The End of an Experiment," Working Paper, 1986.

Pejovich, S. "The Incentives to Innovate Under Alternative Property Rights," *Cato Journal*, 1984, pp. 427-446.

Pejovich, S. "The Labor-Managed Firm and Bank Credit," in J. Thornton (ed.) *Economic Analysis of Soviet-Type System*, Cambridge: Cambridge University Press, 1976, pp. 242-255.

Putterman, L. "On Some Recent Explanations of Why Capital Hires Labor," *Economic Inquiry*, 1984, pp. 171-187.

Rosenberg, N. *Perspectives on Technology*, Cambridge: Cambridge University Press, 1976.

Sertel, M. and A. Steinberr. "Information, Incentives, and the Design of Efficient Institutions," *Journal of Institutional and Theoretical Economics*, 1984, pp. 233-246.

Tornatsky, L. et al. *The Process of Technological Innovation*, Washington, D.C.: National Science Foundation, 1983.

Watrin, C. "Economic and Social Consequences of Socialist Policies in West Germany," Paper presented at Symposium on Socialism, Interlaken, 1985.

# Discussion

## Edited by Michael A. Walter

**Michael Walker** This morning we have a slightly different pattern of affairs, largely because the comment by Tibor Machan in effect amounts to a new point rather than an intervention on the paper by Steve Pejovich. As a consequence, I'm going to go to interventions from the floor now, and I will bring Tibor in at a later stage of the proceedings with his new point.

**Raymond Gastil** I want to make two points. First, earlier we heard that China had no word for individual freedom until very recently. In listening to the discussions around here, it strikes me that maybe there are too many words for individual freedom in our language, because the over-emphasis on the individual doesn't seem to me to accord to the actual reality of the world today. For example, the idea that innovation is strictly an individual thing doesn't accord with the way innovations are now carried on in corporations. I used to work for Battelle Memorial Institute which had 7,000 employees around the world—in very few of those innovations did the return from the innovation go to the person who did the innovation. He received a salary, he worked for the corporation, he got paid whether or not he made an innovation that week. I think an awful lot of innovation today is of *that* sort rather than the entrepreneurial innovation of the individual that is being discussed here.

The second point I wanted to make is that if we are going to discuss the gains and losses of a system, such as the Yugoslav self-management system, as they call it, in relation to something like innovation, then it seems to me that it has to appear as if we are doing a kind of balancing job. Too often in these discussions I haven't seen a balancing job.

Yesterday, Assar tried to look at freedom of choice in the welfare state, suggesting there might be some gains as well as losses in the welfare state as regards freedom of choice. I didn't like freedom of choice as an analytical category; I thought it was very difficult to deal with. Nevertheless, it seems to me that we have to make that attempt more often. In this paper I missed that. I felt you were trying to point out all the ways in which this system made innovation difficult without ever really thinking seriously about whether there might be ways in which it would *improve* the chances of innovation. Unless you do that, I am not very convinced about the paper. For example, it occurred to me that if the managers of the various self-management units are, in fact, the people who run the banks that give money to those units, the argument could be made that if they make the decision that they want to push a certain innovation, they don't have to do what they might have to do in a Western country, which would be to then convince the bank first. They might have some advantage, an ability to short-circuit the process, because they control the banks directly. That's just a thought, but unless these things are brought up, I don't feel very convinced.

**Walter Block** I was puzzled somewhat by the absence of any footnote or citation to Israel Kirzner with regard to entrepreneurship in his book *Competition and Entrepreneurship* and certainly in his other writings. I don't know of anyone who has done more for promoting entrepreneurship and criticizing the neoclassical paradigm for overlooking it.

I also have a different interpretation of what Steve calls the Lange-Mises debate. First, I would call it the Lange-Mises-Hayek debate, because certainly both Hayek and Mises were very instrumental in upholding their end of the discussion, vis-a-vis Lange. The paper implies, if I am reading it correctly, that the whole debate ignores entrepreneurship and incentives and is based pretty much on neoclassical optimal allocation analysis. The way I see it, this is certainly true of Lange but not of Mises and Hayek, who stress entrepreneurship vis-a-vis economizing. Certainly Kirzner's work on entrepreneurship is based upon the Mises-Hayek contribution. I don't think these are crucial points. I think it is a very good paper, but these are perhaps minor oversights.

On the point of innovation by committee versus individuals, I don't think that even in the past there were only individuals working on these things. The inventors of the past always had assistants and people they were working with. But I think the distinction between the committee and the individual is not the crucial one; it is rather between the private and the public sector—the private sector where there is entrepreneurship, where there are gains and losses, where there are incentives, versus the public sector where we have the bureaucratic mentality.

**Svetozar Pejovich** I would like to take the opportunity now to answer a few points.

As an innovation unfolds many people have to say yes. But in its inception, innovation is still the result of an individual's perception. I still think it's the individual who is in the centre of the analysis here. It has to be because innovation is the product of an idea, ingenuity, perception or whatever.

I find myself very reluctant to talk about American-Austrians. I think they are busy trying to tear down something rather than advance their method of thinking. It seems that their major occupation is to be critical of neoclassical theory rather than to make their own case. I happen to be philosophically closer to the Austrian method of looking at economic processes, but I am also turned off by their arrogance and non-intellectual attitudes.

On Lange-Mises, you can look at the debate in two ways. If a planned economy could only replicate the results of a free market, then you have to say that planning is completely unnecessary. However, transaction costs are higher in a planned economy. Suppose the Soviet manager *is* told to maximize profit, and suppose that if he were to do as he were told the outcome would be the same as the free market outcome. But what is his incentive to do so? What is the cost of monitoring his behaviour? If his rewards are associated with a different behaviour and the cost to the state to monitor his behaviour is high, then the Lange-Mises debate was meaningless.

**Milton Friedman**  I have two points; one is just an informational one. I certainly believe that the existence of a large element of the free market is a very essential ingredient for successful use of resources. But I think there is a fascinating case that I want to call your attention to, which suggests that it may be a necessary but not a sufficient condition for innovation. Many years ago Sol Tax wrote a little book called *Penny Capitalism*. I don't know how many of you have seen it. It is a wonderful little book about a tribe in Guatemala which has an absolutely perfect Adam Smithian kind of economy—completely free markets, private property, individual returns proportionate to effort, et cetera. It has a higher standard of living than its neighbouring tribes that have communal arrangements, but it has no progress. It has been absolutely stable for a long time. It is a fascinating case, which I think suggests something about necessary versus sufficient conditions and that what matters is not only the economic arrangement but also attitudes, ideas and so on.

The second point goes partly to what Raymond said. I think the issue about whether you talk about individual innovation or corporate innovation is in large part a purely semantic issue; the real issue is very different. It is, how do you establish arrangements under which somebody has a chance to take a one chance in five hundred? The point is that if you have a bureaucratic organization in which nobody is going to be in a position to get a big windfall if the one chance in five hundred turns out to be successful, that chance is never going to be taken. What is crucial is not whether the decision is made by a corporate board, by Battelle or Mr. Jones, but whether some people at Battelle figure it is worth while risking money in order to have a small chance of a very large return. That is what produces innovation—the fact that there are a lot of people, whether they are individuals or groups, who are in the position where if the one chance in five hundred works, they get a thousand-fold return or a two thousand-fold return. Whereas, in a bureaucratic organization like the Soviet Union or Yugoslavia, if the four hundred and ninety-nine chances in five hundred come out, they are in a bad way; if the one chance in five hundred comes out, maybe their salary is doubled. It doesn't pay them to take the one chance in five hundred. That is why in the Yugoslav case, which I remembered going over many years ago—I spent quite a lot of time in Yugoslavia—I came to the conclusion that the crucial defect in the whole Yugoslavian situation was the absence of a private equity market or the equivalent of it. There was no way in which anybody who took a risk for a large return would be able to get a reward which would make it worth his while to take that risk.

**Herbert Grubel** I hope I am not talking about something that is so totally obvious that I bore you, but isn't there an important distinction between research and the innovation? Britain and the Soviet Union have very successfully done basic research, but the economic success that makes the United States the envy of the rest of the world is the dynamism of the owners of little garage shops that take these ideas and put them to work in risky, innovative applications, all hoping to get rich. I think that is an important distinction. It is at least in part an explanation of the puzzle that there is such a low correlation between the amount of resources that nations spend on research and the actual rate of growth in per capita income. England has one of the highest research expenditures but one of the lowest rates of innovation.

One interesting problem arising in this context concerns the optimum time of protection for innovation. What is sacrosanct about the current fifteen years of copyright or patent protection? How was this length of time determined? Is it the optimum? I wonder whether anyone has any ideas on these matters.

**Michael Walker** Just as a side comment, if you won't regard this as an intervention, the Fraser Institute has published a wonderful little book called *Industrial Innovation* which makes clear the distinction between invention and innovation which, if I may be permitted to say, has not been made in this discussion.

**Ramon Diaz**  I just want to tell you of a conversation I had very recently with one of the executives of an important pharmaceutical company in Switzerland that engages in research in a big way. They have changed their method of how to reward individuals. At first they did not have any pre-arranged reward. They instituted one and have removed it now. They say it is unfair, because a lot of people help the company by knocking out certain projects saying: this is a dead end project; it won't do anything. And he doesn't get anything. So there is a problem, but the corporation is the one that has to create incentives of one kind or another for its staff. The situation is very different if there is no one who is trying to create incentives.

**Walter Block**  I thought it was a mere oversight that Steve didn't mention Kirzner regarding entrepreneurship. I am puzzled to find that it was purposeful and that the ground is that the Austrians' major function is to tear down rather than to build up. I find this to be an inaccurate description of Hayek and Kirzner.

**Svetozar Pejovich**  I said American-Austrians.

**Walter Block**  I don't see any difference between Hayek and Kirzner in this regard. They are both, certainly, trying to plumb the depths of process as opposed to equilibrium. As Steve says, certainly the Austrians are interested in a heterogeneity...

**Michael Walker**  Walter, may I? This is a doctrinal dispute which gets us away from the central issue. I'm going to put it down as a new point, and you can bring it back in later. But I am going to go now to Raymond on the same issue.

**Raymond Gastil**  I just wanted to respond to Milton. I have no doubt that there are large advantages to being willing to take risks and getting rewards for this. What I was objecting to was the discussion as though the people who actually are doing the innovating or thinking up the ideas—this is the point you were making—are necessarily risk-takers. Now Battelle, to take the example, is an organization that is hired to make discoveries which become practical innovations in the marketplace. A corporate president might need a better mousetrap, so he goes to Battelle and says, you figure out a better mousetrap for me. He comes back later, and the corporate executive says, okay, we'll risk so much money on it. That is a very different process, it seems to me, than what was being described here, which seemed to apply to a different era, that's all.

**Milton Friedman** I think it is purely semantic. I think that is really what he is talking about. I don't think there is any difference between you and him.

**Gordon Tullock** The entrepreneurial decision is to hire somebody to do some research, and then it gets factored down. It isn't true that your individual researchers are not taking risks. They, in fact, will get fired if they don't have enough new ideas. This little company I am involved in has just spent, in an entrepreneurial decision, $250,000—which to us is a lot of money—to hire some people to come in and renovate part of our personnel policies. It is going to cost us a lot more because of the workers' morale and so forth while the renovation is going on. Anyway, the decision to do that—hiring a very peculiar type of research work—is an entrepreneurial decision. Frequently, the people who are taking the entrepreneurial risk are not the technicians; they are the people who hire the technicians.

**Tibor Machan** In response to something Milton said, I would like to pose a question somewhat like the Devil's advocate. Suppose this Yugoslav says: "Of course our innovators cannot gain as much as yours do, but they won't lose so much either because we have a safety net and we don't run them into a situation of destitution as your free market capitalist society does. Even if his innovation doesn't succeed, he will be taken care of."

That mitigates some of the points that you might raise. I don't know how that is answered.

**Milton Friedman** Very easily. It changes the whole odds situation, and it changes the character of the innovations that people ought to undertake. It changes them in the direction of undertaking innovations which have very small chances of success, but in which failure is not conspicuous.

**Ingemar Stahl** I don't know if Raymond referred to Batelle or LaRoche, but both firms are well-known for their highly bureaucratic structures. There are some things in the market that create some of the examples. For example, you can sell your ideas to another company, or you can even start a new company. The pharmaceutical company is just a bundle of contracts; and most of the things being done in a pharmaceutical company can be hired in the market.

The second notion is that you can always buy stocks in the company. That might be an indication that LaRoche is too large, because you can't capitalize too much of your own interest in such a huge company. But it is also interesting to note that it has been pretty unsuccessful in innovation during the last 15 or 20 years, whereas modern firms have been much more successful.

A question to Steve, which I don't really think I found covered in the paper: How do I start a new firm, a BOAL? Do I have to register it, or can I just go out into the street and take five people with me and say, "you are a new BOAL." That is the most important thing, because innovations within firms might be a smaller thing than the establishment of new firms.

**Svetozar Pejovich** A group of citizens like you and I meet in a bar and decide to start a new firm. Yes, we can do that. A major problem is that the capital we invest in the firm belongs to the state.

**Assar Lindbeck** If you look at the innovation literature, a typical feature of innovations is that they come in so many different forms and structures and organizations. It is extremely difficult to generalize about it.

One way of generalizing about this complexity is to say that if you want to have a maximum of innovations in society, you should allow a maximum number of organizational forms because different types of organizations favour different types of innovations. If you only allow certain institutional forms, you are likely to get fewer innovations and restriction of the set of innovations.

Another generalization might be that large organizations with heavy research seem to be fairly good at what the Japanese call "improvement engineering." They put known pieces together in new forms and make big systems. Whereas, if you look at completely new ideas, it is remarkable how they come from what we call "outsiders." These are often people in their early twenties, coming from universities or who have jumped off large organizations where their ideas did not fit in. The word "outsiders" is a very usual term in that literature.

A very good book called *The Innovation Millionaires* dealt with the environment in Silicon Valley and around MIT. It turned out that it was a young guy who was able to get money from some millionaire risk-takers. Engineers often get funding this way. A study by a Swedish economist in business administration looked at how successful Swedish firms started. It was very usual that it was one engineer and a businessman or a capitalist— one or two or three persons, very often based on an idea of their own. If you look at path-breaking innovations, they seem to come from single individuals. It is very unlikely that larger organizations generate something completely new. Nylon from DuPont is often mentioned as a counter-example. But otherwise, innovation in the electronics industry and the recording industry mainly comes from newly established firms.

**Walter Block** The Apple computer.

**Assar Lindbeck** Yes, the whole of it, practically. So, if I may end where I began, if you restrict the number of institutional arrangements that are allowed in a society, you are likely to reduce the number of innovations.

**Douglass North** Actually, my comment follows right on Assar's. I have just finished some research on an article that I have sent off to a journal. We have been looking at the interplay between technical change and institutional change historically, and attempting to examine how costly it was to transact at both margins. We would try to observe under what conditions we have had lots of flexibility with respect to institutional arrangements which then would produce the technical changes we are looking at. In this paper we have attempted to demonstrate that the interplay between these two has been very decisive, but that the most fundamental one has been the one that Assar has been talking about. That is, if you maximize the number of alternative ways you can combine yourself—going back to the point I was making about adaptive efficiency the other day, that is, ways that allow you to take chances and to lose as well as to have the losers be eliminated—then you produce a setting which I think fits Milton's point, that then you tend to encourage the kinds of technical change that we are talking about.

**Alan Walters** Those institutional environments that we regard as anti-innovation in fact have always had an enormous incentive for innovation but often of a nonproductive kind. In Africa some years ago it seemed as if the society was completely stagnating, but in fact innovations were coming out of everybody. The innovation was there; it just wasn't being directed the right way.

We see this, for instance, in Britain. The Labour government of 1964 created the British National Enterprise Board which was charged with the task of promoting all risky innovations. The record was almost an un-mitigated disaster. I think it had something like thirty-five promotions. In fact, only one of these thirty-five *did* go right—it was a drug. All the others failed. When they return to power, the Labour Party has it fully in mind to refinance this Board.

Now the general lesson from this is that when we talk about innovation we had better be clear how government drives innovation into channels which are quite unproductive, but nevertheless the innovation is always there.

**Alvin Rabushka**  I think Assar started the right theme here. Living near Silicon Valley, I am reminded of the fact that most new jobs in the United States are created by small firms, not the large, existing firms. When we had the 1978 capital gains tax rate reduction from about 50 to 28 percent, we had a rather substantial increase in venture capital. When Stanford tries to recruit new faculty, they come out and look for housing and they say: "By golly! For $280,000 all you get is a garage!" Of course, garages are where Hewlett-Packard and other new companies are formed, and that is why there is a very high price for buying a garage.

Now, the garage story has a ring of truth in it, because it's just two guys in a garage, fooling around, and lo and behold, you have Hewlett-Packard and Varian Brothers, and on we go. All of this is captured in the equity, and whether or not five guys put together a hundred bucks each or they go to a venture capital group and sell 20 percent of the equity in exchange for X amount of dollars, I think Milton's point was absolutely right. There is a way to capitalize on a very high-risk venture. I think the fundamental reality of these publicly owned systems is that they get in the way of that to varying degrees—some completely get in the way of it, and some partially get in the way of it.

If you think about the single biggest economic experiment taking place on the face of the earth, involving one billion one hundred million people, Deng Xiaoping and his cohorts are trying to figure out how to get the impediments to this out of the way. So, for example, they are starting to experiment with bonds, they are starting to experiment with freely traded stock, they are letting companies go bankrupt, they are letting creative destruction take place. After all, we know in our country that 95 percent of all new products fail, and 90 percent of all new business ventures fail. Socialism is not a system designed to let new business ventures fail; that is not the way the system works. Unless you are prepared to have that, you are not likely to get much innovation. The Chinese are trying to get from here to there. They know where they want to go, and they've got to dismantle it. It's awfully hard to dismantle. It's probably harder to dismantle a control system and get to a free system than it was to have a free system in the first place and keep it.

I keep harking back to what I will call "the Walters-Parkin question" raised very early. It is not just how is it that Hong Kong, Singapore and a few others sustain those free institutions. The bigger question is how is it those that never had them are going to get to them as well? And why is it that places like China, for example, have now decided enough is enough, and yet the Soviet Union has decided it's *still* not enough?

**Armen Alchian** I worked at Rand for several years and spent three or four of those years on innovation research and concluded—and I still believe—we don't know the first thing about research innovation. We know a little bit about what induces it, but beyond that we are a total blank. Some of the methods for enhancing what we call innovation are what we would normally call very restrictive. They look like monopolistic devices, but they are not. So when I see contracts drawn on inventors or in strange areas, I no longer take the attitude that they are necessarily monopolistic devices.

We just don't have any good general theory at all that I know about regarding innovations; it's one of those blank areas. I hear all your comments, and I say, yes, I've been through that before. But I'll be damned if I can make any substantive propositions that are worth carrying around. It just isn't true that small firms are the most inventive; the opposite is true—we don't know which one is true. So I caution you to be very careful about any statements you make that we know about innovation because it's a great mystery, at least it is to me.

**Milton Friedman** May I add a footnote? While the Apple computer was invented in a garage, the Hollerith machine was invented in the Census Bureau in order to carry out the calculations for the census in a government agency.

**Armen Alchian** The idea that you invent something is just crazy. There is a whole string of people involved, and you don't know where the thing gets invented.

**Brian Kantor** I wanted to make Assar's point. I also know nothing about innovation and how you encourage it. But one of the strengths of a free society is precisely that of citizens being able to choose the form of association or organization or contractual arrangement that is most suitable for the purpose. One of the ways in which competition is joined in a free society is precisely over the type of association or organization. You compete—if you are allowed to—in the marketplace, and the marketplace will select, over time, the forms of association that are right for different kinds of activities. That is the key.

I don't think defenders of a free society have to make any presumptions in favour of one kind of organization over another. Equity capital may be most useful for some purposes and may be terribly unsuitable for others. A workers' co-operative might work; an inventors' co-operative might work. A mutual arrangement between managers might work or it might not work. If a society is wise, it doesn't put any regulatory barriers in the way of choosing the form of association that's suitable.

These thoughts occurred to me because in South Africa we have been deregulating the building society movement. Managers in building societies now have an option. They can choose to continue to be a mutual-type organization or turn themselves into an equity-type organization. An argument I made was, give them the freedom and see what happens in the home loans market—what type of organization is best. You will probably have different kinds of associations co-existing in different markets.

**Ingemar Stahl** I think Gordon and I would probably use the same argument on Alchian's point. Of course, there *must* be a mystery around innovation and how to promote it. If there were no mystery, there wouldn't be very much to discover. If we really knew how to do it, of course, we should have been doing it already.

**Douglass North** I wanted to pick up on Armen's query, because it illustrates Armen's point very well. Steve Cheung, who some of us around the room think was one of the brightest economists around, got this whole pile of contracts on innovation out of SEC or somewhere. He was sure that he could sort them all out and come up with some generalizations about innovation and solve this problem just like he'd solved the problem of being the world's greatest photographer or the world's greatest whatever, as Cheung had thought he was before that. It turned out that he just got immensely frustrated, and that was probably the reason he quit being a serious economist. He absolutely could not sort it out and come up with some generalization.

In fact, he came up with one of the points that Armen was just making. He found that some things that on the surface looked like they were monopolies and would be restraints turned out to be ways by which with trade secret things you actually channelled the flow of information in directions that, as he looked at it, turned out to be very productive.

But, there is one very cautious generalization that I think Steve could make, which is that you did allow for a maximum of voluntary contracting arrangements that made possible people working out these very complex things, even though he couldn't rationalize them. I think the generalization that there was a lot of flexibility in the way you could contract was an important point.

**Armen Alchian**  That's like saying, I don't know what to tell you to do; I'll just give you freedom to do whatever you want to do.

**Douglass North**  The point I am making is that that's different from what you can do in a lot of societies where you are not allowed this flexibility.

**Armen Alchian**  Oh, I agree. Yes, we can say that.

**Voice**  Beyond that, not much.

**Tibor Machan**  I was going to comment briefly on Brian's point, which relates to this. One of the most irritating claims in Marx is that free market capitalism implies the wage system—that there is no way to have a capitalist society without a wage labourer/capitalist relationship. I have never been able to understand where he got that idea. Maybe it was because of history or the predominance of hired labourers, but it seems to me you could even have labour corporations work like a law firm rather than individual labourers. I have always felt that it was sad that unions developed as a predominant spokes-organization for labourers. Had they not developed and become such an entrenched part of our society, through collective bargaining and through the legal system recognizing them as a necessity, there would have been all sorts of innovations in the arrangements in the free market which might have usurped the wage system.

**Assar Lindbeck**  I tend to look at innovation about the same way as a genetic mutation process. There is a probability that mutations will arise, but you don't know where. If you look at biological mutations, you have a very one-sided environment. Very few of these mutations will result in anything new growing up. But if you have an extraordinarily variable

environment in terms of soil, climate, et cetera, more of those genetic mutations will result in something new growing up.

That is why I think the society that puts few restrictions on who is allowed to innovate and what type of organizational forms they can choose is
much more likely to generate innovation than a society that says that we are
going to create these ten organizations that are going to innovate, they
employ these persons called "innovators" and assume that innovations will
come from there. A society which requires new firms to get permission
from the government or from somebody else to start up is less likely to
create innovation than one where innovators do not have to ask somebody
else's permission.

A typical aspect of innovation is that often only one or two people
believe in it. If they need permission, then they have to convince other
people to believe in it too. That is often extremely difficult. But if they have
free entry without asking permission, there is a much higher probability of
innovation.

The innovative capacity of Soviet-type countries is extraordinarily low.
They rank much better in allocative efficiency, even if they are bad there.
But I think they are much, much lower in innovation. It is very difficult to
think of innovation there. There are state enterprises in the world that have
made innovations, which shows that innovations are not restricted to
private firms. If you take the steel industry, some new processes after the
war came from the state-owned Austrian steel industry. These examples
just reinforce my point that you should not restrict institutional forms if you
want innovations.

**Walter Block**  If we were to search around for a possible counter-example
to Assar's point (with which I agree entirely), one might mention the space
programme. Here is a situation where the U.S.S.R. is at least competitive
with the American space programme. But I would say that this is not a
counter-example to Assar's very correct point, because in the space
programme in the U.S. we do not have the essence of free enterprise;
rather, we have a central planning type operation. So all that could be said
is that when it comes to central planning, the U.S. and Russia are competitive or perhaps the Soviets are slightly ahead. This would not be a true
counter-example to Assar's insightful hypothesis.

**Brian Kantor**  I want to pick up Herb's point; I think it is important. We
have heard we know nothing about innovations, therefore we have no basis
for deciding what is the best way to protect property rights in knowledge

because we don't know how those affect the outcomes. Whether it should be fifteen years or five years or fifty years or no years at all, we just don't know. So that is one issue.

The other issue is, how do we protect the trade in knowledge across countries? Clearly, it may be advantageous to free-ride on other people's research. Maybe it is optimum for a small country or even a big country to discourage research altogether and free-ride off the improvements in knowledge made somewhere else. I think that is a problem in relations between governments.

**Assar Lindbeck** The problem is that everybody tries to do it.

**Brian Kantor** Yes, that's one of the free-rider problems.

**Michael Parkin** I wanted to complete the Assar point, which I think is an important one. I think Assar is correct, and his analogy is brilliant. I think there is one further feature of it that we have not quite got. It connects to what Alan was saying. Innovation of all kinds is going on all the time. The important thing is the value of the innovation, and the value to whom. If we have a society in mind in which the values that matter are the values of individuals, based on individual willingness to pay, then Assar's observation is clearly correct that maximum variety of institutional forms and freedom to form contractual arrangements will further that goal of innovating in areas and in ways that produce things that are valued by individuals.

If, however, we think that the correct form of society is one in which the views of a small elite are the ones that count and nobody else's count for anything, then indeed we might prefer to organize ourselves in the form of the big space programme or whatever and produce this mass of innovation, as it is highly valued by the relevant group. I think there is an intimate connection between the basic ideals and the fundamental notion that individuals are what matter and the conclusion that the innovative process is best served in an environment in which those individuals are free to form whatever contractual arrangements they elect to.

**Michael Walker** Now we have the opportunity to go to new points. Walter, I will give you 30 seconds at this stage on your doctrinal issue.

**Walter Block** What I was saying is that the Austrians certainly have not just torn down but also built up, although sometimes a part of building up *is* tearing down. But even if the contention were true that somehow the Austrian didn't, this seems to be no reason for purposely avoiding a footnote that should have been made.

Now with regard to the Lange-Mises-Hayek debate, yes, incentives are missing. So it is very difficult for the Soviets to replicate the market. But this was not the point of both sides of the Lange-Mises-Hayek debate; it was just the Lange side. The Mises-Hayek side made the very point that Steve is making very well himself.

**Svetozar Pejovich** Let me start with Walter's statement. It is fine to disagree with me, but I think I have the right to ask you to understand my point. When I referred to American-Austrians, I certainly did not mean Hayek. It is not fair to put them together. Hayek belongs to the same club as Milton, Armen Alchian and Lord Keynes. I have conceived and organized symposia that will be held annually to honour Mr. Hayek.

On asking where Marx got the idea of employer-employee relations, I would say he got it by looking around.

To Alan Walters, in the last five years of his life, Mr. Haggerty—a founder of Texas Instruments—was very concerned with the issue of how to preserve incentives to innovate in a growing corporate firm.

Finally, my point to Ingemar Stahl. I think I have given you an answer which is partially correct about the Yugoslav firm. It is possible in Yugoslavia to have a private firm. But you can have a private firm only in well identified areas like hotels, motels, restaurants. However, they are supposed to employ at most five people. If you go into any Yugoslav restaurant that is privately owned, you will see about thirty people employed there. If you ask whether they are breaking the law, they will say, of course not, they're all family. They are innovators!

# Chapter 9

# Economic Analysis and the Pursuit of Liberty

# Tibor R. Machan

## Connecting Theory with Practice

The connections between the dominant (neoclassical) theory of economic relations and the pursuit of political and civil liberties are of interest to us. Does the dominant economic approach to human affairs, which offers positive grounds for free market systems, give rational support to acting in defence of free societies?

True, the condition of (negative) freedom is an analytic feature of the economic approach to human affairs. Such freedom is a necessary precondition for the pursuit of our subjective utilities or preferences, not itself a utility or preference. But I am more concerned with whether this approach gives rational support to achieving this condition when it has not been fully realized. Putting it simply, does the economic approach to human behaviour provide a rationale for the importance of the kind of political action that would establish and sustain a free society? I am certain that this subject will tie in with our purpose well enough so as to be of interest to us all.

To fend off the charge that I am concerned with a straw man—i.e., a theory no one endorses—let me cite a clear statement of the relevant features of the theory by one of the most prominent neoclassical economists of our time, namely, Professor George Stigler. There are many others who make the point that this theoretical model of market economics and of its assumptions are widely and prominently embraced. Stigler states the point in very succinct terms:

> Man is eternally a utility maximizer—in his home, in his office (be it public or private), in his scientific work—in short, everywhere.[1]

Gary Becker is no less an uncompromising supporter of the approach I have in mind, one sometimes called economic imperialism:

> The combined assumptions of maximizing behaviour, market equilibrium, and stable preferences, used relentlessly and unflinchingly, form the heart of the economic approach as I see it.[2]

### The Self-Defeating Nature of the Model

A criticism of economic defenders of the market is that it is indefensible in its own terms. Quentin Skinner of Cambridge University noted, in his Harvard University lectures, "The Paradoxes of Political Liberty," that "we are very poor guardians of our own liberties." He referred to liberalism's "minimalist view of civic obligation" and lamented the "dangerous privatization" of certain values of Western civilization.[3]

The impeding feature of liberalism is the definition of the concept "human being" employed as the fundamental assumption of economic analysis. Economists differ somewhat on the precise content of their definition of human nature. Yet most share Stigler's view that an understanding of human behaviour is most promising if we assume that everyone is maximizing utilities, pursuing self-interest, trying to maximize wealth, or the like. Some such idea constitutes the basis for a scientific economic conception of human affairs and figures prominently in liberalism's world view.

Why is the economic approach to human behaviour stifling vis-a-vis the pursuit of liberty? Since it defines human beings as relentless subjective utility maximizers, it fails to produce the conclusion that people should make the establishment and maintenance of a system of liberty a priority in their lives. Economic man, then, has no good reason for choosing to be political or patriotic man.

Economic man, as Stigler notes, is also non-scientific man. If one holds that human beings are always in markets and their utilities can only be a purely subjective matter, one must infer that scientists are also utility maximizers as they engage in analysis and research. Any other commitment is derivative. Yet this view undermines the claim that a scientist can be objective since, if falsehood gave the scientific economist greater satisfaction than truth, he would sell out his mission. So, by the economist's own account of human behaviour, the economist would be ready to pursue falsehood if that were utility maximizing. At any rate, the pursuit of truth would have to be regarded as accidental, not necessary, to scientific behaviour. And when Karl Marx criticized economists—even the great ones such as Adam Smith and David Ricardo—he in fact took this line, presumably laid down by economic science itself. He, of course, mercilessly indicted such less well-known economists as Frederick Bastiat and H. C. Carey, for simply espousing notions that serve the vested interest of the economic class to which they belong.[4] This is just the point public choice theorists make about why bureaucrats cannot be trusted with their task, namely, the pursuit of the public interest. This public choice idea means that the pursuit of self- or vested-interest undermines economic scientific work just as it does the work of politicians and bureaucrats.[5]

Of course, there are other complaints about the economic man idea, most prominently that it is ultimately vacuous. If, as Stigler claims, "Man is eternally a utility-maximizer—in his home, in his office (be it public or private), in his church, in his scientific work," what can we even mean if we deny this? Suppose we claim that at least when people sacrifice their lives for some cause that is of no immediate or even long range personal benefit to them, they do not act as economic man. What do we hear in response to this? Milton Friedman gives us the answer when he states:

> every individual serves his own private interest... The great Saints of history have served their 'private interest' just as the most money grubbing miser has served his interest. The *private interest* is whatever it is that drives an individual.[6]

Friedman's idea renders the idea of "private interest" quite meaningless. And it also makes the notion that someone is indeed pursuing his or her private interest wholly unclear, not to mention untestable—a favorite concern of positivist economists.

## The Reason for the High Value of Liberty

Are these valid criticisms? Can they be met? The critics do make a good point. So long as the free market relies solely on economic defences—that is, on neoclassical economic arguments—one of its analytical implications is that people may quite rationally not act so as to defend it. But is there no other way to defend the free market society from a framework that does not have these self-defeating implications? While human beings do indeed—perhaps even should—act as utility maximizers, as (in other words) prudent individuals, this is not all there is to them. They could also be pursuers of certain objective values because they have become convinced of their existence.

This rebuttal to the critics of the economic defence of the free society involves a different idea of human nature, though not necessarily one that is wholly opposed to economic man.

What is to be done? I suggest that we have a perfectly good tradition in which the following are reconciled: science, liberty, morality and utility (or human happiness). This line of thinking has only been advanced recently but has been hinted at in earlier times.[7] It owes a great deal to the Aristotelian tradition. In Aristotle there are two features of human life that are closely linked, namely, liberty and human happiness. He recognizes that individuals must be acting volitionally, of their own free will, in order to be credited, morally, for their conduct. And he identifies moral conduct by reference to its principled pursuit of the happiness of the acting agent. Interestingly, Adam Smith recognized the value of the ancient outlook on morality when he wrote the following:

> Ancient moral philosophy proposed to investigate wherein consisted the happiness and perfection of a man, considered not only as an individual, but as the member of a family, of a state, and of the great society of mankind. In that philosophy the duties of human life were treated as subservient to the happiness and perfection of human life. But when moral, as well as natural philosophy, came to be taught only as subservient to theology, the duties of human life were treated of as chiefly subservient to the happiness of a life to come. In the ancient philosophy the perfection of virtue was represented as necessarily productive to the person who possessed it, of the most perfect happiness in this life. In the modern philosophy it was frequently represented as almost always inconsistent with any degree of happiness in this life, and heaven was to be earned by penance and mortification, not by the liberal, generous, and spirited conduct of a man. By far the most important of all the different branches of philosophy became in this manner by far the most corrupted.[8]

The Aristotelian view of human morality revived and modified by Ayn Rand must, of course, be reconciled with science, specifically with the doctrine of free will. This gives economists a great deal of trouble. Yet their notion of scientific explanation is no longer the sole option.[9] Scientific defences of the free will idea are, furthermore, quite prominent and respected now, as, for example, those put forth by Roger W. Sperry.[10]

In ethics classical egoism, departing somewhat from Aristotle, completes the picture. Here liberalism gains a powerful moral footing: It is indeed morally right for everyone to act so as to become the happiest he or she can be, but here "happiness" is not left undefined but is tied to the nature of human beings and to the individual involved. Thus this is not a subjectivist, subjective-utility oriented idea of human values. Accordingly, to cap it all off, the value of political liberty is an objectively demonstrable priority for every individual, in behalf of which a great deal of effort is morally required.[11]

In this way, it seems, the paradox of liberalism, which made the defence of liberty a mere preference that many people might quite rationally omit from their list of priorities, gets resolved. It is no longer optional whether one should pursue liberty but a prominent civic obligation. If true, this outlook can defend both the free market and the imperative to strive to establish it. Because though one ought to be free to pursue the values one chooses, and this is impossible without economic liberty, one is morally—which does not mean one must be legally—bound to pursue some goals ahead of others. The pursuit of liberty is rationally justified, not merely a subjectively preferred course of conduct some may choose to engage in.[12]

*360*

## NOTES

1. George Stigler, Lecture II, Tanner Lectures delivered at Harvard University, April 1980, pp. 23-4. Quoted in Richard McKenzie, *The Limits of Economic Science* (Boston: Kluwer-Nijhoff Publishing, 1983), p. 6.

2. Gary Becker, *The Economic Approach to Human Behaviour* (Chicago: University of Chicago Press, 1976), p. 5.

3. Quoted in Richard Higgins, "British philosopher says self-interest corrupts Western Liberty," *Boston Sunday Globe*, October 28, 1984.

4. Karl Marx, *Grundrisse,* translated by Martin Nicolaus (New York: Vintage Books, 1973).

5. James Buchanan and Gordon Tullock, *The Calculus of Consent* (Ann Arbor: University of Michigan Press, 1962). See also Mancur Olson, *The Logic of Collective Action* (Cambridge: Harvard University Press, 1965).

6. Milton Friedman, "The Line We Dare Not Cross," *Encounter*, November 1976, p. 11. What this approach to understanding human affairs secures is what Friedman and other positivists desire, namely, a positive science, that is, "a system of generalizations that can be used to make correct predictions about the consequences of any change in circumstances ... by the development of a 'theory' or 'hypothesis' that yields valid and meaningful (i.e., not truistic) predictions about phenomena not yet observed." M. Friedman, *Essays in Positive Economics* (Chicago: University of Chicago Press, 1953) pp. 4-8 in the Phoenix edition, 1966.

   For a meticulous critique of this system see Steven Rappaport, "What is Really Wrong with Milton Friedman's Methodology of Economics," Reason Papers, #11 (Spring 1986), pp. 33-62.

   I should add that I believe that a great deal of the substance of positivist economic analysis could be saved by giving up the way in which the basic assumptions about human behaviour and motivation are treated and substituting conditional statements which could function as value free within the theory but which could give ample room for value considerations when we explore whether the antecedent of the conditional should be put into effect—e.g., if we start by the claim that "If people go to markets, they will pursue their prosperity (in their varied but not purely subjective ways)," this will yield testable hypotheses just as it leaves open the possibility that on some occasions people should not go to markets at all—e.g., when their mother is lying on her deathbed or their son needs parental advice. Instead of this move the positivists prefer obliterating the distinction between concern for prosperity or prudence and concern for others or kindness.

7. Ayn Rand, *Capitalism: The Unknown Ideal* (New York: New American Library, 1966). Rand is sometimes charged with being an a priorist but this is wrong. Her book *Introduction to Objectivist Epistemology* (New York: New American Library, 1979) clearly demonstrates that for her sound theories must be grounded in knowledge of facts. (So does her famous motto, "Check your premises!") For more on this see Tibor R. Machan, "Epistemology and Moral Knowledge," *The Review of Metaphysics*, Vol. 36 (September 1982), pp. 232-49.

   It is particularly important to keep in mind that the metaethical approach of objectivism—whereby a moral judgement is said to be capable of being shown true or false—is no more arrogant—no less lacks humility, if you will—than any scientific approach. No infallibility is implied and the underlying epistemology is not absolutist but contextualist, i.e., admits that knowledge may require updating, revising, etc., given further learning about and changes in reality.

8. Adam Smith, *The Wealth of Nations* (New York: Random House, 1937), p. 726.

9. A good criticism of the Humean doctrine of causality that still dominates positivist social science may be found in Milton Fisk, *Nature and Necessity* (Bloomington: Indiana University Press, 1974). See, also, A. R. Louch, *Explanation and Human Action* (Berkeley: University of California Press, 1969). Of course there are refined versions of positivist social science, such as Milton Friedman's instrumentalism and Ludwig von Mises' a prioristic praxiology (which aims to be a criticism of positivism and which Friedman regards as unscientific). But the point is that in all of these we have a reductionist view of what can count as a natural cause, namely, some materially describable event. (Mises, for example, explains human action by reference to an uneasiness, a feeling of need, on the part of an individual, which then propels the person to act. See Ludwig von Mises, *Human Action* [New Haven: Yale University Press, 1949].)

10. Roger W. Sperry, *Science and Moral Priority* (New York: Columbia University Press, 1983) and "Mind, Brain and Humanistic Values," in J. R. Platt, ed., *New Views of the Nature of Man* (Chicago: University

J. R. Platt, ed., *New Views of the Nature of Man* (Chicago: University of Chicago Press, 1965). From psychologists, who by no means prefer some anti-scientific, existentialist approach, comes another criticism of the passive model of human behaviour. Isador Chein says, for example, that "The image of Man as an impotent being rests on the false assumption that all the determinants of behaviour are included in the constitution and, separately, in the environment, that is, that every determinant of behaviour is either a body fact or an environment fact." Chein adds that a further logical problem with this idea is that "in principle, [the theorist] cannot apply his principles to himself as an actor." (Isador Chein, *The Science of Behaviour and the Image of Man* [New York: Basic Books, 1972], pp. 21-22.) D. Bannister echoes this same objection: "the psychologist cannot present a picture of man which patently contradicts his behaviour in presenting that picture." (D. Bannister, in D. Bannister, et al., ed., *Explanation in the Behavioral Sciences* [New York: Cambridge University Press, 1970], p. 417.) And economists, too, exhibit this problem—often in the respect in which they are dedicated and principled defenders of liberalism and the rights of individuals when it clearly is not of any discernible economic benefit for them to do so. Needless to stress this, but Milton Friedman is a prime example of one such dedicated, courageous defender of the free society. Yet I would have to say that his own economic science makes this defence unintelligible. (The attempt to explain this away is a case of tautologous imperialism that renders the idea of utility maximization vacuous.)

11. For more on this idea, see Tibor R. Machan, "The Classical Egoist Defense of Capitalism," in T. R. Machan, ed., *The Main Debate: Communism vs. Capitalism* (New York: Random House, 1987).

12. It might be argued that there is nothing wrong with subjectivism in values, since all it says is that we are unsure of our grounds when we decide on what is of value to us. But this is not the standard meaning, nor the most widespread understanding of "subjective" in this context. It is that the values and ethical imperatives at issue are derived from the desires of the person making the value or moral judgement.

# Discussion

## Edited by Michael A. Walker

**Michael Walker** Tibor, I am going to give you the opportunity to introduce your ideas now.

**Tibor Machan** I want to apologize to Steve for not really taking up his paper, but I am not an economist. It would not have been fair for me to make a lot of half-educated statements. Had I heard him render his points the way he did, in ordinary language, I think I might have been able to do better. But in the technical language of economics I am "unsurefooted." Let me also say that, though I am not an economist but a philosopher, all philosophers would not agree with me. There are a lot of philosophers who are sympathetic to some of the things that I might criticize. I am not a positivist, I am not a Popperian, I don't go along with a number of those philosophical schools which are much closer to what I take to be at least certain renditions of the neoclassical paradigm in the philosophy of science, and in particular, for economics.

More to the point of my paper, some people have charged the neoclassical liberal defence or defence of liberalism of the free market capitalist system with a certain technical flaw. This applies only to those renditions of it which are imperialistic, that is, which maintain that the language of neoclassical economics sufficiently takes care of everything that needs to be said about the merits and the conditions of a free market economy. There are much more restricted advocates of the marketplace who are economists, accept the neoclassical approach, but do not rule out other approaches. I am thinking of the imperialists as people like Gary Becker, or as Gordon Tullock sometimes proudly announces he is, and George Stigler sometimes is taken to be. I think Steve sometimes speaks as if no other language is really cognitively intelligible beyond that of the positivist framework.

Within this framework we find the idea that human beings are utility maximizers or perhaps, with some alterations, wealth maximizers—or selfish, as some looser versions would have it. This framework maintains that the utilities are subjective, that the preference curves are really arbitrarily set or set in inexplicable ways, and are certainly not rationally disputable. There is no disputing of tastes—there is a famous Latin way of putting it that, as you well know, is the title of a famous essay.

If this is the way to analyse values, then the value of liberty itself would have to be concluded (from within this framework) as merely a subjective preference. Sometimes economists really even talk like that. Armen sometimes says, "I prefer liberty, I like liberty, I have a taste for liberty"—something like that—rather than that "liberty is a good thing of objectively demonstrable value for society" and so on. This is not just a straw man. It is an implication of looking at the world in certain ways and ruling out other ways of looking at it. It is denying that there are different contexts in which different forms of discourse are appropriate.

Isn't it a problem of liberalism if it cannot defend the recommendations of liberty as anything but a subjective preference? I think it is a very serious, limiting problem. Conservatives like Walter Burns and Leo Strauss, neoliberals or neoconservatives like Daniel Bell, Quientin Skinner and George Will have made this point; it is nothing original with me. I just want to reiterate it as a reason for reflecting on a different, somewhat altered way of defending not just the sense or the intelligibility of a free market but also the efforts to secure it. We must have a rational ground for urging people to secure liberty and not to regard it simply as one of their possible preferences. If they don't like it—if they like golf or lots of ice cream or something else more—and then they choose not to spend time defending it, are they equally rational no matter what they do?

I want to propose that the one major way is to change from the concept of subjective utility or subjective values to individual utility or individual values. The reason I recommend this change is that "individual" is an objective fact—there are you and I and the rest of us who are objective facts. Certain things can be good for us or bad for us, and this can be discovered. I, your mother, a friend, or someone who knows you better can say what is good for you or bad for you. You can find it out, certainly, too. Whereas if it is entirely subjective, then the subject *creates* the value and without its creation the value doesn't exist. That may be okay for technical analyses of certain kinds, but not for understanding and, especially, evaluating political alternatives.

This change doesn't alter one important aspect of the subjective utility approach, and that is that there is enormous diversity among individuals. Although there may be objective values, nevertheless there is enormous diversity and pluralism in these objective values. What is good for you may be objectively demonstrable, but it is not generalizable or universalizable over others. Certain clothes might be good for you, certain kinds of hairdos might be good for you, on all sorts of dimensions—aesthetic, moral, prudential, whatever. So the diversity that subjectivism allows for remains; the subjectivity gets abandoned.

This is already provided for in a certain outlook on moral matters, what I call "classical individualism." It derives from Aristotle, though is not reducible to Aristotle. It has a little bit of input from the Randian framework, admittedly, which a lot of people pooh-pooh, but that's too bad. One of the major ingredients of this outlook is that individuals have to be responsible for the goods that they produce. They are the ones who are to be credited or blamed, for either achieving or failing to achieve values. For that, it is an absolute necessity that there be freedom. If there isn't freedom, then an individual's achievement of a value is merely an accident.

So, even though there is this objectivity of values and diversity, it is a necessary condition of the existence of this entire framework that there be freedom. Thus, it becomes one of the prime social values. Thus, it can be rationally defended as a prime social value, advocated as such, and maybe even considered to be a civic responsibility for people to defend their free society. It is no longer a matter of their subjective preference but a civic responsibility, because it becomes a prerequisite of the very system within which objective good values can be pursued.

**Walter Block** I welcome Tibor's point. I think it is very important. It is not fully relevant to Steve's paper, but viewing it as a paper or a point on its own, it harks back to what I was saying about the war of ideas. In this battle, I think it would be much more effective on our part if we had not just one but two products, efficiency as well as liberty. The Marxists, our main competitors, have both. They offer a moral vision as well as a historical vision and an efficiency vision. If we have only the one product, as many value-free economists would have it, then I think we are missing a bet. Certainly the point that liberty is only one argument in the utility function, and you can put liberty on an indifference curve against bananas and have an isoproduct curve and indifference curves and this and that, is part of this moral colour-blindness. There are many people who are, in effect, with regard to morality as if they were colour-blind. The point I would make about that is that liberty underlies all choice. Liberty underlies the entire enterprise; it's just not one more vector in an indifference curve.

So I would say that we should have a division of labour. Not everybody has to specialize in boats. Certainly, there is room in free market advocacy for people who specialize in one or the other or even both. But I think it is very easy to undersell or underestimate the importance of the liberty argument in this war of ideas. Both weapons are of positive use.

**Assar Lindbeck** Suppose that we want to have a private zone for individuals where the individual himself can do what he likes, regardless of what others think. One example is the right to sleep either on your belly or your back. Another example is the freedom to read *Lady Chatterley's Lover*. What needs to be clarified in this issue is that the private zone for individuals is a kind of lexigraphic ordering. That is a priority which is given, and that would mean that other people's preferences have nothing to do with it. Even if other people have preferences in how I sleep, they should not count. My freedom to sleep the way I like comes first. The whole idea of conflict does not make sense. If you decide that the lexigraphic ordering is a private zone, then other people's opinions should not matter.

I am very surprised that philosophers and also some economists, like Arrow and others, take this very seriously. Since we have some philosophers here, I wonder what they think about it. Am I too simple-minded, saying that if it is a private zone that is by definition something in which other people's preferences should not count? That connects to what Block said; we do not make a marginal evaluation between bananas and freedom. We put freedom as a lexigraphic ordering, and the other evaluations come below that.

**Gordon Tullock**  I never understood how Sen's article got published, because if you have two principles it is only coincidence if they are identical in all characteristics, and therefore I would not have expected these two to be identical.

David Friedman gave a lecture at the University of Virginia which was supposed to be "What is Wrong with Sen." There was a typographical error, and in the announcement it was printed "What is Wrong with Sin?" But this has nothing to do with what I really wanted to add.

I could go around and say to somebody, you are making a mistake. Granted the values that you have on other matters, the free market will achieve them better than socialism. You tell me that you want socialism not because you like it, but because you want people to be well off. This is an intellectual error. At that point I would be in the position of the mother telling the child. But in this case I am doing something which I think almost any economist would buy.

On the other hand, I could say to you that the free market is better than socialism, even though you are a high-ranking bureaucrat and if we go to the free market your pension will be endangered. My question is, are you saying both of these or just one of them?

**Tibor Machan**  The latter.

**Gordon Tullock** The latter. That's what I wanted to find out.

**Tibor Machan** I want to be able to defend the position to the bureaucrat and say that by logic and reason, by historical evidence and whatever else you have to adduce, he would have to give in despite the fact that he loses his pension.

**Gordon Tullock** I could tell him that other people would be better off, but it would be very hard to tell him that *he* would be better off.

**Tibor Machan** We're not talking about better off; we're talking about whether it would be right for him to do it.

**Gordon Tullock** Then there is a distinction. But it is true; you have put the objectivity in a place where it can be handled.

**Milton Friedman** I am on Gordon's side on this. I must frankly say that I believe that what Tibor has written in this paper is a caricature of what neoclassical economics or economics is about. I accept his judgement that he is not an economist. But I don't understand what he *does* say. I don't know what it means to say that the value of political liberty is an objectively demonstrable priority for every individual. Objectively to whom? What does the objective mean? Does it mean that you can conduct an experiment which demonstrates it for me? The notion that somehow or other to say that things are subjective is to say they are arbitrary seems to me to be a complete *non sequitur*. Lots of things are subjective which are not at all arbitrary.

It seems to me that you get things all mixed up in this analysis. From one point of view, I am an economist, a scientist, but I am also a human being and in that context I have values. The value that seems to me most important and most neglected in the kind of approach here, and it's what I have mostly against Ayn Rand, is the value of humility. There is nothing else that is more fundamental or more basically justifies a free society than the value of humility in the sense of saying, well, maybe I am wrong. If someone disagrees with me, I don't have any right to do what you want to do—to say that you can objectively, rationally demonstrate to him that he is wrong. I only have the right to argue with him, to try to persuade him. If I don't persuade him, what does it mean to say he is objectively wrong and I am objectively right? I just don't understand the language.

**Walter Block** I would certainly agree with Milton. One of the many shortcomings of Ayn Rand was an extreme lack of humility. I know of no person who had more of this lack of humility than she. There are other libertarians, i.e., people who value and see things not just in terms of an economic defence of the free market as you yourself, who have much more humility than Ayn Rand. In other words, we shouldn't equate lack of humility with libertarianism. Robert Nozick, another libertarian, has even gone to the extreme of arguing against forcing people to agree with you based on logical reasoning.

**Ingemar Stahl** Coming back to this problem of Sen, I think what is mixed up is that he is taking two quite different principles, as Gordon indicated. One principle, the private zone, is a type of social contract which we would like to enter that has to do with relationships between individuals. The other thing is a type of preferential value of certain types of states which just concerns me. If we look upon the private zone as a kind of social contractual agreement for a type of good society before we make further choices, I think we would be on the right track.

Then, of course, you are tricked by all these logicians. You can always find four or six or nine conditions which are reasonable, each by itself, but when you put them all together they are self-contradictory. That is nothing special. That is exactly the same as Arrow's theorem.

**Raymond Gastil** I just wanted to agree with Milton on that issue. One of the reasons for what Tibor is saying—and I found it incomprehensible—is because we need it. We need this subjective base. This is what Walter was saying. But because we need it doesn't mean we can get it, and that seems to be the problem.

**Tibor Machan** Starting with the last first, one can always accuse a person of being blind and just simply promoting his own prejudices and so on. I didn't do this to anyone else, and I find it a little annoying that it is being done to me. I believe this to be objectively demonstrable. I may be wrong about this. I don't think I am being arrogant nor lacking in humility. I don't know why Rand is brought in; it's a red herring. I have made my case and it stands or falls on its own. I may have mentioned Rand, but then people mention people all the time without having to be associated with their character or personality.

I don't think I caricatured anybody; I simply summarized the Becker, Tullock, Stigler view. I gave all kinds of hedges and qualifications. It seems to me there is a prominent trend, but in five pages, and especially even less of a presentation, one cannot write a book. If you want to go to a book, Richard McKenzie wrote a book about this against Gary Becker. Maybe it's not a good book or whatever, but there are all the qualifications there. There are lots of people who don't exactly believe all this. But there are also many who do—as documented in *Economic Imperialism* (Paragon House 1987).

Now, another thing. "Objective" does not necessarily mean "experimentally demonstrable." Mathematics can be objective, and it is not experimentally demonstrable. There are all sorts of different contexts of human inquiry within which standards of objectivity apply, and not all of them adopt the very same *criterion* of objectivity. I simply maintain that in a certain realm, like ethics, there is a criterion of objectivity that is different from physics or chemistry or biology.

Finally, when you argue with someone and you cannot establish your conclusions, I am not sure what the point of arguing with the person is in the first place? Obviously, you argue with someone because you are contending that your reasons ultimately support the conclusion that you support. If you believe from the very beginning that you are wrong—and "may be wrong" is a kind of a hedging thing—and that you are too humble and too inadequate to come to any conclusion about it, you should stop wasting everybody's time and not argue with them.

**Michael Walker** Ladies and gentlemen, that brings the symposium to a close. As the chairman, I want to thank you all for your good behaviour. But, having established the constitutional form at the beginning, I do think it demonstrates the power of constitutions to keep otherwise irascible behaviour under control. I think you have done a masterful job of communicating without unduly running into difficulties that sometimes attend when there are people of strong opinions on every side. I again want to thank you for coming to the symposium.